PRINCIPLES AND MAXIMS

OF

JURISPRUDENCE

BY

JOHN GEORGE PHILLIMORE, Q.C., M.P.

READER ON CONSTITUTIONAL LAW AND LEGAL HISTORY
TO THE FOUR INNS OF COURT.

Ἡμεῖς μὲν κλέος οἷον ἀκούομεν, οὐδέ τι ἴδμεν.

IL. B. 486.

THE LAWBOOK EXCHANGE, LTD.
Clark, New Jersey

ISBN 978-1-58477-177-7 (hardcover)
ISBN 978-1-61619-413-0 (paperback)

Lawbook Exchange edition 2001, 2014

The quality of this reprint is equivalent to the quality of the original work.

THE LAWBOOK EXCHANGE, LTD.
33 Terminal Avenue
Clark, New Jersey 07066-1321

*Please see our website for a selection of our other publications
and fine facsimile reprints of classic works of legal history:*
www.lawbookexchange.com

Library of Congress Cataloging-in-Publication Data

Phillimore, John George, 1808-1865.
    Principles and maxims of jurisprudence / by John George Phillimore.
        p. cm.
    Originally published: London : J.W. Parker, 1856.
    Includes bibliographical references and index.
    ISBN 1-58477-177-1 (cloth : alk. paper)
    1. Legal maxims (Roman law). 2. Roman law--Interpretation and
construction. I. Title.

KJA100 .P49 2001
340.5'4--dc21   2001029071

Printed in the United States of America on acid-free paper

PRINCIPLES AND MAXIMS

OF

JURISPRUDENCE

BY

JOHN GEORGE PHILLIMORE, Q.C., M.P.

READER ON CONSTITUTIONAL LAW AND LEGAL HISTORY
TO THE FOUR INNS OF COURT.

Ἡμεῖς μὲν κλέος οἶον ἀκούομεν, οὐδέ τι ἴδμεν.

IL. B. 486.

LONDON

JOHN W. PARKER AND SON WEST STRAND

1856

LONDON:
PRINTED BY WERTHEIMER AND CO
FINSBURY CIRCUS.

TO

HENRY SINGER KEATING, ESQ., M.P.,

ONE OF HER MAJESTY'S COUNSEL.

MY DEAR AND TRIED FRIEND,

ACCEPT the dedication of these pages, the result of much thought and study, from one who, through many a changing year, has been cheered by your society and instructed by your example.

The grave has closed over the aspirations of many since we first met on that rugged path which you have trodden with so much ability and success.

There lie the kindness and eloquence of Talfourd—there lie the deep learning and powerful intellect of John William Smith —there lie the strength and hopes of many less-gifted sharers in our early struggles.

Your thread is yet unbroken, and your destiny has been fortunate. You inherit an ancient name embellished by military renown, and you have added to it the lustre of great civil reputation.

As in the House of Commons you have shewn that a lawyer can be a patriot, at the Bar your whole life has proved that the vigilant discharge of the duties of an advocate is consistent with the purest morality and the most fastidious honour.

These are your claims upon the esteem of strangers. But whatever belongs to the constant display of qualities for which every succeeding year has heightened my admiration, to goodness that no prosperity can taint, and friendship that no adversity can alter, is due to HENRY SINGER KEATING from

JOHN GEORGE PHILLIMORE.

PREFACE.

Εἰ δέ τῳ μὴ ἀρέσκοι, ταῦτα παραβάλλων τὸ ἄλλων ἦθος πρὸς ταῦτα—
οὕτω κρινέτω.—Xen., *Mem.*, iv. 8.

In this work, I have endeavoured to lay before the reader
some of the luminous and noble principles which informed
Roman jurisprudence. I have first selected several maxims,
to each of which I have annexed a commentary. Then I
have collected several maxims for the interpretation of statutes,
wills and contracts. And lastly, by the enumeration of several
instances, and a detailed analysis of some remarkable laws, I
have shewn the truth of the remark of Leibnitz, 'that the
study of the Roman law, after that of the severer sciences,
was the best discipline for the mind; and that the Fragments
of the Digest furnished the most excellent examples of the
application of the rules of logic to the affairs of civil life.'
The idea of this undertaking was suggested to me by a passage in the works of D'Aguesseau, in which, after remarking
that it is impossible to pay too much attention: 'A remarquer
tout ce qui peut former un axiome ou une règle générale du
droit, soit dans la décision même soit dans la raison de la
décision;' he says, speaking of some defects in the title 'de
regulis juris': 'Si on pouvait corriger ces défauts, on auroit
l'avantage de recueillir dans un très petit volume, toute la
substance et comme tout l'esprit de ces principes généraux qui
sont dictés par la loi naturelle et qui influent dans toutes les
décisions des juges.' Again he says, in his instructions to his
son: 'On ne sauroit trop se remplir l'esprit de ces notions
communes qui sont comme autant d'oracles de jurisprudence
et comme le précis des toutes les reflexions des juris-consultes.'
Some portion of this condensed wisdom will be found in this

volume, and will, it is hoped, atone for the many deficiencies
of its author.

It only remains for me to say, that I have derived very
great advantage from the excellent work of Mr. Broom, on
the Maxims of English Law, from the treatise of Sir F.
Dwarris, on Statutes, and from the ' Science of Legal Judgment,' by Mr. Ram.   I hope that I have always acknow-
ledged my obligations to these learned writers, in the proper
places; but if I have ever omitted to do so, I must ask them
to accept this general acknowledgment of the service which
the works of all (especially that of Mr. Broom, as it is more
immediately connected with the subject) have rendered me, in
the performance of a task, which it has required all my
energies to accomplish.   The works of Faber, of James
Godefroi, and of Pothier, especially of the second, are the
basis of my undertaking; and if I have not cited them in
almost every page, it is because I thought it best at once to state
that my obligations to them can hardly be overrated.   I have
been much assisted also by the work of Antoine, though, in
learning and precision, it is far inferior to the others.   In
conclusion, I will express my earnest hope, that the time is
approaching when we shall groan no longer under the miserable servitude entailed upon a people who live under vague
and unknown laws; when the admirable materials which we
possess, scattered over more than a thousand volumes, will be
extricated from the rubbish by which they are encumbered,
and embodied into a code, in which the same antagonist
elements that are now heaped together in incessant contra-
diction and perplexity, may, when digested by experience and
methodized by reason, form a lucid and harmonious whole—

' alterius sic
' Altera poscat opem res et conjuret amice,'

and when England, paying a tardy homage to reason and to
right, will profit by the example of those for whom the great
teachers of jurisprudence have not written in vain.

CONTENTS.

ERRATA.

TABLE OF CASES.

b

PRELIMINARY DISSERTATION.

NEXT to the possession of Freedom, a wise system of Laws regulating the relations of individuals to each other, is the greatest blessing that any community can enjoy. It does not indeed follow, that the nation which possesses one should enjoy the other; on the contrary, it has often happened that the two blessings have been distinct and separate. It may even be doubted whether a beneficial code of Private Law will not reconcile a degenerate people to the loss of freedom; as it is certain that the security of freedom will induce a magnanimous people, so long as no vexatious privilege is conferred on a particular class, to bear with patience, and almost to cherish with complacency very glaring defects in their municipal institutions.

When a horse was made consul, Rome enjoyed a system of private laws unequalled for wisdom and equity; and when our balanced government had approached as near perfection as perhaps human infirmity will admit, the preliminaries of trial by battle, elaborately arranged by eminent lawyers, actually took place, under the eyes and with the sanction of the first ministers of English justice; at the same time, the language and decisions of our judges on questions of real property and special pleadings, were more like the whimsical extravagance of a goblin allowed by some mysterious dispensation to apply to human affairs the morbid acuteness of a perverted intellect,[a] than the errors and mistakes of beings possessing the

---

[a] Before the reader condemns these expressions, let him first reflect on the language of the law in England down to the reign of George II., of which I subjoin some specimens ; let him consider that these words

B

usual faculties, and invested with the outward appearance, of humanity.[b] So the decision on ship-money alarmed and ex-

---

were not the gabble of Bushmen huddled together in a craal, or dancing round a stake, but of judges and lawyers dealing gravely with human affairs—of the contemporaries of Bacon and Shakespeare, of Dryden, Somers, and Addison. Let him judge of the intellectual and moral state which led to retaining such forms of thought and expression in our courts of justice, while improvement was making rapid progress in every other department of human affairs. All are taken from standard works.

Whether goods taken in Withernam are irreplevisable.

Bastard eignè.

Rumper de prison.

Mulier puisnè.

Exigent de novo.

Reason why a prisoner who had once refused to plead was pressed to death in spite of his repentance.

Ceo sera son diet et ne seroit raison qui per tel repentance le roi seroit tolle del forfeiture.

Fines.—'Sur cognizance de droit sur ceo qu'il a de son done.'

' Sur cognizance de droit.'

' Sur done grant et render sur concessit where the cognizor grants to the cognizee an estate de novo.' ' Si un devise al enfant en ventre matris suæ cest bone devise, autrement est per feoffment, graunt ou done, car en ceux cases il doit estre un del'abilité pur prender maintenant.'—'Il ne poit a lui meme conveyer per heires males, CAR LA MERE (i. e., of the *unborn infant*) EST UN OBSTACLE A CEO !'

Jeofail.—Flemeswit 'hoc est quod habeatis catalla sine amerceamento.' Floatsam Jettsam Fletwit.

' That the seisin to feed Contingent Uses by a Scintilla juris, is in nubibus, in mare, in terrâ, or in custodiâ legis.'

'En qu'eux cases home a cest pur poit aver un atturney et en qu'eux nemy—vies en le lieu devant.'

Next let him refer to the bill of costs in a suit in Chancery *Commission of* 1826 Appendix to the Index tit. Pleading and Demurrer to Meeson and Welsby's Reports, and then let him meditate on the numbers who have been ruined, and (till the Revolution) murdered by the use of this jargon, and the frauds and horrors which it concealed from the public hatred and indignation.

[b] 'Having had doubts upon this Will for twenty years, there can be no use in taking more time to consider it.'—LORD ELDON, *Earl of Radnor* v. *Shafto*, 11 VESEY, p. 453.

If any satirist, desirous of lashing the public mind to fury by exposing a vicious administration of justice, had put such language as this into the mouth of a judge, would it not have been condemned for its

asperated a people, in whom the love of material prosperity had not as yet extinguished more generous feelings; but whole families were steeped in misery, and compelled to drink the cup of affliction to the dregs, by the chicane and delay which made the Court of Chancery,[c] during the time of Lord Eldon most especially, one of the most terrible calamities ever inflicted on this country, before a tardy[d] and inadequate

---

extravagance? Add to this a system contrived for chicane and procrastination, and the reader may form some notion of what 'practical' England endured with patience, while Lord Eldon presided over the Court of Chancery. See ROMILLY's *Life* (passim).

[c] Danda autem opera non solum ut cuilibet jus suum tribuatur sed ET CITO.

[d] *Commission of* 1826. The value of which may be judged of, from a perusal of the names of those who composed it, at the head of which is Lord Eldon himself; and from this passage, p. 9, 'The term *delay* has been so frequently misapplied, as to convey a VERY INCORRECT IDEA with respect to the duration of a suit in Chancery': to be sure, there follows, p.11: 'If the defendant should not put in his answer .... a long line of dilatory and expensive process has hitherto been resorted to, for the purpose of compelling him to do it.' There is a reference in the Appendix, vol. ii. p. 603, of a suit for foreclosure, where there was no defence, the suit lasted four years, and cost in fees to counsel £79 12s. 6d.

Report of Commission, 1850. 'The misfortune to suitors in Chancery is, that the expense of the protection afforded often absorbs the whole of the property protected!

'We have thus explained the course of procedure in the Master's Office; in a simple case, it is obviously calculated to cause unnecessary delay and expense. The system had its origin at a time when the Masters and their clerks were paid by fees. Every warrant, every copy, every report, indeed every proceeding, carried its fee; small, perhaps, in individual amount, but the multiplication of which pressed heavily on the suitor, and yielded large emoluments to the officers. This method of remunerating the Masters and their chief clerks by fees, has been put an end to by the Chancery Regulation Act; but the system still remains, fees are still paid as heretofore, though the amount is carried to the fee-fund, and the effects of the system still remain in the mode of procedure, of which we have given an example.

'In estimating the evils arising from this system, it must not be forgotten, that every warrant and every other step and proceeding which we have enumerated, is attended with professional charges of the solicitors employed.

reformation could be wrung from power, obstinate because it was ignorant, and careless because it was not attacked with sufficient vehemence of indignation.

So, too, the Star Chamber was abolished; but the jargon of our Law Latin, which Cromwell had swept away, was carefully restored—and every stupid fiction,[e] every artifice that could be contrived to prevent or to make unfruitful the triumph of substantial justice in our Common Law Courts, continued to flourish down even to our own times. Thus while, in our Constitutional safeguards and provisions we had succeeded in obtaining that union of liberty and order which the greatest writers of antiquity had declared to be unattainable, citizens were stripped of their property, flung into pestilential jails,[f]

'If in such a simple case as we have described, it is a practice to proceed by so many steps, and with so much delay, it is obvious what must be the course of a litigation carried on and prosecuted in a hostile manner, and in a case of complicated circumstances. Each item in an account may form the subject of a separate investigation of a state of facts, and counter state of facts, each of which may be supported by evidence on affidavit, deposition, or *vivâ voce* examination. Warrants are taken out at intervals, according to the engagements of the Master or his clerk, and to suit the convenience of counsel or solicitors.'—*Report C. C.*, 1850, p. 30.

[e] Ejectment has only just been abolished. Fines and recoveries lasted till 1830. The new rules, which the genius of chicane would not worsen, were framed in 1830, retaining all the worst parts of the old system; aggravated by greater technicality. ' Thus the declaration in Ejectment always states a fictitious demise made by the real claimant to a fictitious plaintiff; and the declaration in Trover uniformly alleges, though almost always contrary to the fact, that the defendant found the goods for which the action was brought.'—STEPHENS *on Pleading*, p. 490.

If any reader wishes to see how far grave absurdity can be carried, let him read the account of negatives pregnant, and of 'giving colour,' as a particular kind of falsehood, encouraged by our Courts, was called in the same work, p. 233, and he will think Rabelais feeble and insipid. 'It would seem,' says a writer on Ejectment, p. 3, 'these fictions are coeval with the law itself,' *i. e.*, the worst times of the worst period of our history, 'and form part of its SIMPLE BEAUTY !'

[f] The savage treatment of prisoners for debt can only be conceived

condemned to pay unjust demands, or barred from the attainment of righteous claims for reasons as unconnected with the merits of their case as the shape of their advocate's dress or the colour of his hair—reasons that none but English reporters have ever stated to be conceivable as the basis of a judicial determination, and the use of which not only lowers the character of the people among whom they were allowed to prevail, but may literally be described as a reproach and scandal to human nature. One cause which undoubtedly tended to establish our civil liberty, is as certainly the reason to which the unhappy state of our Municipal Law is to be attributed, I mean the instinctive suspicion and hostility with which our fathers regarded the Roman Law. Politically speaking, these apprehensions were given wisely and taken usefully. Perverted by the Canonists into an instrument[g] of ecclesiastical ambition and rapacity, wielded in every part of Europe by the clergy, as a means of accomplishing their gigantic schemes of usurpation, used in later times by Laud, the meanest of tyrants, to gratify his meddling presumption, his miserable spite, and his savage temper, it is not surprising that real patriots should oppose doctrines which were put forward ostentatiously by the most determined and implacable foes of English freedom. Meanwhile, the English lawyer, shut out from the school of the great masters of jurisprudence, employed in carrying on verbal disputes in an impure dialect, became narrow-minded, and the English law, moulded by such hands, continued barbarous.

---

by those who read the trials of Arne or Huggins, wardens of the Fleet. The committee found a baronet, Sir William Rich, laden with irons by order of Bembridge, the warden. A prisoner for debt was starved to death in prison in this century.

[g] BRACTON clearly lays it down, *De Corona*, lib. iii. fol. 124, that the sovereign has no jurisdiction over a priest until degraded, ' non habebit Rex de eo prisonam quem judicare non potest': and he says, that a clerk convicted of an offence, whatever it might be, was sufficiently punished by degradation; and, therefore, that no crimes committed by him before degradation could incur any other penalty.

That at one time the vestiges of the civil law in this country were manifest, no one who has opened Bracton, or read Selden's Dissertation on Fleta, will dispute. But as the forms of Common Law Pleading[h] were not framed in such a manner as to comprise the relations between the trustee and the person for the benefit of whom he was the nominal owner of the property, common lawyers absolutely refused to take any notice of Trusts, or Uses, as they were then called; and thus, not recognising a state of things imperiously demanded as a remedy against some of the evils of the social state, contributed by their selfish and purblind obstinacy,

---

[h] 'Use fuit chose en regard per le common ley que avoit aucune effet, power, ou authority, ou nemy qu'eux chose, cestuique use avoit ou poit faire per ceo.

'Quel chose use est ou fuit a le common ley fuit dit que nest aucune chose dont le common ley fuit conusance ou done a ceo aucune vertu ou effect.'—ANDERSON'S *Reports*, p. 318.

I have quoted this specimen of the language in which the Common Law delighted to justify the expressions I have used: it seems scarcely credible that human creatures, the contemporaries of Bacon, Dryden, and Addison, should have persisted in the use of such gibberish;—it means simply that a 'use' was not a thing of which the Common Law took any notice, or to which it gave any virtue or effect. The sentiment is worthy of the dialect; for at this time a vast proportion of English property was in the form of which our judges affected ignorance. 'Uses,' says LORD ST. LEONARDS, in perhaps his most remarkable effort, the Preface to GILBERT, *On Uses and Trusts*, 'evaded without overturning the Common Law'; but surely it was overturned *pro tanto* where it was evaded, that is, where it was made insignificant. 'An Use is nothing else but a trust and confidence, and was not any inheritance by the course of the Common Law, for no mention is made of Uses in our ancient books when the Common Law greatly flourished, as in the time of Edward I. and Edward III.; and also Uses are not subject to the grounds of law."—LEONARD, *Brent's Case*, vol. ii. p. 15.

'44 Edward III., *Year Book*, 256, *en foi demit*': The first mention is 30 Henry VI. in our books, FITZH. 22, in the time of Edward IV., they were frequent, *ib.* MANWOOD, *Justice*, says: 'The reason why no mention is made in our ancient books of Uses is, because men were of better conscience than now they are.' Cestuique Use, however, was sworn on juries.

to the result they most dreaded — the power and importance of Courts of Equity. Selden fixes upon the reign of Edward the Third as the period when all reference to Roman Jurisprudence ceased to be made in our Courts of Common Law, when, if any rule that might be traced to that origin was cited, it was usually cited in an English garb, and very rarely in a Latin shape—a practice, he adds, continued by Plowden, Dyer and Coke, who cite the maxims of the civilians, 'velut in Anglicano natos,' as indigenous, instead of being, as they really were, the growth of a more refined age and a more highly gifted people. One great object of the writer of these pages, is to discharge the debt which Lord Bacon says every man owes to his profession, by contributing as far as his slender abilities, and the industry by which he has endeavoured to supply their deficiencies will allow, to put a stop to a practice which has continued down to our own time, and to dispel a prejudice of which the marks are still too gross to be disputed by any one who has imbibed the first notions of jurisprudence, and too pernicious to be endured by those who aspire to promote the welfare of their country.

Another cause of evil to our law, has been the attempt to comprise in the words of different statutes, everything that can exclude the necessity of an equitable interpretation—an attempt caused by the perverse separation of Law and Equity among us, a system unknown to any other country, and pregnant with the most frightful evils, utterly ineffectual for any good purpose, and creating the very evil it was intended to prevent. To these circumstances, which have given so wrong a bias to our law, I shall have occasion presently to advert more at length; but before I do so, it will be consistent with the object of this undertaking, that I should address myself to more general topics.

The history of the human species, as far as the records of civilized nations enable us to judge of it, resembles the

history of an individual. Different objects engross the energies of man at different periods; none can altogether fix his
thoughts, for this is not their abiding-place.

The first predominant principle that we are able to trace in
the accounts that have been transmitted to us of nations after
they have emerged from barbarism is that of a religious feeling, discovering, in the gloom and servile awe with which it
is accompanied, the nature of its origin, and the causes of its
influence: hence the power of the priesthood, and its establishment as a separate caste.[i] As society advances and refinement
increases, this sentiment is softened and modified, and gives
way to the love of the great and beautiful. This is the youth
of the species; and of this, as we now represent its rapidly
increasing decrepitude, Greece was the representative.

The καλοκἀγαθὸν is the word with which that wonderful
people expressed their veneration for all that is lovely, grace-
ful, and magnanimous, which was embodied in their institutions and exemplified by their history. All that there was of
grand or beautiful in nature, in the creations of art, in the
verse of the poet and the eloquence of the orator, in the wisdom
of the statesman and the conceptions of the legislator, all that
there was on earth of loveliness, or truth, or justice, were, in
the eyes of Socrates and of Plato, but dim and faint revelations
of that ideal excellence which no human sense could penetrate,
and no human thought could comprehend. The noblest acts
of virtue, the loveliest forms of beauty, the sagest institutions
which could embellish civil life, were to them but fleeting
types and shadowy outlines by which man might train and
discipline his mind to the contemplation of that ineffable and
imperishable archetype, of which all that is good on earth was
but a remote and imperfect emanation.

---

[i] The writer does not allude in any way to the Mosaic dispensation,
but to the records of other nations. See CASAUBON's *Notes to Sue-
tonius—Augustus*, 31. The duties of the βασιλεὺς at Athens, and the
rex sacrorum at Rome, illustrate his proposition.

The Greeks were the first nation who ascended from the beauty and order of the external universe to the beauty which exalts the moral sense from the harmony of the physical world to the harmony of thought and action, from taste to virtue, from refinement to philosophy and a love of justice.

Thus the love of right and order developed itself among them, and was placed amid the choir of all the virtues. There, in the height and palmy state of this period of our progress, in the full blaze of intellectual splendour, Plato composed his immortal works, and the principles of justice and of equity were the subjects on which the chosen intellects of that unequalled people were employed perpetually.

But, in the pointed language of Lord Bacon, to the vulgar they 'gave little light, because they were so high.' Justice was taught in the schools of philosophers, and laws were ordained by statesmen; but there was no class of men set apart to enforce the one and to administer the other. Open Plato, and you will see, not only that the separation between public and private law has not yet been correctly made,[k] but also that the provinces of law and morality are considered as identical. The state, it was supposed, had the right to control every thought and act of the individual; and an offence against the duties and charities of private life, was an offence

---

[k] *Private*—ἀγὼν ἴδιος—δίκη ἰδία. δίκη.

Public—ἀγὼν δημόσιος δίκη δημοσία.

At the same time there are some noble passages in Demosthenes, one of which is quoted in the Pandects, on the purpose and efficacy of law. So, in the speech against Midias, he insists with unequalled vehemence that a crime against a man clothed with public functions was a crime against the state. 'I anticipate,' says the great orator, 'that Midias will say, that the charge, being for a personal injury, should not have been laid as a public offence (προβολὴ); that I should have brought an action (βλάβης or ὕβρεως), and certainly not have impeached him (οὐχὶ δημοσία κρίνειν αὐτὸν), and endeavoured to make him pay a fine to the state (τίμημα ἐπάγειν. κ. τ. λ.).' But any one who reads the speeches against Leptines, against Aristogeiton, against Timocrates, against Aristocrates, and against Neæra, will find the truth of my proposition substantially verified by the topics and language of the orator.

against the municipal law, and required the interference of its guardians. The Beautiful and the Good were not distinguished from those plainer and more homely doctrines which bind men together in society, and which it is the especial business of the magistrate to enforce. In Plato's republic a thief would not have been punished with more severity than one 'guilty of irreverence to age.

To develop the science of law, and to weave it into the common affairs of life; to define the different provinces of law, and to assign its different name to each; to distinguish between the relations of the citizen and the magistrate to each other and to distinct communities, was not the task assigned to Greece; but, as the world advanced, became the work of a stern and sagacious people, in whose fate it was to conquer and to civilise the West, and in the character of whom may be seen the impress of the virtues and the vices which belong to increasing years in the species as well as the individual. If the English empire in India were swept away tomorrow, it would leave behind it no monument that denotes the great conceptions or well-timed benevolence which have sometimes been exhibited under an enlightened despotism by such rulers as Richelieu or even Napoleon; nothing to tell mankind that to collect money had not been the sole object of its ignoble rulers. But when every other institution had perished, the Roman law furnished materials for restoring civil life to dignity and splendour. Law, when it is made a science, is imperishable; once placed upon its proper basis, its maxims oppose an immoveable barrier to the caprice and violence of authority. In the Roman empire, an hierarchy of power, skilfully organised, and too often an instrument of oppression, (the members of which, however, never affected, like the hireling champions of our Indian rule, a cynical disregard for the happiness of millions, but professed at least some reverence for justice), bound together the different members of the state, affording shelter and protection to the seed and germ from which the refinement and civility hidden under the ruins and ashes of the social fabric were one day to spring forth.

Many causes contributed to the downfall of the Roman empire. To live by one man's will had been long the cause of all men's misery. The corruption of the metropolis,[1]—the desolation of the provinces,—the extinction of all social and manly virtue,—war[m] become the vilest of trades, carried on by the basest of mercenaries,—the most hideous distress,—the most unbounded luxury,—the sensual habits and concentration on material objects which pave men's hearts, and make them as the highway—all these causes had brought the Roman empire to that downward point from which, in the progress of nations, it is impossible to re-ascend. As well might an individual hope to shake off the diseases of age with the same ease as the disorders of youth, as a people sunk in sloth and cowardice, and aiming only at the command of sensual enjoyments, to resume its place in the scale of nations.

The tide of foreign invaders rose higher every year. The barbarians brought with them new elements of political and social life, but we shall look in vain among them for the presence of any single virtue. Cunning and ferocious, dissolute and brutal, alternately slaves to the most grovelling superstition and the most frantic passion, their story is one of unmixed evil; and he who opens the volume of Gregory of Tours, for instance, or any chronicles that relate the events of that dreadful period, finds an account of all the horrors that lust, cruelty, rapine, wild revenge, unrestrained power, and calculating perfidy can bring down upon a devoted race. 'For there was darkness over the face of the land.' Whatever the barbarians

---

[1] As to this, see GOTHOFRED'S *Notes to the Theodosian Code*, a work of stupendous learning : the substance, so far as relates to the condition of the towns, is embodied by ROTH, *De re Municipali.*

[m] 'Nullum vitæ genus est improbius quam eorum qui sine causæ respectu mercede conducti militant, . . . tanto carnifice detestabiliores quanto pejus est sine causâ quam ex causâ occidere.'—GROTIUS, lib. ii. 25, § 1, 2.

could destroy, perished. But two great elements of regeneration were beyond their reach. The fires that consumed city after city, the sword that mowed down myriads after myriads, the famine that laid waste province after province, could neither annihilate the Roman law, nor obliterate the principles of Christianity.

The Christian faith could not arrest the progress of these calamities; but from the principles it established, from the sublime doctrine that in the sight of God all men were equal, the final emancipation of the enslaved and groaning multitude was sure to follow. The teachers of Christianity were men, and, as men, not superior to the temptation of wealth and power. Those dissensions, schisms, and animosities,[n] of which even in the early church the proofs are sufficiently visible, were multiplied and exaggerated as the doctrines of the church became more complicated and its purposes more secular. Nevertheless, the contests in which the church was engaged against kings and emperors, the interminable disputes as to the limits of secular and ecclesiastical authority, compelled the church and its advocates—more especially in an age when the feudal system had embodied the worst abuses of the time—to balance by moral notions the weight of physical strength, to appeal to the supremacy of right and to maxims of jurisprudence. Law became the favourite study of churchmen. Skilfully adapting the Roman jurisprudence to their purposes, they framed a code which, tainted as it was with the vices of those to whom it owed its origin, is nevertheless, by the example which it furnished to the rude nations among whom it was promulgated, a most important era in the intellectual history of the species.

Then it was that Italy once more asserted her privilege

---

[n] SARPI, *Trattato delle mat. ben.*, c. 6: '6 nel 370 fu fatta la legge . . . che proibiva agli Ecclesiastici l'andar in casa di Vedove e di Pupilli 6 il ricevere per donazione o testamento alcuna cosa dalle donne.'—*Cod.* THEODOS., *de Episcopis et Ecc.*, b.10 ; JEROME, *Epist. ad Eustachium*; MOSHEIM, *De rebus Ecc. ante Constant.*

to instruct and reclaim mankind. In the glorious struggles of her republics, in their institutions and their love of freedom, in the field of Legnano, in the league of Lombardy, we find the beginnings of regeneration for ungrateful Europe; above all, we find the reviving study of the Roman law disentangled from the sophistry of ecclesiastics and the frivolous subtleties of the schools—equally opposed to the open violence of the feudal system and the insidious usurpations of the Roman priest. Nor was the great epoch, memorable for the struggle between the Swabian race of emperors and the Papal See, barren of consequences to mankind. The popes, indeed, succeeded in destroying their mighty enemies. Frederick the Second° was overcome; he died, unable to finish a war which annihilated his race. But he had achieved great things for Europe: in his time were founded those schools of jurisprudence which finally subverted the theocracy that Rome attempted to maintain, and established the complete independence of the civil power. Thus the Roman triumphed over his conquerors; reason, the mistress of human life, compelled the illiterate barbarians to receive his laws, and to pay homage to the noblest application of the principles of natural equity to civil affairs which man has ever been able to preserve. It was to those consummate masters of civil knowledge, that reason unveiled her mysteries; it is their works which every one who aspires to be a jurist must deeply meditate, and it is from them that the maxims are drawn, which are the sure and solid basis of jurisprudence, which contain in themselves the pith and marrow of universal justice, and on which law for the most part rested in the great European community, glimmering forth as through a cloud amid the thick night of feudal ignorance.

° The passage in the *Purgatorio*, where Dante meets Manfred, the son of Frederick, is one of the most beautiful in his poem :—

    ' Biondo era e bello é di gentile aspetto
    Ma l'un de cigli un colpo avea diviso,' etc.

Some of these maxims I have endeavoured in the following
pages to develop and illustrate, as thinking that they furnish
a clue which may lead those intrusted with the administration of justice among us from darkness into light, and
that it is better they should be placed under their eyes in
their pure and native shape, than in the adulterate language
of Coke, encumbered with the counterfeit learning and irrational conceits in which he delighted, and with which alone
the English lawyers of his day, and long afterwards, were for
the most part conversant.

Let it not be supposed that the study of the Roman jurists
is useless, except in countries where the Roman law is the
basis of jurisprudence. Dumoulin is the great oracle of the
French feudal law. He lived about the time of Lord Coke.
The *Coutume de Paris* is the standard of French customary law,
and Dumoulin's treatise on that *Coutume* is reckoned his
greatest work: it fills a closely-printed folio volume; and I
doubt if it contains a page without a reference to the Roman
law. If any one wishes to find an illustration of the value of
the study of the Roman law—quite apart from the wisdom of
its institutions—as an exercise and discipline of the understanding, let him compare the works of Lord Coke with those
of Dumoulin;[p] let him observe the want of method, the ignorance of law as a science, the pedantry, the reliance on positive
law, the indifference to abstract right, the incapacity of gene-
ralisation, the antipathy to all enlarged views, the wild conceits, the scholastic barbarism of the writer on the common
law of England; and the close reasoning, the reverence for
justice, the deep learning, the luminous method, and the clear
perception of analogy which distinguish the writer on the
customary law of France; and, if he be fit for anything but to
argue special demurrers, and to draw up reports for anti-
reforming chancellors in favour of obsolete abuses and

---

[p] Born in 1500; 'l'auteur le plus analytique qui ait écrit sur la jurisprudence.'—D'AGUESSEAU.

restraints, he may be left to draw his own inference. I quote Dumoulin, because he was neither a statesman nor a philosopher, but a lawyer only; and in that respect the fittest person to put in the balance with the prosecutor of Raleigh, and the denouncer of the Jews, whom all succeeding ages have venerated as the oracle of English law. Such a reader will appreciate the labours of the great schools of Bologna, Bourges, and Toulouse (carried on while, among us, Fleming was preferred to Bacon, and the Scintilla juris was asserted by the Gaudys and the Pophams), the admirable codes drawn up under the reign of Louis XIV., the work, in great measure, of the virtuous and profound Lamoignon. To these great events in the intellectual history of the species, growing immediately out of the cultivation of jurisprudence, an enlarged range of thought and study will teach him to join the change wrought in the ideas of men by the works of Bodin, of Machiavel, of Grotius, of D'Aguesseau, and, above all, by those of Montesquieu—an impartial philosopher, profound as a jurist, matchless (in modern times) as an historian, a believer in the majesty of right and virtue amid the shallow clamours of successful scepticism, who taught us how to combine the kindred studies of law and history, to make law elucidate history, and history account for law. In his first chapter, he tells us that if some laws which prevail among intelligent beings are made by themselves, others, which they must obey, are not. 'Laws,' he says, 'are necessary relations arising from the nature of things;' and, in this sense, nothing is beyond their influence or exempt from their operation.

Man's nature bears upon it the stamp and intention of a greater Providence. His soul is the seat of reason; and as the same ocean receives different names from the shores by which it is encompassed, so does reason receive different names from the subject to which it is applied.

Considered in its application to the conduct of men who are limited in their dealings with each other by the rules arising out of their common nature, it is called the law of nature. The same reason, considered in its bearing on the relations of communities to each other, and the rules by which their intercourse is governed, is called the law of nations, and public law; that is, *jus populicum*,[q] the law in the application of which the *populus*, the collective body of citizens as distinguished from Titius and Mævius, has a direct and immediate interest. For the same cause it is called public law when it prescribes the duty of the ruling power towards its subjects, and of subjects to the ruling power and to the laws. Public law is the guardian of those other rules which govern contracts, deeds, wills, and other acts which are the basis of social life among members of the same community, and which are called private or civil law.

The law which made the Roman send back the schoolmaster who betrayed the children of his adversaries into his power, which made Mr. Fox reject the offer to assassinate Napoleon, which was violated by Catherine when she carried fire and sword through Poland, which we violated when we compelled Norway to submit to Sweden in 1814, and which we violate by too many acts of our government in the East,[r] is the law of nature. The treaties concluded between our government and other states, the rights and privileges of ambassadors, the respect shewn by civilized enemies to a flag of truce, belong to that branch of the public law known by the name of the Law of Nations. The right of making a will[s] among the Romans, Magna Charta, the Petition of Right, the Bill of Rights, the Act of Settlement, the Constitution, Privileges, and Power of Parliament, the old Navigation Act, the Habeas

---

[q] SAVIGNY, *System, etc.*, vol.i.

[r] *Report of the Madras Torture Commission; Reports on the Salt Duties in India.*

[s] Testamenti factio non privati sed publici juris est.—*Dig.* 28,1,3. And the will was a public instrument, not the property of an individual, but of the community: 'non unius, hominis sed universorum.' — *Dig.* 29, 41.

Corpus Act, all the criminal law, belong among ourselves to the domain of public law. Every municipal law, written or unwritten, that does not fall within the last class, is part of the municipal or civil law; it is—or, as an Englishman, I fear I should say, it ought to be—'jus civile; i. e., æquitas constituta iis qui ejusdem civitatis sunt.'

The rules of private law vary in each nation. But if men were not divided into nations, or subject to regular law, they would observe certain rules in their intercourse with each other. Some portion of such rules is necessarily incorporated with the civil law of each country; hence the distinction among the Roman jurists between those simple contracts that were called 'jus gentium,' and those of a more artificial and arbitrary character. The rules which modify the 'jus gentium' in a manner peculiar to any country, either by adding to or taking away from it, constitute the civil law of that country: 'jus civile est quod neque in totum a naturali vel gentium jure recedit neque per omnia ei servit—itaque cum aliquid addimus vel detrahimus juri communi, jus proprium, id est, civile efficimus.' As, therefore, much of the law of nature is incorporated with the law of nations, so some part of the law of nations is incorporated with the civil law of every country. The same rule may therefore be distinguished by different names, as it is contemplated under different aspects; and this has given rise to much confusion among the writers on this subject. The law, for instance, that protects minors, generally considered, is a law of nature. Considered with reference to twenty-one years, as the time when that protection shall expire, and qualified by other restraints, it is the English municipal or civil law. Framed in a different manner, it is the civil law of Rome. The pure ore may be cast into moulds of different shape and size, it may even be debased by much alloy, but it is the same metal, nevertheless, in every age and climate.

Therefore Gaius says, with admirable reason, on the instance

c

I have selected: ' Impuberes in tutelâ esse *omnium* civitatum jure contingit, quia *naturali* rationi conveniens est, ut is qui perfectæ ætatis non sit alterius tutelâ regatur.'

The rules of law are clear and concise expressions of what justice requires in particular cases, and every rule has its value in the special case for which it is intended.

Rules are of two sorts; the first class contains those which arise from natural law and equity—the second those which are established by positive law.

That no man shall derive advantage from his own wrong is a maxim of natural law. That the property of a deceased person shall be distributed by a will attested in a certain manner is an arbitrary rule of positive law, varying with the habits and opinions of society.

The eternal and immutable nature of those principles from which all law must spring, and which are transferred from the heart of man to our public codes of legislation, has been questioned sometimes by men of real genius, always by sciolists, and especially by the empirical school, which exercised so great an influence in France during the last century,[t] and is at present so omnipotent in this country.

Supposing, however, man to have a share of reason, it is clear that within the sphere of that reason there is something common to him, and (I say it with reverence) to its Author. That, for instance, triangles on the same base and between the same parallels are equal, is a truth present, as Malebranche observes, to the Deity as well as to His creatures.

Hence the distinctions between truth and falsehood, between just and unjust must exist for every order of intelligence.

---

[t] ARISTOTLE, *Later Analytics*, i. 10, says, with his usual wisdom :—An axiom is not an hypothesis—any man may contradict in words any truth however self-evident, but he cannot really disbelieve it. ἀεὶ γὰρ ἔστιν ἐνστῆναι πρὸς τὸν ἔξω λόγον ἀλλὰ πρὸς τὸν ἔσω λόγον οὐκ ἀεί.

The clearest and most complete refutation of Hobbes, on whose 'steel cap' so many have hammered, will be found in JOUFFROY, *Droit Naturel,* vol. i. p. 32.

When we say that the angles of a triangle are equal to two
right angles, we state a truth independent of time or place, a
truth to which the actual existence of a triangle in any part of
space is absolutely indifferent. When we declare ingratitude
to be a vice, we assert a truth arising out of certain relations
which, as it was a truth

    'Before the hills were made or fountain played,'

would be a truth if man and the heap of dust over which he
crawls, and which he is so proud of measuring and traversing,
were annihilated to-morrow.

As it would be no argument against the physical truth to
shew an ill drawn figure like a triangle of which the angles were
not equal to two right angles,[u]—neither is it any argument
against the moral truth to shew a law or custom by which it is
contradicted.

    ' If black and white blend, soften and unite
      Ten thousand ways, is there no black or white ?'

No man can feel the particular sensation of another, but every
one may see the truth that another contemplates. The reason
is, that the sensation belongs to the individual, and the truth
is the property of the species. Just as when a thousand eyes
behold the sun at once, they see the same individual object.
It is certain, indeed, that it is not easy to lay down an
infallible rule by which the dictates of natural reason may
be distinguished from the creatures of positive law: 'Omnis
definitio,' say the civilians of the civil law—and the same
is true of natural law—' periculosa parum est enim quin sub-
verti possit.' Those who would thus mutilate and disfigure
human nature might have learnt from an admirable passage in
the Politics of Aristotle, that mere juxtaposition does not
make citizens,—that if a state of war had been natural to man
it never would have ceased; nor would man have been ever
able to perceive the benefits of society. But because a sense of

---

    [u] ARIST. *Topics*, lib. i. c. 1, mentions this fallacy : ὁ ψευδογραφῶν.

those benefits is impressed upon his mind, a social state is on
the contrary natural to him, φύσει μὲν ἐστιν ἄνθρωπος ζῶον
πολιτικόν.[x]

Hobbes leaves out of his account altogether the pleasures of
sympathy, which, as Aristotle well observes, would alone and
without any prospect of other advantage, account for the existence of society.[y] 'What tyrant is there,' says Lord Shaftesbury, 'what robber or open violator of the laws of society
who has not some particular set either of his own kindred, or
such as he calls his friends, with whom he gladly shares his
good, in whose welfare he delights, and whose joy and satisfaction he makes his own.'[z] And according to the argument
of those who deny that there is any law but that with which
the feelings, wishes, and instincts of every individual furnish
him, not only is the existence of such words as 'ought' and
'duty' unaccountable, not only is it impossible that any motive
should ever have induced men to form themselves into communities, but there must be a different law of nature for every
member of the species; inasmuch as the views, hopes and
wishes of no two among it are the same.

Human affairs, *quicquid agunt homines*, are so mixed and in-
terwoven with each other, there are so many mediums by which
the light that comes from heaven is broken and refracted upon
earth, that the sophist has abundant scope for his ingenuity in
endeavouring to confound what is variable and accidental with
what is as fixed and eternal as God Himself.

Admirably indeed has it been said by the illustrious man at
whom the minute philosophers of the day have presumed to
cavil: 'Ferme hic quidem evenit quod in mathematicis ubi
quædam sunt notitiæ primæ aut primis proximæ, quædam de-
monstrationes quæ statim intelliguntur et assensum obtinent,

---

[x] ARIST. *Politics*, iii. § 4.—a work which contains more sense in a
page than whole volumes of modern dissertations on the same subject.

[y] Διὸ καὶ μηδὲν δεόμενοι τῆς παρ' ἀλλήλων βοηθείας οὐκ ἔλαττον ὀρέγονται
τοῦ συζῆν.   [z] *Inquiry.* Part ii. § 1.

quædam veræ quidem, sed non omnibus patentes.'—GROTIUS, ii. 20. 46.

And to a superficial observer, the same act may in different ages and countries wear a very different aspect. For instance, to make the breaking down a dam in England a capital felony was justly selected by Blackstone as an instance of the barbarous condition of the criminal law, all amendment in which was so steadily and acrimoniously resisted by *all our judges*. But to break down a dam in Holland was justly visited by the severest punishment, because the safety of the state depended on its preservation. Hume and Montaigne would seize upon such a circumstance and dazzle their readers with every sort of specious fallacy arising from the contrast. But the answer is clear; in the one case the law can be traced up to and connected with a higher law, in the other it cannot; in the one case severity is dictated by a regard for the public weal, in the other it springs from a mistaken view of the interests of a particular class of society and a morbid desire for their welfare; in the one case, therefore, the law is righteous, in the other it is oppressive. In short, the law given to man by man must be justified by the law given to man by God.

In like manner, every positive law that is useful may be defended, even when such a reason cannot be assigned—even when the maxim of the Roman jurist applies: ' Non omnium quæ a majoribus constituta sunt ratio reddi potest.' The argument for upholding such a law rests upon the same foundation. The defender of such a law would argue, in some cases justly, that to change it would involve the destruction of things more precious than itself that were connected with it, and that the evils of change were greater than the benefits of innovation, thereby appealing to the higher principles which the sophist would discard—to those grounds of justice, however, and moral virtue which, as Lord Bacon says, if ' they be well and watchfully pursued, make points of convenience and accommodations for the present' as superfluous as medicine to a healthy

body. But because to combine the principles of justice with
the infinite variety of human concerns is an undertaking too
great and vast for any single intellect, there is the more reason to regret the infatuation of those who, born among an inferior race, have steadily rejected for many centuries the precious maxims preserved for them in the treasury of the Roman
law.

In civil matters, as to provide for every case is impossible;
and as all disputes among individuals must in some way or
other be decided, the text of no law can be in itself sufficient.

This necessity was expressed by the Romans when they said
that the 'jus Prætorium' was introduced ' corrigendi aut sup-
plendi juris civilis gratiâ,' and when they pointed out analogy
or 'ratio juris' as a cardinal principle of interpretation. There
is nothing to which the almost incredible confusion of the
English law is more directly to be ascribed than to the attempt
so truly characteristic of an empirical nation to comprise every
particular case in the very words of the statute; an attempt
which as it has uniformly failed, has given rise to the most
opposite evils, to the most pettifogging and the most arbitrary
system of interpretation; our judges have assumed to themselves powers of legislation utterly incompatible with every
sound notion of their duties, and, in spite of some creditable
exceptions, they have—I speak of no living person—too often
exercised them in the spirit which might be expected in men
raised by the favour of an inferior class, to frustrate the avowed
purpose of the legislature by most vexatious chicane.[a]

---

[a] The Statute *de donis* was repealed by the decision of the judges in
Taltarum's case ; the Statute of Frauds by Russell v. Russell. 1.
BROWN Ch. C.

Lord Eldon says, in so many words, that 'he must not repeal the
Statute farther than it has been repealed by his predecessors,' ex parte
Whitbread, 19 VESEY, 212. Ex parte GREEN, 15 VESEY, 577. Speaking
of 1 Geo. I. st. 2. c. 19. § 11 and 12, he says : ' Though this is the construction, I doubt if it is the intention of the legislature.' Lord Kenyon,
PEAKE, *Reports, Smith v. Armorer,* says : ' The judges have lent their
assistance to repeal this law as much as was in their power.' Judges

Whenever to interpret a law in its literal and obvious meaning would lead to mischievous consequences and to decisions which, if applied indiscriminately to every thing included in the expression, would be unjust,—then the clear proof of such injustice flowing from the deadly letter obliges the judge to look for the healing spirit, and to discover by its purpose the proper interpretation and limits of its language.[b]

Now this method of interpretation always must rest on the manner in which the law to be interpreted is modelled and qualified by some general rule and maxim of jurisprudence, the law derives its truth and value from such a modification. For instance, there was no clearer or more sacred rule in Roman jurisprudence than that by which the person with whom an article was deposited was bound to restore it to the person from whom it was received;—yet if that person turned out to be a thief, or if he lost his senses and came in a fit of raging madness to demand that the money or the sword he had deposited should be restored to him, it is clear that the duty of the person who has received the money or the sword is qualified and controlled by other rules and obligations.[c] So it was a rule

---

repeal a Statute! Such are English ideas of jurisprudence. The Romans said, 'perquam dura est—sed ita lex scripta est.' Our constitution has not invested judges with the power of repealing or making statutes ; and it would be difficult to find a body of men less qualified for such a task. So by the miserable decision on the statute of uses, they frustrated a most beneficial act of Parliament, and made it end as Lord Hardwicke says, in adding three words to a conveyance. It has been necessary for the legislature to rescue the subject from judicial legislation in many cases. Some of the most recent and remarkable are :—
1 Wm. IV. c. 40, on the undisputed residue of the effects of testators.
1 Wm. IV. c. 46, on illusory appointments. The Wills Act, 7 Wm. IV.
1 Vict. c. 26, as to the meaning of the word *Issue*.—VINNIUS, *Selectæ Juris Quæst.*, lib. i. c. 2.   [b] DOMAT, *Loix Civiles*, vol. i.

[c] 'Bona fides quæ in contractibus exigitur æquitatem summam desiderat sed eam utrum æstimamus ad merum jus gentium, an vero cum præceptibus civilibus et prætoriis? Veluti reus capitalis judicii deposuit apud te centum bona ejus deportata sunt, utrumne ipsi hæc reddenda an in publicum deferenda sunt — ? Si tantum naturale et gentium jus intueamur ei qui deposuit restituenda sunt, si civile jus et legum ordinem magis in publicum deferenda sunt.'—*Dig.* xvi. 3. 31.

equally certain and invariable, that the heir succeeded to all the rights of the deceased; but this rule could not be applied to the case of a partner, the heir of whom claimed the right of succeeding to the partnership. For it would be limited by the rule which makes it requisite that partners should select each other. This principle would overrule the first; for it would be unjust that a man should become the partner of others and make them responsible for his acts and dependant on his integrity without their consent and approbation. These examples shew, that the interpretation limiting the effects of one rule is always founded upon another rule, which obliges the judge to give a different interpretation to the law he is required to explain, than that of which in an isolated and irrelative view it would be susceptible.

It follows from these remarks, that to ascertain the meaning of a rule, it is not enough that it should be considered separately and apart from other rules, but the judge must inquire whether it is not circumscribed and modified by others of equal validity and importance. Justice can never contradict justice, right can never be opposed to right. The equity of no rule, therefore, that is founded on sound reason can in reality be opposed to that of any other: each has its proper scope and its full operation within its proper limits. It is the knowledge of this equity, and the general view of this spirit and purpose of the laws, that furnishes the solid basis of usage, as well as the proper rules for their interpretation. Surely, then, it is a flagrant absurdity to establish courts under the name of courts of equity, as a mark of distinction from other courts dealing with the same subjects, and professing to administer a particular kind of justice. Courts applying different rules to the same subject must have a practice discordant and irregular. The Roman equity[d] was 'idem per diversa;' it

***

[d] I cannot help quoting an admirable passage on equity from Dumoulin (p. 595, vol. i. tit. 1. *De Fiefs*, § 51, 85). The question was one of feudal law: how far the act of the patronus immediatus of a feud

applied a different rule to different cases. Divers measures and divers weights are not more against the interests of commerce, than these different estimates of one and the same thing are against the plainest notions of moral justice and the common interests of mankind. Every decision that does not rest on equity is an unjust decision; and it would not be more ridiculous to establish different rules of arithmetic for bankers and other merchants, than to declare that in the same case justice shall be administered in the same country on different principles. Such a system is an outrage upon reason, truth, and justice, unknown to any people but the English, and justly exposing them to the ridicule of all whose minds are tinctured with any notions of the philosophy of jurisprudence.[e]

could affect the lord paramount—patronus superior. ' Sed ne cui forte hoc breviloquis ausam præbeam et veritate vel jure scripto prætextu nudæ et imaginariæ æquitatis discedendi, ostendo primo hanc secundam partem, non esse veram ex *verbis et mente* hujus consuetudinis. Secundo primam partem sub modificatione sequenti esse æquam, *non simplici et informi æquitate quæ non est æquitas sed æquitatis simia* sed plenâ illa et verâ et germanâ æquitate quam graviter et acute descripsit jure consultus in Dig. C. bona fides, sit depositi. Videlicet quæ non tantum ex naturalibus vel juris gentium, sed etiam una cum præceptis civilibus, et prætoriis æstimatur non *ex una circumstantia vel parte rei* sive ex uno certo respectu, sed ex totius rei id est perfectâ et totali æquitate que ex omnibus personis et circumstantiis quæ negotio gesto conjunguntur impletur. Hoc est in summâ que ex plenâ totius juris et totius subjecti negotii symmetrâ consideratione resultat et hanc merito Trypho in Leg. bona fides summam id est undequâque absolutam æquitatem desiderat quasi legalem ipsam ἐπιείκειαν Πολιτικὴν, ARIST., *Ethic.*, lib. v. 1. . . . Non autem de æquitate, apparenti sive sophisticâ.'

[e] ' Discretion is a science to be governed by the rules of law and equity, which are not to oppose, but to be subservient to each other. This discretion, in some cases, follows the law implicitly; in others, assists it, and advances the remedy; in others, it allays the abuse or the rigour of it; but in no case does it contradict or *overturn the grounds and*
' For the plaintiffs, several cases were quoted from the Court of Chancery; to which my answer is, that none of them is of the least avail in a Court of Law, *because the two courts act on different principles;* and that which is the groundwork and foundation of the decision of Courts of Equity is DIRECTLY *repugnant* to every rule and determination of the Courts of Law.'

For this equity which governs the interpretation of law applies to all laws, to the most arbitrary laws as well as to the laws of nature.[f] It is by this principle that we are guided in our endeavours to discover the intention of the legislator. When that intention is clear, equity forbids its violation: 'ita lex scripta est,' is the conclusive and final answer; and a judge who should transgress the statute of frauds among us, or the 'ordonnance De Moulins' in France, by waving the demand of written proof where the law requires it, would violate equity as much as the most absurd construction by which the most narrow-minded pleader ever gave form a triumph over substance. Strict decisions are not to be looked upon as hostile to equity, or to the intention of the legislator, where it is manifest that a rigorous construction is necessary to the law from which it flows, and where to modify the law would be to make it ineffectual. In such cases *Equity* forbids that a great rule should be weakened by a minute tenderness to particular interests. Whatever be the certainty of a testator's intentions, if the will expressing them be not properly signed it must be set aside; and to hold otherwise would be to repeal the law.

To discover, then, the decision which equity demands in a particular case, without regard to its relative fitness, would not be sufficient to this special consideration: the judge must add a general and comprehensive view of that universal equity

---

principles thereof, as has been ignorantly imputed to this court.' This is the language of SIR J. JEKYLL, Cowper *v.* Earl Cowper, 2 PEERE WILLIAMS, 751.

This is the language of MR. JUSTICE BULLER, Fare v. Newman, 4 *Term Reports,* 637.

'Whereas,' says the preamble to 11 Geo. IV. and 1 Wm. IV., c. 46, certain appointments are 'invalid in Equity, though the like are good in Law; and whereas it is expedient that such appointments should be as valid in Equity as at Law,' etc. Can any Englishman read such passages without feeling his cheeks tingle? Can more wretched imbecility be exhibited, or a more complete want of 'practical' sense? Are appointments under a power the only case in which it is expedient that the decisions of Law and Equity should coincide?

[f] DOMAT, *Loix Civiles,* vol. i.

which teaches him to examine in the particular case before him whether, in the conflict of analogies, other rules should not limit and qualify that which seems immediately and directly to bear on the case under review; if the question be one of natural law, to reconcile it with such others as may seem to clash with it; or, if the question be one of arbitrary law, to discover the intention of the legislator.

It is in the exercise of this discriminating spirit that the functions of the jurist particularly consist. ' There are cases,' says Ulpian, ' where the judge ought to release the defendant on his giving adequate security for the substantial performance of his engagement, 'in summâ ÆQUITATEM ante oculos habere debet judex.' ' Laws must receive a mild and liberal construction,' says Paulus, 'that their spirit may be preserved.' All the remarks that have been made as to the fluctuating and uncertain nature of equitable divisions—of Equity that varies with the length of the chancellor's foot—vanish when we consider that they proceed on a false hypothesis; that Equity is as fixed and certain a notion as the law of which it ought to be the pervading soul; that it ought never to be left to the choice of a judge to decide whether he will apply a strict or a lenient interpretation to the same law, or to the same state of facts. He must be determined always by the intention of the legislator and the nature of the case. If the law admits of no latitude, he must decide according to the strict letter; if the law does admit a latitude, he must construe it equitably. In a country where jurisprudence is understood, the rule is as inflexible in one case as in the other; and the judge who disregards it in either, alike violates his duty. Different laws must admit a different latitude of interpretation; but the same law never can, without a grievous outrage on all justice, receive a different construction before the tribunals of the same country; its meaning never can depend on the court in which it is cited. The mere statement of such a proposition is sufficient to shew its absurdity: it follows that the same power of construction ought to belong to every court. Whatever may be the language of bigots, of men whose minds have never been enlarged by science or refined by cultivation, of pettifoggers and barbarians, whatever may be the opinions of eminent solicitors or pleading judges, the great masters of jurisprudence have taught all who will hearken to their voice, that justice and equity are synonymous. Therefore, it is high time that the divorce between Law and Equity, which has so long been the scourge and scandal of this country, should terminate, and that elements which God and reason have joined together should no longer, by the miserable narrowness and ignorance of man, be kept asunder.

To collect some of the more remarkable rules and maxims dispersed through the books of the Roman law is the object of this undertaking. 'Not only,'. to borrow the words of Lord Bacon, prefixed to his collection of the maxims of English law, a work he undertook to silence the clamour of those dunces who, in his age as in every other, have maintained successfully that a man of genius is unfit for business—' not only will the use hereof be in deciding doubt and helping soundness of judgment, but, further, in gracing argument,[g] in *correcting unprofitable*

---

[g] As a specimen of the cast of thought and study which lifted people to the highest offices of the law, I subjoin an extract from the Parliamentary debates, June 29th, 1815. The Speakers were the Lord Chancellor of England, the Lord Chief Justice of England, and a person who had been Lord Chancellor of Ireland. The reader will judge whether more deplorable ignorance could have been exhibited by Hottentots of all that legislators ought to know, and what chance legal science had under such auspices, and what class of practitioners such judges were likely to encourage.

Lord Grey moved the commitment of the Freehold Estates' Bill. He stated the object of the bill to be to make freehold estates liable to the simple contract debts of their possessor.

Lord Redesdale opposed the bill, on the ground that by its operation all the estates in the country would be brought into the Court of Chancery, and subjected to endless litigation—even where the personal estate was ultimately sufficient to meet all the claims of the creditors. Small freeholds would be thus annihilated, and a material feature in the policy of the country—which consisted in the maintenance of this

subtlety, and reducing the same to a more sound and substantial sense of law, in reclaiming vulgar errors, and, gene-

species of property, and which made the possession of a freehold a
qualification for so many offices—must be changed.

The Lord Chancellor argued that, in the first place, no necessity was
shewn for the present measure, because every man who gave credit to
a person of landed property knew that in case of the decease of that
person he had no claim on that estate. Every man might have any
security for his debts which he chose to take. In the next place, as to
the expediency of the measure : it had been the policy of the legislature, from the very infancy of statute law, to hold real property more
sacred than personal, and they had 'always taken care that no interest
in it should be transferred without proper consideration and solemnity.
The statute merchant and statute staple only applied to persons who
consented to carry on their dealings in a manner which rendered their
estates liable to be taken in execution ; but, even by them, the rents
only were taken, and when the debt was liquidated the estate reverted
to the owner. By statute of Elizabeth, one half only of an estate was
liable to be taken, and that only in virtue of a judgment entered ; and
this so far depended on the judgment, and not on the debt, that if the
possessor of an estate sold it the moment before a judgment was
entered, there was no remedy against him. The whole of the law was
in the same policy ; and it formed too material a feature of the whole
constitution to overturn it without necessity, which he had shewn
did not exist, for every one could make a law for his own case by the
precaution of making his debt a specialty. The bill, too, would be pro-
ductive of evil, by inducing persons to give credit to those who walked
over thousands of acres, which on their death would not, even under
the present bill, be assets for their debts. The bill, also, would not
affect copyholds, which at present were not liable even to specialty
debts. It did not affect estates in tail. These were both inconsistencies. Why did not the bill enact that persons possessed of estates in
tail should suffer a recovery for the benefit of their creditors. He said
this to prove to what extent of innovation the present bill would lead.
He should, therefore, oppose the motion.

Lord Ellenborough said, the present notions of innovation would
lead to the universal establishment of gavelkind, and the destruction
of the present system of tenures. He supported and enforced the leading arguments of the noble lord on the woolsack ; and, in conclusion,
observed, that the adoption of such a measure would be like the putting
on, for the sake of a little inconvenience, a huge blistering-plaster
which would corrode and gangrene the whole system.

After Lord Grey had said, with perfect truth, ' that the only principle which the noble lords had established was one which, from all he
had heard and read, he was more inclined to concur in—that the laws
were in such a state as to be a grievance almost intolerable to the people

rally, in the amendment in some measure of the very nature
and complexion of the whole law.   These are, in the language
of the civilians, the 'legum leges.'   The knowledge of them
is especially important to men intended for civil life.   ' Qui
optime nôrunt quid ferat societas humana, quid salus populi,
quid æquitas naturalis, quid gentium mores, quid rerum publi-
carum formæ diversæ, *ideoque* possint de legibus ex principiis
et præceptis tam æquitatis naturalis quam politices decernere.'

Such is that exalted and noble science of jurisprudence, the
knowledge of which sends the student into civil life full of
luminous precepts and generous notions, applicable to every
exigency of human affairs.   Judge succeeds judge; the technical rules and arbitrary forms held sacred by one generation
are derided by another; and, as we advance in life, the fuel
that kept alive our eager hopes and vehement passions is withdrawn.   Everything around us may be a dream and shadow; all
the suggestions of sense may be, as many of them undoubtedly
are, fallacious; but whatever may happen to exterior objects,
we cannot doubt of what passes within ourselves.   The moral
world rests on a foundation that is immutable; and the happiness of man must of necessity depend on his obedience to
those rules of eternal justice which God has written on his
soul, and of which, though heaven and earth shall pass away,
not a tittle can be altered.

---

of this country.   Indeed, what could be a worse state of the law than
one which so teemed with vices, that all the great lawyers in that house
professed themselves unable to devise means whereby a just creditor
could obtain payment of a debt out of a freehold estate, without such
expense that the estate would be wasted to nothing, and the vexation
to the parties not to be endured.'—The motion was negatived without a
division.

PRINCIPLES AND MAXIMS OF

JURISPRUDENCE.

I.

NEMO potest mutare consilium in alterius injuriam.—PAPINIAN.[a]

No man may change his purpose to the detriment of another's legal right.

This is a rule of natural equity in eliciting the doctrines of which there never has been a greater master than Papinian. 'Injuria' is used here in the same sense as in the 'Lex Aquilia.' By the exercise of our will we alter the position of others, and thus confer upon them rights which a change of purpose would destroy. 'Voluntatis est enim suscipere mandatum, necessitatis consummare.'[b] We may abstain from entering into contracts which we cannot renounce, because to do so would inflict an unjust disadvantage on another. 'Sicut ab initio libera est potestas habendi vel non habendi contractus, ita renuntiare semel constitutæ obligationi adversario non consentiente nemo potest.'[c]

Thus the person who, either by a donation or a legacy, had a right of choice between two objects, after he had determined could not change his resolution; 'quia omne jus legati primâ testatione consumpsit.'[d]—*Digest*, xxxiii. 5. 20.

So a person of full age could neither demand the succession which he had repudiated, nor repudiate that which he had accepted. "Major 25 annis delatam repudians successionem

---

[a] 'Injuria est quicquid contra jus.'—ULPIAN, *De injuriis. Digest*, l. *Injuria ex eo.*

[b] *Dig.* xiii. 7 ; xvii. 3.

[c] 5 *Cod. de Oblig. et Act.* 1.

[d] 'Servi electione legatâ semel duntaxat optare possumus.'—*Dig.* xxx. 1. 5.

post quærere non potest, nec quæsitam renuntiando dimit-
tere.'—*Cod. de rep. vel abstin. Hæred.* 4.

So, if the proprietor of land grant Titius a right of way over
his land, he cannot grant Mævius a right of leading water
over the same place.[e] 'Per quem locum viam alii cessero
per eandem alii aquæductum cedere non potero.'

A judge, though on the same day he may fill up any deficiencies in his sentence, cannot rescind it after it has been de-
finitively pronounced, by condemning him whom he had
dismissed, or dismissing him whom he had condemned.
'Paulus respondit rescindere quidem sententiam suam pre-
cedentem Prætorem non posse reliqua autem quæ ad consequentiam statutorum pertinent priori tamen sententiæ desunt,
circa condemnandum Reum vel dimittendum posse supplere—
eodem tamen die.'[f] The same rule holds good with regard
to arbiters. 'Arbiter etsi in sententiam erraverit corrigere
eam non potest.'[g]

In the third book of his Questions, from whence this law is
taken, Papinian treated two subjects:—1. 'De restitutionibus
in integrum;' the other 'de receptis arbitris compromis-
sariis.' Under the 'restitutio in integrum' we find the
case where a person of full age claimed relief against his own
act, on account of legitimate absence or necessary delay.[h] It
might be asked, whether, in the case of voluntary delay, he
could be relieved, to the disadvantage of another person;[i]
and, in the case of an emancipated son of full age, who had
been passed over without mention in a will, and improperly
disinherited, supposing that he had deliberately, *certo concilio*,
accepted a legacy under it, or suffered the legal time to elapse
before he claimed possession 'bonorum contra tabulas?' the

---

[e] And vice versâ.—*Dig.* viii. 3. 14.

[f] *Dig.* xlii. 7. 42.

[g] *Dig.* iv. 8. 20.

[h] And see *Dig.* xviii. 3, 4.—'Eleganter Papinianus libro tertio responsorum scribit statim atque commissa lex est statuere venditorem debere utrum commissoriam velit exercere an potius pretium petere,
nec posse si commissoriam elegerit postea variare.'

[i] *Digest,* iv. 4. 30.

answer was, that he must be supposed to acquiesce in the decision of the testator; and that, for the reason assigned by this rule, he could not change his mind to the detriment of the heir.[k] There are, however, says Papinian, cases in which ' Prætor variantem non repellit et consilium mutantis non aspernatur.'[l] This was when the two circumstances concurred, that the question arose between brothers as to the paternal estate, and that the repentance was not too late, ' si non serâ pœnitentiâ ductus,' if he changed his mind within a year after possession had been delivered; in that case the more benign opinion was, that the brother ought to be restored to his original right.

A third case under the head of Restitution was, where a man had deliberately written that he was a slave, ' servum se esse;' he did not, therefore, become a slave, and he was allowed ' consilium mutare.' Under the head ' de receptis arbitris:' the rule was thus applied — suppose the litigant parties had referred the case to Titius, and Titius undertook the arbitration, he could not afterwards decline the task, ' quoniam non debent decipi qui me tanquam bonum virum disceptatorem inter se elegerunt;' and the writer adds,[m] ' Finge enim post causam semel atque iterum tractatam, post nudata utriusque intima et secreta negotii operta arbitrum vel gratiæ dantem vel sordibus corruptum vel aliâ quâ ex causâ nolle sententiam dicere quisquamne potest negare æquissimum esse, ut officium suum quod in se recipit impleat.' So, if I lend you any thing, I cannot suddenly, and within an unreasonable time, demand its re-delivery.[n] If I undertake, without reward, the management of your affairs, I cannot all at once abandon the task I have imposed on myself, and leave your property to perish, ' neque enim impune peritura deseret,'

---

[k] ' Electo judicio testatoris repudiare beneficium Prætoris videtur.'

[l] The Roman law did not treat men as if they were intended for chests of drawers, or bags of money, but made allowance for human feelings, and the charities of social and domestic life. See *Cod. de Inoff. Test. Paulus Sententia ' De Querelâ Inoff.'* lib. iv.

[m] *Dig.* xviii. 2. 26.

[n] *Dig.* xiii. 7; xvii. 4.

for I have prevented you from employing any one else. If you lend me beams of wood to prop a house, you cannot take them away when you think proper; and if you have lent me your tablets, on which I have a written security, you will do wrong to importune me for them, as, if you had refused to lend them, I might have obtained other means of proving the obligation which they contain, ' ideo invicem propositæ sunt actiones ut appareat quod principio beneficii ac nudæ voluntatis fuerat, converti in mutuas præstationes, actionesque civiles.' I have not been able to refuse myself the pleasure of citing this admirable passage, which may furnish the reader with a notion of the precision, elegance, and compass of the Roman law, as well as of the marvellous intellect of its expounders. There he will find no awkward attempts at misplaced subtilty which entail litigation and misery on generation after generation, no wilful deviations into crooked by-paths, no doubts wantonly flung out, like ' low-born mists,' to spread darkness and confusion every-where, and perpetuate a feeling of insecurity ; no avoiding points which it is for the public welfare to decide; but strong sense in transparent language, confounding sophistry, abounding in happy illustrations, and bearing down obstacle after obstacle, till the path of truth is clear, and the way of justice is made straight.

Illustrations of this rule, in English law, are to be found in the instances of attorneys, who cannot retract after they have once undertaken to act as attorneys for a particular person;[o] and of trustees and executors. ' The defendants having acted as executors to the extent of securing particular legatees, then abandoned the property. The plaintiffs have suffered in consequence. By the defendants acting so far as

---

[o] I cite the case in the inhuman dialect which the framers of our law preferred to the Pandects.—' Auxy lou l'attorney un foits appeare ou imprist sur luy destre attorney pur un auter la, il ne poit retraher lui mesme mais doit appear a son perill. . . . . Tout ceo fuit dit per Foster, C.J. et Swinden, J., dit que fuit Soven temps issiut rule in temps Rolls, C.J.—SIDERFIN, p. 31. Mordecai v. Solomon, SAYER, 173.

executors, and not acting farther, I conceive that this cannot be permitted. Executors must either wholly renounce, or if they take upon them that character, they can be discharged only by administering the effects themselves.'[p]

So, if the relation of cestuique trust and trustee is once established, a voluntary grant cannot be revoked by the grantor.[q] 'As against the party himself, and his representatives, a voluntary settlement is binding' (SIR W. GRANT, Sloane and Cadogan, *cit.* SUGDEN, *Vendors and Purch.* App. 28).

II.

NON debet alteri per alterium iniqua conditio inferri.—PAPINIAN.

The condition of one man ought not to be worsened by the act of another.

The owner of an estate might drain it—i. e., cut trenches for the sake of improving the soil—but he might not turn the water on his neighbour's land. 'Sic enim debere quem meliorem agrum suum facere ne vicini deteriorem faciat.'[r]

It was an especial object of Roman jurisprudence to protect

---

[p] Doyle *v.* Blake, 1 SCHOALE and LEFROY, 245; Chalmer *v.* Bradley, 1 JACOB and WALKER, 227; LEWIN, *On Trusts*, 227; Moorecroft *v.* Dowding, 2 P. W., 314.

[q] 'A trustee cannot by any act of his own denude himself of that character till he has performed the trust.' Ellison *v.* Ellison, 6 VESEY, 656; Pulvertoft *v.* Pulvertoft, 18 VESEY, 84; Edwards *v.* Jones, 1 MYLNE and KEEN, 238.—Equity will not set aside a deed, though it will not carry it into effect: 'If a man will improvidently bind himself by a voluntary deed, and not reserve a liberty to himself by a power of revocation, a Court of Equity will not loose the fetters he hath put on himself, but he must lie under his own folly.'—Villars *v.* Beaumont, 1 VERNON, 10, 9. Why? Where no human creature is a gainer by the restriction, he is irrevocably bound by a mistake which may be at once corrected; and this is 'practical sense;' and such a quaint sentence is a substitute for any shadow of reason. If there is sufficient reason why a deed ought not to be carried into effect, it ought to be set aside. To talk about 'equity,' 'standing neutral,' 'lying down under his own folly,' etc., is the mere cant and dotage of self-complacent absurdity. 'Rei suæ locatio consistere non potest,' said the Roman.

[r] *Dig.* xxxix. 3. 1. § 4.

every man against any pernicious effects that, without any
fault of his, the act of his neighbour might inflict upon him.
' Omnibus modis id consul agit ne cujus deterior causa fiat ex
alieno facto.' [s] The energy and scope of the words sufficiently
prove the earnestness of the purpose. Therefore, as a change
of adversary in the suit might be adverse to the interests of a
party to it, it was provided that any one who, by the alienation
of property in dispute, substituted another adversary for himself, in order to aggravate the difficulties of the person with
whom he was contending, should be liable in an action so far
as the change of parties had deteriorated the condition of his
antagonist. ' Itaque si alterius provinciæ hominum, aut poten-
tiorem nobis opposuerit adversarium tenebitur.' [t] . . . ' Aut
alium qui vexaturus sit adversarium.'

So when, by the ' nuntiatio,' a stop was put to the progress
of a new work—if one of several joint-proprietors, without the
assent of the others, persevered in building after the ' nuntiatio,'
the others were not responsible. ' Neque enim nocere debet
factum alterius ei qui nihil fecit.' So, if one of several heirs
opened a will without the consent or knowledge of the rest
when the law forbade it, the others were not deprived of their
share in the property.[u] So, if by the misconduct of the creditor the debtor lost the money which he was about to pay
him, the creditor lost his claim.[x] So, the oath offered in an
action was only valid against him ' qui jusjurandum detulit,'
and could not affect the rights of others, of which Ulpian gives
the following illustration:—A wife declaring, after the death
of her husband, that she has conceived by him, demands to be
put in possession of his estate. The heir offers her the oath,
which she takes. The heir takes proceedings against her,
declaring that she is forsworn. The question is, whether the
oath so taken could, after the child was born, affect its condition for good or evil. The answer was, that it should not:

---

[s] *Dig.* iv. 7. 1.

[t] ' Quanti nostra intersit alium non habuisse.'—*Dig.* iv. 7. 1, § 2.

[u] *Dig.* xxix. 5. 27.

[x] *Dig.* xliv. 6. 6.

' Alteri enim nec prodest neque nocet jusjurandum inter alios factum, nec partui igitur nocebit.'[y] So, if the owner repudiated the defence of a noxious slave, it might be undertaken by the ' fructuarius,' or the person who held him as a pledge, ' cui pignoris nomine obligatus est,' lest the fraud or negligence of one man should impair the rights of another: ' Ne alterius dolus aut desidia aliis noceat.'[z] So an arrangement, ' transactio,' between the heir and his mother, did not deprive the manumitted slave of his freedom, or the legatee of his action, if the heir had not provided for these liabilities in his bargain: ' Non debet negligentiam suam ad alienam injuriam referre.'[a] So, if the agent died, and through a mistake of his heir, property was improperly disposed of, the employer of the agent was exonerated: ' Neque oporteat eum qui certi hominis fidem elegit ob errorem aut imperitiam hæredum affici damno;'[b] ' for,' said Caius, ' any one may improve another's condition if he thinks proper, and by paying his debt may liberate him; but one man cannot without the sanction of another enforce payment of what is due to him.'[c] ' Naturalis enim et civilis ratio suasit alienam conditionem meliorem quidem etiam ignorantis et inviti facere nos, deteriorem non posse.'

If an agreement between two persons was not allowed to injure their neighbour, much less was it allowed to inflict any injury on the commonwealth.[d]

' Ante omnia animadvertendum est ne conventio in aliâ re facta aut cum aliâ personâ, facta in aliâ re aliâve personâ noceat—nam juri publico per privatorum pacta non derogatur.'[e]

The best illustration of this principle in our jurisprudence will be found in the case of Meadowcroft v. Gregory.[f] ' A marriage had been declared null and void, because the name

[y] *Dig.* xxv. 6. 6 ; xii. 2: 3, § 3 : 'Matris igitur jusjurandum partui neque prodest neque nocet.'

[z] *Dig.* ix. 4. 26, § 6.

[a] *Dig.* ii. 15. 3.

[b] *Dig.* xvii. 1. 17.

[c] *Dig.* ii. 14. 15. 16 ; v. 1. 1.

[d] *Dig.* xliii. 24. 2 ; ii. 14. 2.

[e] D'ARGENTRE, *Avis sur les partages des nobles,* 29, Coutume de Bretagne. *Donellus Comm.,* lib. xxii. c. 5.

[f] PHILLIMORE'S *History of the Law of Evidence,* 113 ; 2 PHILLIMORE'S *Reports,* 365 ; 2 HAGGARD, 207 ; 4 MOORE, P.C.C. 399 ; 10 BEAVAN, 122.

of Widowcroft had been used instead of Meadowcroft in the publication of banns. The elegance of Lord Stowell's language cannot conceal the gross injustice of his decision. The son of the marriage so cancelled, many years afterwards came of age, and sought to obtain a revision of this sentence.' Dr. Phillimore, 'omnis humani ac Divini juris sciens,' was consulted—all efforts in the Ecclesiastical Courts were unavailing.[g] In another shape, Dr. Phillimore brought the case before the Courts of Equity. The Master of the Rolls pronounced against the son. But on appeal, Lord Cottenham decided in his favour; he directed an issue—the suit was compromised; and to every mind familiar with the principles of jurisprudence, it will be evident a grievous reproach was thus removed from the administration of English justice. There was not even a shadow of difficulty in the case, which was so often erroneously decided. In a recent case,[h] however, it was held that a sentence affecting the legitimacy of a child, no party to the suit in which the sentence was pronounced might be impeached on the ground of collusion.[i]

---

[g] There was no objection on the only ground that should have been tolerated in a civilized country ; viz., that the son had acquiesced in the decision by which he was degraded, after he came of age.

There is a passage in the *Rationalia in Pandectas*, of FAVRE, a work of extraordinary acuteness, on L. 60, *de Condict. Indebiti*, which places the cruelty of the decisions in the Ecclesiastical Courts and in the Privy Council in a very clear light. 'Cum exceptio rei judicatæ nullâ æquitate naturali nititur sed civili tantum, apparet non esse illam ex earum numero quæ aut naturalem obligationem possint tollere quæ ex solo naturalis æquitatis vinculo æstimatur ;' but such arguments are not to be found in treatises on practice, nor in the *Reports* of MEESON and WELSBY. In another passage on L. 40, he proves that the authority 'rei judicatæ ' rests on exactly the same ground as the right of prescription ; it exists because 'alioqui nullus esset litium finis.'

Cod. de liberali causâ : ' Ante litem nati suo nomine omnes in questionem vocentur quoniam hos solos qui in lite nati sunt omnem fortunam matrum complecti oportet.'—*Ordonnance*, 1627. Art. 5. Tit. 27.

[h] Harrison v. the Corporation of Southampton, *Law Journal*, vol. xxii., 753.

[i] *Code Civil*, 1351, incorporates the Roman law. To justify the exceptio rei judicatæ, there must be ' Idem corpus, eadem causa petendi, and ' eadem conditio personarum.'—*Dig. de except rei judic.* xii. 13. 14.

III.

GENERALITER cum de fraude disputatur non quid habeat actor sed quid per adversarium habere non potuerit considerandum est.—PAPINIAN.[k]

In questions of fraud, not only is the debt due to the Plaintiff, but the benefit, which but for his adversary he would have possessed, to be taken into consideration.

It was in this case the intention of Papinian to lay down a general rule in all cases of fraud, according to which the injury inflicted by it, whether with regard to the principal sum due, or to damages and interest, might be adjusted.

In the same spirit the same jurist has declared, that where the question turns on the estimate of profits, it ought to be considered not only whether the wrongdoer has enjoyed them, but whether the plaintiff, if he had not been disturbed, might have done so. 'Generaliter autem cum de fructibus æstimandis quæritur constat animadverti debere, an malæ fidei possessor fruitus sit sed an petitor frui potuerit si ei possidere licuisset.'[l]

In conformity with this principle, Ulpian lays it down, that the heir who is bound to give up a legacy ought to pay to the legatee, not only the profits which he the heir has gained by detaining it, but those which the legatee might have derived from its possession. 'Fructus autem hi deducuntur in petitionem non quos hæres percepit, sed quos legatarius percipere potuit.'[m]

Paulus applies the same principle to a sale: if the seller does not give possession to the buyer at the proper time, the seller is bound to make up all the profits which the buyer might

---

[k] GOTHOFRED, *Reg. Juris.;* FABER, *Reg. Juris.;* Sainsbury *v.* Jones, 5 MYLNE and CRAIG, 1 ; Greenaway *v.* Adams, 12 VESEY, 395 ; Todd *v.* Gee, 17 VESEY, 273 ; Andrews *v.* Brown, 3 CURLING, 135 : Liford's Case, 11 COKE's *Reports* ; Coulter's Case, 5 COKE, 30 ; *Code civil,* Liv. iii. tit. 3, 1149, 1150, 1151. 'Les dommages et interêts ne doivent comprendre à l'égard de la perte éprouvée par le créancier, et du gain dont il a été privés que ce qui est une suite immédiate et directe de l'inexécution de la convention.'

[l] 'Fructus percipiendi.'—*Dig.* vi. 1. 62. *Cod. de rei Vind,* 5. 6.

[m] ULPIAN, *Dig.* xxx. 39, § 1.

have made of it, had it been delivered to him at the proper time. 'Cum per venditorem steterit quominus rem tradat omnis utilitas emptionis in æstimationem venit quæ modo circa rem ipsam consistit;'[n] and the person who had not fulfilled his promise of procuring the ratification, by a supposed principal, of what he had promised in his name, was liable for all the loss the person with whom he contracted sustained, and for all the profit that person might have gained 'in tantum competit actio in quantum actoris interest quantum ei abest, et quantum lucrari potuit.'[o] The same rule held with regard to the person who was sued for the restitution of what he had taken with violence; and to all who by fraud and bad faith, have harmed and deprived him of profit that he might otherwise have gained.[p] 'Et fructus non tantum qui percepti sunt verum etiam hi qui percipi potuerunt a fraudatore.'[q]

Courts of Equity award compensation or damages as ancillary to specific performance or other relief, not as a substantive object of their interference. The exceptions to this rule are cases of fraud,[r] and where the person sued has incapacitated

---

[n] *Dig.* xix. 1. 21, § 3. But Paulus limits the consequences to those which naturally and directly follow: 'Neque enim si potuit ex vino negotiari et lucrum facere id æstimandum est, non magis quam si triticum emerit et ob eam rem quod non sit traditum familia ejus fame laboraverit, nam pretium tritici non servorum fame necatorum consequitur.' LORD BACON, *Maxims*, 'In jure non remota causa sed proxima spectatur.'

[o] *Dig.* xlvi. 7. 13.

[p] *Dig.* xlii. 16. 6. 'In interdicto 'Unde vi,' tanti condemnatio facienda est quanti intersit possidere.'

[q] With a deduction of the sum reasonably expended on the property. *Dig.* xlii. 8. 10. 19: 'Sed cum aliquo modo scilicet et sumptus facti deducantur—nam arbitrio judicis non prius cogendus est rem restituere quam si impensas necessarius consequatur.' Courts of Equity with us do not go to this extent, but confine themselves to cases where the true owner has invoked their aid. See STORY, b. 799. 6.

[r] STORY's *Equity*, § 799. Putnam *v.* Richie, 6 PAIGE, *Ch. Reports.* 'I have not been able to find any case in this country, or in England, where the Court of Chancery has assumed jurisdiction, to give relief to a complainant who has made improvements on land, the legal title to which was in the defendant.'—CHANCELLOR WALWORTH.

himself from the performance of his engagement.[s] 'There are,' says Lord Hardwicke, 'cases where the court will decree an account of rents and profits from the time when the title accrued, as wherever the plaintiff has been kept out of his estate by fraud, misrepresentation, or concealment of the defendant.'[t]

'If an equitable owner of land, who is conusant of his right, will stand by and see another improve his land without asserting his right to it, he must be satisfied to recover the value of the land independent of improvements.'

'But the doctrines of the Civil Law are not recognised by the Common Law of England. Whoever takes and holds land, to which another has a better title, is liable to the true owner for the profits which he has received, of whatever nature they may be, and whether consumed by him or not.'[u]

'There is not, says Mons. Duranton, 'a more abstract topic than that of damages, wherefore the law has only been able to lay down general principles, leaving their application to the wisdom of the tribunals.'[x]

Dumoulin says—'In doloso intelligitur venire omne detri-

---

[s] Andrews *v.* Brown, 3 CURLING *Reports*, 135, upholding Denton *v.* Stewart, 1 Cox, 258. MADDOX's *Chancery Practice*, vol. i., page 123, ed. 1837. 'As upon a legal title, no more than six years' mesne profits are recoverable at law. So where an estate in trust is recovered in equity, the account shall not be extended beyond six years (and see 2 and 3 Wm. IV., c. 27, § 42). But in the case of a minor, as every person who enters on the estate of an infant, is considered guardian or bailiff for the infant, the Court will decree an account from the time when the infant's title accrued.'

[t] See Dormer *v.* Fortescue, 3 ATKYNS, 128. 'Nothing can be clearer,' says Lord Hardwicke, 'both in law and equity, and from natural justice, that from the death of his father, the time when his title accrued, he is entitled to the rents and profits.'

[u] Green *v.* Biddle, 8 WHEATON's *Reports*, 27. 'If one disseises me, and cuts down the trees, grass, or corn upon the land, and afterwards I re-enter, I shall have an action of trespass, *vi et armis*, against him for the trees, grass, etc. ; but if he make a feoffment in fee, etc., ... I shall recover all the mesne profits against my disseisor.'—LYFORD's *Case, Reports*, Part 9, 51 a.

[x] *Cours de droit Français*, vol. x., § 480. TOULLIER, liv. iii., tit. 3, c. 3.

mentum tunc et proxime secutum, non autem damnum postea
succedens ex novo casu . . . . quia istud est damnum remotum quod non est in consideratione.'

The English and American Courts stop short of the doctrine
of the Civil Law, and rejecting profits as a measure of compensation, have confined themselves to the damage actually
sustained as the standard of the plaintiff's claim. The cases
on this subject are collected and explained with great care and
ability by Mr. Sedgwick, in his very learned and excellent
work upon this subject.[y] I will only add this rule from
Dumoulin—' Non debet quod extrinsecus interest (dommages
extrinséques in Pothiers paraphrase) excedere fines objecti,
qui verisimiliter apparebant tempore contractus, sive limites
periculi, vel casus prævisi et tacite suscepti non debent
excedi.'[z]

IV.

FRAUDIS interpretatio semper in jure civili
non ex eventu duntaxat sed ex consilio quoque
desideratur.—PAPINIAN.[a]

*It is not from the event alone, but the intention, that the
law draws an inference of fraud.*

The principle of this rule, is that no event, unless intended,
constitutes a fraud; and that to make a fraudulent act two
things must concur, the intention and the event by which that
intention has been followed.

---

[y] *Treatise of the Measure of Damages*, THEODORE SEDGWICK, New
York. Burrows *v.* Wright, 1 EAST, 615. Greasley *v.* Higginbotham,
1 EAST, 636. Boyle *v.* Brandon, 13 MEESON and WELSBY, 738. Ingram *v.*
Lawson, 6 BIN., N.C. 212. In a case of collision, it was held that the
owner of the vessel injured could not recover for profits on the last
voyage. Smith *v.* Carding, 1 HOWARD, 28. Schooner 'Lively,' 1 GAL-
LISON *Reports*, 314. Pothier puts the case of a canon, who, from the
fault of the horse he has bought, does not reach his town in time to
keep residence, and thereby loses a large part of his income. This he
holds to be too much.—*Obl.* 1.2.

[z] *De eo quod interest*, vol. iii. p. 443, § 63.

[a] GOTHOFRED, *Reg. Juris.;* FABER, *Reg. Juris.*

Human justice cannot reach bare intention — cogitationis pœnam nemo patitur.[b] Thus a creditor cannot accuse his debtor of fraud, for having intended to dispose of his goods, if he has not actually disposed of them. 'Item demum revocatur quod fraudandorum creditorum causâ factum est si eventum fraus habuit.'[c]

It follows that in all criminal proceedings the intention qualifies the act, 'voluntas spectatur non exitus.' This Modestinus has expressed in a passage of singular beauty— 'Infans vel furiosus si hominem occiderit lege Corneliâ non teneatur, alterum innocentia consilii tuetur, alterum fati in-felicitas excusat.'

This doctrine, founded on natural justice, has often been allowed to fluctuate in English Courts of Law.[d] I doubt if it would be possible to cite from the criminal code of any country (the ebullitions of fanaticism, civil and religious, of course excepted), a rule more perfectly immoral and absurd than this which I quote from Hawkins, which (where life is concerned) has of late been tacitly abandoned.[e]

'A fortiori, he shall be adjudged guilty of murder who, in the pursuit of a deliberate intention to commit felony, chances to kill a man, as by shooting at tame fowl with an intent to steal them.' That is, although the act done might be as far as possible from his purpose, and although the purpose was as unlikely as possible to bring about the act. Such was the practical sense, the capacity for legislation, and the humanity of the authors of our unwritten Criminal Law. There are two things, one the physical and the other the moral ingre-dient. Instead of saying, the former shall receive its character

---

[b] *Dig.* xlviii. 19. 18.

[c] *Dig.* xlii. 8. 10, § 2 A.

[d] *e. g.* It has been held, that a man eloping with a woman means to steal her clothes! and that a labourer, who gives more corn than he is allowed to his *master's* horses, means to steal the corn!

[e] HAWKINS' *Pleas of the Crown*, vol.i., page 86, § 10. 'It is a general rule, that where a man, intending to commit one felony happens to commit another, he is as much guilty as if he had intended the felony which he actually commits.' Absurdity can go no farther.

from the latter, our law said in the case cited, we will sever
the intention from the act done, and substitute for the moral
element, by which the act is in reality determined,[f] one of a
totally different character.   Lolly's case [g] is still more scandalous, and has been stigmatized in terms of masculine indignation by Lord Brougham from the judgment-seat.   Lolly took
the opinion of several lawyers whether his divorce was valid;
he was assured it was.   He married again and was tried for
bigamy; the case was referred to the judges, who (properly)
held the divorce invalid: and then, as if intention was no element of crime, actually sent the mistaken man to the hulks,
where he remained two years.   Such was the state of our
jurisprudence.   *His* crime, which he had done all he could to
guard against, was venial ignorance of positive law — the
crime of the judges who punished him, was inexcusable ignorance of natural justice, and indifference to common humanity,
and this in a country where a Lord Chief Justice, on the
bench, had stated 'adultery to be venial.' [h]

I turn gladly from such barbarity to Lord Mansfield—'It
makes a great difference whether an act was done (eventus)
and where no act was done.   The intent may make an act
innocent in itself criminal.   Nor is the completion of an act
criminal in itself necessary to constitute criminality. . . . So
long as an act rests in bare intention, it is not punishable by
our laws; but immediately when an act is done, the law
judges not only of the act done, but of the intent with which
it is done; and if it is coupled with a malicious intent, though

---

[f] 'Un fait involontaire ne peut être criminel.'—MERLIN *Répert. de
Juris. Intention.*   What becomes of morality, if this principle is shaken
in Courts of Justice ? and what becomes of jurisprudence, if all moral
notions are confounded ?   'Certum est casus fortuitos *nullo* in judicio
præstari.'—VINNIUS *Selectæ Juris Quæst.,* lib.i. p.9.

[g] Lolly's case, RUSSELL and RY. C.C. 237; 2 CL. and FINN, 567, n.
'Ignorantia legis sicut inevitabilis si sit, tollit peccatum ita cum aliquâ
negligentiâ conjuncta delictum minuit.' GROTIUS, de J.B. and P. ii.
20, 43, § 2; but why cite authorities to prove what every day-labourer
ought to know, and what no moralist, writer, or jurist, was ever so pro-
foundly ignorant as to dispute?

[h] LORD ELLENBOROUGH : 'It may be venial.'

the act would have been innocent, the intent being criminal,
the act becomes criminal and punishable.'[i]

V.

I N totum omnia quæ animi destinatione agenda
sunt non nisi verâ et certâ scientiâ perfici
possunt.—PAPINIAN.[k]

*All acts that require a fixed purpose are incomplete
unless performed with a full and assured knowledge.*

The knowledge required in acts which ought to be the result
of a settled and deliberate purpose of the mind, is ascertained
by this rule of Papinian.[l] The ' animi destinatio' is that fixed
intention which is opposite to sudden and tumultuous impulse
—the προαίρεσις of the Greeks. So a man is said to choose
his domicile ' destinato animo.' As there are some acts which
are valid, though done with precipitation, there are others for
the validity of which the Roman law demanded proof of, or at
least time for, deliberation. Such were—

1. NUPTIÆ. — 'Concubinam ex solâ animi destinatione
æstimari oportet.'[m]

2. DIVORCE.—' Divortium non est nisi verum quod animo
perpetuam constituendi dissensionem fit.'[n]

---

[i] CALDECOTT *Reports*, p. 400. Rex *v.* Scofield.

[k] GOTHOFRED, *Reg. Juris.;* FABER, *Reg. Juris.;* ANTOINE, *Règles de
Droit;* STORY, *Equity Juris.,* vol.i. c.5 ; FONBLANQUE, *On Equity,* bk.i.
c.2, § 7 ; TUDOR, *Leading Cases in Equity,* vol.ii.610, Stapilton *v.* Stapilton ; MERLIN, *Répert. Ignorance.*

[l] It was on this principle that the error of him who imagined that
he was obliged to fulfil certain municipal duties, and therefore undertook to perform them, did not bind him.—*Dig.* 1.1.17 : 'Error ejus qui
se municipem aut colonum existimans munera civilia suscepturum pro-
simit, defensionem juris non excludit.'

[m] To understand this law, it should be recollected that ' concubina,'
was not a word of infamy, it was a ' species matrimonii.' Therefore,
she was not entitled to the name who was taken ' non verâ et certâ
scientiâ sed impetu quodam libidinis.' CUJACIUS, vol.iv. p.643.—*Dig.*
xxv.7 ; *Cod. de Adult.* 18 ; POTHIER (DUPIN), vol.v. p.167 ; *Traité du
Mariage,* p.4, c.1 ; MERLIN, *Consentement, Code N.,* 1109.

[n] *Dig.* xxiv.3, § 3 : 'Non est divortium nisi perseverantiâ apparuerit
non jurgio abactam mulierem.'—CUJACIUS, supra.

3. OBLIGATIONS.

4. CAUSA POSSESSIONIS.

5. CRIMES.

6. DOMICILE.[o]

7. WILLS.—It is laid down, ' De statu suo dubitantes vel errantes testamentum facere non possunt.'[p]   So it is said, if a person condemned to deportation dies before the emperor has confirmed the sentence, his will is valid: ' Quia certum statum usque adhuc habuit.'

Perhaps, however, the ' vera et certa scientia' can hardly admit of illustration from matters resting so completely on individual will as marriages, gifts, and testaments.   Another branch of law supplies a better exemplification of the matter with which we are dealing; that is, the question, often involving very serious responsibilities, of accepting or repudiating an inheritance: ' acquirendæ' or ' repudiandæ hæreditatis.'[q]   Persons, therefore, who were unable to understand the proceeding, or to form a judgment as to the nature of the obligations which they might contract, could not of themselves accept or repudiate an inheritance.   The ' pupillus,' therefore, could not of course do so without the sanction of his ' tutor.'[r]   ' Pupillus si fari possit hujus tamen ætatis sit ut causam acquirendæ hæreditatis non intelligat . . . tamen cum tutoris auctoritate hæreditatem acquirere potest.'[s]   Questions arose as to the knowledge of the heir on the following matters:—

1. De conditione sua.

2. De conditione testatoris.

3. As to the death of the testator.—If the heir, believing the testator dead when he was living, accepted the inheritance, this premature act was not binding.[t]

---

o ' Ubi domicilium habeat animi existimatione esse accipiendum.' ELLENBOROUGH.—*Dig.* 1.1. 27, § 2.   The law of domicile in a sentence.

p *Dig.* xxviii.1.15.

q ' Hæreditas autem quin obliget nos ab alieno etiam si non sit solvendo plus quam manifestum est.'—*Dig.* xxix.2.8.

r *Dig.* xxix.2.5,8,9.

s Evans *v.* Llewellyn, 1 Cox, *Rep.* 340.

t *Id. Ib.* 32: for ' viventis nulla est hæreditas.'—*Dig.* xviii.4.1; Pusey *v.* De Bouverie, 3 P. WILL. 315.

4. As to his own rights.

5. As to whether there was a will.

6. As to the validity of the will.

7. Supposing the heir ' in alienâ potestate,' as to the ' scientia' and ' destinatio animi' of him in whose power he was.

8. As to his share of the inheritance.[u]

9. As to whether he was heir absolutely or conditionally.

10. What the condition was.

11. That there was no other ' JUSTUS hæres.'

12. As to the 'jus accrescendi.'

So, if a person purchase his own property, imagining that it belongs to another, his error makes the bargain null: ' Si error aliquis intervenit in eo qui emit nihil valet quod actum est.'[x]

The rule is general, ' in totum,' says Papinian, ὅλως and ' omnia;' it requires not only assent, which concerns the will, but knowledge, which informs the intellect. It is, therefore, to be distinguished from the error which vitiates an act, and the ' certa scientia' which has become the style of the acts of princes; it is confined to those acts which may legally be done, and of which a ' destinatio animi' is an essential element.

In the case of Cocking v. Pratt,[y] it was held, that an agreement made by a daughter, four months after she was of age, with her mother, concerning the distribution of her father's estate might be set aside. This case was afterwards cited, with approbation, by Lord Brougham[z] in a very elaborate judgment, in which the principle was to a certain extent involved. In a case before Lord Chancellor Talbot,[a] where

---

[u] So the heir to the whole estate, if he supposed himself heir only to a part, and determined to take possession, took possession of the whole. ' Si ex asse hæres destinaverit partem habere hæreditatis videtur in assem pro hærede gessisse.'—*Dig.* xxix. 2. 10.

[x] *Dig.* xviii. 1. 16; xviii. 1. 9. 2 : 'Nullam esse venditionem puto quoties in materiâ erratur.'

[y] 1 VESEY, 400.

[z] Macarthy v. Decaix, 2 RUSSELL AND MYLNE, 622.

[a] Pusey v. De Bouverie, 3 P. W. 315

the daughter of a freeman of London had made a disadvantageous election (though fraud was not imputed to the person
who gained by her mistake), that excellent judge set aside
the arrangement, saying, ' She might know that it was in her
power to accept either the orphanage or the legacy part.
But I hardly think she knew she was entitled to have an
account taken of the personal estate of her father, and first to
know what her orphanage part did amount to, and that when
she would be fully apprised of this, then, and not till then,
she was to make her election, which very much alters the
case.' In another case Lord Kenyon [b] said, ' The party was
taken by surprise; he had not sufficient time to act with
caution; and therefore, though there was no actual fraud, it is
something like fraud, for an undue advantage was taken of
his situation. I am of opinion, that the party was not competent to protect himself, and therefore this court is bound to
afford him such protection, and therefore these deeds ought to
be set aside as improvidently obtained.' In the very remarkable case of Gordon v. Gordon, Lord Eldon says, ' My opinion is, that if James Gordon [c] (the brother in favour of whom
arrangement had been made on the supposition that his elder
brother was illegitimate) knew that there had been a private
ceremony of marriage, and conscientiously believing that it
was not a legal marriage, omitted to communicate that fact to
his brother, the plaintiff would be entitled to relief on the
principle, that though family agreements are to be supported
when there is no fraud, or mistake, on either side, or none to
which the other party is accessory; [d] yet, where there is mistake, though innocent, and the other party is accessory to it,
this Court will interpose." [e]   " In contracts of this sort full
and complete communication of all material circumstances is

---

[b] 1 Cox, *Reps.* 340, Evans v. Llewellyn.
    [c] 3 SWANSTON, *Reps.* Hunt and Rousmaniere; 8. WHEATON, *Reps.* 214.
C. J. MARSHALL'S JUDGMENT,
    [d] A qualification which unsettles the principle.
    [e] 492 P.

is what the Court must insist upon.'[f] For what reason? surely for the reason in the maxim commented upon, that 'vera et certa scientia' is requisite; yet Lord Eldon, though he lays down the premises, stops short of the conclusion. If the person abandoning, waving, or compromising his right, has a right to full and complete knowledge, how, in any view of the philosophy of law, can his right be impaired by the mistake innocent or malicious, of another person? The doctrine, however, is placed on a basis still more narrow by Lord Cottenham,[g] in a judgment in which I must take leave to say, that he betrays a very rude and imperfect acquaintance with the rules of the civil law; of which he, nevertheless, makes mention.

The French lawyers[h] have, I think, stated accurately the rule which ought to govern the decision where the question is, whether consent has been given; 'it is of no value,' they say, 'if it has been given in error, surprised by fraud, or extorted by violence; but the error must bear upon the substance of the thing which is the subject of the agreement, an error as to an accidental quality is not sufficient; thus, according to Barbeyrac and Pothier, an error as to the motive will not invalidate an agreement, unless it appears evident that without the motive the agreement would not have been made.' 'Si in nomine dissentiam verum de corpore constet nulla est dubitatio quin valeat emtio et venditio nihil enim facit error nominis cum de corpore constet—inde quæritur si in corpore non essetne sed in substantiâ error sit;'[i] and it is laid down, that wherever one thing is sold for another, 'aliud pro alio,' the contract is invalid.

---

[f] 'This Court always considers the reasonableness of the agreement.' —LORD HARDWICKE; 1 ATKYNS, 2 Stapilton v. Stapilton; Lansdowne v.Lansdowne, MOSELEY, Reps. 364; Westby v. Westby; 2 D. and W., 516; Harvey v. Cooke, 4 RUSSELL, 58.

[g] Stewart v. Stewart, 6 CL. AND FINN, 911.

[h] Analyse du Code Civil, vol. iii. p. 20.

[i] Dig. xvi. 1. 9. 2.

VI.

IN toto jure generi per speciem derogatur et illud
potissimum habetur quod ad speciem directum
est.[i]—PAPINIAN.

*It is a maxim in all law that particular words de-
rogate from general words, and that those expressions
bear the most commanding sense which point to specific objects.*

The question decided by the maxim under consideration is
this: Supposing a conflict between a clause couched in
general, and a clause couched in specific words, which is to
give way. Is the maxim, ' Specialia generalibus insunt,' to
prevail, or do the special words detract from the effect of the
general clause? and the answer is positive, that the special
words do detract from the effect of the general clause always,
in toto jure, in contracts, in wills, in rescripts, and in laws.

Papinian gives an instance, under the head ' De pœnis.'
If the law imposes a general punishment on an offender, and
afterwards annexes a special penalty to the same crime, the
special and not the general punishment is to be inflicted.
' Sanctio legum quæ novissime certam pœnam irrogat iis qui
præscriptis legis non obtemperaverint ad eas species pertinere
non videtur quibus ipsâ lege pœna specialiter addita est.'[k]

So in private contracts, the ' Doli clausula,' as it was
called, inserted as of course in all stipulations, did not relate
to those points concerning which there was a specific agreement. ' Doli clausula quæ stipulationibus subjicitur non
pertinet ad eas partes stipulationis de quibus nominatim cavetur.'[l]

---

[i] GOTH., *Reg. Juris.:* FABER, *Reg. Juris.;* DWARRIS, *On Statutes;*
BROOM'S *Legal Maxims,* p. 502 ; ANTOINE, *Règles de Droit;* Sandiman
v. Breach, 7 B. & C. 100 ; DWARRIS, *On Statutes,* p. 668 ; LOFFT'S *Reports,*
App., Maxim 419, 2nd edition : ' Clausula generalis non complectitur
ea quæ non ejusdem generis sunt cum iis quæ speciatim dicta fuerant.'

[k] *Dig.* xlviii. 19. 41.

[l] *Dig.* xlv. 1. 119.

So in wills. A husband bequeathed to his wife an estate, specially designated. The wife bequeaths this estate, in express terms, to Titius; and, in another part of her will, she leaves to her son all that her husband had bequeathed to her. It was held by Scævola and Paulus, that the first legatee took the estate. ' Verisimile non est testatricem id quod specialiter uni legavit voluisse ad alium generali sermone transferre.'[m] So, where a testator left to his son the farm and all upon it; and, in another part of his will, left the slaves upon it, by name, to another person; it was held that they did not pass to the son.[n] It is held, that this rule does not apply to cases where a general word is used as a sort of summary after the enumeration of several particular instances, as the general and special meaning are not brought into collision. ' Cum eo plane qui vinum spurcavit vel effudit, vel acetum fecit vel alio modo vitiavit, agi posse Aquiliâ Celsus ait quia etiam effusum et acetum factum corrupti appellatione continetur.'[o] The same rule of construction, as that last stated, applies where, after the mention of several specific articles, a generic word is used; for, in this case, the whole class is included. So Paulus says, that the addition of this phrase, ' Quæ ejus causâ parata sunt,' sometimes extends and sometimes contracts the sense of the words used before. If, for instance, a testator, after leaving several ornaments to his wife, adds, ' quæque ejus causâ parata sunt,'[p] he augments the legacy; if he adds, ' quæ ejus causâ parata sunt,' he contracts it. ' Detractâ conjunctione que quia ex omnibus supra comprehensis ea sola defini contra quæ ejus causâ parata sunt.'[q] And if a general

---

[m] *Dig.* xxxii. 41. § 3.   [n] *Dig.* xxx. 7. 6. 1.

[o] *Dig.* ix. 2; xxvii. 15.

[p] *Dig.* xxxii. 44. See also *Dig.* xxxiv. 2. 30 : 'Si quis ita legaverit uxori meæ mundum ornamentum seu quæ ejus causâ paravi, do lego placet omnia deberi . . . . hoc enim verbum *seu* ampliandi legati gratiâ positum est.'

[q] Platt's case, PLOWDEN, 36 : 'It is not unusual, in Acts of Parliament, to comprehend, by construction, a generality, when express mention is made only of a particular, the particular instances being only examples.'—LORD ABINGER. Pattick *v.* Stubbs, 9 MEESON AND

law was enacted on account of some special event, the statement of the special reason did not limit the general words.
So the edict against Macedonianus applied to all usurers; and
that passed on account of ' Calphurnia improbissima fœmina,'[q]
to all women; and, if the particular articles were mentioned
from ignorance, the general words were not limited. ' Legatâ
supellectili cum species per imperitiam enumeratur ex abundanti generali legato non derogatur.'[r]   And again, to the
same purpose: ' Si quis fundum ita ut instructus est, legaverit
et adjecerit cum supellectile vel mancipiis, vel unâ aliquâ re,
quæ expressa non erat, utrum minuit legatum adjiciendo
speciem an vero non?'[s] *i.e.*, does the addition of a particular
article take away from the power of the general words that
have been used already? ' Et Papinianus respondit non videri
minutum sed potius ex abundantiâ adjectum.'

This qualification of the doctrine expressed in the rule cited
was examined in the ever-memorable case[t] of Entick *v.* Carrington. Lord Camden says, ' In PLOWDEN 37,[u] and 167, and
467, several cases are cited as authorities under these rules of
construction: as that the bishop of Norwich in one act shall
mean all bishops; that the warden of the Fleet shall mean all
gaolers; that justices of a division shall mean all justices of a
county at large; that guardian in *socage*, after the heir's
attaining fourteen, shall be a bailiff in account; that executors
shall include administrators, and tenant for years a tenant for

---

WELSBY, 830. So the Statute of West. 2nd 13 Ed. I. 1—46, enumerates five kinds of buildings, yet the statute is held to include others
TINDAL, 4 BIN. N.C. 83, Strother *v.* Hutchinson.

[q] *Dig.* iii. 1. 5.   [r] *Dig.* xxxiii. 10. 9. PAPINIAN.

[s] *Dig.* xxxiii. 7. 12. 'Non mutavit substantiam rerum non necessaria verborum multiplicatio.' —*Dig.* xxxiv. 2. 33. 1. 'pediculis.' And,
according to our law, general words are not restrained by particular
words inserted ' ad majorem cautelam.'—COMYN, *Digest, Tit. Paroles*,
vol. v. p. 337.   LORD MANSFIELD — ' It is very common to put in a
sweeping clause, and the use and object of it in general is, to guard
against any accidental omission.'—COWPER, *Rep.* p. 12, Moore *v.* Magrath.

[t] *State Trials*, vol. xix. 1058.

[u] Wimbish *v.* Taillbois, PLOWDEN, v. 7, 58 ; and *State Trials*, vol. xix.
p. 1060.

one year or any less time, with several other instances to the like purpose. In the first place, though the general rule be true enough, that where it is clear the person or thing expressed is but by way of example, the judges must fill up the catalogue; yet we ought to be sure, from the words and meaning of the act itself, that the thing or person is really inserted as an example. . . . In all cases that fall within this rule there must be a perfect resemblance between the thing expressed and those implied. Thus, for instance, administrators are the same thing with executors; tenant for half-a-year and tenant for years have both terms for a chattel interest, differing only in the duration of the term; and so of the rest: in all these cases, the persons or things to be implied are in all respects the objects of the law as much as those expressed.'

This rule was thus transformed by our lawyers into their idiom.

' Generalis clausula non porrigitur ad ea quæ specialiter sunt comprehensa,'ᵛ and it has been upheld by the cases cited below.

Under this head also, the rule may be noticed, that where certain things are expressly taken out of the operation of a particular clause, it shall include everything within its meaning that is not excepted. So Paulus says: ' Si cui penus legata sit præter vinum—omnis penus legata videtur, excepto

---

ᵛ Thorpe v. Thorpe, 1 Ld. RAYMOND, 235 ; Reports, vol. iv. Bonham's Case, p. 378, fol. 1186 ; Ibid, Altham's Case, vol. iv. 449, (1546 fol.). The third and principal reason is upon a maxim and principle of the law : ' Quando carta continet generalem clausulam posteaque descendit ad verba specialia quæ clausulæ generali sunt consentanea interpretanda est casta secundum verba specialia ;' and he cites Margery Mortimer's Case, 7 Ed. III. 10a ; WOODESON, Elements of Juris., p. 36 ; Hare v. Horton, 5 B. and ADOLPH, 715, enumeration of particular fixtures held to exclude others, which otherwise would have passed ; Stannard v. Forbes, 6 AD. and ELLIS, 567 ; Merril v. Frame, 4 TAUNTON, 330 ; Cooper v. Walker, 4 B. and C., 46. To which may be added the construction put on the word ' tenement.' R. v. Manchester and Salford, W.W.Cy. ; 1 B. and C., 630 ; R. v. Moseley, 2 B. and C., 226. The Court were satisfied that it was intended only to apply to things ' ejusdem generis.'

vino.'ʷ   So the Prætor said: 'Pacta conventa quæ neque
dolo malo, neque adversus leges, senatus consulta edicta
decreta principum, neque quo fraus cuique eorum fiat, facta
essent—servabo.' ˣ   So in a case where sealing, signing and
delivering were required to be attested, and the attestation
mentioned the sealing and delivery, but was silent as to the
signing, the deed was held insufficient,ʸ whereas in a case
where the attestation was only, 'Witness A.B., C.B., E.B.,'
and signing, sealing and publishing were the conditions under
which the power was to be exercised, the execution of the
power was held valid by the House of Lords, and the cases
distinguished from one where some of the conditions requisite
only were attested.ᶻ

VII.

QUÆ dubitationis tollendæ causâ contractibus inseruntur jus commune non lædunt.—PAPINIAN.ᵃ

*Clauses inserted in contracts to take away all ground
for doubt, do not impede the general operation of
the general law.*

This clause is from the third book *Responsorum Papiniani*,
which related especially to the contract mandati, to the man-
datores, that is, and fidejussores; and in order clearly to
understand its value, we should know the occasion on which
it was introduced.

1st. According to the old Roman Law, the creditor might

ʷ *Dig.* xxxiii. 9. 4, § 6.

ˣ *Dig.* ii. 14. 7.

ʸ Wright *v.* Wakeford, 17 VESEY, Jun., 454. The wretched decision
of the Court of Error, in Doe *v.* Burdett (in which the influence of
special pleading is not to be mistaken), was happily overruled by the
Lords, with the sanction of Maule, J., and Tindal, C. J., among others.
Tindal, C. J., dwells particularly on the point I have endeavoured to
illustrate, that this was *not* a case where some or one of the solemnities
required were mentioned, and the rest omitted. p. 402.

ᶻ Doe d. Spilsbury *v.* Burdett, CLARKE and F., 10. 402.

ᵃ GOTH. *Reg. Juris* ; FABER, *Reg. Juris* ; ANTOINE, *Règles de Droit* ;
BROOM'S *Legal Maxims.*

take measures at once against the mandator or the fidejussor before he had recourse to the immediate debtor, and without having seized upon their pignora.

2ndly. Even if the creditor had taken measures against the principal debtor, he might still have recourse for payment to the mandator or fidejussor. This was the law in the absence of any particular stipulation.

Recollecting these principles, we must suppose a case in which a creditor, having lent money ' mandato' of Mævius to Titius, had inserted in the agreement, that it should be lawful for him to sue the mandator at once and without having taken any measure against the original debtor: ' Uti liceret sibi mandatorem prius convenire seu eligere quam aut reum principalem aut ante pignora distracta.'

Papinian was asked, whether by the insertion of this clause the creditor had deprived himself of the right given him by the Common Law between debtor and creditor, of having recourse to the fidejussor or the mandator after he had endeavoured to recover the debt from the person originally liable. The rule at the head of this section, contains the reason of his answer—that the creditor retained his right, of which it had never been his intention to deprive himself by words introduced only for the purpose of removing all pretext for doubt or cavil;—in the words of the *Basilica*, ' εἰς ἀναίρεσιν ἀπορίας.' Such is the main object of this rule, and the case to which in the first instance it was intended to apply.

In illustration of it may be cited the principle laid down as to testamentary dispositions: ' Veritatis substantiam non mutare non necessariam verborum multiplicationem, et ex abundanti res per imperitiam enumeratas generali legato non derogare.'[a]

This rule, then applies to the needless multiplication, for the imagined security of one of the contracting parties, of ' clauses secundum naturam contractus et juris communis.'

---

[a] *Dig.* xxxiv. 2. 32, 1. *pediculis* ; xix. 1. 17. 6, *si ruta* ; xx. 5. 9. 1, *quæsitum* ; xviii. 1. 68, *si cum fundum* ; xxx. 7. 12, § *penult* ; xxxiii. 10. 9, *legata*.

That is, clauses which enforce what the law would enforce without their help, and that specifically express what would be tacitly understood.

In the words of Gothofred: 'Supervacua cautio non restringit contractum.' [b]

'It is useless,' says Pomponius, 'for the creditor to stipulate that if the property hypothecated for the debt be insufficient he shall recover the rest from his debtor, because such a right is given him by the law.' 'Supervacuum est tale pactum quia ipso jure ita se res habet etiam eo non adjecto.' [c] This clause is no benefit, as the law will imply it from the existence of the obligation: 'Adjectio eorum quæ tacite insunt contractui nihil adjicit.' [d]

There is a distinction between the case for which this rule was intended to provide, and three other kinds of superfluous provisions, which have sometimes been alleged by the interpreters who have commented upon it.

The first, when words were inserted wholly foreign and irrelevant to the contract, as in the instance of a contract which begins, 'Arma virumque cano, spondeo,' etc.

The second, when words were added 'præter necessitatem.' 'Non solent quæ abundant vitiare scripturos.'

The third, when something is inserted, 'contra naturam negotii,' inconsistent with the nature of the contract; in which case the contract is valid, and the clause disregarded altogether.

---

[b] Note on the law 'qui mutuam.' *Dig.*xvii.1.56. MORNAC, in his remarks on the same law, 'qui mutuam,' recommends the insertion of such clauses, as a means of preventing dispute ; adding, 'Concisiores Tabellionum subscriptiones totidem sunt fœturæ litium.' In the debates on the 17 C. 2, c. 2, enacting that certain persons should swear to their abhorrence of taking arms against those that were commissioned by the king, it was proposed to put the word 'legally' before 'commissioned'; but Burnet tells us the lawyers declared that it must be understood.

[c] *Dig.*xx.5.1. 'Pomponius autem.'

[d] GOTHOFRED, ubi cit. *Dig.*xlv.1.65. 'Quæ extrinsecus :' a remarkable law. *Cod. de Testam. et quemadmodum,* 17.*l.* 'Testamentum non ideo.'

The result of these rules is, that the right given by the law is not impaired or affected by merely superfluous clauses—

Whether they are 'secundum naturam rei;'

Or, irrelevant to it;

Or, ' præter naturam negotii;'

Or, 'contra naturam negotii.'

If, however, words are used ' contra substantiam negotii,' as if a priest were to baptize ' in nomine Patris, Filii, et omnium sanctorum,' they would invalidate the rite.

It remains to observe, that though superfluous words do not invalidate an honest transaction, if unusual restrictions are employed they justify suspicion:[e] ' Nimia cautela dolus est.'

There are, of course, cases where the rule ' unius casus expressio alterius exclusio est' applies; that is, where the insertion of a particular case expressly shows that it was the intention of the person contracting to recede from his right in others. Where the argument ἐκ τῆς ἀντιδιαστολῆς, or a ' contrario sensu,' prevails, an argument used by Papinian[f] and Ulpian.[g]

Suppose a father, under the law which gave him back the portion of his daughter if she were divorced or died without children, were to make an express covenant that the portion should be restored to him—first, in case of her death; secondly, in case of her dying without having had children; would he wave the right given to him by the law of recovering her portion, in the first case, if the marriage was dissolved by a divorce? in the second case, if, though she had borne children, none were living at her death? The answer in both

---

[e] Twynes' Case, SMITH'S *Leading Cases*, and 3 *Reports*, 80 ; BROOM'S *Legal Maxims*, p. 217.

[f] *Dig.* i. 21. 1. He says, it is ' fortissimum argumentum.' A magistrate was expressly permitted by the Julian law to delegate his authority in case of absence : 'Non aliter itaque mandare poterit quam si abesse cœperit.'

[g] *Dig.* xxviii. 1. 20. 6 : ' Posse testem esse mulierem argumento est lex Julia de adulteriis quæ adulterii damnatam testem produci vel dicere testimonium vetat.'

cases is, that the father would not be entitled to recover any part of the portion, as by specifying those cases he must be supposed to wave his right in the others.[g]   Proculus says,[h] it was common to insert a clause in contracts, ' Dolus malus a venditore aberit, qui etiam si adjectus non esset, inesse debet.'[i] Labeo puts the case of a purchaser inserting in the contract a clause to the effect that after the price of the land he had purchased was paid, possession of it should be given to him.[j]   Pomponius, cited by Paulus, says, that the clause inserted usually when things were pledged, that if the pledge when sold did not cover the loan the debtor should make good the rest, was unnecessary.[k]

So Dumoulin says—' Aliquando verba ponuntur et congeruntur ad abundantiorem cautelam.'[l]   In French jurisprudence such phrases are called ' clauses de style.'   When the object

---

[g] ' Si quum dotem daret Pater vel extraneus pro muliere in unum casum pepigit vel in divortium vel in mortem dicendum est in eum casum in quem non pepigit, non esse mulieri actionem.'—*Dig.* xxiv. 3.22 ; and xxiii.4.26.

[h] *Dig.* xvii.1.68, § 1.

[i] D'AGUESSEAU, vol. v. p.328 ; PLAIDOYER, 59 ; M. DE BOSSU, *et les Héritiers du Duc de Guise;* MOLINÆUS, vi. 1.2, *De Verb. Oblig.* 1, vol. iii. p.85 et seq., 'Clausulæ inconsuetæ semper inducunt suspicionem'; Twyne's Case, I. W. SMITH, *Leading Cases,* KEATING and WILLES' *Ed.*

COKE, *Litt.,* 191 *a*   If land be let to two persons for the term of their lives, and the words, 'and the survivor of them,' be added, they are useless ; for the law would give the term to the survivor.

BROOM., 'p.518, 2nd ed. ; *Legal Maxims; Reports,* Borough's Case, part iv. fol.73 ; vol. ii. p.466, FRASER, *Ed.* : 'To demise all woods on a manor, and all woods growing and being on a manor, is the same thing ;' they are 'words of abundance ; for without them the law will imply so much, et expressio,' etc. ; therefore, an exception of woods is an exception of the soil itself.—Ives' Case, *Reports,* part v. fol.11 ; Doe d. Scholefield *v.* Alexander, 2 M. and S. 525 ; FRASER, *C.,* vol.iii. p.20 ; Smith *v.* Packhurst, 3 ATKYNS, 139.

[j] *Dig.* xviii.1.78, § 2.

[k] *Dig.* xx.5.91.   So, if the usual clause in the 'cautio mutiana' was omitted, it was considered as if it had been written (see below) : 'Non habetur, pro omisso.'—CUJACIUS, vol.iv. p.1110 ; *Quæst. Pap.,* Ad. L. ; Jus Mutianum.

[l] Vol. i., p.581.

of a phrase is to explain the consequence from what precedes, it is not necessary to search for any farther interpretation.

This rule has been quoted by Lord Coke, 2 Inst., 365, in this form — 'Expressio eorum quæ tacitè insunt nihil operatur.'

Lord Bacon, rule 21, says—'When the act or words do work or express no more than by intendment the law would have supplied, the doubling or iterating of that, and no more, which the conceit of law doth in a sort prevent or preoccupate, is reputed nugation, and is not supported and made of substance, either by a foreign intendment of some purpose to which it might be material, nor upon any cause emerging afterwards, which may induce an operation of these idle words.'[m]

'Here the prohibition is merely superfluous, and has no greater operation in preventing an appropriation of the fund in different proportions, than if the prohibition had been entirely omitted.'[n] 'Expressio eorum,' etc.

VIII.

DONARI videtur quod nullo jure cogente conceditur.[o]—PAPINIAN.

That may be considered a gift which is bestowed without any legal compulsion.

The object of this rule, which has some bearing on the question of voluntary agreements, is to draw the line clearly between gifts and involuntary alienations.

This was important, as not only were certain persons forbidden to give,[p] but gifts beyond a certain amount were pro-

---

[m] COKE *Litt.*, 19, 1 a.

[n] Attorney-General *v.* Ironmongers' Company, 2 MYLNE and KEEN, 576.

[o] MERLIN, *Rêport Tit. Donation.* MERLIN, *Questions Tit. Donation,* p. 48. The topic of 'mortis causâ donationes,' and others as bearing on gifts, will be considered below under the rule 'cujus per errorem dati repetitio est ejus consulto dati donatio est.'

[p] Minors, husband and wife, father and unemancipated son. *Dig.* xli. 6. 1. 27.

hibited by the Roman law.[q] If a testator, after leaving ten
gold pieces to Titius, gave away five of them, and Titius
sued for the entire legacy, the 'exceptio doli mali' was an
obstacle to his demand. But if the testator had been compelled to part with them from any necessity, as for his own
support, or to satisfy a creditor, the legatee might recover the
full value. So if the testator, after leaving a slave to Titius,
parted with him and then re-purchased him, Titius could not
claim the slave, unless he could prove a renewed intention in
his favour on the part of the testator. 'Cum servus legatus
a testatore et alienatus nuper redemptus sit a testatore non
debetur.'

The 'condictio indebiti' was the means by which the payment of what was not due might be recovered by law. The
law of Rome, which was not framed for the particular benefit
of inferior practitioners, provided, as Papinian elegantly
says, this method of retaking from a person what he
had no right to keep. 'Hæc condictio ex æquo et bono introducta quod alterius apud alterum sine causâ deprehenditur
revocare consuevit.'[r]

The question whether a transfer of property shall be considered as voluntary or not, has often occupied our tribunals,
where, upon the decision of that point, it depended whether
or not a transaction should be set aside in favour of those who,
if the property was free from any valid obligation, might

---

[q] *Codex Theod.*, viii. 2. MEERMAN *Thesaurus*, vol. vi., p. 555 : 'Vaticana
juris Fragmenta.' *Dig.* xxxix. 5.   *Cod.* viii. 54 : 'De donationibus.'
WARNKŒNIG, vol. ii., p. 360. SAVIGNY *on the Lex Cincia*, vol. iv., p. 1.
Zeitschrift für Gesch. Wissenschaft. MÜHLENBRUCH, *Doctrina Pand.;*
the *Lex Cincia* lata, A.U.C., 550, did not comprise 'Donationes
mortis causâ.' Under the emperors, it was decreed that gifts above a
certain value should be registered. *Codex Theod. de spons.*, iii. 5. 27.
Cht., lib. xxxvi., § 3. First, those above 200 solidi ; then it was raised
to 300 ; Justinian changed the sum to 500. By the *Coutûme de Paris*,
284, the 'Don mutuel' was to be registered four months after it had
been made. *Ordonnance*, 1539, art. 132. *Ordonnance*, 1731, art. 1,
drawn by D'Aguesseau. *Code*, art. 931.

[r] *Dig.* xii. 6. 66.

enforce upon it their claims against the original owner. The statutes of 13th Eliz. c. 5, and 27th Eliz. c. 4, mark an important period of our social progress. Under the first, a voluntary settlement of real or personal estate may be set aside by the creditors of the settlor, who at the time of making the settlement was in a state of obvious embarrassment; and under the second, such a settlement is void against purchasers for a valuable consideration. The cases of Sloane and Cadogan, of Ellison and Ellison,[s] of Fletcher v. Sedley,[t] and Taylor v. Jones,[u] explain the doctrine on the subject.

In Powell v. Cleaver,[w] stress was laid upon the quantity and kind of gift, as indications whether any change had taken place in the mind of the testator after he had made the gift. In Richardson v. Sedgwick, the putting a bond in suit against the husband was held proof of an intention to revoke the gift of it to the wife.[x] Equity has refused to interfere in favour of a person to whom a bond had been given without consideration.[y] In Lucas v. Lucas,[z] it was held, that the

---

[s] 6 VESEY, 656, and WHITE and TUDOR's *Selections of Leading Cases*, 190, with the note and cases cited by LORD ST. LEONARDS, in the Appendix to his book on *Ven. and Pur.*

[t] 2 VERNON, 490.

[u] 2 ATKYNS, 600.

[w] 2 BR., *Ch. C.*, 516.

[x] 2 BR., *Parl. C.*, 514. 'Si pignus vir uxori vel uxor viro remiserit, verior sententia nullam fieri donationem existimantium, quod sine dubio si in fraudem creditorum fiat, actione utili revocabitur.'—*Dig.* xix. 1. 18. *Just.* 'De actionibus. *Dig.* xix. 2—10 : 'Item si quis si cum mulier fraudandorum creditorum consilium iniisset,' etc.

[y] 4 L.J., C.C., 163, Edwards v. Jones.

[z] 1 ATKYNS. 'A gift is at the will of the donor, and therefore cannot be prescribed for.' See *Prescription* (K), pl. 2.

'If a man puts a robe or other garment on his servant to use, this is a gift in law.'—BR., DONE, etc., pl. 9, cites 11, H. 4. 31.

'If an adulterer clothes the woman, the baron may take his wife and the apparel, and justify both.'—BR. DONE, pl. 9, cites 11, H. 4. 31.

'A, borrowed £100 of B, and at the day brought it in a bag, and cast . it on the table before B; and B said to A, being his nephew, 'I will not have it ; take it you, and carry it home again with you.' Per cur, this is a good gift by parol being cast upon the table, for it was then in the

husband, by taking back into his possession some of many articles he had given to a friend for his daughter, at the request of his wife, did not cancel the previous gift. In Fortescue *v.* Barnett,[a] it was held, that the delivery by the grantor of a voluntary deed assigning a policy, was a complete gift of the policy, though the grantor kept the policy in his own possession.[b]

'A grantor cannot defeat his own grant, and therefore if a man grant twenty of his best trees to be taken in ten years, the grantor cannot cut down trees without the consent of the grantee.'—*Com. Dig.* Tit. Grant. p. 420.

French Maxim: 'Donner et retenir ne vaut.'

'La donation entre vifs est un acte par lequel le donateur se dépouille actuellement et irrévocablement de la chose donnée, en faveur du donataire qui l'accepte.'—*Code. Nap.* 894; *Pothier* (Dupin), vol. vii. 425.

'Levitati perfectam donationem revocare cupientium, jure occurratur.'—*Cod. de Cond. ob Causam.*

---

possession of B, and A might well wage his law. But it had been otherwise if A had only offered it to B, for then it was a *chose en action* only, and could not be given up without a writing.'—Noy, 67, Flowers' Case ; VINER. ab. Tit. Gift, p. 19.

'A bond without any consideration is obligatory, and there is no relief in equity against such a bond, for it is voluntary and as a gift, and no consideration is pretended. If a drunken man gives his bond it binds him. A gift of anything without any consideration is good, but it is revocable before the delivery to the donee of the thing given. Donatio perficitur possessione accipientis. This is one of the rules of law. A is indebted to B, and C to A assigns the debt due to him by C to B, in satisfaction for the debt due by A to B. This is not maintenance.' JENKINS' *Reports,* 109.

[a] 3 MYLNE and CRAIG, 36.

[b] Clavering *v.* Clavering, 2 VERNON, 473 ; Worrall *v.* Jacob, 3 MERIVALE. 'The party mistook the law, and conceived that a deed might be altered or revoked, though no power of revocation had been reserved.' SIR W. GRANT; 12 VESEY, 103 ; Curtis *v.* Price, 'A settlement of this kind is void against creditors, but only to the extent in which it may be necessary to deal with the estate for their satisfaction. To every other purpose it is good.'—SIR W. GRANT ; *Comyns Dig.* Appendix, p. 1030.

IX.

NON videntur rem amittere quibus propria non fuit.—PAPINIAN.[c]

They cannot be said to lose a thing who never held it as their own.

According to the Roman law, and, indeed, most other laws, there are two kinds of property: the one of things which we hold by a precarious and revocable title; the other of things which we possess by a complete, solid, and unalterable title. To the former class belonged, under Roman institutions, the 'peculium' of the slave and unemancipated son,[d] which, though in a certain sense their property, was, nevertheless, 'in bonis' of the master or father. In the work from which this maxim is taken, Papinian treated of alienation and the means by which possession might be lost. He discussed the question, whether possession could be gained by a slave for him who had only the usufruct of his service; also concerning things possessed ' vi, dolo,' or ' precario'; lastly, he laid down rules concerning the ' res peculiaris' of slaves and ' filii familias,' which, he said, they might occupy, but could not, in a legal sense, be said to possess—' Qui in alienâ potestate sunt rem peculiarem tenere possunt, habere possidere non possunt, quia possessio non tantum corporis sed et juris est'; and he uses here the remarkable expression—' Possessio plurimum ex jure mutuatur.' From this it followed that the ' filius familias' who lost his ' peculium,' was not said, in the legal sense, ' amittere,' what had never been his own, and was, therefore, not entitled to the ' interdictum recuperandæ possessionis' for its recovery. ' Rem amisisse non videtur qui adversus nullum rei persequendæ actionem habet.'

Thus, although the ' Lex Ælia Sentia' required, when a minor emancipated a slave, that a sufficient cause should be shewn for it, ' ne promiscuis manumissionibus liceat minori rem amittere,' yet, if the minor did so by his father's command, this proof was unnecessary, for the reason assigned by

---

[c] GOTHOFREDI, *Reg. Juris.*

the rule above. The same reasoning applied to the 'statu liber' and the 'noxæ deditus.' When the time arrived for his emancipation, the heir was deprived of the first, but could not legally be said to lose a right that never had belonged to him; and the same principle applies to the temporary holder of the 'noxæ deditus.'[d]

Another case to which the rule applies is this—Titius, a debtor of Mævius, endeavours to recover from a third person property hypothecated to Mævius. Titius fails; can Mævius enforce his security? In order to answer this question we must make this distinction: either the property did in reality belong to Titius, or it did not. If it did, and the creditor Mævius can prove three things—the debt—the hypothecation for the debt of the thing to be recovered—and that Titius was the owner of that thing, he is entitled to recover. If it did not, the creditor never had a valid lien, because the property on which it rested never belonged to his debtor, and, therefore, cannot be said to lose what never was his.[e]

Again, the rule often invoked in the gloomy days of the Roman empire, when estates were abandoned in despair by proprietors overwhelmed with fiscal exactions—'Si res pro derelicto habita sit statim nostra esse desinit et occupantis statim fit'—applies to this part of the subject.[f] This often happened to those who had availed themselves of the 'jus emphyteuseos,' as the 14 L. of the Code, under the head 'de omni agro deserto,' clearly shews. But unless the person abandoning was the owner, he could give no right to a third person against the interest of the landlord—'Qui non est verus

---

[d] 'Velut proprium patrimonium.'—*Dig.* xv. 1. 39. 'Peculium nascitur, crescit, decrescit, moritur.'—*Ibid,* xl.

[e] *Dig.* xxii. 3. 23 : 'Ante omnia probandum est quod inter agentem et debitorem convenit, ut pignori hypothecæve sit—sed et si hoc probet actor illud quoque implere debet rem pertinere ad debitorem eo tempore quo convenit de pignore aut ad eum cujus voluntate hypotheca data est.' *Dig.* xx. 1. 3, § 15: 'Si superatus quod dicitur de pignoribus et hypothecis.'

[f] *Dig.* xli. 7. 1. and 6 : 'Pro derelicto.'

rei dominus, ut colonus, et quilibet extraneus, non potest rem pro derelicto habere ad hoc ut acquiratur occupanti.'[f] Such an abandonment made by a person to whom the thing abandoned did not belong, is of no avail, nor can it be the basis of a prescriptive title. 'Nemo potest pro derelicto usucapere qui falso existimaverit rem pro derelicto habitam esse.'

Again: the person to whom anything was left under a condition, acquired no title to the thing left before the happening of the condition; and if he died before that event, his claim was at an end: 'Jus conditionale quod per viam ultimæ voluntatis relinquitur, non transmittitur, si ille in favorem cujus dispositio facta fuerat morietur pendente conditione.'[g] Neither the creditor, therefore, nor the heir of such a person, could support any claim to the property so bequeathed.

If property was left to a person on condition that he did not do a particular act, the 'cautio Mutiana' enabled the legatee to take immediate possession: ' Si testator rogasset hæredem ut restituat hæreditatem muliere, si non nupserit, dicendum erit compellendum hæredem si suspectam dicat, hæreditatem adire et restituere eam mulieri etiam si nupsisset. Idem in cæteris quoque conditionibus Julianus noster probat quæ similiter nisi fine vitæ expleri non possunt. Secundum quam sententiam cautione præstitâ his quorum interest ab his quibus restitui sub iisdem conditionibus hæres rogatus est restituet hæreditatem.'[h]

The Roman law held, as the feudal lawyers did, that a condition once gone was gone for ever: ' Conditio semel defecta non resumitur.'

---

[f] Your tenant can never levy a fine so as to injure you, the landlord; and if a party receive possession of an estate through another for a term of years, a fine levied by such a person would be merely void.'— TINDAL, C.J. Davies v. Lowndes. 5 Bin. N.C., 172.

[g] Cod. de CADUCIS tollendis C. et nomen. Sin autem aliquid, 7. Dig. xxviii. § 3, 5.

[h] Dig. xxxvi. 1. 65, 1. 'Mutiana cautio composita est a Quinto Mutio Scævola ut ejus cautionis remedio caperent statim legatarii vel fidei commissarii quæ sibi relicta essent sub conditione non faciendi aliquid quæ nisi morte legatariorum explere non possunt.'—CUJACIUS, Quæst. Pap. ad L. qui Mutianam, vol. iv. p. 1109.

' No rule is better established than that by the death of the devisee of real estate, or of the legatee of personalty, in the life-time of the testator, the testamentary disposition fails,[i] or, as the expression is, lapses.'[j]   So the word ' lapse' is applied to cases where the gift fails by the happening of some event during the testator's life on which it is destroyed; e.g., if a legacy be given to A. so long as she remains unmarried.[k]

X.

JUS publicum privatorum pactis mutari non potest.—PAPINIAN.

The contracts of private men cannot alter a rule established on grounds of public policy.

During the life of the testator, an agreement by the heir, not to take advantage of the Falcidian law, would be nugatory (*Dig.* xxxv. 2. 15).   ' Frater quum sororem hæredem scriberet, alium ab eâ cui donatum volebat stipulari curavit, ne Falcidiâ uteretur et ut certam pecuniam si contra fuisset praestaret.   Privatorum certiore legibus non esse refragandum constitit et ideo sororem jure publico retentionem habituram, et actionem ex stipulatu denegandam.'[1]

Justinian imposed the ' jusjurandum calumniæ' on liti-

---

[i] ROPER, *On Legacies*, vol.i. p.463.—By the 1 Victoria, c. 26, § 32, 33, this rule was wisely limited.   The 32nd section provides that a devise to a person for an estate tail, or an estate in quasi entail, shall not lapse if the donee leave issue inheritable under the entail.   Section 33 enacts. that where any person, being a child or other issue of the testator, to whom any property shall be left not determinable at or before the death of such person, shall die in the lifetime of the testator, leaving issue, and such issue shall be living at the death of the testator, the bequest shall not lapse.   On these clauses see Johnson *v.* Johnson, 3 HARE, 157 ; Griffiths *v.* Gale, 12 SIMON, 354 ; Winter *v.* Winter, 5 HARE, 306.

[j] Brett *v.* Rigden, PLOWDEN, 340 ; Elliot *v.* Davenport, 1 P. WILLIAMS, 83 ; Shuttleworth *v.* Greaves, 4 MYLNE and CRAIG, 35.

[k] Andrew *v.* Andrew, 1 *Coll.* (C.), 690.   As to conditions precedent, see Tattersall *v.* Howell, 2 MERIVALE, 26 ; Neal *v.* Hanbury, *Prec. Chanc.* 637 ; ROPER, *On Legacies*, vol.i. 748.

[1] 'Nemo ideo obligatur quia recepturus est ab alio quod præstit.'— CUJACIUS, *Quæst. Pap.*, lib. ii., vol. iv., p. 19.   Jones *v.* Randall, 1 COWPER.

gants at the beginning of the suit. Could the parties agree to
waive the oath? No; for it was founded on public policy.
So the time when the payment of the 'dos' was fixed could
not be prolonged—'Ut autem longiore die solvatur dos convenire non potest non magis quam ne omnino reddatur.'ᵐ So
the law gave to married people an action 'ob mores,' that is,
the right of keeping back the 'dos ob mores ejus qui divortio
causam dedit.'ⁿ This right could not be waved, neither could
the right of the husband to recall a gift made to his wife
during his life—'Illud convenire non potest ne de moribus
agatur vel plus vel minus exigatur ne publica coercitio privatâ
pactione tollatur—ac ne illa quidem pacta servanda sunt ne
ob res donatas vel amotas ageretur quia altero pacto mulieres
ad furandum invitantur, altero jus civile impugnatur' ᵒ
(*Dig.* xxiii. 4. 5). An agreement to waive a claim arising from
the 'dolus' of one of the contracting parties was invalid.

But where the public weal was not concerned, contracting
parties might agree to waive their rights; that is, they might
agree not to insist upon certain defects in the thing sold,
which, but for that agreement, the Ædilitian Edict would
have made fatal to the sale. Here the maxim, 'Quisquis
potest renuntiari juri pro se introducto,' applies.

This important doctrine was brought under the consideration
of English lawyers in a recent case.ᵖ Lord Bridgewater had
made an elevation in the peerage within a certain time, the
condition on which large estates were to be enjoyed by the
devisee. The question, therefore, to be decided was, whether
the right of an individual to dispose of his estates entitled him

---

ᵐ Lex. 2 *Cod.*, 'jusjur. propter id.' If it consisted of money, the
twelve tables compelled its payment at three fixed intervals.

ⁿ 'Hæres fiduciarius, hæres *fidei commissarius.*'

ᵒ To the same effect is the rule xxx. 1. 55: 'Nemo potest testamento
suo cavere ne leges in suo testamento locum habeant.' So a devise
made on the secret understanding that the property devised is to be
applied, in violation of the Mortmain Act, 9 Geo. II., c.36, will be void.
Strickland *v.* Aldridge, 9 Vᴇsᴇʏ, 516 ; Muckleston *v.* Brown, 6 Vᴇsᴇʏ, 52.
Cᴏᴋᴇ *Litt.*, p.3.

ᵖ The case was argued in the House of Lords before the judges.

to put it in the power of the ministers for the time being to give £70,000 a year to a particular nobleman as the reward of his support.[q] That such a condition was immoral, unconstitutional, and adverse to the most precious social interests —that it was inconsistent with the dignity and independence of the House of Lords, no one, who was at all acquainted with the political history of the country, with its actual condition, or the trusts confided to the House of Lords in our balanced government, could deny.[r] Nevertheless, all the Common Law judges, with two exceptions, and Lord Cranworth, the Vice-Chancellor, held the condition valid; and if I wanted to illustrate the value of the study of scientific jurisprudence, I could find no better topic than such a decision (the arguments in favour of which will not raise us in the opinion of posterity) would supply. Fortunately for the country, there existed a Court of Appeal from the decision by which the will had been upheld; and by that tribunal, consisting of lawyers who had turned their leisure to account —men of sagacious, and *cultivated* minds, practical enough to satisfy the most eminent solicitor—this decision, so humiliating to the whole English Bar, and fraught with so much public danger, in favour of a bequest so strongly marked with the gross and inherent vulgarity of the Saxon race, was set aside.[s]

---

[q] The estates were of the value of £70,000 per annum.

[r] What would have been the decision of the Vice-Chancellor, if the condition had been, that the devisee should support the government for twenty years? It was gravely argued, that it would be wrong to suppose ministers capable of distributing patronage from any but the purest motives; might it not as reasonably be argued, that no government could be supposed unfit for support?

[s] The reader of the arguments and decisions in favour of this preposterous clause will be forcibly reminded of a passage of Mr. Burke— 'Gentlemen have argued . . . . as if the first things in the world were at stake, and their topics belong only to matter of the lowest and meanest litigation.' I doubt if many of our judges have studied D'Aguesseau, but his remarks in the case of Madame de Bossu might be cited word for word in the Bridgewater Case :—'Depuis quand ose-t-on soutenir dans ce tribunal, que l'ordre des jurisdictions, que la conservation de ces précieuses libertés, qui a coûté tant de soins et tant

But though public morals and direct injury to the constitution were not considered by some as adequate reasons for setting aside the will of Lord Bridgewater, the principle on which it was attacked was not unknown to the law of England. True, the sentence I have put at the head of these remarks was not cited, but the necessities of society had extorted its recognition in several cases, *e.g.* :—

Marriage brocage bonds.

Undue restraint of trade.

Maintenance and Champerty.

Bequest to a married woman, on condition that she lives apart from her husband.

Unjust preference given by a secret deed to a particular creditor.

Seaman's insurance of his wages.

Withdrawal of an election petition.

Why cannot a mortgagor, by an express covenant with the mortgagee, deprive himself of the equity of redemption?[t]

'If,' said Lord Mansfield, 'this wager is contrary to principles, it must be contrary either to principles of morality, for the law of England prohibits everything ' contra bonos mores,' or it must be against principles of sound policy; for many contracts, which are not void as against morality, are void as against principles of sound policy.'

XI.

EX his omnibus causis quæ jure non valuerunt vel non habuerunt effectum, secutâ per errorem solutione, condictioni locus erit.—PAPINIAN (*Dig.* xii. 6. 54).[u]

---

de peines à nos pères soient déposées entre les mains des particuliers, que la caprice ou l'intérêt des parties puissent déroger a des lois qui forment une portion si considérable de notre *droit public*.' So spoke the Chancellor of France. PLAIDOYER, vol. v. COKE *Litt.*, p. 3.

[t] COMYN, *Dig. Chancery*, 4 a, 1, 2.

[u] *Code* 1377. 'Lorsq'une personne qui par erreur se croyait debitrice a acquitté une dette, elle a le droit de répétition contre le créancier.'
—' La répétition de la chose non due.'—LOCRÉ, vol. xiii. p. 53.

Wherever money has been paid by mistake, for a cause which the law does not support, or which has been followed by no effect, an action may be brought for its recovery.

The case which this rule was intended to meet is this:—A master bequeaths freedom to his slave, on condition that he shall pay me ten pounds. The will of the testator was invalid, as the son had been omitted from it; but the slave, in ignorance of this fact, induces Titius to give me the ten pounds. It follows that there is room for the ' condictio indebiti,' inasmuch as the money has been for an object which could not legally be obtained; and the question is, by whom is the money to be recovered? By Titius, who has paid the money, or the heir, the master of the slave? It would seem that the right to recover is in the heir, as the money was paid in the name of the slave, and is, therefore, to be considered as if the slave himself had paid it. The master, however, will be obliged to repay the money to Titius. But the Roman law said with great truth—' Tam benignius quam utilius est rectâ viâ ipsum qui nummos dedit suum recipere'; and, therefore, the right of bringing the ' condictio' was given at once to Titius, who paid the money, though not in his own name. It did not always happen either that the payer of the money had the right to bring the ' condictio,' or that the precise thing given could be recovered.[u] The jurist compares the equity of the two rights, and decides in favour of that wherein it predominates, for ' Hæc condictio ex æquo et bono introducta quod alterius apud alterum sine causâ deprehenditur, revocare consuevit' (*Ibid.* 66).

So if an heir paid a legacy bequeathed by an illegal will, he might, when he discovered his mistake, recover the money, because the legacy ' jure non valuit.' For those ' causæ ' are said ' jure non valere' which are null in their origin. Those are said ' effectum non habere' which were valid at first, but

---

[u] The English Law will be pointed out in the commentary on another maxim. CUJACIUS, vol.iv., p.40.

have been destroyed and taken away. The words 'per errorem' deserve notice; for a man who pays money, knowing that it is not due, gives it and cannot recover it again. Nor if he uses the words ' solvo non dono' at the time of payment, does that alter his right; as, on the other hand, the use of the word ' dono' will not turn a payment, or a transaction, into a gift. The purpose, not the words, of the contracting parties is to be considered, if, for instance, the heir ' prudens sciensque,' instead of deducting so much from a legacy, as the Falcidian Law[x] entitled him to take away from it, paid the full amount. He could not avail himself of the ' condictio,' because it was a gift, and supposed to proceed from a religious desire to fulfil the testator's wishes, ' fidum obsequium defuncti presibus præbere.'

XII.

NEMO damnum facit nisi qui id facit quod facere jus non habet.—PAULUS.[y]

No one is a wrong doer but he who does what the law does not allow.

On this principle Ulpian lays down the rule, that a person who has obtained a grant from the sovereign can only avail himself of it in so far as the exercise of his privilege is consistent with the rights of others; a rule which will surprise those whose knowledge of the Roman law is derived from the misrepresentation of it by English writers. ' Merito ait prætor ' quâ ex re quid illi damnum detur,' nam quotiescunque aliquid in publico fieri permittitur—ita oportet ut sine injuriâ cujus quam fiat et ita solet princeps quoties aliquid novi operis instituendum petitur permittere.'[z]

The ' damnum injuriâ datum,' for which the offender might

---

[x] *Dig.* xii. 6. 53.

[y] GOTHOFREDI, *Reg. Juris.* ANTOINE, *Règles de Droit.*

[z] *Dig.* xliii. 8. 2, § 10: ' Ne quid in loco publico.' COMYNS, *Dig.;* GRANT, *Rolls Abridg. Prerogative,* 9 ; ALTON WOODS, 1 *Reports,* 26 : Queen's grant set aside as illegal, though ' ex certâ scientiâ et rubro motu.'

be sued under the Aquilian law, as distinct from the ' actio in factum,' was that act ' quod cum damno injuriam attulerit.'[a]

Lord Coke lays it down, ' Non potest rex gratiam facere cum injuriâ et damno aliorum.'—2 *Inst.*236.[b] ' It sounds in deceit of the king, and is a great indignity to him—propter apices juris—to make his charter, under the great seal, of things which he may lawfully grant, void and of none effect[c]—QUIA APICES JURIS NON SUNT JURA.'[d] ' It cannot be supposed, unless he is deceived in his grant, that the king would grant to A. that which he has already granted to B. If the king is deceived in his grant, it is perfectly clear the grant is void.'[e] Indeed, it so happens that the very case put in the *Digest* is to be found in the year-books: ' If the king give beforehand license to murder a man, or to commit a nuisance in the high road, it is void.'[f] Bracton says, ' Rex non poterit gratiam facere cum damno et injuriâ aliorum, quod autem alienum est dare non potest per suam gratiam.'[g]

But the most remarkable instance of this principle is (the time and circumstances considered) in Cavendish's case, where the judges refused obedience to the reiterated commands of Queen Elizabeth. ' They say, that of necessity they have not performed the commands; but they say, this is no offence to, or contempt of, her majesty, because those commands were against the law of the land, in which case no one is bound to observe such command.'[h] Such was the government which Mr. Hume compares in terms to the despotism of Turkey.

---

[a] *Dig.*ix.49, § 1 : ' Ad legem aq.'

[b] BROOM's *Legal Maxims*, p.45, where, besides many cases, *Cod.* vii. 38.2, is cited.

[c] Earl of Rutland's Case, cit. *ib.*, 57 *a*, part 8, vol. iv. p.251.

[d] A passage in his favourite author, which is not quoted, I believe, in any of Baron Parke's judgments.

[e] Alcock *v.* Cooke, 5 BING., *Reports*, 349 ; BLACKSTONE, vol.iv. p.522.

[f] I put the Norman French in the note, that the reader may compare it with Ulpian's Latin : 'Si le roy voyloit Poiar. done de occider un homme ou de fair nuisance in le haut chemin ceo est void.'—11 H. VII.

[g] BRACTON, iii. 132 ; and the judgment of that great lawyer and upright judge, C. J. Vaughan, Thomas *v.* Sorrell, VAUGHAN's *Reports*.

[h] ANDERSON's *Reports*, 155.

XIII.

HOC jure utimur ut quicquid omnino per vim fiat aut in vis publicæ aut in vis privatæ crimen incidit.—ULPIAN.[i]

Every act of violence is an offence designated as public or private violence.

Violence is defined in the *Digest* as 'vis majoris impetus quæ repelli non potest,'[k] a power which the person to whom it is applied is unable to resist. Violence and right are opposites: 'Vis dicitur quicquid nullo jure fit contra liberum et justum ejus arbitrium.' Legal compulsion is not violence: 'Vim accipimus atrocem . . . non eam quam magistratus recte intulit.' He was guilty of public violence who employed arms, or any other instrument, to injure another:[l] 'De vi publica tenentur qui armis, telis aut alio quolibet instrumento utuntur ad nocendum alicui.'[m] — and who by artifice obstructed the course of justice: 'Qui dolo malo faciunt quominus judicia tuto exerceantur'—who, of his own authority, imposed new taxes: 'Qui nova vectigalia exercent auctoritate propriâ'[n]—and, of course, armed robbers, with their adherents and accomplices: 'Qui res alienas aperto marte et cum armis eripiunt vel raptoribus opem præstant vel res ereptas scienter servant.'[o]

He is guilty of private violence who, without the use of arms, but, nevertheless, drawing together a multitude, commits some excess, not followed by loss of life, against the person of another. 'Hâc lege tenetur qui convocatis hominibus vim

---

[i] GOTHOFREDI, *Reg. Juris.* Bracton has embodied this distinction in his work.

[k] *Dig.*iv. 2: 'Quod metus causâ gestum erit.'   [l] *Ib.*i. §3.

[m] *Dig.*xlviii. 6.1, and L. *armatos*, 9; xlviii.6.10: 'Item qui cum telo dolo malo in concione fuerit, aut ubi judicium publice exercebitur.'
'Telorum appellatione omnia ex quibus singuli homines nocere possunt accipiuntur.'

[n] *Ib.* 1. 12.

[o] *Cod.* 9: Ad Leg. Julianam de vi publicâ vel privatâ 'crimen non dissimile.'

fecerit quo quis verberetur, pulsaretur, neque homo occisus est.'[p]
He who does not claim what is his due through the judge,
but tears it away by his own act—' Qui sibi debitum auctoritate
propriâ non per judicem reposcunt sed per viam facti eripiunt.'
The creditor who entered upon his debtor's land by violence
—' Qui in possessionem fundi debitoris per vim ingreditur.'

The punishment of him who incurred the penalties of the
' Lex Julia de vi publicâ' was deportation or perpetual banishment.   The punishment of him who incurred the penalties of
the ' Lex Julia de vi privatâ' was confiscation of the third
part of his property.

The ' vis Publica' and the ' vis Privata' were both crimes
against the State; and it would be grievous error to suppose
that the words ' Publica' and ' Privata' meant to divide
offences into crimes against the public and against individuals.[q]   The distinction related to such offences as amounted
to an open defiance of public authority, and those which were
not of so grave a character.

The English law on this head bears still abundant marks of
its Gothic origin.   Nothing can be more confused, irregular,
rude and uncertain, with regard to civil rights and criminal accusations.   It delivers this important point of Public Law over
to conflict and controversy.   What is to be the issue, if every
man is to decide for himself whether he is enforcing a legal
right or resisting a just demand?   Surely nothing but bloodshed and violence, where there is equality of strength and
spirit.   The extreme case of self-preservation, where legal

---

[p] *Dig.* xlviii. 7. 2. *Ibid.* 7 : ' Tu vim esse putas esse solum si homines
vulnerentur ?   Vis est et tunc quoties quis id quod deberi sibi putat
non per judicem reposcit.'

[q] HALE *Pleas of the Crown,* c. 8 ; 25 Ed. III. st. 5, c. 2. was passed to
guard against the doctrine of accroaching.   'If any man doth ride
armed, openly or secretly, with a number of armed men, against any
other, to slay him, or to rob him, or to take and detain him until he
pay a fine for his deliverance, it is not the intent of the king and
council that in this case it be judged high treason, but that it be adjudged felony or trespass.'   *Cod.* ix. 8. 5.   36 Geo. III., c. 7 ; 39 and 40
Geo. III , c. 93 ; 54 Geo. III., c. 46 ; 11 Geo. IV., and 1 Wm. IV., c. 66, § 2 ;
11 and 12 Vict., c. 12 ; 3 and 4 Vict., c. 52, § 4 ; 11 and 12 Vict., c. 12.

authority is grossly abused, can alone justify resistance. Our
law justifies, as will be seen by a case in the note, precisely the
act that the Roman Law forbids, which is inconsistent with all
reason, the assertion by a creditor of his own right with a
strong hand.[r] It is clear that this is to make a man judge in
his own case (whether he judge rightly or wrongly is nothing
to the principle), and, therefore, is a direct encouragement to
violence. Lord Stowell's language is far more applicable to
disputes among citizens of the same community than among
nations, where he says—'I take the rule of law to be that the
vessel shall submit to the enquiry proposed, looking with confidence to those tribunals whose noblest office—and I hope not
the least acceptable to them—is to relieve by compensation
inconveniences of this kind, where they have happened
through accident or error, and to redress by compensation-
punishment injuries that have been committed by design.'[s]
Still more shocking to all reasonable construction, and the
general sense of mankind, are the decisions according to
which trifling riots, for the purpose of destroying meeting-
houses, or houses of ill fame,[t] have been held to be a levying
war against the king.[u]

---

[r] Earl of Bristol *v.* Wilsmore, 1 B. and C., 514. See BACON'S *Abridgment* tit. *Rescous,* where we meet with this passage—'The man, *if he
be innocent* [who is to decide that ?], may rescue himself; but he does
so at his peril, for if, in the attempt to make rescue [which, observe, is
permitted], he is, of necessity, slain, it is no felony in the officer; and,
upon the same principle, if the officer is slain, it is murder.' FOSTER'S
Crown Law. COMYN'S *Digest,* tit. *Rescous.* LUDER'S *Considerations on
the Law of High Treason.* Earl of Essex's Case, *State Trials,* vol. i.,
1334.

[s] The Maria, ROB. *Ad. Reports,* 375.

[t] Messenger's Case, KELYNGE, 71. Hale differed from the other judges
in this case. The judges a short time before decided that Charles II.
was king, immediately after his father's death, *de facto* as well as *de
jure!* Damaree *v.* Purchase, 15 *Trials,* 450. HALLAM'S *Const. Hist.,*
c. 15. Lord George Gordon's Case, 21, *State Trials.* Hardy's Case, 24
State Trials.

[u] 'C'est assez que la crime de lèse majesté soit vague pour que le
gouvernement dégénère en despotisme.'—*Esprit des Loix,* xii. 7.

XIV.

REFERTUR ad universos quod publice fit per majorem partem.—ULPIAN.[v]

The public act of the majority is the act of all.

The principle of this law is to be found in many passages of the Roman Law.

In matters which concern a collective body, the opinion of the greater number of its members is taken to be the opinion of all. It is to be the same as if all had taken a part in the proceedings—' Quod major pars curiæ effecerit pro eo habetur ac si omnes egerint.'[w] So Celsus says, that although where three judges are to decide, the absence of one is fatal, yet if that one be present, and express an opinion at variance with that of his colleagues, ' statur duorum sententiæ ';[x] and Pomponius lays down the same rule with regard to arbiters—' Id quod major pars omnium judicavit, ratum est cum et omnes judicâsse palam est.'[y]

There were cases, however, in which a bare majority was not sufficient, and where even two-thirds were requisite. Paulus gives an instance in the case of Decuriones; but he says the person in favor of whom the vote was given might help to make up the required number: ' Plane at si duæ partes Decurionum adfuerint, is quoque quem decernunt, numerari potest.'[z] A rule which appears at variance with the maxim: ' Nemo se ipsum eligere potest.'[a]

This rule has been opposed, on the ground that ' quod omnes tangit ab omnibus debet approbari,' in support of which is quoted, first, an opinion of Celsus, who decides that a servitude cannot be established over an estate belonging to several owners without the consent of all. ' Prohibitio unius vim habet majorem quam plurium concessio.'

Secondly, an opinion of Ulpian, that a water passage can only be established with the consent of all the possessors of

---

[v] GOTHOFREDI, *Reg. Juris.*   [w] *Dig.* l. 1. 19.
[x] *Dig.* xlii. 1. 39.   [y] *Dig.* iv. 8. 18.   [z] *Dig.* iii. 4. 4.
[a] *Dig.* xxvi. 5. 4 : ' Prætor ipse se tutorem dare non potest.'

the soil in which the water rises, and also of those who have the right to use the stream: ' In concedendo jure aquæ ducendæ non tantum eorum ex quorum loco aqua oritur, rerum eorum etiam ad quos ejus aquæ usus pertinet, voluntas exquisitur,'[b] because he says it would be unjust that the consent of any one should injure those who shared in the same right: ' Iniquum enim est consensum unius . . . præjudicium sociis facere.'[c]

But we must distinguish the cases where a man's interest arises simply from the fact that he is a member of a particular body, and those where he has an interest which belongs to him as an individual—as the writers on Roman Law express it—between ' aliquid commune pluribus ut universis,' and ' aliquid commune pluribus ut singulis.'[d]

In the first case, the consent of the majority, in some proportion or other, is sufficient; in the second, that of all concerned is necessary. To the latter case the words of Paulus apply: ' De unoquoque negotio PRÆSENTIBUS OMNIBUS[e] quos causa contingit judicari oportet—aliter enim judicatum tantum inter præsentes tenet.'[f]

To constitute a valid assembly of a select vestry, a majority of the whole number appointed should be present.[g]

The doctrine of majorities was elaborately discussed in the church-rate case,[h] in which most of the decisions applicable to the question were commented upon at great length. It was there held, that the vote of an actual majority of those present was absolutely required to make a valid church-rate.

---

[b] *Dig.* xxxix. 3. 88 ; *Dig.* x. 3. 28 : ' In re pari potiorem causa esse prohibentis constat.'

[c] *Dig.* xxxix. 3. 10.

[d] *Dig.* ii. 14. 7. 19 : 'Hodie tamen ita demum pactio creditoribus obest si convenerint in unum et communi consensu declaraverint quotâ parte debiti contenti sint—si vero dissentiant tunc Prætoris partes necessariæ sunt qui decreto suo sequetur majoris partis voluntatem.'

[e] See R. *v.* Whitaker, 7 B. and C.

[f] *Dig.* xlii. 1. 47.

[g] Brockett *v.* Blizard, 4 M. and R., 641; Golding *v.* Fenn, 7 B. and C., 782.

[h] Gosling *v.* Veley, *Clerk* ; House of Lord's Cases, p. 796.

In the case of jurors, the law of England will be satisfied with nothing less than unanimity. A single corrupt or wrong-headed man has it thus in his power to arrest the course of justice. To quote instances where good has accidentally resulted from the power thus given to a single individual, only proves that there is no evil without some chance under some circumstances of compensation. The experience of every one conversant with legal proceedings will furnish him with numberless instances[i] of the evil thus occasioned; and in human affairs the preponderating evil must turn the scale. No doubt the use of torture led in some cases to the discovery of crime. The most senseless legal quibbles have sometimes arrested injustice, and perhaps there might be cases in which the right of sanctuary protected innocence. The absurdity is derived from a barbarous age, and is peculiar to the English law.

XV.

NON debet cui plus licet, quod minus est non licere.—ULPIAN.[j]

He who can walk ten miles can walk five.   *He who can do the greater can do the less.*

To this rule may be added several others, founded on the same principle. He who may sell against the will of another, may sell without his knowledge. ' Qui potest invitis alienare multo magis ignorantibus et absentibus potest.'[k]

Any one who has power to condemn, has power also to absolve—' nemo qui condemnare potest absolvere non potest.'[l] He who has the right to give, has the right to sell—' cui jus est donandi eidem et vendendi et concedendi jus est.'[m] He who may alienate, may consent to an alienation— ' cum quis possit alienare poterit et consentire alienationi.'[n]

---

[i] 3 LUDER's *Election Cases,* 324; Taylor *v.* Mayor of Bath ; R. *v.* Hawkins, 10 EAST, 211 ; Oldknow *v.* Wainwright, 2 BURROW, 1017; R. *v.* Monday, COWPER, 530.

[j] GOTHOFREDI, *Reg. Juris.*

[k] *Dig. de reg. Juris,* L. 26.   [l] *Ibid.,* 137.

[m] *Ibid.,* 123.   [n] *Ibid.,* 123.

He who has a right of action, may use the facts which give him a right of action, as a defence to an action—' Cui damus actionem, eidem exceptionem competere multo magis dixerit.'[o] He who may put an adulterer to death, may justify contumelious treatment of him—' Qui occidere potest adulterum multo magis contumeliâ potest enim jure afficere.'[p] ' Plus,' say the authors of the institutes, or rather the old civilians, from the works of whom they have transcribed this valuable passage, 'quatuor modis petitur; 1. re; 2. tempore; 3. loco; 4. causâ. 1. Re veluti si quis pro decem aureis qui ei debebantur, viginti petierit. 2. Tempore veluti si quis ante diem vel ante conditionem petierit. 3. Loco plus petitur veluti cum quis id quod certo loco dari stipulatus est alio loco petit. 4. Causâ, as when by the form of action adopted, the plaintiff deprives his adversary of his right of choice—' eripit electionem adversario.' See, too, the law, ' Si ita' (Dig. xl. 7. 3. 15).

If freedom was left to a slave, on condition of serving the heir five years, and the heir would not allow him to serve, the slave could not claim his emancipation until the five years had expired, because the heir might call upon him at any time within the five years to serve for the remainder of the term. ' Is quem non patitur quis sibi servire postea pati potest, intra quinquennii tempus, atquin jam quinquennio ei servire non potest—sed vel minus potest.'

So an unemancipated son, as he might dispose of his ' peculium castrense' by will, might also make of it a ' donatio mortis causâ,' or give it in any other way. ' Qui habent castrense peculium, vel quasi castrense in eâ conditione sunt ut donare et mortis causâ et non mortis causâ possint quum testamenti factionem habeant.'[q]

The minor, who had the extraordinary remedy of the ' in integrum restitutio,' had, ' a fortiori,' the ordinary remedy of appeal.[r] He who had a right to a real action for the whole,

---

[o] Ibid., 198, § 1.

[q] Ibid., xxxix. 5. 7, § 6.

[p] Ibid., xlviii. 5. 22, § 3.

[r] Ibid., iv. 1.

might, if it seemed more expedient to him, bring it for a part.[s]

The judge, in whose power it is to offer an oath as to the whole sum in dispute between the parties, may offer it for a part.[t]

Taking the argument, ' a contrario sensu,' it follows, that where the less is unlawful, the greater is also. ' Qui indignus est,' says Pomponius, ' inferiore ordine, indignus est superiore.'[u] Callistratus says, that the man whom the law exempts from liability to blows, is exempt from the punishment of the mines: ' Est inconstans dicere eum quem principales constitutiones fustibus subjici prohibuerunt, in metallum dari posse.'[v] 'The man,' says Papinian, ' whom the laws forbid to approach the Pomœrium, they forbid also to enter the city.'[w] ' Quod quidem naturalem habeat intellectum ne scilicet qui careret minoribus, frueretur majoribus.' If a woman who has married a second time cannot disinherit her children by the first marriage, even for reasons that would otherwise be sufficient, neither can a mother who leads a notoriously dissolute life.[x] As you cannot by putting him in bonds gain possession of a freeman, neither can you acquire possession of what is his. ' Si vinxeris liberum hominem eum a te possideri non puto quod cum ita se habeat multo minus a te per illum res ejus possidebuntur neque enim rerum natura recipit ut per eum aliquid possidere possim, quem civiliter in meâ potestate non habeo.'[y] As a last instance, we may cite the rule, that what a man cannot do by himself, he cannot do by another: ' Quod quis suo nomine exercere prohibetur id neque per subjectam personam agere debet.'[z]

' Eum qui suo nomine usucapere non potest nec per servum capere posse, ait Pedius.'

---

[s] *Ibid.*, vi. 1. 76.   [t] *Ibid.*, xii. 35, § 7.

[u] And ULPIAN, 'De interdictis et relegatis,' *Dig.*, l. 7 ; *Dig.* i. 9. 4 'De senatoribus.'

[v] *Dig.* xlviii. 19. 28.   [w] *Dig.* xviii. 7. 5.

[x] *Cod. de Revocandis Donat.*, L. 7.   [y] *Dig.* xli. 2. 2. 5.

[z] *Dig.* l. 81. 27.

Neither, if we cannot bequeath to any persons, can we bequeath to their slaves.[a]

The exceptions to the rule are—

1. When particular powers are confided to a magistrate, he cannot go beyond their limits, even if the jurisdiction be less considerable. The Latrunculator, appointed among the Romans to decide cases of theft, could not decide civil cases.[b]

2. The decrees of the judge; e.g., if the prætor allowed the tutor to sell the property of his ward, that did not justify its hypothecation. ' Mea fuit opinio,' says Ulpian, ' eum qui aliud fecit quam quod a prætore decretum est nihil egisse.' [c]

3. The powers of an agent.[d] An agent appointed for a special purpose cannot transgress its limits: ' Mandatarius debet diligenter custodire fines mandati.'

4. The quality of heir was indivisible. An heir, therefore, could not accept part of a testator's will, and reject the rest. He was obliged to take it altogether, or to leave it alone: ' Nemo potest scindere judicium testatoris.'[e]

5. A custom against legal analogy is not to be extended: ' Quod contra rationem juris introductum est, non est producendum ad consequentias.' [f]

In Isherwood v. Oldknow, Lord Ellenborough held it to be clear, that a power to grant leases for twenty-one years included a power of granting them for fourteen.[g] ' This is a grant

---

[a] *Dig.* xli. 3. 8.

[b] 'Latrunculator de re pecuniariâ judicare non potest.'—*Dig.* v. 1. 61. The ' Præses Provinciæ' might inflict a capital sentence, but not deportation.'—*Dig.* i. 18. 6. LORD CAMDEN, in Entick v. Carrington, *State Trials,* 1058, lays down this exactly—this very principle. (See infra.)

[c] *Dig.* xx. 6. 8, § 13: 'A formâ decreti,' says Godefroi, in his note on the passage, 'non est recedendum est enim stricti juris neque extenditur ad similia vel ad minora.'

[d] *Dig.* xvii. 1. 5.

[e] *Dig.* xxix. 2. 1.

[f] A custom inconsistent with the doctrine of resulting trusts was held unreasonable'—Lewis v. Lane, 2 MYLNE and KEEN, 449.

[g] MAULE and S. 393 ; and see Johnstone v. Sutton, 1 *J. Reports,* 519 (arguendo).

for fourteen years, and I think it is within the rule ' omne majus continet in se minus'; in like manner as if there be a license or authority to a man to do any number of acts for his benefit, he may do some of them, and need not do all.'   So a tenant in fee simple may carve out of it such estate, or impose on it such burdens, as he may think fit.[h] In Lord Camden's immortal judgment of Entick v. Carrington,[i] he touches upon this topic, and insists on an exception to the rule. ' Now whereas it has been argued that if you admit a power of committing in high treason, the power of committing for lesser offences follows *a fortiori*; I beg leave to deny that consequence; for I take the rule with regard to all special authorities to be directly the reverse.   They are always strictly confined to the letter; and when I see, therefore, that a special power in any single case only has been permitted to a person who in no other instance is known or recorded by the law as a magistrate, I have no right to enlarge his authority one step beyond that case.'

XVI.

QUOD initio vitiosum est non potest tractu temporis convalescere.[j]—PAULUS.[k]

Lapse of time cannot cure that of which the origin is vicious.[l]

A contract by which Titius agreed that Mævius, not being his heir, should not be required to do a certain action, was

---

[h] ' If malice be a term of law, and import want of probable cause, omne majus continet in se minus, and, consequently, probable cause must be a matter of law.'—BROOM, *Legal Maxims*, p.129, 2nd ed.

[i] *State Trials*, vol. xix.1058.

[j] GOTHOFREDI, *Reg. Juris;* ANTOINE; BROOME'S *Legal Maxims.*

[k] Greek paraphrase—Τὸ ἐξαρχῆς ἀνυπόστατον οὐ βεβαιοῦται τῇ χρομιᾷ παραδρομῇ. NOY, Ed.5, p.4. Bruyeres v. Halcomb, 3 AD. and ELLIS, 381 ; 3 BIN., *N. C.,* 160 ; CUJACIUS, vol.vi. p.93 ; *Ad Leg. de Usucap.* 42 ; Vernon's Case, 4 COKE, *Reports,* 26.

[l] This rule does not apply to marriages : ' La publication des bans et des autres solemnités que l'Eglise a introduites peuvent à la vérité faire

void; and if afterwards Mævius became the heir of Titius, he could not take advantage of it: ' Quia ex post facto id confirmari non potest' (*de Pactis, Dig.* ii.14,17, § 4). So the rule is laid down (*Dig.* l.17. 201), ' Omnia quæ ex testamento profisciscuntur ita statum eventus capiunt si initium quoque sine vitio ceperint.' To the same effect is the law (*ib.* 210), ' Quæ ab initio inutilis fuit institutio ex post facto convalescere non potest.' So the contracts of a minor, made without the authority of his guardian, were void; but the authority must be given at the time, and by himself in person. A subsequent confirmation, or an authority by letter, was of no avail: it is as if I had contracted to do what was physically impossible: ' Proinde ac si ea conditio quæ naturâ impossibilis inserta esset;' nor did it matter that it might afterwards be in my power to fulfil the contract: ' Nec ad rem pertinet quod jus mutari potest et id quod nunc impossibile est postea possibile fieri' (*Dig., de Verb. Oblig.*, xlv. tit.1.137 § 6). It is to this principle that the Catoniana regula relates: ' Si testamenti facti tempore inutile sit legatum non valere id quandocunque testator decesserit;'[m] a rule, fortunately, of no account in our law, as all wills, as a general rule, now speak from the death of the testator. ' On the other hand, if a slave became the property of another, after an injury committed, the ' noxale judicium' lay against the new master' (*Dig., de Noxal. Act.*, ix.4.42, § 2). Again; an ' actio furti' did not lie against a son or a slave; nor, if after the

---

déclarer un mariage nul en certains cas mais parceque les lois qui les ont établies n'ont en vue que certaines personnes en certaines circonstances, lorsque ces circonstances n'existent plus lorsque l'état des personnes est changé et que leur volonté est toujours la même ce qui étoit nul dans son principe se ratifie dans la suite, et l'on n'applique point au mariage cette maxime qui n'a lieu que dans les testaments. Quod ab initio,' etc.—D'Aguesseau, vol.i. p.462, 7 *Plaidoyer.*

' Il n'est pas d'un mariage comme d'un testament et quelques autres actes, a l'égard desquels on cite la maxime commune de droit. Quod ab initio,' etc.—D'Aguesseau, *Plaidoyer* 33, vol.iii. p.11; *Cause des Héritiers du Duc de Guise, Plaid.* 57 ; *ib.* vol.v. p.403.

m Corroborated by this : 'Omnia quæ ex testamento profisciscuntur ita statum eventus capiunt, si initium quoque sine vitio ceperint.'

' Tutor statim in ipso negotio præsens debet auctor fieri, post tempus vero aut per epistolam interpositâ ejus auctoritate, nihil agit' (*Dig., de Auct. Tutorum*, xxvi.8.9, § 5). If by my order a contract was made with the slave of another man, and I afterwards bought the slave, the contract was nevertheless invalid: ' Ne actio quæ ab initio inutilis fuerit, eventu confirmetur' (*Dig.*, *Quod Jussu*, lib. xv.4, § 2). So, if I contracted to sell a court of justice, or a market-place, or a building dedicated to religious worship, the contract was void: ' Ubi omnino conditio jure impleri non potest vel id facere ei non liceat;' as if ' furtum' committed they were emancipated, could the action be maintained: ' Neque enim actio quæ non fuit ab initio nata oriri potest adversus hunc furem' (*Dig. de Furtis.*, xlvii.2.17, § 1). But in certain cases, the law supposed a new and valid contract, as if I pledged the property of another, and it became my own: 'Datur utilis actio pigneratitia creditori' (*Dig. de Pign. Act.*, xiii.7.41)—where the distinction is drawn between that case and the case of the heir: ' Si convenisset de pignore ut ex suo mendacio arguatur improbe resistit.' Papinian says, if a husband sold the land of his wife's dower, the sale was invalid; but if at her death the land became his, 'si tota dos lucro mariti cessit,' the sale was established (*Dig.* xli.3.42). So, though the marriage of a girl under twelve was invalid, it became valid after she had lived twelve years with her husband: 'Minorem annis duodecim nuptam tunc legitimam uxorem fore cum apud virum explêsset duodecim annos'[c] (*de Ritu Nuptiarum, Dig.* xxiii.2.4).

The rule did not apply to conditional and future contracts (*de Reg. Caton., Dig.* xxxiv.6.4): ' Placet Catonis regulam ad conditionales institutiones non pertinere.'[d] So, though 'ea quæ ædibus juncta sunt legari non possunt;' and although if ' ab initio non constitit legatum ex post facto non convalescet,' and the' Catoniana regula jussum legatum impediet,' in such a case; yet, if bequeathed conditionally, ' si sub conditione legatus,' it is valid,

---

[c] See the law 'Si quis,' *Dig.* xxiii.2.27.

[d] 'Legatum quod ab initio vitiosum est ex post facto non convalescit.'

'poterit legatum valere' (*Dig., de Leg.,* xxx. 1, 41, § 2). In these, the energy and operation of the matter is in suspense till the event happens, and therefore the rule does not apply.

To this rule may be added the converse doctrine, that as subsequent events cannot establish what was originally vicious, neither can they impair what was originally valid.[e] So, if a man in his senses makes his will, or marries, and afterwards loses his reason, the will or the marriage is not shaken: 'Furor contractus matrimonium non sinit quia consensu opus est, sed recte contractum non impedit' (*De Ritu Nupt.,* xxiii. 2. 16 § 2). So, if at first, for the requisite time, Titius has used a path neither 'clam,' nor 'vi,' nor 'precario,' he does not lose his right to the interdict, because afterwards he has used it 'clam' or 'precario:' 'Si quis supra dicto tempore anni non vi non clam non precario itinere usus sit verum postea non sit sed clam precariove videndum est an ei noceat et magis est ut nihil ei noceat, quod attinet ad interdictum' (*Dig., de Itinere actuque priv.* xliii. 19. 12); 'for,' says Paulus, 'what is lawfully done cannot be undone by a supervening offence' (*Ibid.* 2): 'Nec enim commissi aut sunt in quod recte transactum est superveniente delicto potest;' and the principle is clearly stated, *Dig.* l. 17, 85: 'Non est novum ut quæ semel utiliter constituta sunt, durent, licet casus extitent aquo initium capere non potuerunt;' and the law 'Barbarius' expressly provides for the case where a person had performed legal functions in the exercise of an office which the law forbad him to hold: 'Si servus, quamdiu latuit dignitate prætoriâ functus sit: quid dicemus? Quæ edixit, quæ decrevit, nullius fore momenti? An fore propter utilitatem eorum qui apud eum egerunt vel lege vel quo alio jure? et verum puto nihil eorum reprobari.'[f] 'If an infant or married woman do make a will, and publish the same, and afterwards dieth, being of full age or sole, notwithstanding this is void.'[g]

---

[e] 'Τὰ ἐξαρχῆς βέβαια ἐκ τῶν ἐπισυμβαινόντων οὐκ ἀκοροῦται.' — CONSTANTINE'S *Greek Paraphrase.*

[f] *Dig.* lib. i. tit. 14, § 3.

[g] NOY.

In the case of Montmorency *v.* Devereux, before the House of Lords, Lord Cottenham says—' Is the transaction actually void in itself? If so, there can be no confirmation of a transaction actually void in itself. But a transaction, voidable only from circumstances, however strong, may undoubtedly be confirmed by a subsequent deliberate act of the party who might originally, probably, have succeeded in declaring it void.' It is difficult, however, to reconcile the principle so broadly laid down with the following passage in the same judgment:—' It appears to me, that although the transaction was questionable in its origin, and suspicious in its commencement, it is not now capable of being complained of'; and still more with the judgment in the case.

Lord Cottenham says, in plain words, that if the transaction, which his judgment established, had been complained of at *first*,[h] it would, as a matter of course, have been set aside in any Court of Equity. But he relies on this circumstance, that, in the case before him, the conduct of the person injured by such flagrant iniquity, though caused by the wrong-doer (and a more nefarious affair can hardly be imagined) debars him from that right. Such reasoning is to me utterly unintelligible. The injury had been inflicted; no compensation had been offered for it; the transaction, on the face of it, was scandalous; and because the offender, taking advantage of his own wrong, prevented his victim for a considerable time from seeking redress, and even extorted from him a recognition of the proceeding, Lord Cottenham held that for the interest of society, and in obedience to the English law,[i] the transaction should be upheld, that the fraud should be successful, and that the additional guilt of the offender should establish his impunity. Such a decision may be wise, sound, and philosophical, and reflect the highest credit on the state of English law; but it certainly is not that at which the author of this

---

[h] That is, in 1829 ; this was 1840.   7 CL. and FINN. House of Lord's Cases, 1838.

[i] 3 and 4 Wm. IV., c. 27. § 26. See also Presbytery of Auchterarder *v.* Earl of Kinnoul. 6 CL. and FINN, 708.

maxim would have arrived. In the case of Pickering *v.* Lord Stamford,[k] it was held that the length of time alone was not sufficient to justify a presumption that the persons complaining had released their rights and acquiesced in their violation. 'Fraud,' says Lord Chief Justice de Grey, 'vitiates the most solemn proceedings of Courts of Justice.'[l] 'No length of time,' said Lord Talbot, 'will bar a fraud.'[m] 'And it is now provided by a written law, that in cases of concealed fraud time shall not run until the fraud shall be, or with reasonable diligence might have been, known, saving the rights of *bond fide* purchasers for a valuable consideration.'[n]

In the case cited below, Sir W. Grant set aside a deed, after seventeen years, executed for an ignorant woman by one who stood in a relation of confidence to her—' I think she has not been guilty of that sort of laches which may sometimes protect from impeachment transactions originally of a very questionable nature.'[o] This decree was upheld by Lord Erskine and and Lord Eldon. In another case,[p] a deed wrung from persons

---

[k] 2 VESEY, 27.

[l] *State Trials,* 20, Duchess of Kingston's Case.

[m] *Cases Temp.,* TALBOT, p. 63. Cotterell *v.* Purchase. Murray *v.* Palmer, 2 SCHOALES and LEFROY, 487. Lord Redesdale lays down the rule that no act will confirm a fraud, unless the person knew the fraud and intended to confirm it by the act. FONBLANQUE, *Treatise on Equity,* 122, and notes ; 2 VESEY, 155 (Lord Hardwicke); 7 VESEY, 211 ; *Code of Louisiana,* § 1854, 1858 ; MILES, *Reports,* 229.

[n] HILL *on Trustees,* 144. In Trevelyan *v.* L'Estrange, Sir C. Pepys set aside a purchase by a steward at an undervalue after a lapse of forty-seven years, *cit. ib.*

[o] Purcell *v.* Macnamara, 14 VESEY, JUN., 113. Pickett *v.* Logpent, 14 VESEY, 215.

[p] 'Length of time,' says Sir S. Romilly, *arguendo,* 'forms a strong objection, where it can be used, to shew acquiescence, but in no other way ; and in cases of fraud it cannot be a bar.' Lord Cholmondeley *v.* Lord Clinton, 2 JACOB and WALKER, 147. Lord Mansfield, Eldridge *v.* Knott, COWPER, 214. Bond *v.* Hopkins, 1 SCHOALES and LEFROY, p. 414. LEWIN *on Trusts.* STORY *on Equity,* § 529. Broadhurst *v.* Balguy, 1 YOUNGE and COLLIER, 32 : 'This is a case in which the length of time that elapsed between the period when the demand arose and the institution of the suit, does not form any positive bar. Great

in extreme distress, and for an extremely inadequate consideration, was set aside, after a lapse of twelve years, by Lord Eldon. 'It is certainly true,' says Mr. Justice Story, 'that length of time is no bar to a trust clearly established; and in a case where fraud is imputed and proved, length of time ought not, upon principles of eternal justice, to be admitted to repel relief. On the contrary, it would seem that length of time, during which the fraud has been successfully concealed and practised, is an aggravation of the offence, and calls more loudly upon a Court of Equity to grant ample and decisive relief. But length of time necessarily obscures all human evidence; and as it thus removes from the parties all immediate means to verify the nature of the original transactions, it operates, by way of presumption, in favour of innocence, and against imputation of fraud.'[q]

This rule has been acted upon in a case where it was held, that a failure in complying with the provisions, 9 Geo IV. c. 22, vitiates the whole proceedings, and made the Speaker's warrant of no effect.[r] 'The whole of the proceedings take place 'coram non judice,' the jurisdiction fails altogether; and with the jurisdiction the whole of the superstructure built upon it by the statute falls to the ground also';[s] and though an acceptance of rent, or other act of waiver, may make a voidable lease valid, it cannot establish a deed, or a lease void 'ab initio.'[t]

'There is, however,' as Lord Mansfield remarks, 'a known

---

effect may be justly due to it as a circumstance in the case.'—V. C. KNIGHT BRUCE.

q Prevost v. Gratry, 6 WHEATON's *Reports*, 498.   Attorney-General v. Fishmonger's Company.   Lord Cottenham, MYLNE and KEEN, 16 : 'Such a doctrine'—that no regard was to be paid to the lapse of 400 years—'was most dangerous, and might, if acted upon, prove destructive to many of the best titles in the kingdom.'

r Bruyeres v. Halcomb, 3 AD. and ELLIS, 381.

s TINDAL, C.J. Ranson v. Dundas, 3 BIN., N.C., 161.   Smith v. Stapleton, PLOWDEN, 432.

t BROOM's *Legal Maxims*, p. 133.   Doe v. Banks, 4 B. and ALD., 409. Jones v. Carter, 15 MEESON and WELSBY, 719.

difference between circumstances which are of the essence of a thing required by an Act of Parliament to be done, and those which are merely directory.' A defect in one of the latter class does invalidate the transaction, or make it 'ab initio vitiosum.' The maxim, also, 'fieri non debuit, factum valet,'[u] applies to such cases where a form has been omitted which is required, indeed, but is not essential, e.g., residence in the parish before the celebration of a marriage. It is a very material direction, but the marriage is good (under Lord Hardwicke's Act) without it.[x]

Again, a deed that is void may, as Noy says, be good in the English law to some purpose; as if A let land that does not belong to him by deed to B; if A afterwards acquire the land, the lease is valid.

XVII.

NEMO plus juris ad alium transferre potest quam ipse haberet.—ULPIAN.

No man can transfer to another rights that he does not himself possess.

This principle is taken from the law which regulates the succession to the estates of intestates; and in conformity thereto, if any one died before the succession of an intestate came to him, as he had acquired no right in it, so he transmitted none to his heirs. ' Proximum accipere nos oportet eo tempore quo bonorum possessio defertur.' The cognatus proximus succeeded where the written heirs rejected a will; and according to this rule, if the cognatus proximus died before the written heirs had announced their intention to reject the will, not the heirs of the cognatus who died, but the cognatus next in succession to him was admitted to the inheritance.

' Si quis igitur proximus cognatus dum hæredes scripti

---

u *Grounds and Rudiments of Law and Equity*, 403.

x Pargeter *v.* Harris, 7 Q.B., 708.

deliberant diem suum obierit sequens quasi proximus admitte-
tur, hoc est quicunque fuerit tum deprehensus proximum locum
obtinens' (*Dig.*, *Unde Cognati*, 38. 8). The words are 'plus
juris,' but there were many cases in which a man could not
transmit to another all the rights of which he was himself
possessed; *e. g.*, if there was a provision in a will to this effect,
L. Titius, and L. Titius only, shall not be liable to my heir
for such a claim; if no such claim was made during the life
of Lucius Titius, the will was satisfied, and L. Titius could
not transmit his immunity to his heir. 'Tale legatum hæres
meus a solo Lucio Titio ne petito ad hæredem Lucii Titii non
transit si nihil vivo Lucio Titio adversus testa mentum ab
hærede . . . sit commissum—quoties enim cohæret personæ id
quod legatur veluti personalis servitus ad hæredem ejus non
transit—si non cohæret, transit' (*Dig.*, *de liber. legatâ*, xxxiv.
3. 8, § 3.

The rule is stated generally, but there werc certain exceptions to it recognised by the Roman Law, as well as ours, for
the sake of public convenience,[y] as our sale in market overt
gives a title to the purchaser which did not belong to the
seller.   So in the Roman Law, the creditor who sold the
'pignus' (which he had no right to sell) gave what he did
not himself possess, a 'causa dominii,' to the bonâ fide purchaser.

'Non est novum ut qui dominium non habeat alii dominium
præbeat nam et creditor pignus vendendo causam dominii
præstat quam ipse non habet' (*De. acq. rerum Dom.*, 41, Tit.
1. 46).   But though the rule is extended by analogy to
other kinds of property, and other means of its acquisition,
it applies immediately and specifically to the relation in which

---

[y] If the legatee dies before the testator, the English law generally
considers the bequest as a lost or lapsed legacy.   But by a most
beneficial clause in the statute of Wills, 7th Will. IV., and 1st Vict.
c. 26, § 33, it is provided, where the bequest is to a child or other issue
of the testator, for an estate not determinable at or before the death of
the legatee, and the legatee leaves issue who survives the testator, and
whom it does not appear from the will that the testator had any wish
to exclude, that the issue of the legatee shall take the legacy.

the heir stood to the deceased, on which topic of ἰσονομία
there are seven rules besides this in the chapter from which
this rule is taken, of which a synopsis may be useful. Thus,
we are told that the 'jus' of the heir is the same as that
of the deceased (L., 5, Tit. 17, § 59).   'Hæredem ejusdem
potestatis jurisque esse quo fuit, defunctus constat' (*Ibid.*, 169,
§ 2). 'Absurdum est plus juris habere eum qui legatus sit
fundus quam hæredem aut ipsum testatorem si viveret;' and the
heir succeeds ' in universum jus quod defunctus habuit' (*Ibid.*,
62). 'Itis qui in universum jus succedunt hæredis loco habentur' (*Ibid.*, 128, § 1).   Again, we are told, ' Nemo plus
commodi hæredi suo relinquit quam ipse habuit' (*Ibid.*, 120).
' That I have no claim to a better condition, than he from
whom I derive my rights' (*Ibid.*, 175, § 1).   'Non debeo
melioris conditionis esse quam ductor meus a quo jus in me
transit;' to the same effect, ' Quod ipsis qui contraxerunt obstat et successoribus eorum obstabit' (*Ibid.* 145). On the other
hand, it is said (156, § 2): 'Cum quis in alicujus locum suc-
cesserit non est æquum ei nocere hoc quod non nocuit
adversus eum in cujus locum successit.'   All these rules apply
not only to the legal and direct, but to the equitable and
fiduciary heir (128, § 2): to all who for whatever reason ' in
universum jus defuncti succedunt.'   The practical value is
exemplified (*Ibid.*, 18. 54) in the ' actio Tutelæ', and the
actions ' soluto matrimonio,' in the ' hereditatis petitione (*Ibid.*,
62), the 'Restitutio in integrum (*Ibid.*, 120), in the 'rei vindic.'
and ' Publicianâ' (*Ibid.*, 128, § 1, *in interdictis*, 156, § 2, and
in exceptionibus, 143, 168, § 2).   The rule was adapted in
cases of the ' bonorum possessio,' and the edict 'unde legitimi,'
of which as well as the head ' unde cognati,'[z] Ulpian treated
in his 4th book on the *Edict*.

---

[z] 'The actual holder of an indorsed bill of lading may undoubtedly,
by indorsement, transfer a greater right than he himself has. It is
at variance with the general principles of law, that a man should be
allowed to transfer to another a right which he himself has not ; but
the exception is founded on the nature of the instrument in question,
which being, like a bill of exchange, a negotiable instrument, for the
general convenience of commerce has been allowed to have an effect at
variance with the ordinary principles of law.' TINDAL. Jenkyns *v.*

XVIII.

1. REGULA est quæ rem quæ est breviter enarrat. Non ut ex regulâ jus sumatur, sed ex jure quod est regula fiat.

2. Per regulam igitur brevis rerum narratio traditur et ut ait Sabinus quasi causæ conjectio est quæ simul cum in aliquo vitiata est perdit officium suum.— PAULUS.

1. *That is a rule which concisely states the actual doctrine of the case. The law is not taken from the rule, but the rule is made by the law.*

2. *A rule, therefore, delivers a compendious decision of the point at issue, and is, as Sabinus says, a succinct explanation of the principle by which the cause should be governed; but an exception puts an end to its efficacy.*

The word ' rem' is used here, according to the interpreters, for ' res proposita,' 'quæcunque materia subjecta' (τὸ ὑποκεί- μενον), the 'quæquæ res' of the edict. So Arist. says, that rhetoric is δύναμις περὶ ἕκαστον τοῦ θεωρῆσαι τὸ ἐνδεχόμενον πιθανὸν. Therefore, it means all the jurisprudence involved in a particular controversy.

The ' conjectio causæ' is a phrase taken from the ancient practice[a]—it corresponds with the προβολὴ of the Athenians.

Usborne, 8 SCOTT, *N. R.*, 523. Every one will see the wisdom of this limitation to the rule. But who can defend its limitation (swept away by 3rd and 4th Wil. IV.c. 74) to wrongful conveyances, which was the cause of incessant litigation ? Prior to the statute cited, if tenant for years made a feoffment, this feoffment vested in the feoffee a defeasible estate, because the barbarians who created our law of real property chose to lay it down as a rule, that every person having possession of land, was considered to be in seizin of the fee ; therefore, if the feoffee levied a fine, the owner was barred after five years. BUTLER'S note (1); COKE *Lit.*, 3306, and see Rawlyn's Case, *Reports* iv. p. 52 ; Sturgeon *v.* Wingfield, 15 M. and W. 224 ; BROOM's *Legal Maxims*, p. 358.

[a] AULUS GELLIUS, 10 : 'Cum ad judices venissent conjiciendæ et consistendæ causæ gratiâ.' ἐν τόντῳ τῷ λόγῳ ἀνακεφαλαιοῦται.—*Rom.*

Before the 'litis contestatio,' under the old system, at Rome, each suitor shortly stated to the judge the grounds of fact and law on which he intended to rely—'ses moyens de droit et de fait.' This was the 'conjectio causæ.'

I have entered into these explanations to justify my paraphrase.[b]

Lord Bacon has expressed his approbation of the passage in the text. 'It is not in the rule,' he says, 'that we are to look for the reason of its being established; it indicates, but does not create the law—'regula enim legem (ut acus nautica polos) indicat non statuit.' In law, as in all mixed sciences, the object must exist before its theory can be known—τὸ ἐπιστητὸν πρότερον τῆς ἐπιστήμης.[c] As language preceded grammar, rude custom must have preceded law. It is, however, in luminous theory as opposed to blind practice, that is, in rules, collected by experience and methodised by reason, that all science must consist, and especially the noblest of sciences, which marks out the domain of human will and action, and says to the proudest of the sons of men 'Thus far, and only thus far, thou shalt rule. Within this boundary thou art absolute; beyond it, impotent. Stay, here thou hast a giant's strength, and mayest use it as a giant, apart from all human interference and control; but go there, and the power which I, and I alone, gave thee is at an end, and the attempt to exercise it shall make thee a scandal and a by-word to thy species.' Take man out of the element of law, by which the social atmosphere is penetrated and purified, his best faculties are paralysed;

---

xiii. 9. 'In quibus causa summatim reperiatur.'—St. August. Cicero, without using the word, illustrates its meaning, *De Orat.* i. 42. 'Ars quæ .... rem divulsam dissolutamque conglutinaret et ratione quâdam constringeret.'

[b] Gothofred. *ad Rubricam*, p. 7. D'Antoine, p. 3.

[c] *De Augmentis*, viii. 385. Savigny, *System, etc.*, i. 1, § 4, 5. Particularly his illustration, 'Die berühmte Frater a Fratre;' there, he says, the only question for the judge is, whether the action will lie or not. But to decide that the whole legal relation must be present to his view—'Muss ihm die Gesammtanschauung des Rechtsverhältnisses gegenwärtig seyn.'

instead of looking before and after, he is the abject instrument of another's will, or the reckless pursuer of his own. The first thing, on the contrary, that strikes us in a state of social order, is the right that dignifies every citizen. When that right is doubtful or disputed, it is ascertained by a judicial sentence.[d] Still such a decision, if considered with reference to the rights of an individual, must be partial and incomplete, it cannot embrace them all—it comprises only that portion of them which happens to be the subject of litigation. But the merit of the decision rests upon a deeper principle, it rests upon the whole legal relation, of which the part considered has only been a detached or isolated member; and in proportion as it is or is not a corollary from the comprehensive and accurate view of those relations, it will be wise and just, or foolish and erroneous. This is the refined and intellectual element of judicial investigation which distinguishes the noble vocation of the jurist from the degrading trade of the mechanical practitioner; drudgery that no success can sweeten, and no reward make honourable.[e] A question of private right can be decided only by reference to a general rule. If, therefore, we pierce through the outer covering and exterior of any case, we shall see that as every legal relation falls under some corresponding principle, by which it is moulded, every sentence must be governed by a certain rule. The principle is constructed, it may be, or modified by the will of the legislator. The state of things which requires its application is beyond his foresight, and arises from the various and shifting combinations to which every day gives birth in the perpetually ceaseless struggles and collisions of daily life. Take, for instance, the case of the Bridgewater property. There were to be considered the right of a testator, the law of conditions, the duties of a peer, the character of our balanced govern-

---

[d] Mr. Hume has most sophistically selected this very circumstance, which establishes the sublime character of law as a proof that it is altogether arbitrary.

[e] 'Mira quædam in cognoscendo jus civile suavitas et delectatio.'— De Orat. i. 43.

ment, the boundaries of private right, and public law; questions which, by a fortunate accident, some of those invested with judicial authority were capable of understanding. Nominally, the question was, whether a particular condition was valid or invalid. But to decide that properly, all the elements I have enumerated were to be taken into consideration; and the rule by which the case was governed, when it was placed in the hands of persons not incompetent to deal with it, was this, 'jus publicum privatorum pactis mutari non potest.' [f]

The end of every rule, then, is to supply the principle of decision. He who can cite a particular rule in his favour, flings upon his adversary the burden of proving that his case is an exception to it—' Qui regulam pro se habet transfert onus probandi in adversarium.' The word 'vitiata' means not that a rule is ever vicious, in the sense in which it is said that a title is vicious, etc., but that it is sometimes inapplicable, as there is hardly any rule without an exception, and that where the exception holds the rule is suspended.[g]

There are five important precautions to be observed in the application of all rules—

1st. When two rules clash, the higher must prevail. Thus the Law of Nature overrules an arbitrary usage. Public law, as in the Bridgewater Case, is to be preferred to private law. ' So jura sanguinis nullo jure civili dirimi possunt.'

2ndly. Care must be taken that the rule is restrained within proper limits. Thus the maxim, that he who does an act in obedience to his parent, or his master, is not supposed to will it—' velle non creditur qui obsequitur imperio patris vel domini'—is limited to cases of physical coercion, and does not include the fear arising from mere respect.

---

[f] *De prob. and præsumpt. Dig.* v. 'Judicio est in promutiando sequi regulam exceptione non probatâ.'—BALDUS. in cap. i., L. *Omnibus modis Dig.* 'De alicui mutandi judicio causâ factâ.'

[g] There is no phrase—not even that of 'practice,' as opposed to 'theory,' which is silliness itself—more trite than this, 'there is no rule without an exception ;' if so, the rule itself is false, as there would be a rule without an exception.

3rdly. The reason of the rule must be understood; *e. g.*, a man obliged to sell his property to pay his debts, cannot avail himself of the rule—'Id quod nostrum est sine facto nostro transferri non potest,' neither could the rule be cited in favour of a proprietor who was compelled to sell his land for the public benefit.

4thly. If the letter of the rule is too severe, equity will soften it. Thus a man is bound to return what he has borrowed; but if you lend me beams to shore up my house, I am not bound to restore them ten minutes after I have turned them to the purpose for which they were borrowed. Neither did the Roman law oblige a debtor to repay money on the very day when it was lent, notwithstanding the maxim—'In omnibus obligationibus in quibus dies non ponitur præsenti die debetur.'

5thly. The circumstances of the case must be carefully weighed before its application is determined. It was a rule that nobody was liable for accidents, by the act of robbers, flood, fire, etc. But if the defendant was 'in morâ,' and had not returned the thing at the proper time, or if he had expressly taken upon himself the hazard of such events, this general maxim was overruled.

XIX.

IN omni parte error in jure non eodem loco quo facti ignorantia haberi debebit, cum jus finitum et possit esse et debeat. Facti interpretatio etiam prudentissimos fallit.—NERATIUS. [a]

In no part of law should ignorance of fact and
ignorance of law be placed on the same footing, since
law may be, and ought to be, comprised within certain
limits. But on the right construction of a fact the
wisest may be mistaken.

This rule contains an exact application of the principle which ought to govern Courts of Justice in their decisions,

---

[a] *Dig.* xxii. 6. 2.   ' Répétition de la chose non due.'—LOCRÉ, vol. vii. 52.

when ignorance of fact or of law is relied upon by the suitor.

Ignorance of fact is a valid plea, if it does not imply supine and almost wilful ignorance—'Nec supina ignorantia ferenda est factum ignorantis ut nec scrupulosa inquisitio exigenda.' Ignorance of law is a valid plea in some cases, and an invalid one in others. If it were always and of itself an invalid plea, it would not be necessary to lay down the rule that ignorance of law was no bar against the 'usucapio,' as is done by the law. xxii. 6. 4—'Juris ignorantiam in usucapionibus negatur prodesse.'

The difficulties which have arisen on this topic have proceeded from confounding the laws of later emperors, which are to be found in the code, and which are too frequently stamped with the impress of corruption and decay, with those which prevailed during the golden age of Roman jurisprudence. Ignorance of law was a valid plea to minors, women, soldiers (propter rusticitatem), to all who were beyond the reach of legal advice and information. More than this, it was a valid plea when the person insisting upon it, sought to recover that to which by the law of nature he was entitled, to save himself from loss. It was not admitted as a plea where the object of the suitor was not to save himself harmless, but to acquire gain. If it was used to acquire, it was of no avail—'Nisi minoribus aliisque quibus etiam in lucro succurritur.' 'In errore facti,' says Cujacius, 'non distinguuntur damna a compendiis, in errore juris distinguuntur'; and the reason of this rule is clearly stated by Cujacius himself—'Alioqui erranti lucro esset ignorantia juris' (CUJAC. *Rep. de* 8, de juris et facti ign.). Like most questions of the sort, it is a matter of compromise. The good of society requires that in certain cases ignorance of law shall be no defence, not because cases of great hardship may not occur even under a rule so qualified, but because, in the majority of instances, more evil than benefit would result from the inquiry. But there is also a large class of cases where, to lay down the rule broadly and coarsely, as English judges have done, would be preposterous and absurd, would

H

encourage pettifogging practice, and lead, in the vast majority
of instances, to the most cruel oppression. In such cases,
then, not only does more benefit than evil result to society
from ripping up and laying open the transaction, but to cancel
and abrogate such iniquity is one of the main objects for which
society was established. The rule laid down by English tribunals involves a denial of these plain maxims:—

In the first place, that it is unjust that any one should profit
by his own wrong.

In the second place, that it is required by the law of natural
equity that no one shall add to his own wealth by loss or injury
inflicted upon another.

' Jure naturæ æquum est neminem cum alterius detrimento
et injuriâ fieri locupletiorem.'

In the third place, that what is ours cannot be transferred
to another without an act on our part (the word act including
consent or crime).

' Id quod nostrum est non sine facto nostro ad alterum transferri non potest.'

(' Facti nomine consensus aut delictum intelligitur.')

In the fourth place, that there can be no obligation without
a cause. Nothing can come of nothing, therefore, if there
was no original obligation, said the civilian, ' Si ab initio non
constitit obligatio quia sine causâ promissum est, ante solutionem ipsa obligatio—post solutionem quantitas soluta con-
dicetur.'   Hence followed the ' condictio sine causâ,' the
' condictio indebiti,' the ' condictio causâ datâ, causâ non
secutâ,' and the ' condictio ob turpem vel injustam causam.'
Hence the rules, that it was the same thing if there were no
cause at all, or an unjust cause, for an obligation. Hence the
rules—

' Sive ab initio causâ promissum est, sive fuit causa pro-
mittendi quæ finita est vel secuta non est dicendum est condictioni locum fore' (1, § 2, de cond. sine causâ).

' Constat id demum condici posse aliquis quod vel non ex
justâ causâ ad eum pervenit vel redit ad non justam causam '
(§ 3, Ibid).

'Ex his omnibus causis quæ jure non valuerunt vel non habuerunt effectum, secutâ per errorem solutione condictioni locus erit' (54, *de cond. Indeb.*).[d]

It must, however, be maintained by the English school, that a man who errs in a point of law, gives a real consent that an obligation founded on no reason, or on a false reason, is valid—that an absolute nullity may produce an effect—that the remedy established by the Roman legislator, to which the name of the 'condictio indebiti' and the 'condictio sine causâ' has been given, is useless and even mischievous, grounded as it is by them on the following principle:—'Hæc condictio ex bono et æquo introducta quod alterius apud alterum sine causâ deprehenditur, revocare consuevit' (*Ib. de cond. ind.*).

The English legist will, of course, say, that a man who errs in a material point does give a consent as effectual as if he gave it with a full knowledge of the facts; and that the law considers ignorance of its details as a crime, which it punishes by the loss of property. Even, however, if a man does deserve punishment for ignorance (imputed, on very solemn occasions, by long-established forms, to the judges themselves), how does his adversary, who has encouraged it, deserve reward?[e] Can it gravely be maintained (out of the Court of Exchequer) that such a reason justifies the legislator in

---

[d] 'Ignorantia legis, sicut inevitabilis si sit tollit peccatum ita etiam cum aliquâ negligentiâ conjuncta delictum minuit.'—GROTIUS, *de Jur. Bell. et Pac.* ii., 20, 43, § 2. CUJACIUS, *Quæst. Pap.*, vol. iv., p. 41. *De condict. Indeb.*, lib. ii. 54.

[e] Writ of error. 'To our justices assigned, etc. Because, in the record and proceedings, and also in giving of judgment in a plaint, . . . as, it is said, manifest error has intervened, to the great damage,' etc.—TIDD. *Practice*, 497. The 64th law, 'de cond. indebiti,' deserves consideration. It lays down the rule, that money paid under a sense of natural obligation, which could not be enforced, cannot be recovered; therefore, when the civilians speak of an 'indebitum,' they mean something not due by the law of nature—'Ita debiti vel non debiti ratio in condictione naturaliter intelligenda est.' 'Qui exceptionem perpetuam habet solutum per errorem repetere potest.'—xii., 6. 41. 7 and 8 PAPINIAN, *Jur. A.*

stripping one man of what does belong to him, and con-
ferring upon another what does not?[f]

The only way of escaping from these uncouth consequences
is by holding that an error juris shall never be profitable, but
that it shall not prevent a man who has been imposed upon
from recovering his own.

To sum up the whole, the man who pays money to another
which he supposes himself obliged to pay, but which he is not
obliged to pay, does so in ignorance of fact, or in ignorance of law.

In the first hypothesis, even our law does not bar his title to
recover it.

In the second hypothesis, the rule of the Roman law was
this:—

Either he sought to make a profit, or to prevent a loss.

If he sought to make a profit, there could be no doubt that
he was (except in particular cases of minority, etc.) prevented
from taking advantage of his error.

If he sought to prevent a loss, either he paid what by the
law of nature was due from him, and in that case he was not
allowed to recover what he had paid; or he had paid what was
due neither by the law of nature nor by the law of man (I put
the case of money paid under an unjust sentence, with a power
of appeal, and the rule 'res judicata pro veritate occipitur'
aside), and then the money paid might be recovered, unless it
had been paid ' pietatis causâ ex quâ solutum repeti non
potest' (*Dig., de Cond. Ind.*, xxxii. § 2).

Our judges, with their usual want of discrimination, confound public and private law. Society would not be secure if
ignorance could be pleaded as an excuse for the transgression
of public law; though even in that case, if the law transgressed was not part of the law of nature, but an arbitrary
regulation—e. g., that the dead should be buried in woollen
or that salt should not be collected by the sea-shore—or if the
person transgressing was from age, sex, or feeble capacity not on

---

[f] ROPER *on Legacies*, 1652, vol. ii. The English law vacillates. Pusey
v. Desbouverie, 3 P. W., 315 ; Wake v. Wake, 1 VESEY, J., 335 ; Kidney
v. Coussmaker, 12 VESEY, 136.

the same footing with the rest of mankind, a righteous judge as Grotius observes, would look upon ignorance as an extenuation of the offence.

But it is clear, also, that it would be against sound policy to allow what was lost from ignorance of public law to be recovered, since such ignorance, far from furnishing any excuse, stands itself in need of one.

To complete the view of English jurisprudence, it must not be forgotten that, at the same time that our tribunals promulgated with so much complacency the doctrine that every man must be supposed to know the law, the law which they were supposed and bound under terrible consequences to know, did not exist. For by an absurdity incredible to any one who has not read LORD COKE and MEESON and WELSBY'S *Reports* with some attention, every statute, till lately, dated back in its operation to the first day of the session, though it was enacted on the last day of it. So that a man who did an act perfectly innocent in February, might be punished for it by a statute making it criminal in the following July; or if he committed an offence exposing him to imprisonment in May, he might be hanged for the same offence by a statute passed two months afterwards: indeed, this case actually happened. Such is the 'simple beauty'[h] of the English law. In another case,[i] it was held that a statute passed in July imposed penalties and forfeitures on a merchant for exporting goods in the preceding June. As a specimen of this judicial legislation, I quote the words of the Court of Queen's Bench: ' By the unanimous decision of the judges, it is determined that the RULE OF LAW [i. e., the law made by the judges], that where no specific day is mentioned from which an act of parliament is to take effect, it commences by legal relation from the first day of the sessions, has been so long settled [by whom ?] that it cannot be

---

[h] ADAMS, *On Ejectments*, p. 3. The lines after 'simplex munditiis' are more applicable :—

' Miseri quibus—
Intentata nites !'

[i] Attorney General *v.* Parnther, 6 BRO., *P. C.* 489.

shaken; and it is to be remembered, that the opinion of the judges was founded on prior determinations, by one of which *the life of a person* was affected.'[k] To which I observe, that it is impossible to find an instance of more wanton, provoking, barefaced, inexcusable, and cruel folly, in the legal annals of any civilised people, the volumes containing the New Rules, our own Reports and State Trials, not excepted. A retrospective law is a phrase which abridges in two words every possible notion of oppression, wickedness, and wrong;[1] and this was the common law of England, according to the unanimous opinion of the judges. The legislature was at last obliged to interfere, in this as in other instances, to save the country from the consequences of the law made by those whose duty it should only be to expound it.[m]

---

[k] Latless *v.* Holmes, 4 *T.Reports*, 660 ; R. *v.* Thurston, 1 LEV. 90.

[1] I do not speak of cases of necessity, cases where practice is facilitated, or cases where a principle of natural justice is recognised.

[m] This absurdity could have proceeded from no cause but the most utter ignorance of principles which, in every other country, are considered as the alphabet of jurisprudence. There was no general rule to be established, which might make it necessary to overlook cases of particular hardship. There was no difficulty to be overcome. It was anomaly for the sake of anomaly—a mere disinterested love of absurdity for its own sake. As the alchemists said, men ought to seek the philosophers' stone for the mere love of virtue, and without any purpose of getting rich. Even in English courts of justice, the argument 'ab inconvenienti' has been allowed. When could it ever have been urged with greater force than against such a scandalous outrage on common sense ? But where the principles of Roman jurisprudence had taken hold of the minds of men, such a doctrine could not have been promulgated without awakening a tempest of indignation. In England, however, men repeated their brainless panegyrics on the common law, while the statute-book contained such damning sentences as these, inserted with the utmost complacency by the panegyrists themselves : ' Whereas every act of parliament doth commence from the first day of the session in which such act is passed, and WHEREAS THE SAME IS LIABLE TO GREAT AND MANIFEST INJUSTICE,' etc.—33 Geo.III., c.13.

But the very title of the act proves the state of our jurisprudence. What is the legal mind of a country in which it is necessary to pass an act truly described in this way : 'An Act to prevent Acts of Parliament from taking effect FROM A TIME PRIOR TO THE PASSING THEREOF' ?— BACON, *Abridgment,* Statute c.

The English law professes to refuse its protection not only to those who are ignorant of law, but to those from whom money has been extorted in ignorance of *fact*, and under circumstances of the most grievous wrong. In the case of Hamlet *v.* Richardson,[n] the jury found that the money sought to be recovered had been made without knowledge, or reasonable means of knowledge, of the facts on which the demand had proceeded, yet the Court set aside the verdict in favour of the plaintiff. If this jurisprudence is right, that of every other civilised country, without exception, is erroneous. Lord Mansfield, indeed, thought otherwise, and made an attempt, which, after his death, was speedily overruled, to overcome that incorrigible bias in favour of pettifoggers which is wrought into the stamina of the English law. Lord Mansfield (a reverence for whose name as a jurist will be one of the first symptoms of the progress of legal science among us) said—'Money may be recovered under a right and legal judgment, and yet the iniquity of keeping that money may be manifest, upon grounds which could not be used by way of defence against the judgment.'[o] Lord Kenyon gravely gives as a reason for stamping a legal sanction on such atrocious chicane, that, otherwise, cases might be tried twice over. On this question, if the language of Equity is the same as that of the Common Law Courts, its interpretation of that language is very different from that adopted on the other side of Westminster Hall; and its assistance has been afforded in cases which can hardly be reconciled with the broad assertion, that ignorance of law is never, except in the case of heirs, entitled to relief.[p]

---

[n] 9 BINGHAM, 644.

[o] Moses *v.* Macfarlane, 2 BURROW, 1006. And a doctrine better suited to their purposes, than that money, paid under compulsion of legal process, cannot be recovered, it is not possible to imagine. This is entirely peculiar to our law. Lord Mansfield argues 'ex æquo et bono,' words 'unmusical to pleading ears.' Marriott *v.* Hampton, SMITH'S L.C., Keating and Willes, ed., vol.i., p.238.

[p] STORY, *Equity Jurisprudence*, vol.i., ch.v., p. 139, § 114.

XX.

SEMPER qui non prohibet pro se intervenire mandare creditur. Sed et si quis ratum habuerit
quod gestum est, obstringitur mandati actione.—
ULPIAN.

*He who knows, and does not prohibit what is done on
his behalf, is taken to command it; and, moreover, if
he ratifies what has been done, he is liable to an action,
such as would lie for an agent against his principal.*

The word 'intervenire,' used in this maxim, includes all
instances wherein one man has undertaken, without express
authority, the management of another's business.[q] Thus it
comprises the case where one man has substituted himself as
the principal debtor, instead of another—where one man has
appeared for another before a Court of Justice, 'intervenire
dicitur qui pro alio consistit injudicio.'[r]

Whatever, therefore, the transaction may be, it will create
an obligation in him on behalf of whom the interference, not
repudiated, has taken place, if it was with his knowledge, and
if he has derived from it any benefit. ' Si passus sum,' says
Ulpian, ' aliquem pro me fidejubere vel alias intervenire mandati teneor.' So if a man knows that his friend has employed
agents to borrow money for him, he is as liable to their engagements as if he had employed them himself. ' Qui patitur
ab alio mandari ut sibi credatur, mandare intelligitur.'[s]

But a man is not liable for what has been done in his name
if he has repudiated the interference of his self-appointed
agent, nor he who has suffered injury in consequence of what
another has done in his name.

' Nisi pro invito quis intercesserit,' says Ulpian.[t] Paulus

---

q CUJACIUS, vol. viii., 784 ; GOTHOFREDI, *Reg. Juris.;* D'ANTOINE, *Règles.*

r *Dig.* xlvii. 10. 11., § 3.

s *Dig.* xvii. 1. 18 ; 1. 6, § 2 : 'Mandati vel contra.

t *Dig.* xvii. 1. 6. 2 ; 1. 18: 'Qui patitur ab alio mandari ut sibi credatur mandare intelligitur.'

holds the same language. It is on this principle that the creditor, who knows that his debtor has alienated the land hypothecated for his debt, is not, therefore, supposed to waive his rights over the thing alienated, because his claim follows the property, and cannot be taken from him without his express consent. ' Non videtur autem consensisse creditor si sciente eo debitor rem vendiderit cum ideo passus est venire quod sciebat ubique pignus sibi durare.' But the master or charterer of a merchant vessel was held liable for what was done by him whom he had entrusted with its management, and for what was done by any one who performed his functions, provided it was not without his knowledge, nor against his will. ' Cæterum si sit et passus est eum in nave magisterio fungi ipse eum imposuisse videtur.'

So from the possession of an article by the buyer with the knowledge of the seller the law implied, that the knowledge the law implied, that the possession was lawful, ' licet instrumento non sit comprehensum.'

Ratification, which is a subsequent assent, has the same effect as if consent had preceded the transaction to which it is given. A father is taken to receive the loan made to his un-emancipated son, as soon as he sanctions and approves it: ' Si servus tuus tuo mandato precario rogaverit vel tu ratum habueris quod ille rogavit tuo nomine, teneberis quasi ipse precario habeas.'[u] Marcius asserts, that he who ratifies the hypothecation made without his knowledge of his property by a third person, is to be considered as if he had hypothecated it himself, supposing that he is of full age and entitled to the management of his property. ' Si nesciente Domino res ejus hypothecæ datæ sunt, deinde postea dominus ratum habuerit dicendum est hoc ipsum quod ratum[v] habet voluisse eum retro recurrere ratihabitionem ad illud tempus quo convenerit—voluntas eorum et fere servabitur qui et pignori dare possunt.'[w] And when my agent has without my

---

[u] *De precario*, 13, *Si Servus Dig.* xliii. 26.

[v] *Dig.* xx. 1. 16. 1.   [w] *Dig.* xlvi. 3. 12. 4.

sanction delegated his authority to another, against the well-known rule, ' Delegatus non potest delegare,' if I ratify the acts of my agent's deputy, they bind as much as if I had authorized them in the first instance. ' Sed et in ipsum procuratorem si omnium rerum procurator est, dare debet institoria, sed et si quis meam rem gerens præposuerit et ratum habuero, idem erit dicendum.'ᵂ

A debtor who pays to a person pretending to be an agent of his creditor, is nevertheless released from his debt, if the creditor ratify the payment. ' Etsi non vero procuratori solvam, ratum autem habeat dominus quod solutum est; liberatio contingit.'

So if the principal approve of the proceedings taken in his behalf by one who was not his agent, he will make them valid. ' Si quis cum procurator non esset, litem sit contestatus deinde ratum dominus habuerit, videtur retro res in judicium deducta.'ˣ

Ratification may be given by acts as well as words: ' Non tantum verbis ratum haberi potest,'ʸ says Scævola, ' sed etiam actis.' So Gothofred observes: ' qui agit ex contractu ipsum contractum probare intelligitur;' a strong illustration of this principle is to be found in this law: ' Si pupilli tui negotia gessero non mandatu tuo, sed ne tutelæ judicio tenearis,'ᶻ *i.e.*,

---

ᵂ *Dig.* xiv. 3. 6. 7 ; *Year Books* vii. H. 4. 35. Gascoigne said, 'that if the defendant took the beasts without command of the lord for services due to him, and the lord afterwards agreed to the taking, he should be adjudged his bailiff, though he had never been his bailiff before.' So in GODBOLT, 109.

ˣ *Dig.* v. 1. 53 ; 'Ratihabitio mandato æquipollet.' POTHIER, *Pandect*, xvii. 1. 19 ; xiv. 3. 18.

ʸ 'Gerere atque administrare tutelam extra ordinem tutor cogi solet.'—*Dig.* xxvi. 6. 1.

ᶻ ' Debet pater si actum filii sui improbat continuo testationem interponere contrariæ voluntatis.'—L. 16, *Dig. de S. C. Macedoniano.* ' Verum non tam epistola ipsa habetur pro ratihabitione quam tacitus consensus patris accipientis epistolam missam a filio qui certe pro ratihabitione est.'—CUJAC. ad l. 59, *penult; Dig., mandati,* lib. 4, *respons,* PAULI.

CUJACIUS, *ib.* : 'Continuo accipe cum spatio aliquo.' ' Cette recepto save you from the consequences of your neglect without express authority: ' negotiorum gestorum te habebo obligatum;' and not you only, but your pupil also: ' Sed et pupillum modo si locupletior fuerit factus.'[a] This maxim relates not only to tutors and guardians, but to those who were responsible for the management of corporate or municipal property—' universitatis seu municipii '—duties which have entailed heavy burdens and most serious liabilities.[b] A distinction of little importance to us was taken as to whether an action ' mandati ' or ' negotiorum gestorum' should be brought under certain circumstances.[c]

According to our law,[d] if an agent has made a contract without authority, and it is afterwards ratified, the principal ' may sue and be sued thereon, as if he had given the authority.' ' Where an act is beneficial to the principal . . . and amounts generally (as in the case of the tutor cited above) to the assertion of a right on the part of the principal, the rule is generally applicable.'[e] The exceptions to the rule are cases where, if the ratification was not given, the rights of the person affected by it would be altered. No man is obliged to act upon an uncertainty, or to do an act on the speculation that the assent of another may confirm it.[f] In Hagedorn v.

---

tion de la lettre non, contredite est parmi les negocians un acte positif d'approbation.'—EMERIGON, c. 5, § 6.

' Receptio litterarum est actus positivus.'—STRACCHAE, *Gl.* 11. 247.

[a] *Dig.* iii. 5. 6, § *Item quæsitur.*

[b] *Dig.* l. 8 : ' De administratione rerum ad civitates pertinentium,' 1, coupled with 2, § 4. ' Sui frumentaria pecuniæ in alios usus quam quibus destinata est conversa fuerit . . . licet ex bonâ fide datum probatur compensari quidem frumentariæ pecuniæ non oportet, solvi autem a curatore reipublicæ jubetur.'

[c] GOTHOFRED, p. 256.

[d] STORY, *On Agency,* § 244.

[e] So it was held that a subsequent ratification established a notice 3 BARN. and ALD., 689; Goodtitle *dem* King v. Woodward : ' Subsequent recognition by all the lessors of the plaintiff gives effect to the authority.'

[f] On this head: Right v. Cuthell, 5 EAST, 491 ; Doe v. Walters, 10 B. and CR., 626 ; LLOYD'S *Paley,* On Agency, 190, note c. Even here there has been wavering, and the principle has been broken in

Oliverson, Lord Ellenborough said—' The plaintiff had a right
to effect an insurance on the chance of its being adopted for
the benefit of all those to whom it might appertain . . . he
might insure for those who were interested, and those who
might become interested. Schrœder was interested, and might
become privy to the benefit of this insurance by subsequent
adoption.'[g]

Dampier, Justice, says: ' If he had an interest his subsequent
adoption will be good.' ' A subsequent assent,' says the lamented
J. W. Smith, in his excellent work *Mercantile Law*,[h] ' by the
principal to the agent's conduct, exonerates the latter from
the consequences of a departure from his orders; in like manner it will render the principal liable for contracts made in
violation of such orders, or even without any previous re-
tainer or employment; such an assent may be implied from
the conduct of the principal, who cannot confirm a transaction
in part and repudiate it as to the rest.'[i] The assent of the
principal may be implied from his conduct, as in the Roman
law his silence may amount to a ratification in certain cases.[k]
Lord Kenyon says: ' Although the assignees may either affirm
or disaffirm the contract of the bankrupt, yet if they do affirm
it they must act consistently;[l] and as the assignees in this case

---

upon. Roe *v.* Pierce, 2 CAMPBELL ; Doe *v.* Goldwin, 2 AD. and ELLIS, 143,
N.R., 96 ; STORY, § 247 ; VINER's *Abridgment*, Assumpsit 7.

[g] Hagedorn *v.* Oliverson, 2 MAULE and S., 491 ; Lucena *v.* Craufurd,
13 EAST, 274 ; Routh *v.* Thompson.

[h] SMITH'S *Mercantile Law*, p. 217, by G. M. DOWDESWELL. 'The assent must be given to the act *really* done,' Horsefall *v.* Fauntleroy, 10
B. and C., 755 ; BULLER's *Nisi Prius*, p. 130, 6th Ed.
Defendant was nurse to plaintiff's intestate, and when he died ab-
sconded with the money. Parker, C.J, said he would presume a
subsequent agreement to make a contract, and bringing the action is
an admission of such consent.

[i] STORY, 258.

[k] Prince *v.* Clark, 1 B. and C., 189, was decided on this ground.
Casaregis, 20. 63 : 'Prima est mandatorem habentem certam scientiam
de excessu suo mandati, eique neque facto neque verbis contradicentem
haberi pro approbante,' p. 95.

[l] Smith *v.* Hodson, 4 T. *Reports*, 216. 'If the agent effects an
insurance for his principal without his knowledge or authority, and the

treated the transaction as a contract of sale, it must be pursued through all its consequences . . . Now here by bringing this action on the contract, the assignees recognised the act of the bankrupt, and must be bound by the transaction in the same manner as the bankrupt himself would have been.'

' It seems to be well settled,' says Judge Oakley, ' that a contract for the benefit of a third person without his knowledge and authority, is a binding contract, and may be enforced by him for whose benefit it was made. The defendants having made this policy and received the premium, cannot be permitted to shew any want of authority in the plaintiff to act for Foster. It follows, therefore, that the defendants are bound, unless Foster has disaffirmed the act of the plaintiff in such a manner as to release them from the contract.'[m]

principal afterwards adopts the act, the insurer is bound, and cannot object to the want of authority.'—KENT, *Comm.* vol. iii. § 260.

' It is proved that the defendant pursuing his own purpose of bringing these sales to a conclusion, asks Smith whether delay will arise by his absence, and was told by him that he was in the habit of allowing his clerks to sign contracts and conduct his business ; and upon the evidence it is impossible to say that the defendant did not give his assent to that.'—Coles *v.* Trecothick, 9 VESEY, 252 ; Thompson *v.* Davenport ; SMITH's Leading Cases, Keating and Willes, p. 212, vol. ii.

Schemerborn *v.* Vanderheyden, 1 JOHNSON's *Reports in the Senate of New York*, p. 139 ; Pigott *v.* Thompson, p. 139 ; 3 Bos and PULLER, note ; Maclean *v.* Dunn, 4 BINGHAM, 722.

[m] Bridge *v.* Niagara Insurance Co. of New York, HALL's *Sup. Court Reports*, 250.

' And the act of the agent may be good pro tanto, and void as to the excess by the French law.'—VALIN, art. 3, *Titre des Assurances,* EMERIGON, c. 5, § 6 ; *Dig., Mandati ubi supra,* 3 and 4 ; POTHIER, *Traité du Contrat de Mandat,* ED. DUPIN, vol. iv., p. 260.

'Dans tous les cas auxquels nous avons dit que le mandataire excedait les bornes du mandat si ce qu'il a fait outre ou même contre la tenure de ce qui est porté par la procuration a été fait au vu et su du mandant qui l'a suffert ce qu'il a fait doit être jugé valable et doit obliger le mandant tant envers le mandataire qu'envers les tiers avec lesquels le mandataire a contracté au nom du mandant qui la suffert—on doit en ce cas présumer une extension ou une réformation tacite de la procuration.'

XXI.

IN maleficio ratihabitio mandato æquiparatur.—
ULPIAN.°

*In offences against the law, a ratification is equivalent
to a command.*

These words are taken from the interdictum, 'unde tu
illum vi dejecisti.' Ulpian asserts that he has committed the
offence who has ordered another to commit it; and, moreover,
that he is to be treated as the offender who has ratified the
violence of another. 'Dejicit et qui mandat—dejicit et qui
ratum habet.' This is the principle of the last rule applied to
another branch of the law. Indeed, Gothofred says—'De
ratihabitione spectatur veritas istius regulæ passim toto jure,'
especially in matters to which the interdicts belong. It applies,
as we have seen, to contracts—it applies to loans, to pledges,
to the consequences of carrying a corpse upon the field of the
person affected (for his subsequent assent made the spot sacred),
and to the restitution of an inheritance, 'ex senatus consulto
Trebelliano'; therefore, if any one has turned my neighbour
out of possession in my name, and I ratify the act, I am as
responsible as if I had given express directions. 'But,' says
Cujacius, 'if any one commits a murder for my sake, and I

° *Dig.* xliii. 16. 1. 14. 'Rectius dicetur in maleficio ratihabitionem
mandato æquiparari.'—ULPIAN, ad edictum. CUJACIUS, vol. viii., p.784.
GOTHOFRED, *Reg. Juris. Dig.* xliii. 16. 1. § 12 : 'De vi et vi armatâ.'
'Dejecisse autem etiam is videtur qui mandavit vel jussit ut aliquis
dejiceretur, parvi enim referre visam est suis manibus quis de dejiciat
an vero per alium, quare et si familia mea ex voluntate meâ dejecerit,
ego videor dejecisse.' *Ib.* 14 : 'Sed si vi armatâ dejectus es sicut ipsum
fundum recipis, etiam si vi aut clam aut precario eum possideres—ita
res quoque mobiles omni modo recipies.' *Ib.* 15 : 'Si vi me dejeciis
vel vi aut clam feceris quamvis *sine dolo et culpâ* amiseris possessionem
—*tamen damnandus es, quanti mea intersit—quia in eo ipso culpa tua
præcessit,* quod omnino vi dejecisti aut vi aut clam fecisti.' *Ib.* 3, § 10 :
'Cum procurator armatus venit et ipse dominus armis dejecisse videtur
sive mandavit sive ut Julianus ait ratum habuit. Hoc et in familiâ
dicendum est, nam si familia sine me armata venit, ego non videor
venisse sed familia, nisi jussi, vel *ratum habui.*'

ratify it afterwards, am I responsible for the murder?' and he answers in the affirmative.[p] Those acts were exempted from the operation of this rule in which the law specifically related to the origin and commencement of them. So the father, who allowed his son to marry 'intra annum luctûs,' was infamous; but if the son married without his father's knowledge, 'intra annum luctûs,' the father's subsequent assent to the marriage did not make him so. For the time to be considered was the time when the marriage was contracted. ' Patris voluntas etiam prius spectatur in prohibendis nuptiis cum posset nec ratihabitio sufficit.' Toleration is in some cases equivalent to a command, if, for instance, my colonus has erected a work on my estate, to the injury of my neighbour, ' ex quo aqua vicino noceat'; and when I am informed of it, I do not take active measures for its removal (as my ' patientia' must perpetuate the evil), an action may be brought against me ' pluviæ ascendæ.' If I had ordered the work, I should be liable to an interdict.[q]

---

[p] The law of England takes a different view of such an offence in criminal matters. It wisely holds, 'that the offence of an accessory before the fact is of a much deeper dye than that of the accessory after the fact.'—R. *v.* Banridge, 3 PEERE WILLIAMS, 440. ' It is an uncontroverted rule, that whatever will make a man an accessory in felony will make him a principal in treason.'—HAWKINS' *Pleas of the Crown*, vol. i. p. 15. ' Accessory after the fact is he who, knowing that a man has committed a felony, receives, comforts, or assists him.'—1 HALE, 618, 4 BLACKSTONE'S *Com.*, 37. 11 and 12 Vict., c. 46. ' In offences under felony there are no accessories after the fact.'—1 HALE, 623. ' If A advise and procure B to murder C, A, by this, is an accessory before the fact ; and if D receives and conceals A from justice, D becomes an accessory.' I must say that I do not think the text in the Digest quite warrants the inference o Cujacius. Limited to cases of tort, the rule is sound, nor does any case that I have been able to discover in the Pandects carry the doctrine farther.

[q] *Dig.* xxxix. 3. 5 : ' De aquâ et aq. pluviæ arcendæ.'

XXII.

QUOD contra rationem juris receptum est non est
producendum ad consequentias.—PAULUS.[r]

*Consequences are not to be drawn from anomalies in
law.*

Quæ propter necessitatem recepta sunt non debent in
argumentum trahi.—PAULUS.

*Necessity justifies no argument beyond the case it has
enforced.*

The first rule relates to the ' Jus singulare,' which is described
by Paulus (*Dig.* i. 3. 16)—' Quod contra tenorem juris . . . .
introductum est,' for the sake of some particular exigency, or
from some inevitable necessity.   So Modestinus says that
there are certain personal privileges, ' quæ personæ sunt,' and
which, therefore, are not transmissible to the heir; and
Paulus lays it down as a universal rule, that where the
condition of the person is the cause of the indulgence, where
that condition ceases the indulgence is at an end—' In omnibus
causis id observatur ut ubi personæ conditio locum facit beneficio ibi deficiente eâ, beneficium quoque deficiat.'[s]   The advocate of the 'jus singulare,' therefore, is cut off from all
arguments founded on analogy—from all corollaries which, in
other cases, where the law was regular and not exceptional, he
might be entitled to draw.[t]   Thus the general rule was, that
one person could not acquire property for another without his
(the other's) knowledge.   An exception to this was allowed in
the cases of slaves and ' filii familias,' who were allowed to
acquire the right of ' usucapio,' and to complete the 'usucapio,'
for their masters and fathers, ' ex causâ peculiari'; *i. e.*, from a
cause connected with the 'peculium' which they were permitted to possess—' item possessionem acquirimus per servum

---

[r] Παρὰ Κάνονας νόμων.

[s] 'Quod non ratione introductum est sed errore primum deinde consuetudine ostentum in aliis similibus non obtinet.'

[t] 'Propter utilitatem promiscui usus.'—*Dig.* xiv. 3.

aut filium qui in potestate est et quidem earum rerum quas peculiariter tenent etiam ignorantes.'[u] This is the especial privilege of the 'peculium,' otherwise, Papinian observes, it would be necessary for the father or master to enquire at every moment into the 'peculium' of his son or slave (*Ibid.* 44, *Peregrè*). The permission once given to acquire the 'peculium' is sufficient. Therefore you may possess, but you cannot acquire a prescriptive title to what your procurator has taken possession of in your name—'Si emtam rem mihi procurator ignorante me meo nomine apprehenderit, quamvis possideam tamen eam non usucapiam quia ut ignorantes usucapiamus in peculiaribus tantum rebus receptum est' (*Dig.* xlii. 4. 46).

It has been asked, says Papinian,[y] why 'peculii causâ,' in cases of 'peculium,' a slave should acquire property for his master without his knowledge: 'Dixi utilitatis causâ, jure singulari receptum ne cogerentur domini per momenta species et causas peculiorum inquirere.' And the same author gives another instance of the 'jus singulare,' to which he joins the same caution:[z] 'Etiam fidei commissaria libertas a filio post certam ætatem ejus data, si ad eam puer non pervenit ab hærede filii præstitutâ die reddetur—quam sententiam jure singulari receptam ad cætera fidem commissa porrigi non oportet.'[a] To sum up the whole, anomalies make no precedents.

Very much to the same effect, and closely connected with the last, is the second rule, 'Quæ[b] propter necessitatem recepta sunt non debent in argumentum trahi:'[c] man must yield to

---

[u] *Dig.* xli. 25.

[y] *Dig.* xli. 3. 44, § 1.

[z] *De Fid.,* lib. xl. 5. 23, § 3.

[a] See, too, the law, *Dig.* xl. 5. 23, *de Fidei Comm.,* § 3: 'Etiam fideicommissaria libertas a filio post certam ætatem ejus data, si ad eam puer non pervenit, ab hærede filii præstituta die reddatur—quam sententiam jure singulari receptam, ad cætera fideicommissa relicta porrigi non placuit.'

[b] Χρειῶδες.

[c] Convention Parliament. Speech of Somers, 1670, April.—GREY'S *Debates.*

Ship money. Old law of pressing. Habeas Corpus Act.

necessity; but the law of necessity is locked up in the solitary case that it establishes, and can never furnish a precedent where its motive does not prevail. That which arises from necessity is indivisible, like its parent: ' Necessitatis nulla est pars.' As an instance of this rule, we may take the case where two heirs had been obliged by their testator to emancipate a slave. There is no principle, generally speaking, more powerful than this: ' Res inter alios acta nemini nocet;'[d] yet on this occasion it gave way to a superior equity. For if the slave succeeded in establishing before the prætor his right to freedom against one of the heirs, he might use the judgment pronounced in his favour against the other; for he was either a freeman or a slave; he could not be a slave with regard to one heir, and a freeman with regard to another. So, if the use of the same thing was left to two persons, the prætor gave a pecuniary compensation to one, and the thing itself to the other: ' Si usus tantum noster sit, qui neque venire, neque locari potest, quem-admodum divisio potest fieri in communi dividundo judicio, videamus? Sed prætor interveniet et rem emendabit: ut si judex alteri usum adjudicaverit, non videatur alter qui merc-edem accepit, non uti—quasi plus faciat qui videtur fieri, quid hoc propter necessitatem fit.'[e]

The necessity spoken of here is almost synonymous with the ' utilitas publica,'[f] which is best consulted in most cases by an inflexible adherence to general rules, though a departure from such rules may on very rare occasions be requisite to avoid a greater evil: ' Jus singulare est quod propter aliquam utili-tatem, contra tenorem rationis, auctoritate constituentium in-

---

Attainder.

Land taken for public works.

Goods thrown over in a storm.

The Emperor Constantine allowed the father in extreme distress to sell his son.

Cod. de patribus qui filiis suos distraxerunt. ' Si quis propter nimium.' De usu et habit.

[d] *Dig.* xliii. 2. 29.   PAPINIAN.

[e] *Dig.* x. 3. 10, § 1.

[f] ' Juste *prope* mater et æqui.' What a rebuke for modern sciolists

troductum est.'ᵍ So the rule with regard to the putative slave, which made his acts enure to the benefit of his master, as if he had been a real slave, was not extended to the case of a son by a supposed and irregular adoption. The acts of such a person did not enure to the benefit of him who, if the adoption had been regular, would have been his father, and entitled to take advantage of them as acts done by a son not emancipated; and the reason given by Papinian is, that the same necessity did not exist, although the father, 'justo errore ductus,' imagined the adoption to be regular, and the person therefore really to be in the place of an unemancipated son: 'Non enim constitutum est in hoc,' that is, the supposed son, 'quod in homine libero, qui bona fide servit placuit—ibi;' in the latter case, 'propter assiduam et quotidianam comparationem servorum ita constitui, publice interfuit, nam frequenter ignorantiâ liberos emimus—non autem tam facilis, frequens, adoptio vel arrogatio filiorum est.'ʰ So the two cases are contrasted (though the reason is not given) in another part of the *Digest*: 'Per eum quem justo auctus errore *filium* meum et in meâ potestate esse existimo, neque possessio, neque dominium nec quisquam aliud ex re meâ mihi quæritur. Per *servum* in fugâ agentem, si neque ab alio possideatur, neque se liberum esse credat, possessio nobis ad quiritur.'ⁱ

Grotius has dwelt upon the topic of necessity in one of the most striking passages of his great work.ʲ 'Can,' he asks, 'one man ever have a right to make use of the property of another? A question,' he says, 'that will appear extraordinary; but it is not so; for we ought to consider what the intention was of those by whom private property was introduced. Their purpose must have been to depart as little as possible from natural equity; for if this is the rule for the interpretation of written laws, much more ought it to govern

---

ᵍ *Dig.* i. 3. 16.

ʰ *Dig.* xli. 3. 44. So, in another case, the same law, clause 6, the reason given is, 'utilitate suadente.'

ⁱ *Dig.* xli. 2. 50, § 1.

ʲ *De Jure Belli ac Pacis*, Q. 1. 6.

custom which is undefined by writing.' From hence he infers
that, in extreme necessity, the right revives of using things as
if they were still in common: 'Quia in omnibus legibus
humanis ac proinde in lege dominii summa illa necessitas
videtur excepta.' So in a sea voyage, if food was wanting, the
crew and passengers might take the corn on board belonging
to another;[k] so houses may be pulled down to arrest the progress of a conflagration; and if my ship is driven among nets
and ropes, I may cut them away if I cannot otherwise extricate it. 'Quæ omnia lege civili non introducta sed exposita
sunt.'[l]

Instances of the 'jus singulare' in our law may be found in
the prerogatives of the crown. Such, for instance were the
old laws of purveyance; and the maxim, 'nullum tempus
occurrit regi,'[m] by means of which Lord Bute, in the beginning of George the Third's reign, endeavoured to strip the
Duke of Portland of a considerable portion of his property—
an instance of atrocious iniquity which led to the alteration of
the law.[n] So, that the crown pays no costs, is still the law.
The attorney-general, representing the crown, has the right of
reply in criminal cases. So, if after the sheriff has seized
under a writ of ' fi. fa.,' a writ of extent is delivered to him,
the crown has the priority over the private debtor. Neither
can the right of lapse prevail, where the right of presentation
to a benefice[o] is in the crown. The liability of innkeepers to
have soldiers billeted upon them—of sailors to be pressed—the
law as to heirs; ' catching bargains,' as to minors and married
women—the exemption of members of parliament from arrest

---

[k] *Dig.* xiv. 2. 2, *Lex Rhodia:* ' Cibaria eo magis quod si magis ea defe-
cerint in navigationem quod quisque haberet in commune conferret.'

[l] GROTIUS, ii. 16.

[m] 'The King's Plea,' HOBART, 347 ; Lambert *v.* Taylor, 4 B. and C. 151.
VINER's *Abridgment Statuti, E.* 10 ; BACON's *Abridgment,* tit. *Prerogative,*
7 *E.* Burke and Junius both allude to this case.

[n] 9 Geo. III. c. 16 ; Doe *v.* Roberts, 13 M. and W. 520.

[o] R. *v.* Sloper, 6 PRICE, 114 ; Attorney General *v.* Walmsley, 12 M. and
W. 179 ; Giles *v.* Grover, 9 BINGHAM, 128 ; BROOM's *Legal Maxims,* 49 ;
6 *Reports,* 50.

—the right of a peer to give his vote by proxy, his judicial sentence upon honour, and to enter a protest against the vote of the body to which he belongs—are all instances of the 'jus singulare.'

So the English law allows magistrates to plead the general issue in answer to civil actions brought against them for their official acts, thereby admitting the abominations of the system of special pleading, to which other members of the community are forced to submit.[p] For if special pleading is the best means of eliciting truth, why is it not applied to the case of magistrates? If it is not, why is it applied to other suitors? This is one of the countless proofs of the vicious empiricism, the incapacity of embracing a general principle, which is the original sin that taints the mind of England, and especially the mind of those to whom the task of making and expounding laws has been entrusted.[q]

As instances of the second rule may be cited the case of Sir John Fenwick, in William the Third's time; the case of Lord Strafford, which can be defended on that ground only; the proceedings against Bishop Atterbury, the proceedings of the convention parliament, the alien acts, the proceedings in consequence of George the Third's insanity, the taking land for railways and public works, bills of indemnity to witnesses against public delinquents, the suspension of the Habeas Corpus Act, the levying foreign mercenaries—stopping the exportation of corn, all which must be vindicated on the same principle. The venal lawyers of the Stuarts justified on the same ground

---

[p] So the danger of allowing special pleading in actions where the title to land was concerned was especially insisted upon by the common law commissioners in 1830, while it was carefully retained in other actions. It is needless to comment on such proofs of the *practical* wisdom which is held up as an excuse for the fact that jurisprudence, in the proper sense of the word, is unknown among us.

[q] Among other instances of this I may quote the Spanish law mentioned by JOVELLANOS, in his *Lex Agraria*, by which a right of passage was maintained for sheep from one end of Spain to another, because the change of pasture, at certain seasons of the year, was necessary to preserve the fineness of the fleece.

the levying ship-money, the dispensing power, and the right of arbitrary imprisonment.[r] 'J'avoue pourtant,' says the great man whom writers among us, where law is a chaos, have presumed to speak of in a tone of depreciation; ' pourtant que l'usage des peuples les plus libres qui aient jamais été sur la terre, me fait croire qu'il y a des cas ou il faut mettre un voile sur la liberté comme l'on cache les statues des Dieux.'[s]

XXIII.

CUM principalis causâ non existit ne ea quidem quæ sequuntur locum habent.—PAULUS.

When the principal cause has no existence, the consequences of it cease.

As the accessory shares in the nature and qualities of the principal, it follows that the destruction of the former follows the destruction of the latter: ' Quæ accessorium locum obtinent, extinguuntur cum principales res peremptæ sunt.'[u] Therefore, if the legacy of a slave is revoked, or made of no effect by his emancipation, the bequest of the peculium which was its accessory, ceases also. ' Servo legato cum vel peculio et alienato vel manumisso vel mortuo, legatum etiam

---

[r] So were justified the proscriptions of Sylla and the triumvirs: 'Vous diriez qu'on n'y a d'autre objet que le bien de la république tant on y parle de sang froid, tant on y montre d'avantages tant les moyens qu'on prend sont préferables, à d'autres tant les riches seront en sureté tant le bas peuple sera tranquille tant on craint de mettre en danger la vie des citoyens, tant on veut appaiser les soldats tant enfin ou sera heureux.'—MONTESQUIEU, *Esprit des Loix*, xii.18.

[s] *Esprit des Loix*, xii.19.

[u] ' Accessorium sequitur suum principale,' is one of the many rules of the canon law that has found its way into our own. Ulpian gives a mark by which to distinguish the principal from the accessory. 'Semper cum quærimus quid cui cedat, illud spectamus quid cujus rei ornandæ causâ adhibeatur, ut accessio cedat principali.'—*Dig. De auro legato*, 20 § *Perveniamus.*

Cod. 'Per quas personas nobis acquiritur'—the law in the 'actio personalis' which is the principal—governs the law in the 'pignoraticia actio.' *Dig.* xxxiii. 8. 2.

peculii extinguitur.'ᵛ So there were cases where the garden, though not actually touching it, followed the legacy of the house.ʷ ' Qui domum possidebat hortum vicinum ædibus comparavit ac postea *domum* legavit, si hortum domus causâ comparavit, ut amœniorem domum ac salubriorem possideret, aditumque in eum per domum habuit, et ædium hortus additamentum fuit domus legato continebitur.' So the release of the principal debtor, exonerated his surety. ' Debitore liberato,' says Papinian, 'per consequentiam fidejussor dimittitur.'ˣ If the marriage of a woman does not take place, the promise of a dowry to her, on account of it, it is no longer binding: ' Neque enim dos sine matrimonio esse potest.'ʸ So if a woman, or a 'pupillus' 'without the authority of his tutor, or any other person whom the Roman law declared incapable of making a valid contract,ᶻ gave a ' pignus' as an security for any engagement into which they had entered, it might be withdrawn at pleasure: ' Quia pignus nullum fuit.'ᵃ And in conformity to this rule, Ulpian lays it down, not only that all agreements contraryᵇ to law are invalid, but all that has been done in consequence of them.ᶜ So if the house of which I have 'usufruct' falls, I lose the right to the area: ' Certissimum est nec areæ nec cementorum exustis ædibus usumfructum deberi.'ᵈ So the easement followed

---

ᵛ *Dig.* xxxiii. 8. 1.

ʷ *Dig.* xxxii. 91, § *Qui domum.*

ˣ *Dig.* iv. 3 19 ; see also 5 *Institit., De pupillari substitutione.*

ʸ *Dig.* xxiii. 3. 3.

ᶻ *Dig.* xli. 3. 12 : ' Si ab eo emas quem prætor vetuit alienare idque tu scias usucapere non potes.'

ᵃ *Dig.* vi. 1. 39.

ᵇ *Dig.* ii. 14. 7, § 16 : ' Et generaliter quoties pactum a jure communi remotum est, servari hoc non oportet, nec legari, nec jurisjurandum de hoc adactum 'ne quis agit' servandum—Marcellus . . . scribit si stipulatio sit interposita de his pro quibus pacisci non licet servanda non est sed omni modo rescindenda.'

ᶜ *Dig.* xlv. 1. 69 : · Si homo mortuus sisti non potest nec pœna rei impossibilis committetur quem admodum si quis stichum mortuum dare stipulatus, si datus non esset pœnam stipuletur.'

ᵈ ' Rei mutatione interire usumfructum placet veluti ususfructus mihi ædium legatus est—ædes corruerunt vel exustæ sunt, sine dubio extinguitur;' and see *Dig.* xix. 1. 54, § 1, *Si dolia,* etc.

the land: ' Si partem fundi mei certam tibi vendidero, aquæ-
ductus jus (etiam is alterius partis causâ plerumque ducatur) te
quoque sequitur.'[e] So if I have the right ' stillicidii,' on your
area, or of way over your field, and I allow you to build on the
area, or to carry on any work over the path, I lose my right:
' Si stillicidii immittendi jus habeo in aream tuam et permisero
jus tibi in areâ ædificandi, stillicidii immittendi jus amitto, et
similiter si per tuum fundum via mihi debeatur, et permisero
tibi in eo loco per quem via mihi debetur aliquid facere, amitto
jus viæ.'[f] In another passage, Paulus qualifies the maxim by
the addition of the word ' plerumque,' intimating that there
are cases in which it does not apply.

Such are the cases of merely personal exceptions which the
' fidejussor' could not employ because the principal could[g]—
the case where Titius brings an action against Mævius for the
recovery of a slave belonging to him.   If the slave die pending the action, the plaintiff may still demand the profit of
his labour, and if the debtor of the slave has given sureties,
his death does not exonerate them.   ' Si homo ex stipulatu
petitus post litem contestatam decesserit, absolutionem non
faciendam et fructuum rationem habendam placet.'[h] Papinian
says that the bonâ fide holder of land in mortgage, though
obliged to give up the land to the real owner, is not obliged
to give him back the profits which he has taken from it while
it was in his possession.[i] So the penal clause might be valid
when the original stipulation was of no avail: ' Pœnam enim
cum stipulatur quis non illud inspicitur quid intersit (which
was the question in stipulations), sed quæ sit quantitas quæque
conditio stipulationis.'   By the old law, if a testament was
set aside as inofficious, the legacies it contained fell to the

---

[e] *Dig.* viii. 3. 25 ; and see *Dig.* viii. 3. 35, *De servitutibus Præd. Rust.*
[f] *Dig.* viii. 6. 8.
[g] *Dig.* xliv. 1. 7 : ' Exceptiones quæ personæ cujusque choærent non
transeunt ad alios veluti quam socius habet exceptionem non competit fidejussori.'
[h] *Dig.* xlii. 1. 8, PAULUS.
[i] *Dig.* xx. 1. 1, § 2.

ground. Justinian ordained, that though the testament was invalid for other purposes, it should be effectual in so far as related to the legacies: ' Sola institutio evacuatur, cætero firma manent.'[j] This alteration, though like most of Justinian's enactments it strongly proves the decline of jurisprudence, could not be passed over in dealing with the subject.[k]

When a law is abolished, all the precautions and provisions to which it gave rise were abolished also. That odious hypocrite, Augustus, enacted that the heir by will should pay a twentieth part of his inheritance to the public treasury. With a view to this law, and to prevent delay in the payment to the treasury, Adrian enacted, that the heir should be put in possession within a year after the death of the testator.[l] The law of Augustus was abolished, and therefore it was held that the edict of Adrian ceased to operate. ' Quia,' says Justinian,[m] in that affected and impure style, which in Rome as in England, is one sign of a degenerate period, ' vicesima hæreditatis pars a nostrâ recessit republica.'[n] So if a farm could not be recovered by the ' Publiciana actio,' neither could the soil added to it by the force of waters—' Quod per alluvionem fundo cedit simile fit ei, cui accedit et ideo si ipse fundus Publicaniâ peti non potest nec hoc petitur—si autem potest et pars quæ per alluvionem accrescit.'[o] Papinian gives another instance: ' Titio centum relicta sunt ita ut Mævium uxorem ducat—conditio non remittetur—ideo nec cautio remittenda est.'[p] Another striking illustration of the rule is given in this law: ' Cum instrumentum, omne legatum esset *excepto pecore*, pastores oviliones, ovilia quoque legato contineri—

---

[j] *Dig.* xlv. 1. 38, § 17, *Alteri*, etc.

[k] BROOM's *Legal Maxims*, p. 368, 2nd ed. ; Lord Buckhurst's Case, Chanel *v.* Robotham, YELVERTON ; Regina *v.* Stoke, 1 *Reports*, BLISS, 6. 2, B., 158.

[l] *Inoff. Test.* v. 2. 13, *Titia filiam*, etc. : ' Probat autem Paulus nec fideicommissa ab intestato data deberi, ut ademente.'

[m] 1. 3, *Cod de Edicto Divi Hadriani tollendo in principi.*

[n] *Cod. de Liberis Prœteritis.*

[o] *De Public. in rem actione, Dig.* vi. 2. 11, § *quod tamen.*

[p] *Dig. de condit.* and *Dem.*, 69, § 1, *Titio centum.*

afilius non recte putat;'[q] because the 'oviliones,' etc., were accessary to the ' pecus.'

Instances of this maxim are of course extremely common in English Jurisprudence. If the marriage was invalid there was no right of dower. Among these may be cited the right of the purchaser of land, conveyed to him in fee to the title-deeds as incident to the land, though the conveyance is silent as to them; heir-looms, and things in the nature of heir-looms, which are transmitted with the inheritance; an advowson which passes by the grant of a manor 'cum pertinentiis'; estovers to the owner of the house for which they were granted to be used;[r] a millstone which passes by the grant of the mill, though severed from it—common of pasture, which is the right of the owners or occupiers of arable land appendant to a particular farm, passes with the grant of the farm[s]—covenants running with the land—and the fact that if the plaintiff cannot recover the principal sum, he cannot recover the interest.[t]

So where an original estate determines by the nature or terms of its limitations, or is defeated by a condition, the leases made by the conditional owner, or by the owner of the particular estate, determine also in conformity to this rule,[u] the exceptions to which cause many difficulties in the investigation of title.

---

[q] *Dig. de instrumento legato,* l. '*fundi,*' 26 *fin.* ' Pupillare testamentum pars et sequela est paterni testamenti adeo ut si patris testamentum non valeat, nec filii quidem valebit.'—*Inst. de pupill. substit.*

[r] Wild *v.* Pickford. 8 M. and W., 443 ; SHEPHERD'S *Touchstone,* 90.

[s] COKE, *Littleton,* 231 : ' Transit terra cum onere.'

[t] Clark *v.* Alexander, 8 SCOTT, *N. R.,* 165 ; Chappell *v.* Purday, 15 L. J. CHANC., 261 ; BACON'S *Abridgment* ; GRANT, 1. 4 ; COKE, *Littleton,* 152. *a* ; 3 *Inst.,* 139 ; 4 BLACKSTONE'S *Com.*

[u] 1 PREST, *abs. title,* 248 ; BROOM'S *Legal Maxims,* p. 372.

XXIV.

NIHIL tam naturale est quam eo genere quidque dissolvere quo colligatum est; ideo verborum obligatio verbis tollitur, nudi consensus obligatio, contrario consensu dissolvitur.—ULPIAN.

Nothing is so natural as that what served to tie should loosen; therefore, an obligation made by words is put an end to by words; an obligation arising from the simple agreement of the persons contracting, is dissolved by an opposite agreement.

The same means that serve to create may be employed, 'ipso jure,'[s] to destroy an engagement. When the will discovers itself in any particular manner, it must in the same manner declare its change of purpose. If the external act is simple, an act of equal simplicity is sufficient for its revocation. If it is of a more formal and solemn character, it can be cancelled only by an act which purports to have been the result of equal care and forethought.

The Roman jurisprudence recognised four means by which contracts might be made binding:—

1st. They might be established 're' by the delivery of the object of the contract.[t] Of such contracts there were five: the mutual loan, the gratuitous loan, the payment of what was not due, the deposit, and the pledge. These contracts were completed only by the actual delivery of the thing; until that took place, no legal obligation arose from them. A promise to lend was not a loan; it became such only by the payment of the money or the delivery of the article; and therefore it was by repayment or by re-delivery that the debtor could exonerate himself

---

[s] *Dig.* ii. 14. 27, § 2.

[t] 'Prout quidque contractum est ita solvi debet ut cum re contraxerimus re solvi debet veluti cum mutuum dedimus ut retro pecuniæ tantundem solvi debet.'—*Dig.* xlvi. 3. 80.

'Fere quibus cumque modis obligamur iisdem in contrarium actis liberamur cum quibus modis acquirimus, iisdem in contrarium actis amittimus.'—PAULUS.

from his obligation: ‘Cum re contrahimus re solvi debet contractus.’

2ndly. By words.[u] The ‘stipulatio’ consisted in the proposal made by one of the parties, and the formal assent to that proposal by the other: ‘Spondes, Spondeo; Fidejubes, Fidejubeo,’ etc., in the presence of witnesses.

3rdly. ‘Litteris,’ by writing.[x] These were called ‘nomina’ by the Romans, and constituted a proof against the debtor which could be repelled only by a written receipt.

4thly. ‘Consensu,’ by consent.[y] The four contracts that were complete by consent only were buying and selling, hiring and letting—hypothecation, partnership, and agency; and as they were binding without writing or part-performance, they could be cancelled by the consent of those by whom they had been created.

This maxim did not apply to contracts only. A verbal declaration of a testator, in the presence of seven witnesses, that it was his wish to die intestate, was not a revocation of his will without some authentic act. To conclude with the doctrine of the modern law, ‘Contraria contrariis actibus dissolvuntur.’

Marriage is the great exception to the rule.

There are two other rules on this head of the ‘ortus’ and ‘interitus’ of civil rights. Papinian has touched upon it, as

---

[u] ‘Acceptum fieri non potest nisi quod verbis colligatum est, acceptilatio enim verborum obligationem tollit, quia et ipsa verbis fit neque enim potest verbis tolli quod non verbis contractum est.’—*Dig.*xlvi. 4. 8, § 3.

[x] *Inst. quibus modis tollitur obligatio; Inst. de obligationibus,* § *Sequens Divisio.*

[y] ‘Rebus scilicet adhuc integris.’—GOTHOFRED.

‘Ab emptione, venditione, locatione conductione cæterisque similibus obligationibus, quin integris omnibus consensu eorum qui inter se obligati sunt recedi possit dubium non est.—*Dig.*ii.14. 58.

‘Emptio et venditio sicut consensu contrahitur, ita contrario consensu resolvitur antequam fuerit res secuta.’—*Dig., de Rescindendâ Venditione,* xviii.5.3; *Dig.* xix.2.1.

Dig. xlvi. 3. 80 : ‘Quoniam consensu nudo contrahi potest etiam dissensu contrario dissolvi potest.’

bearing upon the difficult topic of possession, in one of his refined explanations of the laws: 'Quamvis saltus proposito possidendi fuerit alius ingressus tamdiu priorem possidere dictum est, quamdiu possessionem ab alio occupatam ignoraret— ut enim eodem modo vinculum obligationis solvitur quo quæri adsolet—ita non debet ignoranti tolli possessio quæ solo animo tenetur.'[z]

The other two rules on the same subject are: 'Fere quibus- cumque modis obligamur iisdem in contrarium actis liberamur, cum quibus modis acquirimus iisdem in contrarium actis amit- timus;' and 'Omnia quæ jure contrabuntur contrario jure pereunt.'[a]

The last of these, notwithstanding the commentary of Godefroi, I take to be general. The second relates more par- ticularly to possession.

The law of servitudes affords abundant illustrations of it. We lose by the same means that we acquire, when they are inverted.

The owner of land can only acquire a right of servitude over the land of another. If, therefore, he becomes himself the owner of the land over which he had the right of ser- vitude, his right ceases, because the two rights are incompati- ble: 'Res sua nemini servit.' The servitude sinks into the proprietorship: 'Quia rebus nostris utimur non jure servitutis sed jure domini.'

The English law has not adopted the simple and salutary rule of Roman jurisprudence on which these remarks have been written but has (in imitation of the French law,[b] enacted more than a century before) required certain contracts to be in writing. The Statute of Frauds, in which this doctrine was incorporated— bad in itself, and worse by its interpretation—has been so con- trived that (our law of real property, to which the place of honour is due, and the proceedings in equity, always excepted)

---

[z] *Dig.* xli. 2.46.

[a] 'Ut enim nulla possessio acquiritur nisi animo et corpore ita nulla amittitur nisi in quâ utrumque in contrarium actum.'

[b] *Ordonnance de Moulins*, 1561.

the ingenuity of man could hardly have devised a more prolific cause of mischievous litigation, or one that could place the qualities of our system and its expounders in a more disadvantageous light.

In considering the three kinds of obligation—by record, by specialty, and by simple contract[c]—it is enough, with regard to the first, to remark, that in the year of grace 1840, or thereabouts, it was clearly settled that an obligation by record might be discharged by a release under seal.

With regard to specialties, Lord C. J. Tindal says, ' I apprehend no rule of law is better established than this, that a covenant under seal can only be discharged by an instrument of equal force and validity; quodque,' etc.[d] Here it may be remarked, that instead of making the plain distinction between written and unwritten contracts, the English law, with a confusion all its own, has thought fit to annex a mysterious sanctity to instruments under seal, whereby it has created an amount almost infinite of chicane, and uses the word ' parol' to describe verbal and written contracts. If to this be added the new rules, and their various expositions, the net will be as nearly inextricable as Ch. J. Saunders could desire.

Now the opinion of Ch. J. Tindal is far too clear and simple to convey a correct idea of our law. Upon it must be grafted the doctrine, that where there has been a breach of such contract, accord with satisfaction of the damages will be a good plea to an action on the specialty; in other words, that a covenant under seal can be put aside in another way than that stated by the Chief Justice;[e] and that, after an instrument has been reduced to writing, it may be dissolved before breach by an new contract not in writing, or it may be qualified and varied by a merely verbal agreement.[f] The dissertation on special

---

[c] Barker v. St. Quentin, 12 M. and W., 453.

[d] West v. Blakeway, 3 SCOTT, N. R., 199. 'Fiunt Scripturæ ut quod actum est per eas facilius probari possit.'—Dig. xxii. 4. 4 ; again, xx. 1. 4.

[e] Blake's Case, Cumber v. Wane, 1 STRANGE, Reports, 426 ; 6 Reports, 43.

[f] Goss v. Lord Nugent, 5 B. and ADOL. 64 ; SMITH, J. W., On Contracts, 2nd ed., Malcolm.

pleading, in Heath *v.* Durant,[g] completes the sketch of English law upon this subject.

A parol contract may, before breach, be waved by parol.

Where the statute requires a contract to be in writing, it cannot be varied by any subsequent verbal agreement. But on this intelligible rule must be grafted the practical exception, that the statute does not prevent a verbal waiver or abandonment of a contract which it requires to be in writing.

On the general principle, the cases and text-books cited in the note will furnish the clue to its illustration, as far as a doctrine, so wantonly perplexed and made ambiguous, can be described by such a word.

XXV.

NUPTIAS non concubitus sed consensus facit.— Ulpian.[h]

Consent, not physical intercourse, constitutes marriage.

This famous and most salutary rule furnishes us with a test by which, according to the Roman law, the existence of a

---

[g] Heath *v.* Durant, 12 M. and W. 438; Giraud *v.* Richmond, 2 C. B. 835; Sibtree *v.* Tripp, 15 MEESON and WELSBY (qualifies Cumber *v.* Wane); COKE, *Litt.* 212; Rennell *v.* Bishop of Lincoln, 8 BING, 490; BROOM'S *Legal Maxims*, 690.

In Longridge *v.* Dorville, 5 B. and ALD. 117, and Wilkinson *v.* Byers, it was held that if the original claim was for unliquidated damages, or was disputed, the accord of the creditor to take a security for a smaller sum certain, and abandoning the excess, was valid. So you may give a negotiable note in satisfaction of a large demand, but not money.— Cooper *v.* Parker, 5 C. and B., *Reports*, 825.

I quote this passage from the *Reports*, that the reader may compare the views of our judges with those of the Roman jurists: Counsel loquitur: 'Another rule is, that the satisfaction must appear to be reasonable.' COLERIDGE, J. Is it not the rule, that it must not appear to be unreasonable? (!!!)—Notes to Cumber *v.* Wane, SMITH'S *Leading Cases*, vol. i. 146.

[h] *Dig.* xxiii. 21: 'Nuptiæ sunt conjunctio maris et fœminæ consortium omnis vitæ, divini et humani juris communicatio.' LOCRÉ, *Legislation de la France*, cap. 11, *De Præsumpt.*, vol. iv. p. 481; VAN ESPEN, *Jus Eccl. Univ.*, vol. 1. p. 562; *Synodus Trident*, sess. 24, case 1; POTHIER,

marriage is to be determined.   The language of Ulpian here,
as in the passage cited below,[i] is general and comprehensive.
In the same strain Papinian speaks of the 'maritalis honor et
affectio.' 'Neque enim,' he adds, 'tabulas facere matrimonium.'[k] As in another place he speaks with chivalrous deli-
cacy[l] of Cassianus, 'Qui Rufinam ingenuam honore pleno
dilexerat.'[m] It was this which made the distinction between
the 'uxor'[n] and the 'concubina.' As cohabitation, therefore, was of itself no proof of marriage, so separate houses were
no proof that it was dissolved.[o] The 'destinatio animi' was
the test.

For proofs of this purpose of the mind, Papinian alleges—

1st. A comparison of station and character, 'personis com-
paratis.'[p]

2ndly. The 'conjunctio vitæ.'

3rdly. Repute among neighbours.   Marriage was inferred
when the woman was taken into the house: 'Quasi in domicilium matrimonii.'[q]

4thly. Aquæ et ignis acceptione.   'Prius quam aquâ et igne
acciperetur.'[r]

---

vol. v., ed. Dupin; 'Ainsi les enfans qu'une femme sauvage aurait eus
d'un sauvage dans un pays ou il n'y aurait point de lois établies seraient
regardés comme légitimes même parmi nous.'—MERLIN, *Mariage Repertoire;* Dalrymple *v.* Dalrymple, HAGGARD, *C. R.,* vol. ii. p. 114.

[i] 'Non enim coitus matrimonium facit sed maritalis affectio.'—*Dig.*
xxiv. 1. 32, § 13.

[k] *Dig.* xxxix. 5. 31.

[l] What would he have thought of those disgusting actions, peculiar
to us, that every year sully our courts of justice, and place the coarse-
ness of our law and country in so glaring a light, in which a husband is
forced to make money by matrimonial affliction and disgrace.

[m] *Dig.* xxxiv. 16. 1.

[n] *Dig.* xxxii. 1. 49, § 4: 'Sane enim nisi dignitate nihil interest.'

[o] *Dig.* xxv. 7. 4; *Menochius de Præsumpt.,* lib. iii. c. 1, § 73.

[p] *Dig.* xxiii. 2. 24: 'Le mariage ne consiste pas dans le simple rap-
prochement des deux sexes.'—PORTALIS.

[q] 'Causa efficiens et perficiens matrimonium est mutuus contrahentium consensus.'—VAN ESPEN, vol. i. p. 562. This was the universal law
of civilised Europe, drawn from the fountains of Roman jurisprudence
before the Council of Trent.—*Dig.* xxiii. 2. 5.

[r] *Dig.* xxiv. 1. 66, § 1.

5thly. By the written documents, or ' tabulæ,' containing the stipulations concerning the ' dos;'[s] which, however, as the passages cited above show, were not essential.[t]

Such were the proofs from which a marriage might be inferred. When complete, it gave the wife, though cohabitation[u] had never taken place, a vested right to her ' dos;' or if money had been left to her on condition that she married, it became due.[x] So Ulpian held that a woman who lost her husband on the first day of the marriage was bound not to marry within the year: ' Maritum qui rediens a cænâ juxta Tiberim perierat, ab uxore esse lugendum.'[y]

' At all times, by the common law of England,' it has been said, on the other hand, by C. J. Tindal,[z] ' some religious ceremony was necessary to complete the marriage contract; nor was the religious rite sufficient in the eyes of the church to constitute a valid marriage, unless it was performed in the presence of an ordained minister.' On this point, then, Lord C. J. Tindal differs from the opinion of Lord Stowell, ' that when the natural and civil contract was formed, it had the full essence of matrimony, without the intervention of a priest.' In the case cited,[a] it

---

[s] *Dig.*xxxv.1.15 : ' Cum fuerit sub hac conditione legatum si in familiâ nupsisset videtur impleta conditio statim atque ducta est uxor.'

[t] *Dig.*xx.1.5.

[u] ' Nihil obstat eandem esse et virginam et uxorem.' Milton speaks of the ' seven times wedded maid.'

Dig. xxiii. 2. 7 : ' Ideoque potest, fieri ut in hoc casu aliqua virgo et dotem et de dote habeat actionem.'

[x] *Dig.*xxiii. 2, § 6.

[y] Cap. 23, 10, pl.1, c. 31, *de Sponsalibus :* ' Sufficiat ad matrimonium solus consensus illorum quorum quarumque conjunctionibus agitur. The church held a marriage ' inter infideles verum,' but not ' ratum'— ' ratum efficit conjugii sacramentum.' It is singular that this should never have been cited in the case of the Queen *v* Millis, 4 CL. and FINN.

[z] KENT'S *Commentaries*, sect. 26, vol.ii. p. 83.

[a] The Queen *v.* Millis, 10 CL. and FINN., 654 ; BRACTON, v.19 ; ix.304 ; iv. 8, 303 ; v. 420. ' Et quia convictum est per assisam istam quod prædictus Johannes del Heith nunquam desponsavit prædictam Catharinam in facie ecclesiæ, per quod sequitur quod prædictus W.

was held by all the judges that the form of the religious ceremony could not atone for the want of the proper minister, and
that no subsequent cohabitation could give a validity to the
marriage which it did not before possess.

It is in vain to say that this judgment, pronounced by an
excellent man, a deeply-learned lawyer, and a most careful
judge, does not shake Sir W. Scott's decision in Dalrymple v.
Dalrymple, and so far unsettle the marriage law. Can that be
a sound state of jurisprudence in which, act of parliament after
act of parliament having been passed, decision after decision
having been pronounced, the judges of England, on being
called upon to deliver their opinion, not on a remote or subtle
point, but on a question lying at the root of social order,
' acknowledge themselves unable to trace or define with absolute certainty the boundary of marriage itself'?[b] And will
Englishmen always be content with repeating ludicrous panegyrics on their coarse, slovenly, confused, and incessantly
vacillating laws, instead of seeking to digest them into some
state, if not equal to the finished system of Rome, less scandalous at least to civilised men?[c]

---

filius Johannis nihil juris clamare potest in prædictis tenementis.'—
EDW. I. 34.

(Beau) Fielding's Case, 14 *State Trials*, 1327 : first marriage was not
disputed. Jesson v. Collins, 2 SALKELD, 436. Marriages ought to be
celebrated according to the law of England to entitle the wife to dower,
thirds, etc., HOLT, C.J. 6 and 7 William III., c. 6, 163 : ' Pretended
marriages between Jews and Quakers. 12 Charles II., c. 33 : Act for
Confirmation of Marriages. 26 George II., c. 33, § 18 ; Cawdry's Case,
5 *Reports*, 1 ; HALE, *Hist. of the Common Law*, c. 2 ; *Le Case de Com-
mendams*, DAVIES, *Reports ;* WILKINS, *Concilia*, 367. ' A mass priest
shall, with God's blessing, bind the union to all prosperity.'—*Law of*
KING EDMUND.

[b] Queen v. Millis, 4 CL. and F., 700. ' The highest names in the law
stand opposed to each other.'—LORD COTTENHAM, *ib.* LEE, *Reports*
edited by DR. PHILLIMORE, Baxter v. Buckley, 57. In this case a marriage in ' facie ecclesiæ ' was held void, and the heir set aside, in consequence of a previous marriage ' per verba de præsenti.'

[c] 'Quid dicendum de procreato a parentibus qui sponsalia quidem
inivere sed propter mortem forte alterutrius, sponsi scilicet vel sponsæ
solenni copulatione ac benedictione sacerdotali nuptias non celebrârunt ;

If the opinion of the judges in R. *v.* Millis (on which the law lords were equally divided) be law, all marriages to which Lord Hardwicke's Act[c] did not extend, not solemnised by a person in holy orders (of course, including all marriages before 1835 between Jews and Quakers), were absolutely void. What must be the state of men's minds on subjects of jurisprudence? What must be the character of their studies, what the complexion of their reasoning habits, where such a decision is possible? Such is the result of incessant study of a labyrinth of detail, without the faintest ray of principle.

The argument of Lord Brougham against this doctrine, p. 705, from the practice of the Ecclesiastical Courts, who until the Legislature interfered, compelled persons who had contracted ' per verba de præsenti' to clothe their contract with religious solemnities, is powerful, and to the mind of the writer, conclusive. For as Lord Brougham asks, what was the contract between the making of it civilly and its alleged completion?[d] How could the parties be bound indissolubly and yet to do nothing? I much wish that my limits would allow me to cite the whole of this luminous, eloquent and learned argument, to which I particularly invite the attention of the reader.[e]

—anne iste in feudo succedet —quod affirmandum existimamus cum ista solemnitas ecclesiastica non ad ipsam matrimonii essentiam pertineat.'—STURVII, *Juris Feudalis Syntagma,* c. ix. § 3, p. 307.

[c] Bunting *v.* Lepingwell, 4 *Reports,* 29. Roger North complains of Lord Hale for allowing a special verdict to be found in favour of a Quaker's marriage, which, that meanest of all men except his brothers, says, could not be good without the liturgy, and was therefore a violation of the Act of Uniformity.

Mr. Hargrave, in a note to COKE, *Littleton,* 34 *a,* p. 209, cites Lord Hale's opinion, that a gift to a wife ' post affidationem et carnalem copulam,' was void, which could only be because the marriage was valid.

[d] 'I am not prepared to say, or to admit, that before the Marriage Act the marriages of Jews and Quakers were good by the law of this country. Surely the Act left them where they were.'—LORD ABINGER, R. *v.* Millis. But see Macadam *v.* Walker, 1 Dow., 148 ; 1 HAGGARD'S *Cons. Reports,* App. 9 ; Dean *v.* Maris, 1 MOOD. and M., 361.

[e] Jesson *v.* Collins, 2 SALKELD, 437 ; Lindo *v.* Belisario, 1 HAGGARD, *Cons. Reports,* 242.

K 2

Lord Holt distinctly declared, that a contract 'per verba de præsenti' amounted to as valid a marriage as if it had been pronounced in 'facie Ecclesiæ.' Lord Ellenborough[f] says, 'Certainly a contract of marriage 'per verba de præsenti' would have bound the parties before the Marriage Act.' C. J. Gibbs[g] says, ' It appears that a contract of marriage entered into 'per verba de præsenti' is a valid marriage,' i. e., at Madras where the Marriage Act did not reach. ' Our law,' says Blackstone, ' considers marriage in no other light than as a civil contract; the holiness of the matrimonial state is left entirely to the Ecclesiastical Law.'[b] 'As I understand the law,' said Lord Tenterden, ' before the Marriage Act, a marriage might be celebrated without a clergyman, upon a declaration by the parties that they were man and wife accompanied by cohabitation.'[i] Chancellor Kent says: ' No peculiar ceremonies are requisite by the Common Law to the valid celebration of marriage; the consent of the parties is alone required, if the contract be made 'per verba de præsenti,' or if made 'per verba de futuro;' if it be followed by consummation it amounts to a valid marriage, and it is equally binding as if made in 'facie ecclesiæ.' This is the doctrine of the Common Law.' Lord Campbell,[j] in his able argument, puts the case of the person who officiates as priest never having been ordained.

---

[f] Rex v. Brampton, 10 EAST, 282. 'I think, though I do not wish to be bound, that even an agreement between the parties 'per verba de præsenti' was 'ipsum matrimonium.'—LORD KENYON. Reed v. Passer, PEAKE, N. P. Reports, vol. i., 309. By what fatality is it that the narrow view always triumphs among our judges ? will they always act in defiance of the rule 'Rapienda occasio est, præbendi BENIGNIUS responsum.' As to the maxim, 'Communis error facit jus,' see Cadell v. Palmer, 1 CL. and FINN., 372, where it was pointedly applied.

[g] Lautour v. Teasdale, 8 TAUNTON, 830.

[h] BLACKSTONE'S Com., vol. i. p. 437.
'Les juris consultes n'y voient que le contrat civil.'—PORTALIS, vol. iv. p. 479, LOCRÉ, Leg. de la France.

[i] Beer v. Ward, cit. CLARK and FINNELLY, vol. iv. p. 607, 611 ; Wright v. Elwood, 1 CURTIS, 67.

[j] LORD CAMPBELL Argument, 776, 4 CL. and FINN. ; KENT, Com. vol. ii. p. 83 ; STORY'S Conflict of Law, c. 5, says : 'The Common Law of England considers marriage in no other light than as a civil contract.'

This is provided for by the celebrated Roman Law 'Barbarius;'[k] but how is it to be answered by the advocates of the doctrine held by all the judges on this occasion. Lord Stowell repeatedly expressed an opinion that such marriages would be valid; nor can there be, I think, any doubt that they would be so, even under our law,[l] abandoned as it has been to Special Pleaders. ' Ut conjugium consistat non aliud natura requirere videtur quam ut talis sit cohabitatio quæ fœminam constituat quasi sub oculis et in custodia maris, ad hoc in homine accedit fides, se fœmina mari obstringit.'[m] So the Common Law.[n] If two persons marry under the age when consent can be given upon coming to that age, they may treat the marriage as a nullity; but if at the age of consent they agree to continue together, they need not be married again.[o]

By the Act of Dr. Phillimore, 3rd Geo. IV. c. 75,[p] the law as to banns, marriages and consent, where unions were concerned, was regulated. Provision was also made therein for

---

[k] *Dig.* i. 14. 3.

[l] The last Earl of Oxford, of the stock of De Vere, the first of our nobles, went through the ceremony of a sham marriage, celebrated by a pretended priest, with an actress, who died of a broken heart, in the time of Charles II. CROKE, 775, Costard *v.* Waidet : ' It would be mischievous if all acts by such averments were drawn in question ; and every one agreed that all spiritual acts done by such a one while he is parson are good.'

[m] GROTIUS, *de Jure Belli et Pacis*, l. 2, c. 5, § 8. 9.

[n] COMYN'S *Dig.*, *Baron and Feme*, B., 1 ; COKE, *Littleton*, 34 *a*, note 1, citing Hale, MSS. and 16, H. III., and 13, Ed. I., 117 ; 12, C. II. 33, 1659 : ' Marriage shall be before a justice of the peace, and confirmed by him,' yet see SIDERFIN, 1. 64.

[o] STEPHENS' *Blackstone*, ii. 241 ; REEVES' *History of the English Law*, vol. iv. p. 53, l. 4, tit. 2, qu. 3 ; see 6 and 7 Will. IV. c. 85 ; 7 Will. IV. and 1 Vict. c. 22 ; 3 and 4 Vict. c. 72 ; 14 and 15 Vict. c. 97, § 25.

[p] This Act, amending Lord Hardwicke's, was so maimed and mutilated in its passage through the Lords, that Mr. Canning expressed his delight at the escape of any portion of it. ' We have got our bill again,' he said, ' let us take care how we send it back to its enemies.' 4 Geo. IV. c. 76.

CRUISE'S *Dignities*, vol. iii. tit. 29, c. 2. 3 ; *Scotch Marriages*, 8 CL. and F., p. 318 ; STEWART and MENZIES ; 9 CL. and F., p. 347, Hamilton *v.* Hamilton.

the case where the person whose consent was required was ' non compos.'

Connected with this subject, is the absurd and unconstitutional measure, called the Royal Marriage Act, which is still censured and maintained. The admirable protest against it was drawn up by Mr. Dunning:[q] ' To make a man's power of contracting marriage dependant neither on his own choice nor on any fixed rule of law, but on the arbitrary will of any man or set of men, is exceeding the power permitted by Divine Providence to human legislators; it is directly against the earliest command given by God to mankind; contrary to the right of domestic comfort and society, and to the desire of lawful posterity, the first and best of instincts implanted in us by the Author of our nature, and utterly incompatible with all all religion natural and revealed; and, therefore, a mere act of power having neither the nature nor the obligation of law.' An excellent exposition of this statute will be found in the judgment of Lord C. J. Tindal, in the case of the Sussex Peerage.[r] It was said by the Court of Exchequer,[s] ' That the House of Lords had decided in the case above cited, that a contract of marriage ' per verba de præsenti,' in the presence of a minister not in episcopal orders, did not constitute a valid marriage.' Probably the reader will think that some of the words of the protest against the Royal Marriage Act are not inapplicable to such a law as that laid down by the judges in Rex v. Millis; and that, in favour of a harsh and narrow construction, it runs counter to the best authorities on the subject.[t]

As every man is supposed to know the law, and as Lolly after taking counsel's opinion was sentenced to transportation,

---

[q] *Parl. History,* vol. xvii. p. 391 ; BURNS' *Ecc. Law,* DR. ROBERT PHILLIMORE'S Edition, vol. ii. p. 433.

[r] See 3 and 4 Vict. c. 52, § 4.

[s] 11 CLARK and FINNELLY, 143.

[t] 13 MEESON and WELSBY, Catherwood v. Caslon. ' A husband suing for adultery, must prove his marriage by direct testimony ; repute and cohabitation are not sufficient.' 4 BURROW, Morris v. Miller, 2057.

and kept for two years on the hulks among the worst of mankind for doing what he was advised by them he had a right to do, I subjoin a list of some of the statutes on the law of marriage, which might be contained in five lines, and which the subject is supposed to know:—25 Hen. VIII. c. 21, altered; 4 Geo. IV. c. 76; 32 Hen. VIII. c. 38; 2 and 3 Ed. VI. c. 21; 5 and 6 Ed. VI. c. 12; 15 Geo. II. c. 30; 26 Geo. II. c. 33: 21 Geo. III. c. 53; 44 Geo. III. c. 77; 48 Geo. III. c. 127; 57 Geo. III. c. 51, altered; 5 Geo. IV. c. 68; 58 Geo. III. c. 84 (to remove doubts!); 58 Geo. III. c. 45, § 27, § 28; 59 Geo. III. c. 134, § 6; 3 Geo. IV. c. 72, § 18; 3 Geo. IV. c. 75; 4 Geo. IV. c. 5; 4 Geo. IV. c. 17; 4 Geo. IV. c. 67; 4 Geo. IV. c. 76; 4 Geo. IV. c. 91; 12 and 13 Vict. c. 68; 5 Geo. IV. 32; 6 Geo. IV. c. 92; 11 Geo. IV. and 1 Will. IV.; 1 Will. IV. c. 66, § 20; 3 and 4 Will. IV. c. 102; 4 and 5 Will. IV. c. 28; 5 and 6 Will. IV. c. 54, § 1, retrospective; 6 and 7 Will. IV. c. 24; 6 and 7 Will. IV. c. 85; 6 and 7 Will. IV. c. 86; 6 and 7 Will. IV. c. 92 (for marriages in St. Clement's, Oxford!), suspending 6 and 7 Will. IV., § 85 and § 86—7 Will. IV., and 1 Vict. c. 1, explaining and amending ditto, 7 Will. IV., 1 Vict. c. 22; 3 and 4 Vict. c. 72; 3 and 4 Vict. c. 92 (Fleet and Curzon-street!); 4 and 5 Vict. c. 42 (Winterbourne, Gloucestershire); 5 and 6 Vict. c. 65, § 3 (Forest of Dean!); 6 and 7 Vict. c. 37, § 15; 7 and 8 Vict. c. 96; 8 and 9 Vict. c. 70, § 10; 9 and 10 Vict. c. 72; 10 and 11 Vict. c. 58 (caused by the absurd case of the R. v. Millis) retrospective; 10 and 11 Vict. c. 98, continued by 11 and 12 Vict. c. 67; 12 and 13 Vict. c. 39; 13 and 14 Vict. c. 47; 14 and 15 Vict. c. 2; 15 and 16 Vict. c. 17; 13 and 14 Vict. c. 38 (law for Upton cum Chalvesly!); 14 and 15 Vict. c. 40; 14 and 15 Vict. c. 97, § 25, besides the law relating to the royal family.

This is the state of things which a people who boast of being practical, and abridge every idea of scorn, dislike and distrust, in the word theorist, as negroes call the devil white, prefer to a code. No wonder that on a very simple question affecting a contract which is the foundation of society, three law lords hold one opinion and three another; and that we read in the statute-books such passages as that below inserted, with the most perfect simplicity and obvious unconsciousness of the bitter reproach they brand upon our legislation.[u]

This is the reason, 'holy just and pure,' of our law, and the way in which it provides for the dignity of that sacred tie,[x] the origin and nurse of all civility, the source of all the charities of social life, which the heathen jurist described as being ' omnis divini et humani juris communicatio.' When disorder is the effect of the passions, which—

> ' Shake
> The private state, and render life unsweet,'

it may be cured by law; but when it springs from the law, the disease is incurable, for the remedy is part of it. Our law of divorce is in keeping with the law of marriage; it is perfectly indefensible, inaccessible to the poor, and only to be attained by the very rich, after asking aloud for a pecuniary compensation for an act, which if money could atone for it, would be no injury at all. The rules of the canon and French law before the Revolution on this subject, will be found in D'Aguesseau.[y] He says that the rule, ' Quæ ab initio non valent non possunt tractu temporis convalescere,' does not apply to marriage, because ' Il s'agit d'une question d'Etat et qu'il n'y a rien de si important que de l'assurer a ceux qui en jouissent par une

---

[u] ' Whereas doubts have been entertained as to the validity of marriages amongst the people called Quakers, and amongst persons professing the Jewish religion, solemnized in England before the first day of July, One thousand eight hundred and thirty-seven, or in Ireland before the first day of April, One thousand eight hundred and forty-five, according to the usages of those denominations respectively, and whereas it is expedient to put an end to such doubts.' 10 and 11 Vict. c. 58.

[x] ' Le public est donc toujours partie dans les questions de mariage.' —PORTALIS, *Discours Prél.* ; LOCRÉ, vol. i. p. 286.

[y] *Œuvres de* D'AGUESSEAU ; and *Sixième Plaidoyer*, vol. i. p. 400 ; *Cause de Jacques de Senlis*, 43 ; *Plaidoyer*, vol. iv. p. 240. He distinguishes between two kinds of nullities, Les unes absolues essentielles, irreparables, les autres relatives,' *ib.*, 241 ; *Cause de la dame de Chabert, Plaidoyer*, 33 ; *Cause de Louise de Bury*, vol. iii. p. 10 ; LOCRÉ, *Législation*, vol. iv. p. 512.

possession longue et paisible aux yeux de public;' a maxim which, if our judges had thought it worth attending to, might have saved us from the scandal of such an act as 10 and 11 Vict. c. 58.

' Il faut pourtant,' says Portalis, ' qu'il y ait une régle et une régle générale.' The English law, like the Sibyl's sayings (except, indeed, as to inspiration), is not only written on detached leaves, and in obscure language, but blown into disorder by the puff of every new decision. In the case which involved the social happiness of thousands, one of the judges,[z] whose opinion was hostile to the opinion on which men had acted since the Conquest as the law of this country, said: ' The highest names in the law are opposed to each other. The many great authorities who have expressed opinions adverse to those held by the judges, the presumption that the law of this country, previous to 23 G. II., had been the same as prevailed in other countries, which derived their law from the same source, and a CONSIDERATION OF THE GREAT EVILS NECESSARILY ATTENDANT UPON A CONFIRMATION OF THE THE OPINION OF THE JUDGES, had raised in my mind a strong opinion that the judgment was erroneous, and no slight wish that it might be so.' And then he deliberately confirms a judgment which carried misery and dismay to many a peaceful hearth, and declared thousands of his fellow-subjects, happy in the confidence and purity of domestic life, to be living in concubinage, and their issue to be illegitimate.

Such are the consequences of substituting treatises on Special Pleading for the Pandects; of relying on mechanical empirics for legislation, and of supposing that because Titius cannot comprehend a general principle, he is a man of common sense and practical ability.[a]

---

[z] LORD COTTENHAM.

[a] ' All this I know well enough will sound wild and chimerical to the profane herd of those vulgar and mechanical politicians, who far from being qualified to be directors of the great movement of empire, are not fit to turn a wheel in the machine.'—BURKE, *Speech on Conc. with America*, vol. iii. p. 126.

XXVI.

SECUNDUM naturam est commoda cujusque rei eum sequi, quem sequuntur incommoda. — PAULUS.[a]

It is natural equity, that he who suffers the inconvenience should enjoy the benefit.

This is a principle which applies to every part of law—contracts, inheritance, donations, usufructs, dowry, to the paternal authority, adoption, guardianship, and generally to all kinds of acquisition, by the law of nations as well as by the civil law.[b] So, as the deterioration of land by flood after the sale fell upon the buyer, the benefit it gained by alluvion was his also : ' Namque et si totus ager post emptionem flumine occupatus esset periculum esset emptoris sic igitur et commodum ejus esse debet.'[c] So it is laid down in the *Institutes,* that if the thing sold loses its value after the sale, or, indeed, if it is destroyed altogether, if the seller is not to blame, the loss must fall upon the buyer: ' Quidquid sine dolo et culpâ venditoris accidit in eo venditor securus est.'[d]

Exceptions to this rule:—

---

[a] Γλαῦκε, τίη δὴ νῶϊ τετιμήμεσθα, μάλιστα
'Εδρῃ τε, κρέασίν τε ἰδὲ πλείοις δεπάεσσιν ;
 * * · *   *

Τῷ νῦν χρὴ Λυκίοισι μετὰ πρώτοισιν ἐόντας,
'Εστάμεν, ἠδὲ μάχης καυστειρῆς ἀντιβολῆσαι·
"Οφρα τις, etc.

[b] *Pro socio, Dig.*xvii. 2, 29, § 1 : 'Ita coiri societatem posse ut nullam partem damni alter sentiat lucrum vero commune sit Cassius putat. Quod ita demum valebit, ut et Sabinus scribit si tanti sit opera quanti damnum est plerumque enim tanta est industria socii ut plus societati conferat quam pecunia—item si solus naviget, solus peregrinetur, pericula subest solus.'

· ' Post perfectam venditionem omne commodum et incommodum quod rei venditæ contingit ad emptorem pertinet.'—1 *Cod. de periculo et commodo rei venditæ.*

[c] *Dig.* xviii. 6. 7, § 1.

[d] ' Quum autem,' 3 *Inst. de empt. et vend.* ' By common law, he who has the use of a thing, is bound to repair it.'—LORD MANSFIELD, 2 DOUGLAS, 745.

1. Where the seller had given a guarantee; as in the law, ' Frumenta quæ in herbis erant quum vendidisses—dixisti te si quid vi aut tempestate factum esset præstaturum, ea frumenta nives corruperunt si immoderatæ fuerunt et contra consuetudinem tempestatis agi tecum exempto poterit.'[e]

2. Where the seller is ' in mora.'[f]

3. Where there is any ' dolus' or negligence on his part.[g]

4. When the sale is conditional, and the thing perishes before the condition takes place.[h]

5. When, before the sale is complete, the articles sold are to be weighed, measured, counted, verified, etc.: ' Necessario sciendum et quando perfecta sit emptio tunc enim sciemus cujus periculam sit nam perfectâ emtione periculum ad emtorem respicit—et si id quod venierit, appareat, quid, quale, quantum, sit, et pretium et pure veniit perfecta est emtio.'[i]

A partnership in which all the gain was to be on one side, and all the loss on the other, was unjust: ' Aristo refert, Cassium respondisse societatem talem coiri non posse ut alter lucrum tantum alter damnum sentiret, et hanc societatem leoninam solitum appellare, et nos consentimus talem societatem nullam esse.'[k] In the absence of any particular stipulation, the loss was divided in the same proportion as the profit. So we are told: ' Bonorum possessio commoda et incommoda tribuit.'[l]

If a father make a gift to one of his children, and his circumstances afterwards become so far reduced that the other children do not inherit their ' légitime,' they may reduce the gift so far as will make up their ' légitime': ' Donatio tunc reducitur ad legitimum modum sive ad quantitatem legitimæ ne scilicet legitimarii defraudentur portione suâ in bonis paternis.'[m] The same rule, by parity of reason, applies to the' dos.'[n]

---

[e] *Dig.* xviii. 1. 78, § 3.

[f] *De peric. et com. rei venditæ, Cod.* 4, ' *cum inter.*'

[g] *Inst. ubi supra.*   [h] *Cod. ubi supra.*

[i] *Dig.* xviii. 6. 8, *de per. et com. rei venditæ.*

[k] *Dig.* xvii. 2. 29, § 2.   [l] *Dig.* xxxvii. 1. 1.

[m] *Cod. de Inoffic., Don I. L.* ' Si liquent. l. non convenit.'—CUJACIUS, lib. v. observ. tit. 14.

[n] *L. Unicâ Cod. de Inoff. Dot.*

If a testator leave a thousand pounds to Titius, on condition that Titius shall give a picture to his heir, the testament is cancelled as inofficious by Mævius. It is to Mævius, and not to the heir, that Titius must apply for his legacy: " Quia absurdum est illum commoda hæreditatis habere alium onera sustinere in præstando legato.' °

Hence it was an incontestible maxim in Roman law, ' Portio hæreditaria vacans accrescit cohæredi invito et cum onere.'ᴾ If, then, of two heirs chosen by the testator, one should die before him, or repudiate the inheritance, the other, whether he like it or not, if he accept the portion of the inheritance bequeathed to him, must accept with its inheritance that portion which was bequeathed to the other: ' Tacite ei deficientium partes etiam invito crescunt.'�q And again: ' Tacito jure partes ei accrescunt.'

With regard to estates. From its situation, the lower land receives the water from higher districts by a kind of natural servitude: ' Inferiores agri superioribus naturaliter serviunt.'ʳ But if the soil of the lower land was improved, this was entirely for the benefit of its proprietor: ' Incommodum aquæ defluentis ad eum compensatur pinguedine terræ quæ ad eum decurrit.'ˢ So the holders of land in Egypt were to contribute to the public burdens of mounds, dykes, dams, reservoirs, etc., in proportion to the benefit which they derived from the inundation of the Nile: 'Cui de flumine quid dimminuitur eidem tributi onus decrescat—e contra vero cui alluvione emolumentum adjicitur eidem onus tributi adcrescat.'ᵗ On the same principle, the usufructuary was bound to keep the property of which he reaped the profit in moderate repair:

° *Dig.* xxxvii. 5.15, § 4.

ᴾ *Dig.* xxix. 2. 35, *De acq. vel omitt. Hæred.*; xxix. 2.52, § *Qui ex.*

q Onera realia sequuntur rem quocunque ierit.

ʳ *De aqua, et aqua pluv. arcen.*

ˢ *Dig.* xxix. 3.1, § 1; xxix. 3.1,29, *Denique*: 'Si tamen lex non sit agro dicta agri naturam esse servandam et semper inferiorem superiori servire.' Talbot *v.* Earl of Radnor, 3 My. and K. 252; Messenger *r.* Andrews, 4 RUSSELL, 478.

ᵗ *Si quos Cod. de alluv. et palud.*

' Quoniam igitur omnis fructus rei ad eum pertinet reficere quoque eum ædes per arbitrum cogi Celsus scribit . . . hactenus tamen ut sarta tecta habeat.'ᵘ So with regard to the ' dos,' all the profit of the ' dos' belonged to the husband, in consideration of his supporting the family of which he was the head: ' Omnia quæ fructum nomine continentur ad mariti lucrum pertineant pro tempore matrimonii.'ᵛ And if the ' dos' had been improved, it fell to the widow, as compensation for the enjoyment of it by her husband: ' Augmentum datur in compensatione fructuum dotis quos maritus facit suos.'ˣ So the rule was, that he who was heir was obliged to accept the ' tutela:' to this example women were an exception: ' Quo tutela redit eo hæreditas pervenit nisi cum fœminæ hæredes intercedunt.'ʸ The same doctrine, under Justinian, applied to minors.ᶻ

By a parity of reason it is held, ' Ex quâ persona quis lucrum capit ejus factum præstare debet.' The master for the act of the ' institor,' the ' exercitor navis' for the act of the ' magister,' the hirer for the hireling, the ' publicanus' for the act of the slave.ᵃ So the ' usufructiarius' was bound to pay the taxes, and the ' emphyteuticarius' the ' canonem' or sum at which his property was assessed. So the father and master were bound to make good the act of the son unemancipated and of the slave. This rule, ' Ex quâ,' etc., is, especially according to Gothofred, to be referred to cases in which the interdict, ' Quorum bonorum' (given to the heir or the possessor 'bonorum,' against him who possessed any part of the inheritance ' pro hærede' or ' pro possessore'), and the interdict, ' Quod

---

ᵘ *Dig.* vii. 1. 7, § 2 : ' Si qua tamen vetustatæ corruissent neutrum cogi reficere.' *Ib.*, and again : 'Subsere re cogitur arbores.'

ᵛ *Dig.* xxiii. 3. 7, *de Jure Dotium.*

ˣ 9 *Cod. de rei uxoriâ actione, L. unicâ,* § *Cumque ex.*

ʸ ' ὅπου κληρονομία ἐκεῖ καὶ ἐπιτροπή.'

ᶻ *Inst. de excus. tutorum,* § *Et minores; Inst. curatoribus,* § *Interdum; Inst. de legitimâ aquatorum successione,* § *Penult.*

ᵃ George *v.* Clagett, 7 *T. Reports,* 359 ; Carr *v.* Hinchcliff, 4 B. and C. 359 ; Sims *v.* Bond, 5 B. and AD. 393 ; Waugh *v.* Carver, 2 H. BL. 246 ; SMITH's *Leading Cases.*

legatorum' (given to the heir against the legatee who had taken his legacy without the assent of the heir), were applicable. To the same effect are the rules, ' Quod ipsis qui contraxerunt obstat et successoribus eorum obstabit,' and ' Qui in jus vel dominum alterius succedit eo jure ejus uti debet.'

In the Dean and Chapter of Windsor's case, it was adjudged, ' that the action of covenant did lie, although the lessee had not covenanted for him and his assigns; for such covenant which extends to the support of the thing demised is ' quodammodo' appurtenant to it, and goes with it; and in respect the lessee has taken upon him to bear the charges of reparations: the yearly rent was the less, which goes to the benefit of the assignee, and ' qui sentit commodum sentire debet et onus.' [b]

' If neither case nor covenant is maintainable, the consequence would be, that the plaintiffs, who have been sued, and who have paid large damages for breaches of covenant after they assigned, would have no remedy; and the defendant, although he had the benefit of the estate, would not be bound either to pay rent or perform the covenants.' [c]

' The defendant was to hold the premises, subject not only to the payment of rent, and to perform the covenants. It is true, he entered into no express covenant or contract that he would pay the rent and perform this covenants. . . . If we should hold that no action will lie, the consequence will follow, that a man having taken an estate from another, subject to the payment of rent and performance of covenants, and having thereby induced an undertaking in that other that he would pay the rent and perform the covenants, will be allowed to cast that burden upon another person. Reason and common sense shew

---

[b] Cheetham v. Hampton, 47 Reports, 318; Dean and Chapter of Windsor's Case, 5 Reports, 25, DYER, 136, No. 67; Russell v. Shenton. 3 Q. B. Reports, 429; Tenant v. Goldwin, 1 SALKELD, 21, 360.

[c] Burnett v. Lynch, 5 B. and C. 607; HOLROYD, J. ABBOTT, C. J.; Wolveridge v. Steward, 1 W. and M. 644; Humble v. Langston, 7 MEESON and WELSBY; Tremeere v. Morison, 1 B. and C. 98.

that never could be intended; and if the law of England allowed any such consequence to follow, it would *cease* to be a rule of reason.'[d]

In another case,[e] Lord Ellenborough said, 'The county was bound to repair by the statute of Henry VIII. But here the statute gives power to the company to take and alter the old highway for their own purposes: and if they do not perform the condition, they are not entitled to do the act. . . . When the company thought proper for their own benefit to alter the highway in the bed of the river, so that the public could no longer have the same benefit of the ford, they were bound to give another passage over the bridge, and to keep it for the public.' It is a rule, 'that wherever a grant is made for a valuable consideration which involves public duties and charges, the grant shall be construed so as to make the indemnity coextensive with the burden: ' Qui sentit onus sentire debet et commodum.' In the case of a ferry there is a public charge and duty. The owner must keep a ferry in good repair; . . . he must keep sufficient accommodation for travellers; . . . in return, the law will exclude all injurious competition, and deem every new ferry a nuisance which subtracts from him the ordinary custom and toll.'[f]

If a person take advantage of a contract made by another in his name without authority, he cannot adopt it in part, but

---

[d] Papinian says, ' Non videntur rem amittere quibus propria non fuit.' —This was in 1826. Trial by battle had begun in the court where the judge who said this presided, 1820.

[e] R. *v*. Inhabitants of Kent, 13 EAST, 227. 'So here the power of substituting the new for the old drains was a power conferred upon the undertakers for their own benefit, and therefore the maxim of law will apply, ' Qui sentit commodum sentire debet et onus.'—Priestly *v*. Foulds, 2 SCOTT, *New Reports:* MAULE, J., *ib.* ' A part of the consideration for the act was, that the undertakers should give the landowners a more efficient drainage than they had before.'—Stourbridge Canal Company *v*. Wheeler, 2 B. and ALD. 792.

[f] JUSTICE STORY, Charles River Bridge *v*. Warren Bridge et al.,PETER'S *Supreme Court, Reports*, vol. xi. p. 630 ; COMYN'S *Digest*, vol. v. 363, Piscary B. Ferry.

must take or reject it altogether.[g] ' If you adopt De Baume as
your agent, you must adopt him throughout, and take his agency
cum onere.'[h] So, again, the principle upon which the doctrine
of election in Equity is founded is, that he who adopts a
benefit under an instrument cannot reject that part of it which
is disadvantageous to him;[i] e.g., a man cannot reject a bur-
densome lease and accept an annuity under a will.[k] ' That an
heir to whom an estate is devised in fee may be put to an
election,[l] although, by the rule of law,[m] a devise in fee to an
heir is inoperative, I should have thought perfectly clear,
independent of Lord Cowper's decision; for if the will is in
other respects so framed as to raise a case of election, then not
only is the estate given to the heir under an implied condition
that he shall confirm the whole of the will, but, in contemplation of equity, the testator means, in case the condition shall
not be complied with, to give the disappointed devisees a
benefit out of the estate over which he had a power, corre-
spondent to that of which they are deprived by such non-com-
pliance. So that the devise is read to the heir absolutely if he
confirm the will; if not, then in trust for the disappointed
devisees, as to so much of the estate given to him as shall be
equal in value to the estate intended for them.' Lord Rosslyn
said, ' The principle of these cases of election is very clear.
The application is more frequent here, but it is recognised in

---

[g] 4 TYRWHITT, 486, Burn v. Morris ; SMITH's *Mercantile Law*, by Dowdeswell, p. 137.

[h] Howill v. Pack, 7 EAST, 166 ; BULLER, *N. P.*, 131 ; Billon v. Hyde,
1 ATKYNS.

[i] WHITE and TUDOR, *Leading Cases in Equity*, vol.i. p. 233 ; Streatfield v. Streatfield.

[k] Messenger v. Andrews, 4 RUSSELL, 478 ; Talbot v. Earl Radnor,
3 M. and KEENE, 254 : ' As it was the plain intention of the testator that
his estate should no longer be subject of the leasehold house, the
legatee could not disappoint his intention and retain the benefit given
by his will, but must take the benefit cum onere.'

[l] Welby v. Welby, 2 VESEY and B., 190.

[m] But see 3 and 4 William IV. 106, § 3, which makes the case stronger
against the heir. Blake v. Bunbury, 1 VESEY Junior, 523 ; Noys v. Mor-
daunt, 4 BRO. C. C., 24.

courts of law every day. You cannot act, you cannot come forth to a court of justice, claiming in repugnant right.'[n]

Such is the language of justice, reason, and morality; but it is not the voice of the common law. As Mr. Swanston[o] observes, in one of his admirable notes, fraught with so much deep learning and solid reason, ' In courts of law, the suitor is permitted to assert rights which, so far as the intention of the parties constitutes repugnance, are confessedly repugnant.' This position is abundantly proved by the cases cited in the note, which rest on the principle so worthy of our law, ' that a freehold right shall not be barred by collateral satisfaction.'[p] ' The like assertion of rights morally repugnant,' says Mr. Swanston, ' has been sanctioned in many of the cases in which the courts have overruled a plea of accord and satisfaction;[q] the plaintiff being permitted, on *technical* grounds, to enforce a claim for which *he had* received compensation.' Where was he permitted to perpetrate an act of such oppression and barefaced wickedness? In what cavern of banditti, in what country, smarting under the yoke of what Eastern despot, was such an abomination sanctioned? It was in an English court of justice. And what gave him a power so hideous and shocking to all good men? ' The perfection of reason,' as Lord Coke calls it, ' the English common law.' These were the evils and cruel outrages which Lord Mansfield atoned for his political errors by endeavouring to expunge from our

---

[n] ' The equity of this court is to sequester the estate till satisfaction is made to the disappointed devisee.'—Lady Cavan *v.* Pulteney ; Goodtitle *v.* Bailey, COWPER, 601 ; 2 VESEY Junior, 560.

[o] Gretton *v.* Howard, 1 SWANSTON's *Reports*, p. 426 ; COKE, *Litt.* 366. A case where A. gave lands for the use of B.'s wife for life, in satisfaction of her dower. This is not within the statute, and *she shall have her dower also.*'—4 COKE, 2 B ; WILMOT's *Opinions*, 188. So, if A disseise B. of the manor of Sale, and give B. and his heirs the manor of Dale in compensation for it, which B. *accepts*, yet B. may enter into the manor of Sale, or recover it in a real action.'—4 COKE, 1 B. Can any pleader imagine worse injustice ?

[p] COKE, *Litt.*, 3 b ; *Doctrina Placitandi*, 17.

[q] Peyton's Case, *Reports*, 9, 77 ; Grymes *v.* Blofield, CROKE, Eliz. 541 ; COKE, *Litt.*, 212.

law, by which he earned a lasting title to the gratitude of his
country, and the hatred of all who admire special pleading
and a different rule of law for the same case in different courts
of Westminster Hall.

XXVII.

B ONA fides tantumdem possidenti præstat quantum
veritas, quoties lex impedimento non est.—
PAULUS.[r]

*Good faith gives the possessor the same rights as a valid
title, where the law has not otherwise provided.*

It is one of the most difficult tasks of jurisprudence to
provide for the difficulties that beset the cases to which this
rule applies. The Roman law refused to the 'bonâ fide' possessor the title of proprietor. But it was due to his good faith
that he should be allowed to enjoy many of the privileges
belonging to such a person. ' Quia licet dominus non sit
attamen se putat dominum justâ de causâ.' For this purpose
the law supposed him to be the proprietor, for the fictions of
Roman law, unlike those which were the disgrace of our
fathers, and will be the amazement of their posterity, amounted
in fact—except where they were designed to mitigate the
harshness of extreme cases in law, and to promote the happiness of individuals in the case of adoption, &c.—to no more

---

[r] Civil Code of Louisiana, 3391, 3393, 3399, 3411; 3 BOUVERIE'S
Institutes, 2640.

This must be coupled with the maxim 'non videtur possessionem
adeptus qui ita nactus est ut eam retinere non potest,' de acq. poss.,
as to what is 'bona fides.'—*Dig.* 1. '*non videtur.*' Hildreth *v.* Sands,
2 JOHNS' *Ch. Reps.* p. 43 ; Beatle *v.* Guernsey, 8 JOHNS' *Reps.* 446 (sale
void made to defeat execution though full price was paid); WINGATE'S
Maxims, 37 ; Stone *v.* Grubham, 2 BULSTRODE, 225, 2 VESEY, Jun., 292,
LORD COKE ; Codwise *v.* Sands, 4 JOHNS' *Reps.* 586.

'Fictiones locum habent in his quæ sunt juris civilis ut in post-
liminio . . . . sed ea quæ sunt facti seu juris naturalis fictionem non
receperint.'—*Alteserræ opera,* vol. vi., cap. 3, p. 3. What would he say
to a fiction which dated laws sometimes months, and always several
weeks before they had been enacted.

than this, that a suitor should be supposed to possess those rights and qualities which it would be dishonest in his adversary to deny.[s] A directly opposite principle appears to have governed the fictions at length exploded of the English law.[t] The Roman maxim is thus expressed in one place, ' Fictio in casu ficto idem operatur quod veritas in vero.'[u]

Therefore the possessor ' bonæ fidei ' might have recourse to the same actions, and avail himself of the same exceptions as the real owner against all wrong doers. In that respect their condition was alike, so if he was turned out of possession he might recover it by means of a real action, which had the same effect as the 'revendicatio,' and was given him by the prætor against all but the real owner of the property of which he had been deprived by a merely wrongful act. So, if he was disturbed in his possession, he might oppose his title as a sufficient bar against all others besides the lawful owner. This was one of the most refined parts of the noble and wise system we are now considering, and one which offered an impregnable barrier to the machinations of chicane.[x] So the pignus and hypotheca given by the ' bonâ fide ' possessor for the security of his creditor were valid. ' Si ab eo qui Publicianâ uti poterit quia dominium non habuit, pignori accessi; sic tuetur me per Servianam prætor, quemadmodum debitorem per Publicianam.'[y] Moreover, the produce and fruits which he gathered and consumed during his ' bonæ fidei ' possession were lawfully his,[z]—' Bonæ fidei possessor fructus industriales

---

[s] 'Fictio non admittit presumptionem contrariam.'—*Alteserræ op.* vol. vi., cap. 4, p. 5, 'De Fictionibus Juris.'

[t] 'The meaning of confessing lease entry and ouster is to bring the matter to the mere question of the defendant's possessing title.'—LORD MANSFIELD, Oates *v.* Brydon, 1894; BURROW, vol. iii.

[u] See the whole chapter 'de Publicianâ in rem actione.'—*Dig.* vi. 2.

[x] LORD HARDWICKE has enumerated the frauds in which equity will give relief, 2 VESEY, 155. MALLEVILLE'S *Analyse de la discussion sur le code civil.'* 1 FONBLANQUE'S *Treatise on Equity,* 122, notes.

[y] *Dig.* xx. 1. 18.

[z] 'Fructus percipiendo uxor vel rei ex re donatâ (that is, an invalid gift) suos facit illos tantum quos suis operis acquisierit veluti serendo— nam si pomum decerpserit vel ex silvâ ceciderit non fit, sicut nec

consumptos lucratur pro, culturâ et curâ.' And again, ' Post
litem contestatam etiam fructus venient in hoc judicio nam et
culpa et dolus exinde præstantur—sed ante judicium percepti
non omni modo in hoc judicium (finium regum donum)
venient aut enim bonâ fide percepit, et lucrari eum oportet
si eos consumsit—aut malâ fide et condici oportet.'[a] Rent,
freight, the services of slaves and cattle were placed in the
same category. 'Mercedes plane a colonis acceptæ loco sunt
fructuum—opere quoque servorum . . . . . . item vecturæ
navium et jumentorum.'[b] There were, however, cases where
the law refused these privileges. On the subject of prescription Pomponius remarks, ' Ubi lex inhibet usucapionem
bona fides possidenti nihil prodest.' So some things were
considered imprescriptible. ' Aliquando[c] etiam si maxime quis
bonâ fide rem possederet non tamen illi usucapio ullo tempore
procedit,' say the institutes.[d] Among these things were the
goods of a pupil. ' Dotal' property—the property of him who
was absent on public service—the right of the debtor to
redeem his pledge;[e] things with regard to which the maxim
applied ' adversus non valentem agere non ausit præscriptio.
Things that were stolen—' res fisci ' ' res sacræ,'[f] sanctæ, publicæ, populi Romani et civitatum—to which when Chris-

---

cujuslibet bonæ fidei possessoris, quia non ex facto ejus, is fructus
nascitur.'—*Dig.* xxii. 45. But generally the rule is, 'Bonæ fidei emptor
non dubie percipiendo fructus etiam ex re alienâ suos interim facit non
tantum eos qui diligentiâ et operâ ejus pervenerunt sed omnes ; quia
quod ad fructus attinet loco domini pene est.'—*Dig.* xli. 1. 48. This
rule is stated and explained *Dig.* xxii. 1. 25, § 1, 'in alieno fundo quem
Titius bonâ fide mercatus fuerat frumentum sevit,' &c. See *Dig.* 'de
religiosis,' 2. § 1.

[a] *Dig.* x. 1. 4. 2.

[b] *Dig.* v. 3. 29.

[c] *Dig.* xli. 3. 24.

[d] § 'Sed aliquando Inst. de Usucap. et longi temp.

[e] So the 'Manilia Lex' made the space of five feet on the limits of
' estates imprescriptible.'

[f] *Dig.* xli. 3. 9. For an instance where the situation of the 'bonæ
fidei' possessor was better than that of the real owner, see *Dig. aq.
et aq. pluv. ar.* xxxix. 7. § 1.

tianity became the religion of the empire, property dedicated
to the Church and monasteries, was, for a time, added.

It is the maxim of our law that every person in possession has
a good title until the contrary is proved. This rule, which properly qualified, is just, has by the coarse and indiscriminate manner in which it has been applied, occasioned much litigation.
The Roman law, as we have seen, would not acknowledge all
kinds of possession. If even the rightful owner had obtained
possession by violence or fraud, the Roman law would not allow
him to gain any benefit by his tortious act, but obliged him to
replace the person, whom he had displaced, in his original
situation, before it proceeded to examine the question of right.
Our law, abounding in mischievous subtleties, was guiltless of
such refinement.[g] Possession gave a right, no matter how it
was acquired, and the protection of the maxim that the plaintiff
in ejectment was to recover, by the strength of his own title
and not by the weakness of that of his adversary, operated in
cases where, the first act of the prætor would have been
to make the plaintiff and defendant change places, and to
give the former the protection which a fraudulent or violent
act under our law afforded to the latter. To this must be
added the doctrine arising from the judicious civil war perpetuated in our courts, that no equitable title could avail in a
court of law.[h] Lord Mansfield, foully slandered by Junius for
the avowed reason that he was acquainted with Roman law,
endeavoured to change this barbarous anomaly.[i] But this
voice of reason was soon stifled, ' and it was a fixed principle
that a trustee (who has no right, and in whom the attempt is
infamous) may maintain ejectment against his own ' cestui-

---

[g] The Code of Louisiana distinguishes between the cases where
possession is changed, with and without the consent of the possessor.
A possessor of an estate loses possession against his consent when
another expels him from it, or *succeeds in usurping* possession during
his absence and preventing him from re-entering.

[h] Doe *v.* Pott, DOUGLAS, 721.

[i] Keech *v.* Hall, 1 DOUGLAS' *Reps.* 21 ; Moss *v.* Gallimore, 1 DOUGLAS'
Reps. 279 ; Lade *v.* Holford, 3 BURROW, 1416.

que' trust (who has a perfect right), and that an unsatisfied term in trustees would bar the heir-at-law, even though he claimed subject to the charge. Such a state of things prevailed against Lord Mansfield's declaration 'that the trust estate shall not be set up in an ejectment to defeat the trust.'[k] 'Though,[l] in general, it is only from the owner of goods that any property in them can be derived, yet, in some cases, they may be effectually purchased from a vendor who has himself no title; and, therefore, the rule of law is that all sales and contracts of anything vendible in markets overt, or fairs, shall not only be good between the parties, but binding on all those that have any right or property therein.' 'But if my goods are stolen or wrongfully taken from me, and sold out of market overt, my property is not altered, and I may take them wherever I find them.'[m] The liabilities of owner, as distinct from those of occupier, are discussed in the cases in the note.[n] 'By common law,' said Lord Mansfield, 'he who has the use of a thing is bound to repair it.'[o]

XXVIII.[p]

CONTRACTUS quidam dolum malum duntaxat recipiunt quidam dolum et culpam dolum tantum, depositum et precarium. Dolum et culpam, mandatum commodatum venditum, pignori acceptum, locatum, item dotis datio, tutelæ, negotia gesta in his quidem et diligentiam. Societas et rerum communis

---

[k] On this point see SUGDEN's *Concise View, etc.*, pp. 355 ,489, 490 ; *Blackstone's Comm.* by STEPHEN, vol. ii. p. 67.

[l] An exception has, as usual, been introduced inconsistent with the rule, 7 and 8 Geo. 4. c. 29. COMYN's *Digest Market E.* 5 *Reps.* 83.

[m] Pawnbrokers act, 39 and 40 Geo. 3. c. 99 (of course) amended 9 and 10 Vict. c. 98. Peer *v.* Humphrey, 2 AD. and ELLIS, 495.

[n] Brent *v.* Haddon, 7 MEESON AND WELSBY, 456 ; Rex. *v.* Kerrison, 1 M. and S., 435, Lord Ellenborough objected strongly to the words 'owner and occupier' in an indictment ; Payne *v.* Rogers, 2 H. Bl. ; Rex. *v.* Sutton, 3 AD. and ELLIS.

[o] Taylor *v.* Whitehead, 2 DOUGLAS, 745.

[p] LOCRÉ, vol. xii. p. 18.

et dolum et culpam recipit—sed hæc ita si nisi quid
nominatim convenit—legem enim contractus dedit,
excepto eo quod celsus putat non valere convenerit
ne dolus præstetur hoc enim bonæ fidei judicio contrarium est et ita utimur, animalium vero casus,
mortes quæ[n] sine culpâ accedunt fugæ servorum qui
custodiri non solent, rapinæ, tumultus, incendia,
aquarum magnitudines, impetus prædonum, a nullo
præstantur.—ULPIAN.

*In every contract, 'dolus malus' makes the person
guilty of it responsible. So in some contracts does
the 'culpa.' 'Casus fortuitus' never.*

This a law of Ulpian,[o] who more perhaps than any other
of the Roman jurists, whose works have been transmitted to
us, devoted his time and labours to questions concerning the
liabilities of parties to contracts. This law is taken from the

---

[n] This is clearly the correct reading, though the common reading
is 'quæque'; but the Greek paraphase is—Καὶ τὴν χωρὶς ῥαθυμίας
θάνατον.

Dig. Com. v. § 2 : 'In contractibus in quibus utriusque utilitas versatur . . . et dolus et culpa præstatur.'

Dig. xxx. 108, § 12 : 'In contractibus bonæ fidei servatur ut si quidem utriusque commodum versetur etiam culpa—sive unius solius
dolus malus tantummodo præstetur.'

[o] The law (*Dig.* xlvii. 2. 12) is taken from ULPIAN's *Commentary* :
'Itaque fullo qui curanda polienda vestimenta accepit semper agit;
præstare enim custodiam debet;' as is the other law, *ib.* xlvii. 2. 14 : 'Eum
qui emit si non tradita est ei res furti actionem non habere sedad huc
venditoris esse actionem celsus scripsit—mandare eum plane oportebit
emtori furti actionem et condictionem et vindicationem ; et si quid ex
his actionibus fuerit consecutus, id præstare eum emptori oportebit.'
Besides others from his *Commentary on the Edict, Dig.* xlvii. 2, § 5, 2
to § 11. *Donellus Commentar jur. civ.,* lib. xvi. c. 6, 7. The learned
treatise of HASSE, *Die Culpa des Römischen Rechts,* Kiel, 1815.
Zeits. für Gesch. W. 4, No. 5. *Essai sur la Prestation des Fautes,* LE
BRUN, Paris, 1813. ELVERS, *Doctrinæ jur. civ. über die Culpa Lineamenta.*
Jones On Bailments, THEOBALD's Edition. MÜHLENBRUCH, *Doctrina
Pandect,* 352. STORY *On Bailments. Code,* Art. 1148.

29th book of his *Commentary on Sabinus*. Herein he treated among other topics, ' De præstationibus in contractu empti venditi;' when he takes occasion to discuss the liabilities of those who have in their custody property belonging to another, ' aliquo eorum periculo.'[p] In the same work he treated of the question when a ' furti actio' might be brought by those who hold transient possession of another's property; and after laying down the rule that every one had a right to the ' furti actionem,' who had an interest in preventing a theft of the property, he fortifies his doctrine by examples.[q] And in the 14th law of the same chapter, which consists of eighteen paragraphs, he enters into a minute examination of the sub-ject, discussing separately almost every contract falling under the rule which applies when the chattel of another is in our possession and of value to us. He considers the ' depositum,' par. 3 and 4; the ' precarium,' 11; the ' mandatum,' § 9, 17; the ' commodatum,' 8, 10, 14, 15, 16; ' de venditione' at the be-ginning, etc., § 1; ' de Pignore accepto,' § 5, 6, 7, 16; ' de locato,' § 12, 16. So there may be added the ' colonus,' 2; the ' right of the commodator on the death of the bailee,' etc., § 17; the ' interest in an intercepted letter.' All these explanations contri-bute materially to a right understanding of the text. The sub-ject matter of the law relates to contracts, and contracts ' bonæ fidei,' ' quibus,' in the words of Cicero, ' vitæ societas contine-tur,' under the word ' contractuum.' Ulpian[r] includes every sort of obligation and ' quasi contractus,' as ' tutela negotia gesta, rerum communionem.' Another division of the contracts

---

[p] *Dig.* xlvii. 2. 14, § 16 : ' Qualis ergo furti actio detur ei cui res com-modata est quæsitum est et puto omnibus quorum periculo res alienæ sunt,' etc.

[q] *Dig.* xlvii. 2. 29 : ' Cujus interfuit non subripi is actionem furti habet.' Compare this concise and complete rule with a sentence in our Acts of Parliament, or a sentence from Meeson and Welsby. Again: Quis ergo furti aget ? is cujus interfuit cum non subripi [in the case of the letter] id est ad cujus utilitatem pertinebant ea quæ scripta sunt.' *Dig.* xlvii. 2. 14, § 17.

[r] ' Omnem obligationem pro contractu habendam existimandum est, ut ubicunque aliquis obligatur et contrahi videatur.'—PAULUS, *Dig.* v. 1. 20.

mentioned, is with reference to the persons making them. Some
contracts are exclusively for the benefit of him who gives;
others for that of him who receives; some are for the benefit of
both. Another division turns upon the purpose for which the
property of another is in our possession. This may be:—

1. For the sake of safe keeping; as in the case of the
' depositum,' or where the thing sold, after the sale is complete,
remains in the care of the seller.[s]

2. For the sake of the use, or the ' usufruct'; as in the case
of the ' precarium—commodatum—locatum—dotis datio.'

3. For our own security; as in the case of a pledge.

4. For the sake of management and administration; as in
the instances of the ' mandatum susceptum,' ' tutela,' the ' negotiorum gestio.'

5. For community and partnership; as ' societas,' and ' rerum communio.'

Such are the causes, titles, or motives which may give us an
interest in the property of another.

The rule tells us that certain contracts imply certain obligations—' præstationem aliquam recipere.' The question to be
settled is, How far and in what respects is the possessor of
another man's chattel liable to the owner, from the nature of
the contract made? This is the limit of the inquiry, for there
is no question put as to the liability of the owner himself to
the person having the care or custody of his property; and
the question is as to the obligation imposed on the possessor
from the nature of the contract.—φυσικῶς πρέποντα, in the
words of the Greek paraphrase—as to the requisite amount of
diligence, and the circumstances which are followed by loss or
risk to the contracting party. Ulpian's word is ' præstare,'[t]

---

[s] *Si vestimenta—depositi* ii. 1.

[t] I have a great respect for Mühlenbruch ; he is a careful and learned
writer. But as I think Cicero (and indeed Bossuet and Montesquieu)
knew more about Roman History than Niebuhr, so I prefer Ulpian's
exposition of the Roman law to that of Hasse ; and when Mühlenbruch
seeks shelter in what he calls the rhetorical amplification of men, who

to make good, which is employed by the Roman jurists, and
by Cicero,[u] to express the liability of any one to repair or to
compensate the loss sustained in consequence of any neglect
on his part, by the owner of the chattel, hence the word
'præstationes,'[x] used in the passage cited in the note, and by
Papinian (*Dig.* xxii. tit. 1, § 5). Certain 'præstationes' were
were inherent in the nature of every contract;[y] 'recipere,'
the word used in the text, means 'to exact,' or 'to
admit,' from its nature, and is appropriated to this sense
by the civilians;[z] and so is 'periculum,' in the sense that a
thing is at our risk—the cause which exposes us to the chance
of loss.[a]

Ulpian proceeds to point out the nature, extent, number,
and degrees of these 'præstationes,' or responsibilities, and he
enumerates finally three kinds, 'ob culpam admissam,' having,
at the outset of the law, stated only two. 'Some contracts,'
he says, 'make the possessor responsible for 'dolus malus' only;
others make him responsible for 'dolum et culpam.' In the
course of the law he states a third ingredient, which the possessor is bound to make good, *i.e.*, 'diligentiam'; and in
the same commentary on Sabinus, cited *Dig.* xxx. 47. 5, *de
legatis*, he says, speaking of the liability of the heir—'Culpa
autem qualiter sit æstimanda videamus, an non solum ea quæ
dolo proxima sit verum etiam quæ levis est, an numquid et
diligentia quoque exigenda est'; and Paulus enumerates also
the 'dolus, culpa, et diligentia.' 'In rebus dotalibus virum
præstare oportet tam dolum quam culpam . . . sed etiam

---

wrote with the elegance of refined critics, and the precision of mathe-
maticians, never using a word in vain, he shews, I think, the weakness of his cause. 'Amplificationem quandam orationis extollendæ
gratiâ ab Ulpiano usurpatam,' are the expressions of Mühlenbruch to
which I allude, § 354.

[u] *De Officiis*, 3. Quintus quidem Scævola.

[x] *Dig.*1. 17. 152, § 3: 'In contractibus quibus doli præstatio inest,
hæres in solidum tenetur.'

[y] *Dig.* xix. 1. 11. 1.

[z] 'Actus legitimi qui diem vel conditionem recipiunt.'

[a] *Dig.*1. 17. 77.

diligentiam præstabit quam in rebus suis exhibet'.[b] — *Dig.* xxiii. 3. 17.

'Dolus,' or 'dolus malus,' then, differs from 'culpa': the former implying intention; the latter, want of due care and foresight. Papinian (*Dig.* xli. 1. 52, § 1) uses the words 'fraus vel nequitia,' to denote both.[c] 'Culpa,' as opposed to 'dolus,' is described by Gaius (*Dig.* xvii. 2, 72) — 'Socius socio culpæ nomine tenetur id est desidiæ atque negligentiæ. Culpa autem non ad exactissimam diligentiam dirigenda est: sufficit et enim talem diligentiam communibus rebus adhibere qualem suis rebus adhibere solet.' Thus 'culpa' is throughout distinguished from 'dolus.' In spite of the various dissertations by which German writers, abusing the leisure afforded to them by servitude, have darkened a subject tolerably clear in itself, I agree with the old interpreters, that there are three degrees of 'diligentia'—

1st. The 'diligentia communis omnium hominum' (*Dig.* l. 16. 213). 'Lata culpa est nimia negligentia, id est, non intelligere, quod omnes intelligunt.'[d] 'Negligentia crassa' (*Dig.* xxii. 6. 6).[e] 'Dissoluta negligentia,' which 'prope dolus est' (*Dig.* xvii. 1. 29),[f] in some instances 'dolus'

---

[b] *Dig.* xlvii. 9. 11 : 'Si fortuito incendium factum sit venia indiget, nisi tam lata culpa fuit ut luxuriâ aut dolo sit proxima.'

[c] It is the case of guardians neglecting to obtain compensation from the goods of an insolvent surety. 'Fraus vel nequitia tutoribus qui persequi judicatum potuerunt damnum dabit.'

[d] 'Lata culpa' (xvii. 8. 10), where the agent ordered to make a purchase, '*dolo* emere neglexit, aut si *latâ culpâ* . . . . tenebitur.'

[e] 'Nec supina ignorantia ferenda est factum ignorantis.' An instance is given (*Dig.* xiv. 3. 11, § 3 ; xxvi. 7. 7, § 2), 'competet adversus tutores actio tutelæ, si male contraxerint : hoc est si prædia comparaverint non idonea, per sordes, aut gratiam.' Other examples are—a man who sets fire to his weeds in a high wind, in consequence of which his neighbour's crops are burnt (*Dig. ad leg. Aquiliam*, 30) ; of the master of a ship, who trusts her to a current without a pilot—'et tempestate ortâ temperare non potuerit, et navem perdiderit.'—*Dig. Locati Conducti* (xix. 2. 13, § 2).

[f] *Dig.* xxxvi. 1. 22, § 3 : 'In dolo proxima.'

(*Dig.* xvi. 3. 32). 'Quod Nerva diceret latiorem culpam dolum esse, Proculo displicebat, mihi verissimum videbatur.'— *Celsus.*

2nd. The 'diligentia' which you employ in your own affairs, and which you ought to give to the property of another entrusted to you. Opposed to this is the 'culpa levis.' [g] 'Non tantum dolum sed et culpam [h] in re hæreditariâ præstare debet cohæres,[i] quoniam cum cohærede non contrahimus sed incidimus in eum—non tamen diligentiam præstare debet qualem diligens paterfamilias . . . . . . talem igitur diligentiam præstare debet qualem in rebus suis.'—*Dig.* x. 2. 25, § 16.[k]

3rd. The last and highest degree of diligence is that beyond the 'communis omnium hominum diligentia'—beyond the 'diligentia propria contrahentis'—a more exact and vigilant care than a reasonable man always exerts in his own affairs. Such was the diligence required from the borrower without interest, and from the seller who retained possession of the goods sold—'Custodiam autem venditor talem præstare debet, quam præstant in quibus res commodata est, ut diligentiam præstet exactiorem quam in suis rebus adhiberet.' To this is opposed 'levissima culpa,' an expression that occurs only once in the fragments of which the Pandects are composed. It is the want of the care of a 'diligens paterfamilias.' 'Culpa autem,' says Ulpian, 'qualiter sit æstimanda videamus an non solum ea quæ dolo proxima sit, verum quæ levis est— an numquid et diligentia quoque exigenda est ab hærede; quod

---

[g] 'Rebus suis consueta negligentia.'—*Ib.*

[h] 'Culpa,' used alone, means 'levis culpa.'

[i] That is, it is no choice of ours that such a person is our 'cohæres,' and, therefore, he is bound to exercise more diligence than a person selected by ourselves. 'Quia qui parum diligentem socium sibi acquirit de sequeri debet.'—*Dig.* xvii. 2. 72.

[k] I cannot help quoting the remarks of Heraldus on this very point, as not quite inapplicable to the German writers, and as very applicable to many discussions in our books—'Qui sint casus fortuiti quærunt doctores et male explicant de quibus neque quid sint quæreret neque interrogatus male responderet Bubulcus.'—*Animadv. in Sat,* 15 c, vol.i.

et verius est' (*Dig.* xxx. 1. 47, § 5). So Gaius (xliv. 7. 1, § 4). ' Is vero qui utendum accepit si majore casu cui humana infirmitas resistere non potest velut incendio, ruinâ, naufragio, rem quam accepit amiserit, securus est alias tamen exactissimam diligentiam custodiendæ rei præstare compellitur nec sufficit ei eandem diligentiam adhibere quam suis rebus adhibet—si alius diligentior custodire poterit.' [1]

It now remains to consider the twelve contracts mentioned by Ulpian. They may be divided into three classes. In one class the contracting party is responsible for the ' dolus' only. This class includes the ' depositum'[m] and 'precarium.'[n] In the second he is responsible for the ' dolus culpa ' and the want of 'diligentia.' This includes the ' mandatum,'[o] ' commodatum,'[p] ' venditum,'[q] ' pignori acceptum,'[r] ' locatum,'[s] ' dotis datio,'[t] ' tutelæ,'[u] ' negotia gesta.'[v] The third class makes the person

---

[1] 'In lege Aquiliâ et levissimam culpam venire."—*Ad leg. Aquiliam.* ἀκριβεστάτην καὶ ὑπερβάλλουσαι παραφυλακὴν.—THEOPHILUS.

[m] 'Depositum' (*Dig.* xvi. 3), and the § *Papinianus*, xix. 5. 17, § 2.

[n] 'Precarium est,' *Dig.* xliii. 26 : 'quod precibus petenti utendum conceditur quamdiu is, qui concessit, patitur.'

[o] 'Mandatum,' *Dig.* xvii. 1 ; 'Mandatum,' xvii. 1. 8.

[p] 'Commodatum,' *Dig.* xiii. 6. 2.

[q] 'Venditum,' when the seller remains in possession of the thing sold. *Dig.* xviii. 6 : 'De periculo et commodo rei venditæ.' xviii. 6. 3 : 'Custodiam autem venditor talem præstare debet, quam præstant hi quibus res commodata est; ut diligentiam præstet exactiorem, quam in suis rebus adhiberet.'

[r] 'Pignori acceptum.'—*Dig.* xiii. 6. 5, § 52. *Cod. de Pignoribus*, 1. 5. 6. 7. 19 ; *Inst. quibus modis re contrahitur obligatio*, § 5. *Dig.* xiii. 7. 13, § 2, *de Pignor. act.*: ' Venit autem in hâc actione et dolus et culpa ut in commodato, venit et custodia, vis major non venit.' 'Vis major quam Græci (Θεοῦ Βίαν) id est vim divinam appellant.'

[s] 'Locatum.' *Dig.* xix. 2. 25, § 7 : 'Culpa abest si omnia facta sunt quæ diligentissimus quisque observaturus fuisset.'

[t] *Dig.* xiii. 6. 5, § 2 ; xxiii. 3. 1. The word 'contrahitur' is used.— *Ib.* 1. 17, *In rebus.* *Dig.* xxiv. 3 ; xxv. 1 : 'Soluto matrimonio dos quem admodum petatur.'

[u] *Dig.* xxvii. 3. 18 : ' Tutelæ.'

[v] 'Negotia gesta.' *Dig.* iii. 5. 11 : ' Si negotia absentis et ignorantis geras ; et culpam et dolum præstare debes : sed Proculus interdum etiam casum præstare debere.'

contracting liable for the ‘dolus’ and ‘culpa.’   This includes
the ‘societas’[x] and ‘rerum communio.’[y]

The second part of this law relates to special agreements,
and to those accidents for which no man is responsible.   The
part we have hitherto considered relates to those obligations
which flow from the very nature of the contracts themselves,
without any positive stipulation.   ‘Hæc ita,’ says the rule,
‘nisi quid nominatim convenit.’   A person may, by an express
contract, make himself liable for the ‘culpa’ and ‘diligentia,’
where the nature of the contract would bind him for the
‘dolus’ only; or he may limit his responsibility to the ‘dolus,’
where, by the nature of the contract, he would be liable only
for the ‘dolus.’   But a contract that exonerated either of the
parties from the consequences of the ‘dolus,’ was immoral—
against the ‘jus publicum’—and, therefore, invalid.   ‘Illud
non est probandum dolum non esse præstandum, si convenerit;
nam hæc conventio contra bonam fidem contraque bonos mores
est, et ideo nec sequenda est.’[z]   In other respects, the special
agreement of the parties was the law of the contract, ‘pacta
legem contractui dant’ (*Dig.* ii. 14. 7).   ‘Nothing,’ says
Ulpian (*Dig.* xix. i. § 11), ‘is more conformable to good
faith than to maintain the obligations entered into by those
who have made the contract; but in the absence of any such
agreement, ‘ea præstabuntur quæ naturaliter insunt hujus
judicii potestate.’—*Dig.* xix. 1. 11.

To this rule, however, the ‘dotis datio’ was an exception,
as an agreement that the husband should be responsible for the

---

[x] ‘Pro socio societas.’   *Dig.* xvii. 2, 63, § 8 : ‘Voluntaria societas.
‘Voluntarium consortium.’—xvii. 2. 52. 8. PAPINIAN.

[y] ‘Communio rerum.’   ‘Societas involuntaria’ made ‘re’ not ‘consensum.’   *Dig.* x. 2. 25, § 16 : ‘Non tantum dolum sed et culpam in re
hæreditariâ præstare debet cohæres, quoniam cum cohærede non contrahimus sed incidimus in eum, non tamen diligentiam præstare debet
qualem diligens pater familias . . . . talem igitur diligentiam præstare
debet qualem in rebus suis.   Eadem sunt si duobus res legata sit ;
nam et hos conjunxit ad societatem non consensus sed res.’

[z] *Dig.* xvi. 3. 1, § 7.

'dolus' only was invalid. 'Pomponius ait maritum non posse
pacisci ut dolum solummodo in dotem præstet, videlicet propter
utilitatem nubentium.'[a]

The last head of this rule relates to accidents 'casus fortuiti,'
which 'a nullo præstantur.' Seven are enumerated; but the
person cannot rely on one of these 'casus fortuiti' for his
defence who has contributed to them through his own negligence—'sed ita scilicet hoc dici potest si ipsa ruina vel incendium sine vitio ejus acciderit.' The case put in the law by
Gaius is that of a 'negotiorum gestor,' who has provided all
that was requisite for the safety of what was entrusted to him,
which is afterwards destroyed by fire, or some other form of
destruction. So if the guardian,[b] instead of selling the property of his ward, or depositing it in a proper place, suffers it
to remain in his own house, which house is burnt down, he
must bear the loss himself. So the 'commodatarius' was
liable, if the accident happened through his negligence. So
'is qui utendum accepit si majore casu cui humana infirmitas
resistere non potest veluti incendio ruinâ naufragio rem quam
accepit amiserit, securus est . . . . sed et in majoribus casibus
si culpa ejus interveniat tenetur.'—*Dig.* xliv. 7. 1, § 4.

1. The 'tumultus'; 2, the 'incendia'; and 3, the 'impetus
prædonum,' are those among the casualties stated which are
most interesting to an English jurist. The 'incendium' mentioned in the text must be a fire caused by the act of strangers.
Where the 'colonus' bargained to give back the villa 'incor-
ruptam præter vim et vetustatem,' and it was burnt down by
the slave of the 'colonus,' it was held that the 'colonus' was
responsible for the accident. 'Non videri eam vim exceptam,
respondit sed extrariam vim utrosque excipere voluisse.'

The leading case on this subject in English law, is Coggs
v. Bernard.[c] The English law holds that a gratuitous agent

---

[a] *Dig.* xxii. 4. 5.

[b] *De peric. tut.*, § 3.

[c] *Doctor and Student*, Dialogue, 38 ; Writ ' de Pipâ vini carriendâ,'
Reg. Origin, 110, Jones, p. 59 ; Miles *v.* Cattle, 6 BINGHAM, 743.

is responsible for gross negligence—' lata culpa'; that where
the bailment is solely for the benefit of the bailee, he is bound
to the very strictest diligence; that, in short, he is responsible
for the ' levissima culpa.' That where the bailment is for the
benefit both of the bailor and bailee, an ordinary degree of
diligence only is expected from the latter. Lord Stowell gives
this instance of gross negligence: ' If I send a servant to a
banker, and he carries it with proper care, he would not be
answerable for the loss though his pockets were picked in the
way. But if instead of carrying it in a proper manner and
with ordinary caution, he should carry it openly in his hand,
thereby exposing valuable property, so as to invite the snatch
of any person he might meet in the crowded population of this
town he would be liable, because he would be guilty of the
' negligentia malitiosa' in doing that, from which, the law
must infer, he intended that which has actually taken place.'[d]

Bailment.—BACON'S *Abridgment* ; 2 LORD RAYMOND ; SMITH'S *Leading Cases,* ED. KEATING and WILLES, 82.

Pawnbrokers.—Nickesson v. Trotter, 3 M. and W, 130 ; Wallen v.
Smith, 5 B. and ALD. ; BRACTON, 99, *ab cit.* Coggs v. Bernard.

Bailee for Hire.—Leck v. Mertaer, 1 CAMPBELL, 138 ; Wood v. Curling, 15 M. and WELSBY, 626 ; 16 *ib.* ; Clarke v. Earnshaw, 1 GOWER, 30.

Innkeepers.—Calye's Case ; SMITH'S *Leading Cases,* and notes.

Carriers for Hire.—Palacer v. Grand Junction Canal Company, 4 M.
and W., 149 ; Pickford v. Grand Junction Railway Company, 10 M. and
W., 399 ; 8 M. and W., 373 ; Parker v. Great Western Railway Company,
7 SCOTT, *N. Reps.,* 835.

Walker v. Jackson, 10 M. and W., 179 ; Hinton v. Dibbin, 2 Q. B. ;
646 ; STORY, p. 87, comments with just severity on the English
law, as laid down with regard to depositaries, in Holiday v. Camsell,
1 *T. Reps.,* 685.

[d] *The Rendsberg* 6 ROB. *Adm. Reps.* ; MERLIN, *Repertoire Bail.* ;
POTHIER, *Contrât de Depôt,* 27, § 29 ; *Prêt à usage,* 31. 33. 73. 74 ;
Code of Louisiana, 2908, 2909 ; *Code Napoléon,* 1937, 1939 ; STORY,
Comment on Bailment, 93 ; KENT, *Comment. Sec.* 40.

Booth v. Wilson, 1 BARN. and ALD, 59. It was held gross negligence
in a gratuitous bailee, to put a horse into a pasture where there was
danger. Batson v. Donavon, 4 B. and ALD., 21 ; *American Jurist,* Jan.,
1839.

Kemp v. Coughtry, 11 JOHNSON'S *Reports,* p. 108 : ' It is no longer to
be questioned, that owners of vessels, employed in the transportation

' Every man,' says the same great judge, ' who undertakes a commission, undertakes all that belongs to the prudent and honest execution of that commission. Then the question comes, what is a prudent and honest execution of that commission? . . . The commissioner must provide a competent number of persons to guard the property; and having so done, he has discharged his responsibility, unless he can be affected with fraud or negligence, amounting in legal understanding to fraud. If he knowingly takes a master and crew dishonest or negligent, that is ' dolus' or ' negligentia dolo proxima'; if losses happen in consequence, he may become answerable, because he has not executed his trust; he becomes answerable in that case for his own wrong doings, and not for that of others, against which he has used honest and reasonable caution.'

In another part of the same judgment, he translates the very words of the Roman law. ' A common carrier, or a master of a barge, is answerable for embezzlement and robbery; but the case of such persons constitutes an exception to the general rule, founded in necessity, and confined to persons carrying for hire in their general occupation. Being a person unknown to his employers, and not employed in special confidence, the public conductor, ' rerum vehendarum,' is to be liable for all risks, otherwise there would be no possibility of guarding against combinations between this unknown person and others with whom he might collude. ' I agree,' said the judge, in Tracy v. Wood,[e] ' to the law as laid down at the bar, that in cases of bailees without reward, they are liable only for gross negligence.' Such are ' depositaries ' and ' mandataries.'[f]

---

of property, are to be considered common carriers.' ' A person may be a common carrier of money as well as of other property.'

[e] MASON'S *Reports*, 132.

[f] POTHIER, *Observation Générale Traité des Obligations*; Tompkins v. Saltmarsh, 4 SERG. and RAWL., p. 282; DUMOULIN, *De eo quod interest*, n. 185; NOY'S *Maxims*, 91; BACON'S *Abridgment*, carriers, a; EMERIGON, c. 12, § 14.

M

XXIX.

DOMICILIUM, re et facto transfertur, non nudâ contestatione.—PAULUS (*Dig.* 1. 1. 20).[g]

Change of domicile is proved by facts and actions, not by a simple declaration.

Few questions were of more frequent occurrence under the jurisprudence of Imperial Rome, than those which affected the domicile of its subjects. As the burdens and obligations of each separate municipality devolved upon those whom birth or choice had fixed within its limits, and as to evade those burdens, which increased with frightful rapidity during the empire, was the object of every one who could by any means withdraw himself and his family from their overwhelming weight, the utmost refinement and ingenuity were employed to settle and ascertain the principles by which responsibilities of such vast importance were to be decided. The privileges of a Roman citizen, during the glorious days of the Republic, had led, as we know from the beautiful speech of Cicero for Balbus, to similar investigations.[h] But when submission to a military despotism, that most terrible condition to which God in his wrath can reduce a civilized people, had been substituted for the Rome of Cato and Cicero, for the country ' pro quâ mori et cui nos totos dedere et in quâ nostra omnia ponere et quasi consecrare debemus,' when the question of domicile was, as it became in the sad days of Rome, a question of

---

[g] BOULLENOIS, *Traité de la Personalité et de la réalité des Loix,* ' Observations sur, etc.' ; FELIX ; STORY, *Conflicts of Law* ; PHILLIMORE (ROBERT), *Law of Domicile* ; MERLIN, *Répertoire Domicile.* The account of personal, as opposed to territorial, law, is given by SAVIGNY, *Geschichte des R. R.,* c. 3 : ' It oftens happens,' says Agobardus in a letter to Louis le Debonnaire, 'that five men are together, each of whom is under a different law,' *cit. ib.*

[h] ' Ego mehercule et illi (Catoni) et omnibus municipibus duas esse censeo patrias, unam naturæ, alteram civitatis, ut ille (Cato) quum esset Tusculi natus in populi, Romani civitatem susceptus est—ita quum ortu Tusculanus esset, civitate Romanus habuit alteram loci patriam alteram juris.' *De Legibus,* 2. 2, *Pro Balbo.*

existence; when laws were made obliging criminals as a punishment to undertake the highest functions of municipal magistrates; and when men fled to the barbarians to avoid the certain ruin and probable degradation which attended them, in spite of every sort of artificial privilege granted to those who would incur their responsibility,[i] it excited far deeper interest, and was canvassed with very different emotions. Even in the chapter of the *Digest* from which the sentence at the beginning of these remarks is taken, we find this ominous extract from the works of Paulus, which must have been written long before the darkest hours of municipal servitude, and shews that men were even then anxious to escape from the ruinous honours which an iron despotism obliged them to undergo. ' Incola jam muneribus publicis destinatus nisi perfecto munere, incolatui renuntiare non potest.'[j] Therefore, as

---

[i] It is curious to observe the reluctance of the law to exclude persons from the station of decurio, which was to the other inhabitants of the city what the patrician class was to the plebeian, in the early period of Roman history. People who sold goods for a livelihood, though they might be scourged by the ædiles, were not excluded. *Dig.* l. 2. 11, *de decurionibus.* ' Spurios posse in ordinem allegi nulla dubitatio est' (*ib.* l. 2. 3, § 2). ' Expectes litterarum decurionis munera peragere non prohibent jura' (*Cod. de decur.*, l.). ' Qui ad tempus ordine renovetur . . . . impleto tempore decurio est' (*Dig.* l. 2. 2, § 1). and see notes to the *Theodosian code.*

[j] *Dig.* l. 1. 34. Origin, manumission, adoption, and domicile gave the ' civitas.' The ' civitas ' entailed the discharge of certain functions. The character imposed by the ' origo,' and the liabilities consequent upon it, were indelible. ' Jus originis in honoribus obeundis ac muneribus suscipiendis adoptione non mutatur; sed novis quoque muneribus filius per adoptivum patrem astringitur' (*Dig.* l. 1. 15, § 3). These passages shew the tenacity with which the law clung to its victim, even in the better days of the empire. ' In adoptivâ familiâ susceptum . . . muneribus civilibus apud originem avi quoque naturalis respondere D. Pio placuit; quamvis in isto fraudis nec suspicio quidem interveniret' (*ib.* l. 1. 17, § 9). ' Municipes sunt liberti et in eo loco ubi ipsi domicilium suâ voluntate tulerunt, nec aliquod ex hoc origini patroni faciunt præjudicium; et *utrobique muneribus astringuntur*' (*ib.* l. 1. 22, § 2). ' Incola et his magistratibus parere debet apud quos incola est et illis apud quos civis est—nec tantum municipali jurisdictioni in utroque municipio subjectus est, verum etiam omnibus publicis muneribus fungi debet' (*ib.* l. 1. 29).

the question is one which often occupies our tribunals, and is seldom discussed in a manner that is satisfactory, I have thought that it might be useful to collect the maxims of the Roman law, as it has been transmitted to us on the subject. Those from the *Digest* will be found in the chapter to which I have already had occasion to refer.

A man may be without a domicile.[k] 'Si quis domicilio relicto naviget vel iter faciat quærens quo se conferat, hunc puto sine domicilio esse' (*Dig.* xxvii.).

A man may, generally speaking, choose his domicile. 'Nihil est impedimento quominus quis ubi velit habeat domicilium quod ei interdictum non sit' (*ib.* xxxi.).

A man may have two domiciles. 'Viris prudentibus placuit duobus locis posse aliquem habere domicilium si utrobique ita se instruxit ut non ideo minus apud alteros se collocâsse videatur' (*ib.* vi., § 2).[l]

The meaning of the word 'domus' is thus explained (*Dig.* l. 16. 203, *De verb. sing*): 'Igitur quæri solere utrium ubi quisque habitaret sive in Italiâ sive in provinciâ an duntaxat in suâ cujusque patriâ domus esse recte dicetur—sed de eâ re constitutum est eam domum unicuique nostrum debere existimari ubi quisque sedes et tabulas haberet, suarumque rerum constitutionem fecisset.'

In the code of Justinian, it is said with more elegance and propriety than is common in that work (*De incolis* l. vii.):[m] 'In eodem loco singulos habere domicilium non ambigitur ubi quis larem rerumque ac fortunarum suarum summam constituit,[n] unde rursus non sit discessurus si nihil avocet, unde cum profectus est peregrinari videtur.'

A married woman was the 'incola' of the 'civitas' where

---

[k] Hardly according to our law, 5 VESEY, 587 ; 10 PICK, 77 ; 3 ROBINSON, 191 ; or the American law.

[l] N. GAIUS, *Instit.* i. 56, 57 ; iv. 37, 105.

[m] There is an express exception of students—'Nec ipsi qui studiorum causâ aliquo loco morantur domicilium ibi habere creduntur nisi decem annis transactis eodem loco sedes sibi constituerint' (*Cod. de incol.* l. 2).

[n] 'Le Français conserve toujours l'esprit de retour.'

her husband lived.[n] A soldier if he had no home where he served[o]—a person relegated to a distant spot[p]—might keep his ancient domicile. The 'filiusfamilias' might establish a separate domicile by his own choice.[q]

The mere possession of a house,[r] or transient residence on a spot, did not establish a domicile.

It is of course important to keep the distinction clear between domicile and residence—there may be residence without domicile, and domicile without residence—residence is preserved by the act, domicile by the intention; and where the maxim—'actor sequitur forum rei,'[s] is upheld with strictness, it is the domicile not the residence of the defendant that determines the place of litigation.

Domicile is of three kinds,

1. Domicile of origin. This is not the place where a man happens to be born, but the home of his parents.[t]

2. The domicile given by law. This includes those to whom the law assigns the domicile of others on whom they depend; e.g., the wife during marriage; the minor, etc.; it comprises also the case of some public servants. Embassadors and their families preserve their native domicile.[u]

---

[n] *Dig.* v. 1, 65 : 'Exigere dotem mulier debet illi ubi maritus domicilium habuit non ubi instrumentum dotale conscriptum est.'

Dig. l. 1. 38, § 3 : 'Mulierem rescripserunt . . . quamdiu nupta est, incolam ejusdem civitatis videri cujus maritus ejus est.'

[o] *Dig.* l. 1. 23. 1 : 'Miles ibi domicilium habere videtur ubi meret, si nihil in patriâ possideat.'

[p] 'Domicilium habere potest est relegatus eo loci unde ascetur.'

[q] *Dig.* l. 1. 3, 4 : 'Placet etiam filiosfamilias domicilium habere posse.' 'Non utique ibi ubi pater habuit sed ubicunque ipse domicilium constituit.' The French law is different ; MERLIN, *Reports, Domicile*, § 2.

[r] *Dig.* l. 1. 17, § 13 : 'Sola domus possessio quæ in alienâ civitate comparatur domicilium non facit.'

[s] 'Qui in agro permanet incola esse non existimatur.'—*Dig.* l. 1. 35. 'Non tamen ibi sedem suam habens.'—CUJACIUS. 'Contraxisse unusquisque intelligitur in eo loco, in quo ut solveret se obligavit.'—*Dig.* xliv. 7. 21.

[t] *Code Civil, Du Domicile*, 102, *seq.*

[u] 2 Bos. and P., 231, note ; 3 VESEY, 198 ; 1 BINN, 349. There is an

3. The domicile of origin, which is kept till another is acquired. In order to change it there must be an actual removal, with an intention to reside in the place to which the person whose domicile is in question removes. Mere intention to remove is not sufficient; upon a return with an intention to reside, his original domicile is restored.

The French law[x] distinguishes between a political and civil domicile; one may exist, as, for instance, in the case of women and minors, who have a civil but not a political domicile without the other.

The political domicile is the spot in which a person is entitled to exercise the political rights annexed to his condition as a citizen.[y]

The civil domicile is the spot which a person chooses as the seat of his business, of his fortune, of his habitual residence. Mere absence does not interrupt a domicile. A man may change it when he thinks fit. Every question of domicile is one of law and fact. The French[a] law carefully lays down the

---

eloquent passage in Lord Shaftesbury, who writes in a very different style from that which is now fashionable, on this subject, vol. iii. misc. 3, c. 1 : ' If, unhappily, a man had been born either in an inn, or in some dirty village, he would hardly, I think, circumscribe himself so narrowly as to accept a denomination or character from those nearest appendices or local circumstances of his nativity, etc. It is a wretched aspect of humanity which we figure to ourselves, when we would endeavour to resolve the very essence and foundation of this generous passion into a relation to mere clay and dust, exclusively of anything sensible, intelligent or moral.'

[x] *Code of Louisiana*, tit. ii., § 42 to 49 ; POTHIER, *Introd. aux coutûmes*, § 8 to 20 ; TOULLIER, *Droit Civil Français*, 1. 3, § 362, § 378 ; 3 MERIVALE, 79 ; KENT, *Comment.*, 1, § 74 to 80 ; 2, § 348.

[y] *Théorie du Code Civil*, LOCRÉ, vol. i. p. 298 ; vol. ii. p. 130.

[a] I have thought myself obliged more than once in the course of this work to comment on the effects of the unhappy narrowness, arising, partly from nature, and partly from the character of the heap of contradictions and unmeaning subtleties which go by the name of law in England, that characterises too many of those who have made, and almost invariably those who (I speak not of any now living) have interpreted, laws among us. Among the proofs that an incapacity of comprehending general principles is not always a certain sign of practical sense, and that attornies are not infallible guides in matters

rules by which the real domicile of a citizen is fixed, as thinking, that for all judicial purposes, and for the daily intercourse of life, that the distinct knowledge of a citizen's domicile, or at least of the rules by which it may be ascertained, is most important. The proof of intention, which is the turning point in question of domicile, is thus prescribed by the Civil Code, 104, 'La preuve de l'intention resultera d'une declaration expresse faite tant à la municipalité du lieu que l'on quittera qu'à celle du lieu ou l'on aura transféré son domicile;' 105, 'à défaut de déclaration expresse, la preuve de l'intention dépendra des circonstances.'

That debts and contracts affecting personal property, have no 'situs,' but follow the domicile of the owner, is an universal rule, 'mobilia inhærent ossibus domini.' 'It is clear,' says

of legislation, I would mention a question arising out of the subject in the text discussed in a manner peculiar to ourselves, and placing our practical sense in the clearest view. I mean the question of settlement. Millions were spent not in feeding, or clothing, or employing, but in discussing the settlement of paupers. The sum so spent in a few years after the close of the war would, perhaps, if properly laid out, have prevented the necessity of a future poor rate ; it went into the pockets of attorneys and barristers. The discussions lasted several weeks in the year, entangled with every sort of absurdity, before the country gentlemen, and the disputes were then brought up in a great number of instances to be discussed over again in Westminster Hall, whence they were again sent to Sessions, and sometimes brought back again to Westminster Hall. The evil became so great that a change was made which led, as might be expected from its authors, for some time to more wretched quibbling than before. I say nothing of the mischief done, irreparable as it often was, to those trained in such a school of litigation, or of the undue power and influence it gave to the lower branch of the profession. Those are mere theories; but as a simple estimate of expense, I would ask with the utmost phlegm whether in the notions of civilised countries it is possible to find an absurdity parallel to that of paying millions to attorneys for suggesting quibbles about the residence of paupers ? This went on while we were boasting 'ad nauseam' of our superiority in practical sense to every other people and, of our antipathy to theorists. Is there in Laputa an example of more provoking and grosser folly invented by the scorn of Swift, lashed by vexation to misanthropy, than this specimen of 'the simple beauty' as the author of the treatise on 'Ejectment' has it of the English law !

Mr. Justice Bayley,[b] from the authority of Bruce v. Bruce and
Somerville v. Somerville, 'that the rule is that general property
follows the person, and is not in any respect to be regulated
by the situs[c] . . . . Wherever the domicile of the proprietor
is, there the property is considered to be situate.'[d]

'Adeo recepta sententia est,' says one of the greatest masters of
public law, 'ut nemo audeat contra hiscere.' It is[e] an established principle, in spite of a mischievous and absurd decision of
Sir John Nichol, betraying the most profound ignorance, or
the most corrupt disregard of public law, overruled in the
Court of Delegates, that a will of personal or moveable property regularly made according to the forms and solemnities
required by the law of the testator's domicile, is sufficient to
pass his moveable or personal property in every country. The
same doctrine is established in America.[f]   Very difficult and

---

[b] 1 CR. and JERVIS, Re Ewin, 156.

[c] STORY, *Conflict of Laws*, c. 11 : LORD LOUGHBOROUGH, Sill v. Wors-
wick, 1 H. BL. 690 ; ABBOTT, C.J., Doe v. Vardill, 5 B. and C., 438, 2 CL.
and FINN., 671.

[d] BYNKERSHOEK, *Quæst. Priv. Juris.* lib. i. c. 16. 'Tel a toujours été
le sentiment presqu'unanime des autres et des cours de justice.
Témoins, Dumoulin, Chopin, Bretonnier D'Argentré, Brodeau, Le
Brun, Poullain du Parc, Burgundus, Rodenburg, Abraham a Wesel,
Paul Voet, Jean Voet, Sande Christin, Gail, Carpyor, Wernher, Mevins,
Franzke Boullenois, Pothier Struve, Seyrer, Huber, Hert, Hommel,
Doug, Glück, Thibaut Merlin, Mittermaier Hauss, Meier, Favard,
Duranton, Stony, Wheaton, Rocca et Burge.' FELIX, *Revue, Étranger et
France*, 1840, tom. ix. p. 222. STORY, *Conflict of Laws*, § 470, &c. ;
VATTEL, book ii., c. 8, § 111.

[e] The case of Swift v. Swift, decided by the same judge, was still
more crying.

D'AGUESSEAU considers the absurdity of the principle maintained by
Sir John Nichol as so manifest, that to argue it would be a waste of
time.—*Plaidoyer*, 54. 'Let us leave,' he says, 'to others arguments on
so clear a point.' 'Pour vous disons, avec Monsieur d'Argentré, que ces
questions . . . . ne seroient pas même dignes d'occuper un moment
l'attention de ceux qui ont le moins d'étude et de savoir,' p. 637, 4to. ed.,
vol. 4.

[f] 1 BINNEY, *Reps.*, 336, Deserbats v. Berquier ; Pottinger v. Wight-
man, 3 MERIV. 59 ; 2 BOULLENOIS, Ch. i., pp. 2, 54, 57 ; J. VOET *ad
Pandect.*, lib. xxviii., tit. 3, vol. ii., § 13, p. 293.

perplexing questions, however, may still arise as to what the
domicile is of a person who is a native of one country, and has
long been[g] resident in another. The validity of every disposition of real estate depends on the law of the country in which
that estate is situated.[h] This is the rule maintained by our
courts and those of America, as well as by a great preponder-
ance of foreign authorities.[i] Grotius sums up the law thus:
'Ubi de formâ sive solemnitate instrumenti agitur respici
locum conditi testamenti—ubi de personâ antestari jus domicilii—ubi de rebus quæ testamento relinqui possunt vel non
respici locum domicilii in mobilibus in rebus soli situm loci.'
Epist. 467. 'A will,' says Lord Lyndhurst, 'must be interpreted according to the law of the country where it is made,
and where the party making it has his domicile.[k] . . . . . It
appears to me that where a will is executed in a foreign
country, by a person having his domicile in that country, with
respect to that person's property, the will must be interpreted
according to the law of the country where it is made.'

There yet remain to be considered two questions: first, if a
a person make a will, being a native of one place, and domiciled in another; secondly, if he make a will in one and have
his domicile in another,—by what law is the will to be
governed? And the answer is, by the law[l] of his domicile.

---

[g] STORY, *Conflict of Laws,* p. 399.

[h] Coppen *v.* Coppen, 2 P. W., 291; 3 PETERS' *Reps., appendix,* p. 501
to 503; Curtis *v.* Hutton, 14 VESEY, 537; 2 FONBLANQUE *On Equity,*
445, note; 4 BURGE, *Comm. on Foreign and Colonial Law,* part 2,
c. xii., p. 217; FELIX ubi supra; STORY, *Conflict of Laws,* c. xi., § 474.

[i] 'Statutum agit in rem et quæcunque verborum formulâ utatur,
semper inspicitur locus ubi res sita est.' 'Quoties statutum princi-
paliter agit in personam non extenditur ad res sitas in locis ubi jus
communæ vel statutum loci diversum est.' DUMOULIN, *Oper.* tom. iii.,
p. 556; *Comment. ad Cod.,* lib. i., 1., c. 1.
'Bona defuncti immobilia et quæ juris interpretatione pro talibus
habentur deferri secundum leges loci in quo sita sunt.' VOET *ad Pand.*
lib. xxxviii., 17, § 34. VATTEL, 2. 7. § 85, 8, § 103, § 110, § 111.

[k] Trotter *v.* Trotter, 4 BLIGH, N.S., 502 ; Yates *v.* Thompson, 3 CL.
and FINN., 544.

[l] STORY, p. 401, ch. xi. § 479 ; BURGE, ch. xii. 4, p. 2 ; ch. ix. p. 855,
&c.; Harrison *v.* Nixon, 9 PETERS, *Reps.,* 483, 505 note. BOULLENOIS,

In the absence of any express contract in cases of marriage, the law of the matrimonial domicile governs the rights of parties as to their property in that place, and their personal property elsewhere; their immoveable property will be governed by the rule laid down before.[m] The law of domicile, as it affects divorce, gives rise to questions as delicate, and of as transcendant importance as any within the range of jurisprudence. Here, if any where, the judge, 'incedit per ignes Suppositos cineri doloso.'

The possession of estates, and what is more, the honour of families, may be concerned in the litigation of strangers. To the scandal of Great Britain, the Law of Marriage and Divorce is different on different sides of the Tweed. Marriages are valid in the north, under circumstances that would not make them valid in the south. Divorces are refused in the south for causes that would be sufficient in the north; and it has been held that a marriage contracted in England may be dissolved, for reasons that would not be sufficient in England, by Scotch judges, between parties domiciled in Scotland. Thus it has been determined, that a contract may be followed by consequences excluded by the law of the land from the consideration of the parties by whom it was made at the time

---

Observ., 46, p. 494, 503; DUMOULIN, *Opera*, tom. iii., ubi supra; tom. i., 'de Fiefs,' § 33, p. 88; Lansdowne *v.* Lansdowne, 2 BLIGH, *Reps.*, 60.

[m] STORY, *Conflict of Laws*, § 186; POTHIER, *Traité de la Comm.*, art. 'prél.,' p. 14, 15, 16.

'Hinc infertur ad quæstionem dotis et matrimonii quotidianam qui censetur fieri non in loco in quo contrahitur sed in loco domicilii viri, et intelligitur non de domicilio originis sed de domicilio habitationis ipsius viri.' DUMOULIN, tom. iii., p. 555.

'Non is locus spectatur,' where the contract of marriage is celebrated, 'sed is in quem sit migratio. Hac ratione mulier non agit ubi matrimonium contraxit sed ubi ex matrimonio migravit.' CUJAC. *ad Legem*, 'Exigem Dotem,' tom. ix. p. 164.

HUBER, i. tit. 3, c. 60; Le Breton *v.* Nonchet, 3 MARTIN, *Reps.*, 60; Robinson *v.* Bland, 2 BURROW, 1077; 2 KENT, *Comm. Lect.*, 39; Lampe *v.* Barker, 3 WHEATON, *Reps.*, 101.

'Le veritable principe dans cette matière est qu'il faut distinguer si le statut a directement les biens, pour objet ou leur affectation a certaines personnes.' D'AGUESSEAU *Plaid.* 53, 'Maréchale de Créqui.'

when it was made; and that the maxim, 'Nihil tam naturale est quam eo genere quidque dissolvere quo colligatum est,' in the most sacred of all contracts, is set aside. If two English persons, married in England, were to be domiciled in a country like Prussia, or where incompatibility of humour is a sufficient ground for a divorce, would such a divorce be sufficient to cancel the tie of an English marriage? Such, however, is a corollary from the doctrine maintained in the case of Warrender v. Warrender.[a]

XXX.

UNICUIQUE mora sua nocet.—PAULUS.[b]
Every one must bear the consequences of his own delay.

Delay entailed many responsibilities. In the first place, the risk of the thing which the person who delayed was bound to deliver. So if the buyer of wine did not carry it away at the time appointed, the seller, unless guilty of ' dolus malus,' was exonerated from the risk—' Si per emptorem steterit quominus ad diem vinum tolleret, postea nisi quod dolo malo venditoris interceptum esset non debet ab eo præstari.'[c] Secondly. The fluctuations of price in the thing to be delivered were to the disadvantage of him who had been guilty of delay—' Si per venditorem vini mora fuerit quominus traderet condemnari eum oportet utro tempore pluris vinum fuit vel quo venit vel quo lis in condemnationem deducitur.'[d] Thirdly. He was bound to compensate the loss which his adversary had suffered from the delay—' Si moram fecerit in homine reddendo possessor et homo mortuus sit; et fructuum rationem usque ad rei

---

[a] BLIGH's *Reports,* 89. 2 CLARKE and FINN., 488. Hopkins *v.* Hopkins, 3 *Mass. Reports,* 158 ; Carter *v.* Carter, 6 *Mass. Reports,* 268.

[b] MÜHLENBRUCH, *Doctrina Pand.,* § 371. D'ANTOINE, *Règles du Droit Civil.* GOTHOFRED.

[c] *Dig.* xviii. 6.5. 'Debitor tenetur etiam de casu fortuito quando ejus mora præcessit interitum rei quia mora perpetuat obligationem.' —ii. *de b. Ob.* 23.

[d] *Dig.* xix. 1.3, § 3.

judicatæ tempus spectandum esse.'[e] 'Is qui fideicommissum debet post moram non tantum fructus sed etiam omne damnum quo adfectus est fideicommissarius præstare cogitur.'[f] Besides these general consequences, the debtor was liable for interest, for penalties, and for the destruction of the thing, though this last liability was so far mitigated, that the debtor was ex- onerated from the risk where the thing would equally have perished in the hands of the creditor.[g] On the other hand, if the creditor was guilty of delay, the debtor, after giving him proper notice, might exonerate himself from all farther respon- sibility, by depositing the money due to him, and by aban- doning or pouring away the goods or wine he was bound to receive.

'Licet venditori effundere vinum si diem ad metiendum præstituit nec intra diem admensum est . . . . si tamen cum possit effundere,' says the Roman jurist, with that humanity which our legists seem to think incompatible with sense, 'non effundit, laudandus est potius.'[h]

Delay was purged, when the person guilty of it did the act he was bound to do before litigation had begun—'verum est eum qui interpellatus dare noluit offerentem postea, periculo liberari.'[i] So if I contracted with you to build, and the time in which you contracted to do the work has past—'quamdiu

---

[e] *Dig.* vi. 1. 17, § 1.

[f] *Dig.* xxxii. 26, and especially xxxii. 35, where the 'tribus' was be- queathed to a freedman by his patron ; and it was held, that the heir of the freedman might claim not only the value of the 'tribus,' but of the 'commoda et liberalitates quas libertus ex eâdem tribu usque in diem mortis suæ consecuturus fuisset' from the patron's heir, who had delayed to purchase it.

[g] *Dig.* xvi. 3. 14, § 1 : 'Sive autem cum ipso apud quem res deposita est actum fuerit sive cum hærede ejus et suâ naturâ res ante rem judi- catam interciderit, veluti si homo mortuus fuerit, Sabinus et Cassius absolvi debere eum cum quo actum est dixerunt, quia æquum esset naturalem interitum ad actorem pertinere, utique cum interitura esset ea res, etsi restituta esset actori.'

[h] *Dig.* xviii. 6. 1, § 3 ; xviii. 6. 18, § 1: 'Ante pretium solutum dominii quæstione motâ pretium emptor solvere non cogetur.'

[i] *Dig.* xlvi. 3. 72, § 1.

litem contestatus non sim posse te facientem liberari placet, quod si jam litem contestatus sim nihil tibi prodesse—si ædifices.'ʲ It is on occasion of this doctrine, as to the manner in which delay may be extinguished, that the Roman jurist pronounces a severe and memorable rebuke on pettifogging —'Esse enim hanc quæstionem de bono et æquo, in quo genere plerumque *sub auctoritate juris scientiæ* perniciose erratur.'ᵏ This is the language of Celsus, quoted by Paulus. Let the readers of Saunders and Meeson and Welsby say whether words could have been found more exactly describing the mischievous quibbles, paring down great principles to the razor edge of chicane, which were long adored as genuine learning in our Courts of Justice. While on this subject of 'mora,' I may remark, that the old maxim was 'Dies interpellat pro homine,' that no specific demand was requisite when a fixed day had been agreed upon, a doctrine still valid in our law. An opposite rule has been adopted in France, in the absence of an express stipulation the other way—' Le débiteur est constitué en demeure, soit par une sommation ou par autre acte equivalent, soit par l'effet de la convention lorsqu'elle porte que sans qu'il soit besoin d'acte, et par la seule échéance du terme le débiteur sera en demeure.'ˡ

XXXI.

QUI sine dolo malo ad judicium provocat non videtur moram facere.—JULIANUS.

He who appeals to law without a fraudulent purpose is not guilty of delay.

In order to prevent vexatious litigation, the Roman jurisprudence exacted from the suitors an oath, called 'juramentum

---

ʲ *Dig.* xlv. 1. 84.

ᵏ *Dig.* xlv. 1. 73, § 2 : 'Stichi promissor post moram offerendo purgat moram, certe enim doli mali exceptio nocebit ei qui pecuniam oblatam accipere noluit.'

ˡ 1139, *Code Napoléon* ; ROGRON, 1273 ; DONELLUS, xvi. c. 2 ; NOODT, *De Usuris*, lib. iii. c. 10 ; THIBAUT, *Archiv. Civ. Praxis*, b. ii.; SOULLIER, *Droit Civil*, tom. vi. § 244.

de calumniâ,' which is mentioned in the Institutes[a] and the Code,[b] and in which he declared his belief that his cause was founded on reason. And if the defence was not unusual, it was to be presumed that the person who availed himself of it, did so with no dishonest purpose. 'Juste enim dicitur provocare qui id facit quod communiter fieri solet,' are the words of Gothofred in his commentary on this rule. If, for instance, the debtor being ready to pay, the creditor for some reason was unprepared to receive—if the debtor was absent on public service—if, before payment could be made, accounts were to be examined—in all these cases delay was innocent. 'Mora[c] sua est inculpata,' says Papinian, and though delay there be, as far as the debtor is concerned, it shall be as if there were none, for he is innocent of it. 'Nam etsi reverâ moram faciat non videtur tamen moram facere qui a mora est justa ideoque danunandus ipse[d] non est.'

Paulus proposes the case of a person who refuses to give up the property that has been deposited with him, because the person demanding it in the name of the depositor cannot prove his authority, or establish his title as the heir if the depositor be dead. 'Si quis inficiatus sit non adversus dominum sed quod eum qui rem depositam petebat verum procuratorem non putaret, aut ejus qui deposuisset hæredem nihil dolo malo fecit.'[e] But the benefit of the rule does not extend to mere wrong doers, to thieves, and trespassers. 'Fures sunt in perpetuâ morâ;'[f] and Tryphonius held that if the

---

[a] 'Hæc autem 3 de pœnâ temere litigantium. Ecce enim Decret. 1.

[b] 'Cod de jurejur. propter calumniam dando.'

[c] *Dig.* xxii. 1. 9.

[d] 'Sciendum est,' says Ulpian, 'non omne quod differendi causâ optimâ ratione fiat, moræ a numerandum,' *Dig.* xxii. 9. 21. 'Sed et si . . . defensionem sui mandare non possit moram facere non videbitur,' xxii. 1. 23.

[e] *Dig.* xvi. 3. 13.
'Si quis solutioni moram fecit judicium autem accipere paratus fuit, non videtur fecisse moram.' xxii. 1. 24.

[f] *Dig.* xiii. 1. 8. 'Si ex causâ furtivâ res condicatur cujus temporis æstimatio fiat quæritur : placet tamen id tempus spectandum quo res unquam plurimi fuit. Maxime cum deteriorem rem factam fur dando non liberatur. Semper enim moram fur facere videtur.'

thing stolen perished in the hands of the wrong-doer, or his heir, before the owner had attempted to recover it, the delay in endeavouring to recover could be of no service to the defendant.[g] 'Quia videtur qui primum invito domino rem contractavit, semper in restituendâ eâ quam nec debuit auferre moram facere.'

If after a divorce[h] the wife demanded, as generally speaking she had a right to do, the restitution of her 'dos,' and the husband believing that he had, as he might have, a legal ground of resistance to her demand, disputed it ineffectually but bonâ fide, in a court of law, he was not in 'morâ,' and therefore not liable for interest during the delay; and if the heir, in the 'bonâ fide' belief that the Falcidian law had been violated, refused to pay the legacies, he was not in 'morâ,' nor bound to pay the interest of the legacies during his unsuccessful litigation.

XXXII.

NULLA intelligitur ibi mora fieri ubi nulla petitio est.—SCÆVOLA.

Where there is no right of action there is no delay.

The principle maintained in this rule is, that where an obligation is, ipso jure, null, or useless, because of the pleas by which it may be encountered, the person sued as the debtor cannot be in morâ.

An obligation may be null, either because it is not clothed with the requisite formalities, such as was the case of a mere verbal promise 'nudum pactum,' which conferred no right of action, because it was not supposed to have emanated from a deliberate consent, 'huic enim præsumitur non evenire plenum et perfectum consensum, sed promissionem ex lubrico lingue fuisse emissum;' or it may be null on account of the person making it, as if a pupil were to make a contract without the sanction of his tutor. From all this it follows, that the de-

---

[g] See the remarkable law, *Dig.* v. 3. 40. de hæred. petitione.

[h] Cod. l. 2 de usuris et fruct. leg. *Dig.* xxxi. 78.

mand is without effect; and because it is without effect, the person who does not comply with it cannot be 'in morâ.'

Indeed, Ulpian is still more indulgent, 'Quid enim,' he says, 'si amicos adhibendos debitor requirat vel expediendi debiti, vel fidejussoribus rogandis—vel exceptio aliqua allegetur? Mora facta non videtur.' But to return to the original instances: the obligation gives the right of action, the right of action gives rise to the claim for delay; therefore, where there is no obligation, there is no right of action, and where there is no right of action, there is no delay. 'Ex obligatione petitio, ex petitione mora nascitur, ideoque ubi nulla obligatio est ibi nulla petitio, et ubi nulla petitio ibi nulla mora.' Clearly to appreciate this rule, we should bear in mind these three principles of law: first, that a man become a surety (and, therefore, liable to an action) for the fulfilment of a purely natural obligation; secondly, that the surety is answerable for the delay of the surety; thirdly, that the obligation contracted by a 'pupillus,' without the sanction of the tutor is merely a natural obligation. Then let it be supposed that a 'pupillus,' without the authority of his tutor, has engaged to deliver a certain animal to Titius, and that Caius is his surety. The 'pupillus' does not fulfil his contract at the appointed time, and while he is in 'morâ' the animal dies. Is the surety, Caius, liable? This is what Scævola denies. The doubt arose from the fact that, in ordinary cases, a surety was responsible for delay; but this is only the law in those cases where the debtor is legally liable, which is the 'ipsissima sententia' of this very rule.[i] The definition of a debtor is 'a quo invito exigi pecunia potest,' 108, 'De Verb Signif.' But in this instance, the debtor was not liable; there was no 'petitio,' and, therefore, no 'mora.' Nor do the texts which lay it down that, 'ubi nulla petitio fiat,' there may still be 'mora' made against this rule, for the question here is one not of

---

[i] 'Adhiberi autem fidejussor tam futuræ quam præcedenti obligationi potest ; dummodo sit aliqua vel naturalis futura obligatio.' *Dig.* xlvi. 1. 6. § 2.

fact, but of law; and, therefore, does not refer to what actually happens, but to what would happen if the attempt was made to establish the right; viz., that it would be in vain. 'Non enim[k] in morâ est is a quo pecunia propter exceptionem peti non potest.' It should be borne in mind that this question was discussed by Scævola on the edict 'de jure deliberandi,' where the 'prætor,' during the time asked, in the name of the 'pupillus,' for deliberation as to the acceptance of an inheritance, forbids any diminution of the property.[l]

XXXIII.

BONA fides tantundem possidenti præstat quantum veritas, quoties lex impedimento non est.—PAULUS.

Good faith gives the possessor the same rights as the fact, unless the law prevent it.

If Titius, not being the proprietor of a horse (or anything else) had placed it, 'ex justâ causâ,' in the possession of Mævius, who believed Titius to be the owner of it, this rule, in ordinary cases, gave Mævius the rights of a legitimate proprietor. 'Bonæ fidei emptor videtur qui ignoravit alienam esse; aut putavit eum qui vendidit jus vendendi habere putavit procuratorem aut tutorem esse,' says Modestinus (109, *Dig. De Verb. Sig.*). 'Si modo eas bona fide acceperimus quum crederemus eum qui vendiderit dominum esse,' says Gaius (*Inst.* 2, § 43). 'Si ab eo emas quem præter vetuit alienare idque tu scias usucapere non potes,' says Paulus (*De usurp. Dig.* 112). I do not think it necessary here to enter into discussions as to 'res mancipi,' or 'res nec mancipi,' or the distinctions between the property acquired 'ex justâ causâ,' and that held 'bonâ fide.' It is only requisite to know, so far as this maxim and the place from which it is taken is concerned,

---

[k] *Dig.* xii. 2. 40, de rebus creditis. The celebrated law, 'Lecta.'

[l] 'His verbis prætor non tantum alienationem impedit, verum etiam actiones exerceri non patitur, est enim absurdum ei cui alienatio interdicitur permitti actiones exercere.' *Dig.* xxviii. 8. 7.

that if the 'bonâ fide' purchaser of property from a person
not the owner—'a non domino'—lost it before his title by
'usucapio,' *i.e.* by prescription, was complete, he might employ
the 'actio Publiciana' for its recovery, as the passage from the
Edict shews: ' Si quis id quod traditur, ex justâ causâ a non
domino, et nondum usucaptum petet, judicium dabo.' It is
probable that these words, 'a non domino,' are an interpolation
of Tribonian, as, otherwise, the repetition of them in the commentary of Ulpian would be superfluous: ' Proinde hoc me
sufficit me bonæ fidei emptorem esse quamvis a non domino
emerim.' He would hardly have written thus, if these very
words had stood as part of the text which he was explaining.
The words 'nondum usucaptum,' he proceeds to remark, are
significant; for if the 'usucapio' had taken effect, the possessor
would have been protected by the civil law: ' Merito prætor ait
nondum usucaptum nam si usucaptum est habet civilem actionem nec desiderat honorariam.' Nor was this protection
confined to the 'bonæ fidei emptor,' but it extended to others
—' Ut puta ei cui dotis nomine res tradita est necdum usu-
capta . . . . item si res ex causâ judicati sit tradita.' So we
are told, in illustration of the same principle, that the creditor
who took an article in payment might acquire a title by
'usucapio'—' Pro soluto usucapit qui rem debiti causâ recipit
et non tantum quod debetur sed quod libet pro debito solutum
hoc titulo usucapi potest.' Pomponius puts the case still more
clearly. ' If,' he says, ' when I took the thing in payment of
the debt, I knew that nothing was due to me, I cannot acquire
a title to it by 'usucapio'; if I did not, I can.'—' Si scissem
mihi nihil deberi usu eum non capiam—quod si nescio verius
est, ut usucapiam quia ipsa traditio ex causâ quam veram esse
existimo sufficit ad efficiendum ut id quod mihi traditum est
pro meo possideam.' Paulus says: ' Si existimans me debere
tibi tradam ita demum usucapio sequitur si et putes debitum
esse.' He proceeds to make a distinction, to which another
rule refers, between the case of ' emptio' and other kinds of
contract. In other contracts, the time of payment only is
considered; and if the 'bonâ fide' belief then exists, it is suf-

ficient—'Diversitatis causa in illo est quod in cæteris causis solutionis tempus inspicitur — neque interest quum stipulor scium alienum esse, necne, sufficit enim me putare tuum esse quum solvis.' But in the case of the 'emptio' it is otherwise, the time of the contract and of payment are both to be considered; and he who has not made a 'bonâ fide' purchase when he bought, and did not when he paid 'bonâ fide,' the article to have been the property of the seller when he bought it, cannot establish a title by 'usucapio'—'in emptione autem et contractus tempus inspicitur et quo solvitur, nec potest pro emptore usucapere qui non emit, nec pro soluto sicut in cæteris contractibus'[m] (*Dig. de usurp. et usucap.*, xlviii.).

The 'Publiciana actio' then enabled the 'bonâ fide' possessor to recover the property from third parties (wrong doers) —from any one, that is, but the lawful owner, who relied on the strength of his own title. He, the real owner, was allowed to question the 'usucapio': 'Publiciana actio non ideo comparata est, ut res *domino* auferatur.'[n] What would have been fraudulent in another was righteous in his case, so carefully and with such refinement did the Roman law discriminate: 'Ejusque rei argumento est, primo æquitas deinde exceptio si ea res possessoris non sit' (*Ib.*). In conformity with this principle, the pledging or hypothecation by the 'bonâ fide' possessor of what he so possessed, was lawful: 'Si ab eo qui Publicianâ uti potuit quia dominium non habuit, pignori accessi, sic tuetur me per Servianam prætor, quem admodum debitorem (that is, the mortgagor, or pledger) per Publicianam.'[o] The 'bonæ fidei' possessor, before the suit, was entitled to the produce which he had consumed while ignorant that his title

---

[m] Compare with the law, *Dig. de adq. poss.*, iii. § 21 : 'Genera possessionum tot sunt, quot et causæ acquirendi ejus quod nostrum non sit veluti pro emptore, pro donato, pro legato, pro dote, pro hærede, pro noxæ dedito, pro suo sicut in his quæ terrâ, mari, cæloque vel ex hostibus capimus vel quæ ipsi, ut in rerum naturâ essent fecimus—et in summâ magis unum genus est possidendi, species infinitæ.'

[n] *Dig.* vi. 2. 17.

[o] *Dig.* xx. 1. 18.

was defective: 'Bonæ fidei possessor in percipiendis fructibus id juris habet quod dominis præliorum tributum est.'[p]

The rule is limited by the words ' quoties lex impedimento non est.' For there were cases in which the law forbad ' usucapio' altogether: ' Ubi lex inhibet usucapionem bona fides possidenti nihil prodest.'[q] Possession was of no avail against rights that were imprescriptible. Such were the goods and property of a pupillus, of him who was absent on public service, the right of a debtor to redeem his pledge—cases where the maxim, ' Adversus non valentem agere non cernit præscriptio' (which, to the disgrace of our tribunals, was so often disregarded in the case of Gregory v. Meadowbank, cited above) applies. Things that belonged to the ' fiscus' and ' res sacræ, sanctæ, publicæ, populi Romani, et civitatum, et liberi homines, res furtivæ'[r]—the space round the hedge.[s]

This is a maxim which often would apply to questions of public law after great revolutions. The intermediate profits of the livings, from which the episcopal clergy had been expelled during the great civil war, were not claimed from those who had received them, even by the intolerant and vindictive majority of the Parliament that succeeded the convention Parliament, which allowed the judicial murder of Sir Henry Vane, and passed the Act of Uniformity.[t]

The question of prescription is one that has always engrossed a considerable share of the thoughts of jurists. It is one of the frontiers where law and philosophy touch each other; and as some definite period must be fixed at which it

---

[p] *Dig.* xxii. 1. 25, § 1 ; xli. 1. 48. 'Bonæ fidei emptor non dubie percipiendo fructus etiam ex alienâ re suos interim facit,' κ.τ.λ.

[q] *Dig.* xliii. 24.

[r] *Dig.* xli. 3. 9.

[s] Borrowed from the law of Solon, which is quoted in the *Digest.*

[t] Lord Coke, in his third Institute, maintains, a king, who hath right, and is out of possession, not to be within the statute of treason. It is only necessary to mention the statute of Henry VII., which gave full indemnity to all persons who obeyed the king for the time being. The number of French emigrants at the revolution was 123,789. PAILLET, *Droit Public Français,* 335. Bagot's Case, 9 Ed. IV.

must begin to operate, at which the proprietor exchanges his title deeds and material evidence for that moral security which, after the lapse of a certain period of duration, must be the ground of all known property, there is of course abundant room for the sceptical sophist to exercise his ingenuity in demanding why sixty years are fixed upon rather than fifty-nine and three-quarters, and other questions of the same nature. But such men fix their thoughts on the transitory element in this great doctrine, and not on that part of it which is perpetual, which is not the creature but the author of the law in which it is embodied, and which has caused jurists to describe it as the tutelary guardian of the human race— ' patrona generis humani.'[u] Without it human life would be a scene of incessant violence and confusion; for, as Mr. Burke observes, to that all property in the soil must ultimately be traced. Though we use prescription in a generic sense, the Romans employed the words ' usucapio' and ' præscriptio' in senses very different. In the early ages of Rome, the Twelve Tables said: ' Usus auctoritas fundi biennium cæterarum rerum amicus usus esto.' The possessor of three acres would not be very long in discovering that another had taken possession of one of them. But when the possessions of the Romans increased, the term of prescription was extended to ten years. The ' usucapio' applied only to land in Italy, and moveables of which the ownership was transferred by delivery, ' res mancipi.'[v] Land in the provinces was termed ' res nec mancipi,' and the owner, ' dominus bonitarius.' To them possession of ten years gave a title: this was ' præscriptio.' In truth, as we know from the institutes of Gaius, ' præscriptio' was a word taken from the heading of a plea which barred the adversary. This the wonderful sagacity of Cujacius enabled him to surmise: ' Præscrip-

---

[u] *Instit.*, lib.ii. c.6; *Dig.* xli.3; xliv.3; *Code*, lib.vii. 26 and 39; *Novell.* 119, c. 7 and 8; MALEVILLE, *Analyse*, vol. iv.; DUNOD., *Traité des Prescriptions, Code Napoléon*, art. 22, 19, paraphrases, ' Minimâ agnitione debiti tollitur præscriptio.'—Art. 22, 21.

[v] ' Usucapio est adjectio dominii per continuationem possessionis temporis lege definiti.'—*Dig.* iii. *de Usurp.*

tionis nomine,' says the great commentator, ' nihil aliud quam exceptio significatur.'[w]   Justinian abolished the distinction between ' res mancipi' and ' nec mancipi,' and, therefore, between ' usucapio' and ' præscriptio.'[x]   In the 129 *Novell.*, with his usual folly, he calls this most general and recognised title between man that is known in public or municipal jurisprudence, ' impium præsidium.'   He fixed three years for moveables, ten years for immoveables, unless in case of absence, in which case twenty years were requisite for a bonâ fide holder. After undisturbed possession of thirty years, no suit could be instituted against the holder.   The prescription against the church was prolonged to forty years; against the church of Rome, to a hundred.[y]   In the cases of easements and servitudes, the application of this principle is incessant; but into them the limits of this work will not allow me to enter.[z]   I will only add a striking expression from Grotius: ' Nihil fit *a* tempore, quanquam nihil non fit *in* tempore.'[a]   The studies which formed such a man are at least as useful to mankind as those which formed the Gaudys, Flemings, Cokes, Saunders, and Eldons.[b]

---

[w] CUJACIUS, *Paratitl. Code de Præscript. longi temp. ;* D'AGUESSEAU, vol. ii. p. 22, vol. xiii. p. 92.

[x] *Cod. de Usucap. trans. L. anis.*   2 and 3 William IV., c. 71 ; STEPHENS' *Blackstone,* i. 658.

[y] *Cod. de Præscript.,* 30 vel 40 : 'Quas actiones cod. de sacrament. Ecc.' *Code Civil,* lib. iii. § 20, art. 22, lib. 29 ; DOMAT, *Loix Civiles,* iii. 291; BURKE, vol. ix. 351; VAN ESPEN, vol. i. 663, vol. iii. 594 ; *Code of Louisiana,* 3420 to 3527.

[z] Luttrell's Case, 4 *Reports,* 47 ; Newman *v.* Anderson, 1 BAR. and ALD., 258 ; *American Jurist,* vol. xix. p. 106.

[a] *De Jure Belli ac Pacis,* lib. ii. c. 4.

[b] We do not compare them for a moment with those from which the judgments on points of special pleadings in Meeson and Welsby have issued :—

'Nil oriturum alias, nilortum tale fatentes.'

XXXIV.

QUI dolo desierit possidere pro possidente damnatur quia pro possessione dolus est.—PAULUS.

He who has fraudulently transferred his possession is to be condemned as if he were in possession, because his fraud is equivalent to possession.

The meaning of this rule, is clear: it is, that he who for a fraudulent purpose gets rid of his possession, shall be in no better condition than if he were actually the possessor. ' Pro possessione dolus *est.*' With the same emphasis it is said, ' latior[a] culpa dolus *est.*' It is a rule founded on equity; and, therefore, general in its application. So: 1. in the chapter of the Digest, ' de petitione hæreditatis,'[b] we find this passage: ' ait senatus eos qui bona invasissent quæ scirent ad se non pertinere etiamsi ante litem contestatam fecerint quominus possiderent perinde condemnandos, quasi possiderent . . . . § 8, merito nam is qui dolo fecit quominus possideret ut possessor condemnatur, accipiens, sive dolo desierit possidere, sive dolo possessionem noluit admittere.' 2. Under the head ' De rei vindicatione,'[c] it is written ' is qui ante litem contestatam dolo desiit possidere tenetur in rem actione.' 3. Under the head ' ad exhibendum,'[d] ' Julianus scribit si quis hominem quem possidebat occiderit sive ad alium transtulerit possessionem, sive ita rem corruperit ne haberi possit ad exhibendum tenebitur; qui a dolo fecit quominus possideret.' 4. In the chapters on the interdicts ' quorum bonorum,'[e] ' Ait prætor quorum bonorum ex edicto meo illi possessio data est—quod de his bonis pro hærede aut pro possessore possides—possideresve si nihil usucaptum esset—*quod quidem dolo malo fecisti uti desineres possidere id illi restituas.*' The interdict ' quod legatorum,'[f] ' quod ait prætor aut dolo desiit possidere sic

---

[a] *Dig.* xvi. 1. 32. Gothofred. de reg. Juris. p. 353.
[b] *Dig.* lib. v., tit. 7.   [c] *Dig.* vi. 1. 27. § 3.
[d] *Dig.* x. 4. 9.   [e] *Dig.* xliii. 2.
[f] *Dig.* xliii. 3. § 7.

accipere debemus desiit facultatem habere restituendi.' The
interdict 'De tabulis exhibendis.'g The interdict 'De liberis
exhibendis.'h 5. 'In noxali actione.' For the master of a
slave who had been guilty of 'noxa' was liable for the offence
of the slave, not only if the slave was still in his power, but if
he, the master, had fraudulently got rid of him;i and this, as
the word 'damnari' shews, is the particular case to which this
rule was intended to apply. 'Damnari' means to be condemned to a specific, precise, defined act; whereas, the owner
of a noxious slave, who acted 'bonâ fide,' might, by delivery
of the slave, escape the payment of damages. And so averse
was the Roman law to fraud, that if a man not really the
possessor, was sued as possessor, and defended himself without
repudiating the character, he made himself responsible. 'Is
qui se obtulit rei defensioni sine causâ cum tamen non possideret, non est absolvendus.'k

XXXV.

NON est novum ut quæ semel utiliter constituta
sunt durent licet ille casus extiterit a quo initium
capere non potuerunt.—PAULUS.

*It is not without precedent, that what is once beneficially
established, should continue in spite of an event which
would have made the original existence of such a
state of things illegal.*

There are many things to be considered in this rule, which,
as it apparently contradicts the maxim already considered in

---

g *Dig.* xliii. § 5.

h *Dig.* xliii. 30. To these may be added the rule, 'Parem esse conditionem oportet ejus qui quid possideat vel habeat atque ejus cujus
dolo malo factum sit quominus possideret vel haberet,' 150. 'Semper
qui dolo fecit quominus haberet pro eo habendus est ac si haberet,'
157.

i 'Si bonâ fide possessor servum . . . dimiserit ne agri cum eo noxali
causâ possit obligari eum actione quæ datur adversos eos qui servum
in potestate habeant aut dolo fecerint quominus haberent—quia per
hoc adhuc possidere videtur,' *Dig.* ix. 4. 12.

k *Dig.* 'De rei Vindic,' § 25.

these pages, ' Quod initio vitiosum est non potest tractu temporis convalescere,' has much embarrassed the interpreters.

Paulus, the author of the rule, has thus expressed himself in
another part[1] of the Digest—' Etsi placeat extingui obligationem si in eum casum inciderit a quo incipere non potest,
non tamen hoc in omnibus verum est.' That the principle it
involved gave rise to much controversy even among the Roman
jurists, we know from the law 'existimo,' (*Dig.* xlv. 2. 98);
' Si fundi dominus sub conditione viam stipulatus fuerit, statim
fundo alienato evanescit stipulatio et maxime secundum illorum
opinionem qui etiam ea quæ recte constiterunt resolvi putant
cum in eum casum reciderunt, a quo non potuissent consistere.'
The words ' non est novum' indicate, as Cujacius remarks, that
the rule is rather to be considered an exception to other rules
than a general and independent principle. In the same way
it is said, ' non est novum ut priores leges ad posteriores
trahantur.'[m] ' Non est novum ut duæ obligationes in ejusdem
personâ de eâdem se concurrant;'[n] and, again, ' non est novum ut qui dominium non habeat aliis dominium præbeat.'[o]
The first step towards light in the difficulties which have given
rise to so much debate, is to put aside all cases which are
' ab initio inutilia et vitiosa,' as this rule is in terms confined
to the opposite category to those which are 'utiliter constituta.'
This at once removes the difficulty arising from the rule, ' Quod
initio,' &c.; and, in the second place, the particular cases
which Paulus had in view are to be considered. There were
the cases of ' nuptiæ' and ' tutelæ;' now in both these the rule
we are now discussing is paramount. ' Patre furioso nihilo
minus liberi in patris sui potestate sunt.'[p] Again, ' Furor
quin sponsalibus impedimento sit plus quam manifestum
est, sed postea interveniens sponsalia non infirmat,'[q] and
' Furor contrahi matrimonium non sinit quia consensu opus
est sed recte contractum non impedit.'[r] The rule applies to

---

[1] *Dig.* xlv. 2. 140. § 2. [m] *Dig.* i. 4. 26.

[n] *Dig.* xix. 1. 10. [o] *Dig.* xli. 1. 46.

[p] *Dig.* i. 6. 8. [q] *Dig.* xxiii. 1. 8.

[r] *Dig.* xxiii. 2. 16. 2.

magistrates who after they had entered upon their functions were overtaken by some infirmity which would have rendered them ineligible. 'Melius est ut dicamus retinere cæptum magistratum posse, adspirare autem ad novum penitus[s] prohiberi, idque multis probatur exemplis.' So it applies to the burdens imposed on municipal magistrates.[t] To 'servitudes,' 'Si prædium tuum mihi serviat sive ego partis prædii tui dominus esse cæpero, sive tu mei per partes servitus retinetur, licet ab initio per partes acquiri non potest;'[u] 'per partem dominionum servitus acquiri non potest acquisita tamen conservatur et per partem domini, κ. τ. λ.'[x] To wills, 'Is cui lege bonis interdictum est, testamentum facere non potest, et si fecerit, ipso jure non valet. Quod tamen interdictione vetustius habuerit testamentum,[y] hoc valebit.'

The difference must always be recollected between those acts which depend only on the present moment for their validity, and those which have not only once happened, but which are usefully established, which are perfect and consummate, before the circumstance occurs which would have prevented their existence; e.g., the instances above alleged of the magistrate, and of marriage. The exceptions to this rule are—where, although the thing was 'utiliter initio constitutum,' such a change has taken place in its status, as to give it an entirely opposite character, and make the object for which it was done unattainable. e.g., I stipulate for the delivery of slave, Stichus, or of a thing in ordinary use; if the thing becomes sacred, or Stichus acquires his freedom, the stipulation, though originally valid, ceases to be of any avail.[a] 'Nam et cum quis rem profanam aut Stichum dari promisit

---

[s] *Dig.* iii. 1. 5.

[t] *Dig.* l. 6. 5. § 7. Hoc circa vacationes dicendum est ut si ante quis ad munera municipalia vocatus sit quam,' he attained an exemption 'compellatur ad honorem gerendum.'

[u] *Dig.* viii. 1. 8. § 2.

[x] *Dig.* xlv. 2. 140. § 2.

[y] *Dig.* xxviii. 1. 18., and see 'PAPINIAN,' *Dig.* xxxv. 2. 5., and *Inst. de legatis,* § 'Ex contrario.'

[a] *Dig.* xlv. 1. 83, 5.

liberatur si sine facto ejus res sacra esse cœperit aut Stichus ad libertatem pervenerit;[b] and 'e converso' if I stipulate for a thing dedicated to the public or sacred, or a freeman, the stipulation is useless, though the thing afterwards become profane or private property, and the freeman a slave. I believe that all the differing opinions may be reconciled, by keeping steadily in view the distinction between the cases where, before the act is established and complete, the event happens which would have been fatal to its existence, and those cases where the event happens after the act is consummated and perfect. The former class are excluded from the rule we are now considering, and the latter are within it. Thus Ulpian tells, that though the heir must produce the will under which he claims, yet if the will has once existed after the testator's death, the loss of it will not affect his right to the property bequeathed. ' Semel autem extitisse tabulas mortuo testatore desideratur tametsi extare desierint, quare et si postea interciderunt bonorum possessio peti potest.'[c] Modestinus gives us this example of a case, where the rule which we are now considering does not apply. He suppose Titius to have stipulated for a right of way from his estate over that of his neighbour. Afterwards, Titius sells that part of his estate which adjoined his neighbour's. This sale destroys the right of way, which is indivisible, and, therefore, never could have existed if things had been in their actual state when it was created: ' Pro parte neque adimi neque acquiri via potest.'

Another singular instance is given by Ulpian. Two individuals, in order to terminate a law suit actually begun, agree that one shall adopt the other; this at once puts an end to it: ' Quonian inter eos lis ab initio non potuit consistere.' It must be borne in mind, however, that ' erat negotium inchoatum non perfectum,' for otherwise it would not have been altered by the adoption ' perfecta semel durant.'

The question of prescription which, as Mr. Burke remarks,

---

[b] *Dig.*xlv.1, 5.   [c] *Dig.* xxxvii. 11. 1, § 3.

is the great basis of property, and which is a striking instance of the compromise between absolute justice and imperfect right, incident to the infirmity of clinging to all that is human, is touched upon by this rule.

It is laid down in the *Institutes*, that the possession of the deceased may be added to that of the heir, in order to complete a prescriptive title, if the possession of the deceased was bonâ fide,[c] even though the heir was aware of the defect in his title. This at variance with the Canon Law, which for reasons sufficiently obvious (inasmuch as probably at one time or other, two-thirds of the soil of the most civilized parts of Western Europe had been wrung from its owners by the gripe of Ecclesiastical avarice), established it as a rule, that if at the last minute before the prescription was complete, the possessor came to the knowledge that his title was defective, he became a possessor 'malæ fidei.' ' Si bonæ fidei possessor exeunte ultimâ die incideret in malam fidem, hæc supervenientia malæ fidei totam retroactam possessionem vitiaret.'

XXXVI.

SOCII mei, socius meus non est.—ULPIAN.[d]

The partner of my partner is not my partner.

The Roman lawyers held consent to be the essence of partnership. The means by which that consent was proved, were manifold. Modestinus tells us that there can be no doubt that a partnership may be established between the present or the absent, by word of mouth or by writing, by facts, or by the intervention of a messenger: ' Societatem coire et re et verbis et per nuncium posse nos dubium non est.'[e] From this it followed, that a partner chosen by Titius, was only the

---

[c] § *Diutina possessio,* 12. *Institut. de Usucap. et longi temporis proscriptione.*

[d] *Code Civil,* art. 1832; *Analyse du Code Civil,* vol. iii. tit. 9.

[e] *Dig. pro socio,* xvii. 2. 4; LOCRÉ, vol. xviii. p. 88; *Inst.* iii., § 25; *Dig.* xvii. 2. 37, *pro socio*; POTHIER, *Traité du contrat de société, Code* iv., DUPIN, Ed., pp. 443, 560; GLÜCK, *Commentar.,* tom. xv. p. 371; MEERMAN, *Thesaurus,* t. iv. p. 103; GAIUS, *Comment.,* § 148.

partner of him by whom he was chosen, and not of those with whom Titius was in partnership: ' Qui admittitur socius ei tantum socius est qui admisit et recte cum enim societas consensus contrahitur socius mihi esse non potest quem ego socium esse nolui—quid ergo si socius meus eum admisit? et soli socius est.'[f] No man could become the partner of another by accident, by the force of circumstances, without his knowledge and deliberate assent, and therefore partners though the engagement was not general, but for a single specific purpose, were liable to each, not only for dolus, but for the omission of anything that it was in their power to do to promote the common object. ' Verum est quod Sabino videtur etiamsi non universorum bonorum socii sunt sed unius rei attamen in id quod facere possunt, quodve dolo malo fecerint quo minus possint, condemnari oportet, hoc enim summam rationem habet, cum societas jus quodammodo fraternitatis in se habeat.'[g] The interpreters point out three distinctions between this ' societas,' which must be the result of choice, and the ' communio rerum,' which may be the effect of accident:—

1st. The latter happens, for instance, if a testator bequeath the same estate to two or more persons, or appoints several co-heirs; such a legacy or appointment, or a gift of the same kind, produces among these objects of the same bounty a joint interest and obligation even without their knowledge and in their absence: ' Etiam inter absentes et ignorantes quorum nullus est consensus'; it is a ' quasi contractus,' as we are told in the *Institutes*.[h]

2ndly. Partnership ' societas' is a personal engagement, for the reasons above stated. ' Communio rerum ' is, on the contrary, a real engagement issuing from the thing itself, and from its quality of being common to many.

3rdly. ' Societas ' gives rise to a merely personal action—an

---

[f] *Dig.* xvii. 2. 19.

[g] *Dig.* xvii. 2. 63.

[h] *Instit. de Oblig. quæ quasi ex contractu, nascuntur.*

action 'pro socio.' The 'communio rerum' gives rise to a
mixed action: 'Actio communi dividendo'; real, because
each proprietor of a common thing may claim his share of it;
personal, because such a state of things draws after it the
personal liabilities, viz., 1. 'Damni dati res arciendi. 2. Fructuum communicandorum. 3. Impensarum refundendarum.
1. Compensation for injury to the common property. 2. Share
in the produce and benefits accruing from it. 3. Contribution
to the expenses of putting in it repair.

The vocabulary of vituperation might exhaust itself, without adequately describing the unmeasurable follies and frightful
evils of the English law of partnership[k] (to which a very
feeble remedy has at length, after the most virulent opposition, been applied); and the means by which an endeavour has
been made, by 'privilegia,' to shelter a very inconsiderable, and
by no means the most meritorious part of the community from
its pernicious consequences. Deep and ineffaceable is the stain
which these transactions have branded on the English name.
As in the case of divorce, instead of laying down a general
rule co-extensive with the subject, to which all classes might
apply, special privileges have been granted to some favoured
persons to do what is inexorably refused to others: and if
with this be coupled the proceedings in Chancery under the old
system, which at last from the multiplication of parties made all
legal succour impossible, and enabled any one dishonest or liti-
gious partner to ruin every one of his associates; in a vast number of cases, the reader may judge of the *practical* wisdom of our
legislation.[l] The truth is, the law was exactly what a sheriff's
officer would have wished it to be, and if substantial justice was
ever blundered upon, it was in spite of its provisions, and the
scholastic mind of its interpreters.[m]

---

[k] 'Unius vero rei societas ad hanc tantummodo pertinet.' WARN-
KŒNIG, vol. ii. p. 291, § 642.

[l] *Report of Committee on the Law of Partnership.*

[m] In the case of Vansandau *v.* Moore, one of the shareholders of a
joint-stock company filed a bill against the directors and other shareholders, in order to have the partnership dissolved, and the proper

'I have always,' says C. J. Tindal, 'understood the definition of partnership to be a mutual participation in profit and
loss.'[m] An actual partnership is held to exist wherever there
is a participation of profits, even though the person so made
a partner may have guarded with the most earnest and anxious
solicitude against such a relation.[n] So wide is the discord
between the views of Roman and of English lawyers. 'It is
clearly settled,' says Lord Eldon, 'that if a man stipulates
that he shall have as the reward of his labour, not a specific
interest in the business, *but a given sum of money even in proportion to the profits*, that will *not* make him a partner; but if
he agrees for a part of the profits as such, giving him a right
to an account, *though having no property in the capital*, he is as
to third persons a partner . . . The cases have gone to this
nicety, and *upon a distinction so thin*, that I cannot state it as
established on due consideration, that if a trader agree to pay
another person for his labour in the concern, a sum of money

---

accounts taken. Fourteen of the directors appeared, and filed fourteen
separate answers, with long schedules to each—the court holding that
that the defendants could not be bound to answer jointly; and there
was no reason, in fact, why the whole three hundred shareholders
might not have answered separately. The result was, that it became
impossible to proceed with a suit in which the plaintiff might, as a
preliminary measure, have had to take office copies of three hundred
answers, each with a long schedule, and where on every alteration of
the firm by death, etc., he would have to revive his suit, etc. Lord
Eldon's remark shows that he felt the jurisdiction of the court was not
suited to such partnerships. He observes, 'Another consideration is
this—ought the jurisdiction of the court, which can be administered
usefully only between a limited number of persons, to be employed for
a purpose which it cannot by possiblity accomplish? Here is a *bill
with nearly three hundred defendants;* how can such a case ever be
brought to a hearing? And if the plaintiff cannot show a probability
of getting a decree, with what purpose, except that of oppression, can
the proceedings have been instituted? In such a suit the plaintiff can
do nothing, except put himself and others to enormous expense.'—*Appendix to Report from Select Committee on Joint-Stock Companies.
Parliamentary Papers*, 1844, vol. vii., *Report*, c. 3.

[m] Green *v.* Beesley, 2 B. and C., 112.

[n] Bond *v.* Pittard, 3 W. and M. 357.

even in proportion to the profits, equal to a certain share, that will *not* make him a partner; but if he has a specific interest in the profits themselves, he *is* a partner.' [o]

Such are the luminous views and practical sense which shines forth in our reports; and to these wire-drawn distinctions—too thin for Lord Eldon—to these stupid distinctions to these mock refinements, have the mercantile portion of society been sacrificed for centuries—thus have their hard-earned gains been scattered to the winds, the sport and prey of interminable litigation of the harpies of the law, their wives and children reduced to beggary, themselves driven, in spite of industry and its reward, success, to bankruptcy, that they might furnish a theme for quirks and cavils—the blot and curse of England—not embellished by a solitary ray of ingenuity, not redeemed by a grain of solid learning, not methodized by the faintest attempt at legal science, such as nothing but the most abject pettifogging could invent, and nothing but the most inveterate hatred of jurisprudence ever suffer to prevail in a court of justice.[p]

In the French law there are three kinds of partnership:—

1. Collective—where the name of the firm contains the name of some or all of the partners.[q]

---

[o] Ex parte Hamper, 17 Vesey, 112.

[p] Wainwright *v.* Waterman, 1 Vesey, jun., 311; Crawshay *v.* Collins, 15 Vesey, 226 (legal property survives, not beneficial interest); ex parte Digby and ex parte Bucton, 1 Deacon, 345; 2 Mont. and Ay., 735; Jeffreys *v.* Smith, 3 Russell, 158; ex parte Hodgkinson, 19 Vesey, 291; Waugh and Carver, 2 Hen. Bl., 235; Smith's *Leading Cases,* vol. i. p. 506, note and cases cited, Keating and Willes Ed.; Smith's *Mercantile Law,* Ed. Dowdeswell, p. 19.

[q] *Exposé de Motifs,* Regnaud : 'S'il importait de favoriser la société en commandite, qui permet à tout propriétaire de capitaux de s'associer aux chances commerciales, qui donne un aliment à la circulation, qui ajoute à son activité—qui multiplie les liens sociaux, par une communauté d'intérêts entre le propriétaire foncier et le fabricant, entre le capitaliste et l'annateur, entre les premiers personages de l'état et le commerçant le plus modeste—il importait d'empêcher les spéculations frauduleuses faites avec audace sous un nom inconnu, l'interdiction de toute question aux commanditaires sous peine de solidarité absolue, la publicité et l'affiche du contrat de société pour qu'on connaisse la somme donnée ou promise par le commanditaire, et consé-

2. Partnerships ' en commandite '—where one or more persons are general partners, and jointly and severally responsible to the full amount of their property, and others are liable only to the amount of the capital they have contributed. The business is carried on in the name of the general partners.[r] This system has been generally adopted from America, and was invented by the Italian Republics in the Middle Ages whom it furnished with the means of the most amazing exertions and raised to unexampled wealth.

3. ' Société anonyme,' in which all the partners are engaged; there is no social name or firm, but a name describing the object of the association. The business is managed by syndics.[s]

' Le contrat de société,' says the wise and learned Domat, ' diffère des autres contrats en ce que chacun des autres contrats a ses engagements bornés et réglés par sa nature particulière et que la société a une étendue générale aux engagemens des différens commerces, et de diverses conventions ou entrent les associés; ainsi leurs engagemens sont généraux et indéfinis comme ceux d'un Tuteur ou de celui qui entreprend les affaires d'un autre dans son absence ou a son insu, et aussi la bonne foi a dans son contrat une étendue proportionnée à celle des engagemens.'[t]

---

quemment la mesure des ressources et du crédit du commandite sont les principales règles établies par la loi.'—LOCRÉ.

[r] KENT, *Comm.*, 34.

[s] POTHIER, *Traité de Société*; DUR., *Droit Civil*, 5; PARDESSUS, *Droit Commer.*, h.t. ; MERLIN, *Répertoire*, h.t. ; *Code de Commerce*.

[t] DOMAT, Liv. i., § 2 : 'Cest cette solidarité passive qui distingue principalement la société en nom collectif de la société en commandite —et de la société anonyme' (*Esprit du Code de Commerce*, LOCRÉ, vol. ii. p. 74).

TROPLONG : 'Société en commandite : cette société a trois caractères particuliers qui la distinguent de la société en nom collectif. Elle se forme entre les personnes dont les unes ne donnent que leur argent et ne doivent pas même donner leur travail, et dont les autres donnent leur argent ou leur travail tout à la fois, ou leur travail seulement. 2nd. Elle n'établit pas de solidarité passive entre les associés qui administrent et ceux qui ne fournissent que des fonds en commandite ; ces derniers ne sont tenus des pertes que jusqu'à concurrence de leur mise. 3rd. L'associé commanditaire peut demeurer inconnu.'

O

Even in the English law, the choice of contracting parties is so far considered of the essence of partnership, that executors and representatives of deceased partners do not in their representative capacity succeed to the state or condition of partners.[u] But an agreement that the personal representative or heir of a partner shall succeed him in the partnership, is valid.[x] By the law of Louisiana, partnerships are divided into commercial partnerships and ordinary partnerships; art. 2796, ordinary partnerships are divided into particular or universal partnerships; art. 2797, universal partnerships are contracts by which the parties agree to make a common stock of all they respectively possess; they may extend it to all property, real and personal, or restrict it to personal only. They may agree that the property shall be common stock, or the fruits only. But property that may accrue to one of the parties after entering into the partnership by succession, donation, or legacy, does not become common stock, and any stipulation to that effect previous to the obtaining of the property is void (art. 2800). Particular partnerships are formed for business not of a commercial nature (art. 2806). This must be conducted in the name of all the persons concerned, unless a firm is adopted by the articles of the partnership, reduced to writing and recorded, as is prescribed with respect to partnerships ' en commandite,' art. 2808.

Partnership ' en commandite,' is formed by a contract by which one person or partnership agrees to furnish another person or partnership to a certain amount, either in property or money, to be employed by the person or partnership, to whom it is furnished in his or their own name or firm on condition of receiving a share in the profits, in the proportion determined by the contract, and of being liable to losses and expenses to the amount furnished and no more (art. 2810).

---

[u] Crawshay *v.* Collins, 15 VESEY, 225 ; 2 VESEY, 34 ; ex parte Hodgkinson, 19 VESEY, 291 ; 11 VESEY, 3 ; BOUVIER, *Law Dict.*, h.t.

[x] COLLIER *on Partnership*, 1, c. 1, § 1 ; GOV. *on Partnership*, 268 ; STORY *on Partnership*, 3.

XXXVII.

CUM amplius solutum est quam debeatur cujus
pars non invenitur, quæ repeti possit totum esse
indebitum intelligitur, manente pristinâ obligatione.—
PAULUS.

When an indivisible thing has been given in payment of
a debt, beyond the value of the debt, the whole thing
so given may be recovered, and the original obligation
remains as it was.

This rule, and that which follows it, relate to the 'condictio
indebiti,'[y] or the recovery of that which has been paid erroneously. I owe you a hundred aurei, and supposing that I owe you
two hundred, I give you an estate of that value. In this case I
have a right to bring my action for the recovery of the whole
estate so given, leaving the original demand untouched. The
case would be different if I had given two hundred measures
of corn instead of one hundred; for then I should only be
entitled to recover the excess, as we are told: ' Idem Marcellus
ait si pecuniam debens oleum dederit pluris pretii, quasi plus
debens, vel cum oleum deberet, oleum dederit, quasi majorem
modum debens, superfluum olei esse repetendum, non totum,
et ob hoc peremptam esse obligationem.'[z] All the creditor
has a right to do in the first case, is to keep the estate till his
debt is paid. ' Ager retinebitur donec debita pecunia solvatur,'
says Ulpian. The same rule applies to all things that are
indivisible, such as servitudes: ' Ideo autem servitutes indivi-
duæ sunt quia consistunt in usu, usus autem in necessitate et
necessitatis nulla est pars.' The law is thus summed up by
Ulpian: ' Si centum debens quasi ducenta deberem fundum
ducentorum solvi—competere repetitionem Marcellus scribit
et centum manere stipulationem—licet enim placuit rem pro
pecuniâ solutam parere liberationem—tamen si ex falsâ debiti
quantitate majoris pretii resoluta est, non fit confusio partis rei

---

[y] *Dig.* xii. 6. 21, *De Cond. Ind.* ; vii. 6. 60 ; xii. 6. 66, PAPINIAN.
[z] *Dig.* xii. 6. 26, § 5.

cum pecuniâ—nemo enim invitus compellitur ad communionem sed et condictio integra rei manet—et obligatio incorrupta.'ᶻ

XXXVIII.

IS naturâ debet, quem jure gentium dare oportet cujus fidem secuti sumus.—PAULUS.

He on the faith of whom we have relied, being bound to us by the law of nations, is our debtor according to the rules of natural justice.

Engagements differ according to the nature of the principles from which they flow. Some, called 'duties of imperfect obligation,' rest wholly on natural equity; and, as they depend for their support on good faith only, and are not clothed with the formalities of the civil law, do not give rise to any right of action. 'In hocᵃ versatur æquitas naturalis quid enim tam congruum fidei humanæ quam ea quæ invicem placuerunt servari.' On this principle, he who has received what is due to him simply by the law of nature, may retain though he could not have sued for it. 'Habet soluti retentionem quamvis non habeat debitiᵇ petitionem.' And as the secondary rights, arising from the law of nature, are primary rights in the law of nations, the jurist says that he who is bound to another by the law of nations, is also bound to him by the law of nature, as both are founded on the same basis of equity, and the obligations of both are so far identical. 'Nemo jure gentium debet quin et naturâ debeat, nihil enim jure gentium æquum est, quod etiam naturâ æquum non sit.'

In the maxim itself Paulus first explains what is meant by a natural obligation or a natural debt, and then assigns the reason why such an obligation is a bar to the recovery

---

ᶻ *Dig.* xii. 6. 26, § 4, *De Condict. Ind.*

ᵃ *Dig.* xiv. 1.

ᵇ *Dig.* xii. 6. 19., *ib.* 38, § 2. *Dig. ad Leg. Fal.* xxxv. 2. 17. 'Id quod naturâ hereditati debetur et peti quidem non potest, solutum vero non repetitur,' κ. τ. λ.

of money paid on account of it. 'Is naturâ debet quem jure gentium dare oportet,' is the first branch. 'Cujus fidem secuti sumus' is the second; as if Paulus had said, *that* is a natural debt which rests wholly on equity, and the principle of the law of nations, which tells us that *he* is bound to keep his faith, to the faith of whom we have trusted. 'Naturalis obligatio,' says Papinian, 'ut pecuniæ[c] numeratione ita justo pacto, vel jurejurando ipso jure tollitur, quod vinculum æquitatis, quo solo sustinebatur conventionis æquitate dissolvitur,' and if a real debtor, exonerated by an erroneous judgment from the debt, afterwards paid the money, he could not recover it. 'Julianus[d] verum debitorem post litem contestatam manente adhuc judicio negabat solventem repetere posse, licet tamen absolutus sit, naturâ tamen debitor permanet.' In the same sense Ulpian says, 'Hoc edicto prætor favet naturali æquitati qui constituta ex consensu facta custodit quoniam grave est fidem fallere.'[e]

Thus the distinction between natural or imperfect obligations and legal or perfect obligations is, that the person to whom they are due can enforce the latter and not the former. 'Obligatio naturalis est vinculum juris naturalis quod nos necessitate solvendi non astringit. Obligatio civilis vinculum juris civilis quod nos necessitate solvendi astringit.'[f] The English law upon the subject has fluctuated very much. As the Roman law, in many cases, interferes to support the charities of private life, and recognises the sanctity of particular relations, prohibiting the wife to ruin the husband, and the child from dragging the parent before a court of justice, but is firm and inflexible when the rule is once established, saying,

---

[c] *Dig.* xlvi. 3. 95, § 4.

[d] *Dig.* xii. 6. 60. and *ib.* xxviii. 'Judex si male absolvit et absolutus suâ sponte solverit repetere non potest.'

[e] 'De constitutâ pecuniâ,' *Dig.* xiii. 5. 1. 'Creditores accipiendos esse constat eos quibus debetur ex quâcunque actione vel persecutione vel jure civili sine ullâ exceptionis perpetuæ remotione : quod si naturâ debeatur non sunt loco creditorum.'—*Dig.* l. 16. 10.

[f] CUJACIUS, *Quæst. Pap.*, vol. iv., p. 727, in leg. 'Naturalis.'

' perquam durum est sed ita lex scripta est,' our law which seems to delight in setting at defiance all the sympathies of life, as if they were not as real things and as important to the public as a right of way, or the settlement of a lunatic pauper, has been from the natural operation of human feelings twisted into a variety of contortions by men who,[g] not being sheriffs' officers,[h] were shocked by its brutality. 'The cases,' says Lord Denman, ' in which it has been held that under certain circumstances a consideration, insufficient to raise an implied promise, will, nevertheless, support an express one, will be found collected and reviewed in the note to 'Wennall v. Adney,'[i] and in the case of 'Eastwood v. Kenyon.'[j] They are cases of voidable contracts subsequently ratified, and of equitable and moral obligations which, but for some rule of law, would of themselves have been sufficient to raise an implied promise.[k] Lord Mansfield said, 'It is the case of a promise made upon good and valuable consideration which, in all cases, is a sufficient ground of action; it is so in cases of obligations which, otherwise would only bind a man's conscience, and without such promise, he could not be compelled to pay.' Again, ' where a man is under a moral obligation which no court of law or equity could enforce, and *promises* the rectitude and honesty of the thing is a consideration—as if a man promise to pay a just debt, the recovery of which is barred by the statute of limitations—or, if a man, after he comes of age, promise to

---

[g] 'Gensque virûm truncis et duro robore nata.'

[h] Just in the same way the savage criminal law which really was written in blood was mitigated by perjury. Jurors were encouraged to find property stolen below its value. One prosecutor declaring in great wrath that the fashion of the article alone was worth more than the value suggested, 'Gentlemen,' said Lord Mansfield to the jury, 'I hope we shall not hang a man for fashion sake.' All alteration in this law was bitterly opposed by Lord Eldon, Lord Ellenborough, and all the Judges. Sir S. Romilly and Sir J. Macintosh, each in his memoirs, mention Lord Grenville's speech urging its reformation, in reply to Lord Eldon as the most admirable specimen of reasoning they had ever heard.

[i] 3 Bos and PULLEN, 249.   [j] 11 AD. and ELLIS, 438.

[k] Cocking v. Ward, 1 C.B., 858.

pay a meritorious debt contracted during his minority, but not for necessaries—or if a bankrupt, in affluent circumstances after his certificate, promise to pay the whole of his debts— or if a man promise to pay a secret trust, or a trust void for want of writing by the statute of frauds; in such, and many other instances, though the promise gives a compulsory remedy where there was none before either in law or equity, yet, as the promise is only to do what an honest man ought to do, the ties of conscience to an upright mind are a sufficient consideration.'[1] The exact principle of the Roman law is laid down by the same great judge, in a case not alluded to in the more recent decisions.[m] 'The rule had always been that if a man has actually paid what the law would not have compelled him to pay, but what in equity and conscience he ought, he cannot recover it back again in an action for money had and received. . . . . But where money was paid under a mistake, which there was no ground to claim in conscience, the party may recover it back again by this kind of action.' The same rule (while our courts were floundering in darkness of their own creating) has been adopted in America. 'The old rule,[n] that an action will not lie where the consideration is past has received a rational explanation from the liberal ideas (qy.) that actuate modern courts of justice. Though the service has been rendered prior to the promise, yet, if the party be under a legal or moral obligation to pay, the promise

---

[1] Atkins v. Hill, COWPER, 288. But Lord Mansfield did not think that every thing which a sheriff's officer could not appreciate was 'humbug.' Hawkes v. Sanders, ib. Truman v. Fenton, COWPER, 544. It is only in our courts of justice that it could be doubted, much less denied, that a father was bound by his promise to pay for the maintenance of an illegitimate child.—ESP., N.P., 94. Atkins v. Banwell, 2 EAST, 505 ; Barber v. Fox, 2 SAUNDERS, 136.

[m] Bize v. Dickason, 1 T. Reps. 286.

[n] 'The opinions of the English judges,' says Judge Putnam, 'appear to have been varying for a long series of years on this subject.'

'Mills v. Wynam, 3 PICKERING, Reps. 212; Greeves v. MacAlister, 2 BINNEY, Reps. p. 592; Farmer v. Arundel, 2 BL. R., 825; Lowrey v. Bourdieu, 452 DOUGLAS.

will bind him.' 'A moral obligation is sufficient consideration for an assumption.'° 'Where the party, with a good conscience, might receive the money, and there was no deceit or unfair practice in obtaining it, although it was money which the party could not recover by law, this action (for money had and received) has never been so far extended as to enable the party who paid the money voluntarily to recover it again.' ᴾ

XXXIX.

CUJUS per errorem dati repetitio est—ejus consulto dati donatio est.—PAULUS.

That, which if given away in error, entitles me to an action for its recovery, is, if given deliberately, a donation.

The distinction asserted by this rule between the ' per errorem' and the 'consulto datum' is marked by the grant or the refusal of the action for the ' condictio indebiti': ' Si quis indebitum ignorans solvit per hanc actionem condicere potest sed si sciens se non debere solvit cessat repetitio' (*Dig.* xv. 6).

The Roman law gave certain privileges to the master who voluntarily enfranchised a slave, over him after his emancipation. Those privileges, however, did not exist where the slave was emancipated as the condition of a gift, or sale, or legacy. Now, if the slave so emancipated, believing himself liable to the same services as he who was emancipated by the spontaneous act of his master, promised to perform certain acts, in lieu of those services, for his former owner, the law released him from the obligation (1 *Dig. de legalis*, xxx. tit. 1, 95). ' Videndum tamen est numquid si vice operarum rogaverit eum aliquid debeat hoc valere—quod nequaquam dicendum est quia nec operæ imponi hujus modi possunt nec impositæ exiguntur.' So 'de bonis libertorum' (*Ib.* xxxviii. 2. 29). ' Qui

---

° Clark *v.* Herring, 5 BINNEY, 36.

ᴾ Morris *v.* Tavin, 1 DALLAS, 159; Irvine *v.* Hanlin, 10 S. and R , 220 ; Mathers *v.* Pearson, 13 S. and R., 258 ; Bogart *v.* Nevins, 6 S. and R., 369; Mills *v.* Wynam, 3 PICKERING, *Reps.*

ex causâ fidei commissæ,' etc.; and the plain inference from
the law (*De Cond. Indebiti,* xii. 6. 26, § 12).

Money, morally due, but paid under a mistake, could not be
recovered; it was not a 'donatio,' but a 'debiti solutio.' If
the ward made a promise, without his guardian's sanction, and
the guardian afterwards sanctioned it, the promise was
binding (*Dig.* xxxix. 5. 19. 4). So the real debtor, who
paid money after a sentence in his favour, could not recover
it; and, therefore, a suitor, who really owed money, and
paid it 'pendente lite' to his creditor, never could recover
it, for he was bound to pay it if the sentence had been against
him, and if it had been for him, he could not recover it
when paid. 'Julianus rerum debitorem post litem contestatam manente adhuc judicio negabat solventem repetere posse
quia nec absolutus, nec condemnatus repetere posset; licet
enim absolutus sit, naturâ tamen debitor manet similemque
esse ei dicit qui ita promisit, sive navis ex Asiâ venerit sive
non venerit' (*Dig.* xii. 6. 60). Money given for a reason past
could not be recovered, though the reason was false—money
given for a thing to come could be recovered, if the thing did
not happen. 'Damus aut ob causam aut ob rem, ob causam
prætentam veluti cum ideo do quod aliquid a te consecutus
sum vel quod aliquid a te factum est, ut etiam si falsa causa
sit repetitio ejus pecuniæ non est—ob rem vero datur ut aliquid
sequatur, quo non sequentæ repetitio competit' (*Ib.* xii. 6. 52);
and again (*Ib.* 65, § 2): 'Id quoque quod ob causam datur,
puta quod negotia mea adjuta ab eo putavi licet non sit factum
quia donari volui quamvis falso mihi persuaserim repeti non
posse.' It is clear, therefore, that the Roman law, as a general
rule, enabled a person, who, in ignorance either of fact or law,
had paid money which he was not bound to pay, to recover it.
It was the opinion of those great jurists—of Sabinus, and
Ulpian, and Papinian—that the legislator should do what he
could to prevent what was unjust from being profitable. The
rule was built by them on this strong and universal principle.
That this is so is clear, first, from the law, so well worthy of a
great people, and so directly opposite to that most immoral

rule laid down by Lord Ellenborough and Lord Eldon, in which Ulpian sanctions the opinion of Sabinus expressed emphatically in *Dig.* xii. 5. 6 : ' *Perpetuo* Sabinus probavit veterum opinionem existimantium *id quod ex injustâ causâ apud aliquem sit posse condici.*' That no man should be allowed to keep what he was possessed of unrighteously; confirmed by Papinian : ' Hæc condictio ex æquo et bono introducta quod alterius apud alterum sine causa deprehenditur revocare consuevit' (*Dig.* xii. 6. 66). The words of Papinian are full of energy, and comprise law as well as fact.[b] But Ulpian, in the passage I am about to cite, puts the question still more clearly : ' We hold that what is not due has been paid, not merely where no debt at all is due, but where, on account of a perpetual ' exceptio' (which includes law as well as fact), it could not be recovered, unless the person, knowing he is guarded by such an ' exceptio,' has paid it—' Indebitum autem solutum accipimus non solum si omnino non debeatur sed et si per aliquam exceptionem perpetuam peti non poterat, quare hoc quoque repeti poterit nisi sciens se tutum exceptione solverit' (*Dig.* xii. 6. 26. 3).

To lay down as a rule, in a system so destitute of all general principle, and so abounding in snares and pitfalls as ours, that the act of a person who pays money under a mistake of law— which is to be extracted from thousands of volumes, written in a style, compared with which the worst jargon of the schoolmen was elegant—was irrecoverable, was a doctrine as much at variance with the best interests of society as immorality and and want of reason could make it. Nor is the flippant reason of Lord Ellenborough, cited with so much delight by many writers, likely to reconcile to it those whose ideas of jurisprudence go beyond TIDD'S *Practice* and CHITTY *on Pleading.*

Bad as it was, however, it was admirably adapted to promote the interests of lawyers—objects, to which it seemed, at no

---

[b] PAPINIAN, l. 17. 10 : 'Error ejus qui se municipem aut colonum existimans munera civilia suscepturum promisit, defensionem juris non excludit.'

very distant period, admitted on all hands that every other should be sacrificed. 'These things exist,' says Lord Hobart, 'that the law may be an art.' And why is the law an art? for the welfare of society. Is that promoted by such a rule?[c] To return, however, to the Roman law.

So, e. g., a person who was obliged by the natural ties of justice and equity to make property over to another, was not in the strict sense of the word a donor; for the law of nature and of conscience was held to be a valid law, and to take away from that absolute freedom of the will which was requisite for a donation. If a man gave money to a slave, and the slave became free, and promised to repay the money, this was not a 'donatio,' but a 'debiti solutio' (*Dig.* xxxix. 5. 19. 4). So it was held the duty of a parent to provide for his child; e. g., to find the 'dos.' By the 35th paragraph of the Julian law, parents were compelled to provide a suitable portion for their children; and by a law of Severus and Antoninus, those who did not choose to give a dower, 'qui dotem dare non volunt,' might be compelled by the proconsul: 'Præses provinciæ liberos in matrimonium collocare et dotare' (*Dig.* xxiii. 2. 19). So, too, payments made in conformity to the law of nature, and out of reverence to its obligations only, were valid, and could not be reclaimed. 'Id quod naturâ debetur solutum repeti non posse,' said the heathen jurist. An obligation founded on the law of nature, though it gave no right of action, furnished a good defence: 'quod pupillus sine tutoris auctoritate mutuum accepit et *locupletior* factus est, si pubes factus solvat — non repetit' (xii. 6. 13, § 1); and the law 'Julianus' (*ib.* 60), which I have cited elsewhere. So a master who paid his debt to a slave after his enfranchisement could not recover it: 'Si quod dominus servo debuit, manumisso solvit quamvis existimans ei se aliquâ teneri actione tamen repetere non poterit, quia naturale agnovit debitum' (*ib.* 64). This was defined in the law (*Dig.* xxxv. 2. 1, § 17),

---

[c] 'Omnia,' etc.
[d] Hunter *v.* Atkyns, 3 M. and C., 139.

' Id quod peti quidem non potest solutum vero non repetitur'
(*Ad Leg. Falcidiam*). It was the aim and end of the jurist, by
insisting on this rule, to show that there were certain equitable
obligations which rested exclusively on the law of nature. To
same effect Papinian says (*Dig.* xlvi. 3, 95, § 4), ' Naturalis
obligatio ut pecuniæ numeratione ita justo pacto, vel jurejurando ipso jure tollitur quod vinculum æquitatis quo solo
sustinebatur conventionis æquitate dissolvitur.' 'Grave est
fidem fallere,' says Ulpian (*De Pec. Constit.*, xiii. 5. 1).[e] Thus,
where a young man, Aquilius Regulus, wrote to his old hereditary friend, Nicostratus: ' Quoniam et cum patre meo semper
fuisti et me eloquentiâ et diligentiâ tuâ meliorem reddidisti
dono et permitto tibi habitare in illo cænaculo eoque uti;'
after the death of Aquilius, an action was brought against
Nicostratus for his residence. 'Cum de eâ re mecum con-
tulisset,' says Papinian; ' dixi posse defendi non meram donationem esse: verum officium magistri quâdam mercede remune-
ratum Regulum ideoque non videri donationem sequentis
temporis irritam esse' (*Dig.* xxxix. 5. 27). So, ' Si quis aliquem
a latrunculis vel hostibus eripuit et aliquid pro eo ab ipso
accipiat hæc donatio irrevocabilis est' (*Dig.* xxxix. 5. 34, § 1).

So a bonâ fide possessor, who was only bound to repay his
actual profit, ' in id duntaxat, quo locupletior factus est,' and
was not accountable for the waste and dilapidations made,
' dum re suâ abuti putat,' was not responsible for his donations,
' nec si donaverit completior factus videbatur,' unless—and the
distinction illustrates the rule—he had given that he might
receive again: ' Plane si ἀντίδωρα id est remunerationes acceperunt dicendum est eatenus locupletiores factos, quatenus
acceperunt' (*Dig. de Pet. Hæred.*, v. 3. 25, § 11). So Gaius
says, that an ' actio furti' would lie against him who lent gra-
tuitously to another what he had borrowed for his own use,
' furtum fieri si quis usum alienæ ei in suum usum con-
vertit;' adding, with that fine sense of legal analogy and
beauty of language so amazing to the reader of our reports,

---

[e] 'Donationes in concubinam.'—*Dig.* xxxix. 5. 32. SAVIGNY, *Fect-
schrift*, 4, 1, *Lex Cincia.*

' Species enim lucri est ex alieno largiri, et beneficii debitorem sibi acquirere' (*Dig.* xlvii. 2. 54, § 1). And Labeo, quoted by Ulpian (xxxix. 5. 19, § 1), says, ' Extra causam donationum esse talium officiorum mercedes: ut puta si tibi adfuero, si satis pro te dedero, si quâlibet in re operâ vel gratiâ meâ usus fuerit.'

By the English law, a gift[f] of real property is a voluntary conveyance; i.e., a conveyance not founded on any consideration of natural affection or of interest. A gift must be testified by deed, or accompanied by actual delivery of possession.[g] When once made, however, it is not in the donor's power to retract it, unless it be prejudicial to creditors, or the donor were under any legal incapacity, or drawn in, circumvented, or imposed on by false pretences, ebriety, or surprise. Gifts are divided into gifts ' inter vivos,' and those ' mortis causâ'[h] (see *Code of Louisiana*, 1455, *Inst.* 7, *de Donationibus*, where the illustration is given from the *Odyssey*). A donation 'mortis causâ' is, by the civil law, a gift made under apprehension of death, on condition that if the donor dies, the donee shall absolutely possess it; but if he survives, the donor may recall it at his pleasure. Such a donation, as M. Bouvier observes, is now brought, as nearly as possible, to the condition of legacies. It resembles a legacy, inasmuch as, in the legal phrase, it is ambulatory during the life of the giver: it differs from a legacy, because it is not the subject of administration, and requires no assent from the executors to make the title of the holder valid. The Roman law allowed a ' donatio morti

---

[f] ' Give' is the apt word in a feoffment.—COKE, *Litt.*, 9 *a* ; 2 *B. C. Comm.* 310.

[g] Irons *v.* Smallpiece, 5 B. and ALD., 551 ; otherwise the gift is void in law, and equity will give no assistance to the donee. Miller *v.* Miller, 3 P. WILLIAMS, 356. See Ellison *v.* Ellison, 6 VESEY, 656 ; Edwards *v.* Jones, 1 MYLNE and CRAIG, 226 ; Antrobus *v.* Smith, 12 VESEY, 39 ; ex parte Dubort, 18 VESEY, 140 ; Dillon *v.* Coppin, 4 MYLNE and CRAIG, 647.

[h] ' Ubi ita donatur . . . ut nullo casu revocetur, causa donandi magis est, quam mortis causâ donatio, et ideo prinde haberi debet, ut alia vivis donatio.'—*Dig.* xxxvi. 6. 27.

causâ' to be in writing.[i] A 'donatio mortis causâ' can only be of personal property. The *Code of Louisiana* only allows it to be made by will (1563). From utter ignorance of the Roman law, our judges have annexed two conditions to a 'mortis causâ' donation, quite unknown to the writers in the Pandects, and, as may be supposed, not founded on any very luminous notions or extensive knowledge of jurisprudence, requiring, by that sort of fatality which may be traced in almost every branch of judicial legislation—not only the actual delivery of the thing given, but that the donor should die of the malady under which he was labouring when he bestowed it;[k] thus showing that they had never even read the passage in the Institutes on which the law is founded. By the Roman law, as well as by ours, a 'donatio mortis causâ' made to the wife is valid,[l] and thus specifically different from a gift 'inter vivos.' It is now settled, that exchequer bills, bills of exchange, bank notes, bonds and mortgages, may be the subject of donations 'mortis causâ.' A 'donatio mortis causâ,' by the civil law, might be the subject of a trust.[m]

---

[i] 'Avunculo suo debitori mortis causâ donaturus quæ debebat ita scripsit 'tabulæ vel chirographum tot ubicunque sunt inanes esse' neque eum solvere debere. Quæro an hæredes si pecuniam ab avunculo defuncti petant, exceptione doli mali se tueri possint. Marcellus respondit posse, nimium enim contra voluntatem defuncti, hæres petit ab eo.'—*Dig.* xxxix. 6. 28.

[k] WILLIAMS, *On Executors*, pt. ii. b. ii. c. 2, § 4, vol. i. ; Ward *v.* Turner, 2 VESEY Sen., 430; LORD HARDWICKE'S *Remarks ;* STORY, *Equity Jurisprudence*, 606 ; 2 KENT'S *Comm.*, 354 ; ROPER, *Legacies*, ed. White, i. § 2, p. 2 ; 1 BEAVAN, *Reports*, 605; 3 WOODESON, *Lect.* 60, p.513 ; 1 MILES, *R.*, 109 ; Nicholas *v.* Adams, 2 WHARTON, *Reports*, 17.

[l] *Dig.* xxxvi. 6. 27 ; Duffield *v.* Elwes, BLIGH, *Reports*, 493, where Lord Eldon, in an elaborate judgment, delivers an erroneous opinion as to Roman law, and of course impairs the utility of Lord Hardwicke's decision in Ward *v.* Turner.

[m] *Dig.* xxxi. 1. 77. 1 : ' Eorum, quibus mortis causâ donatum est, fidei committi quoquo tempore potest.' Hambrooke *v.* Simmons, 4 RUSSELL, *Reports*, 27.

XL.

QUIDQUID in calore iracundiæ vel fit vel dicitur non prius ratum quam si perseverantiâ appareat animi judicium fuisse.—PAULUS.

Nothing said or done in the heat of passion is irrevocable, until perseverance shews that it was the deliberate purpose of the mind.

Therefore, a wife who had left her husband's house in the heat of passion, but returned to it speedily, was as if she had not quitted it: ' Ideoque brevi reversa uxor, nec divertisse videatur.' And hasty words did not bring the speaker under the penalties of the ' Lex Julia Majestatis;' a circumstance that those who utter common places against the Roman law as hostile to freedom, might occasionally derive some benefit by recollecting. *Dig.*xlviii.4. 7. 3: ' Hoc tamen crimen a judicibus non in occasionem ob principalis majestatis venerationem habendum est sed in veritate—nam et personam spectandam esse, an potuerit facere et an ante quid fecerit, et an cogitaverit, et an sane mentis fuerit, nec *lubricum linguæ ad pœnam facile trahendum est.*' As to the illustration of the rule from the intention of the wife to make a divorce, Ulpian says, ' Divortium non est nisi verum quod animo perpetuum constituendi dissensionem fit, non autem per calores iracundiæ vel frigusculum.'[n]

Paulus gives rather a singular example of this principle. It is from the vehemence of bidders at an auction. He will not allow offers made in the heat of competition to be binding, without security is given: ' Locatio vectigalium quæ calore licitantis ultra modum solitæ conductionis inflavit ita demum est admittenda, si fidejussores idoneos et cautionem is qui licitatione vicerit offerre paratus sit.'[o]

---

[n] *Dig.* v. 16. 13, *de Divortiis.*

[o] *Dig.* xxxix. 4. 9. Those who have read Mr. KENNEDY's valuable *Digest of Evidence on the Tenure of Land in Ireland,* will be at no loss to find modern instances where the same check might be useful.

The Roman law made much more allowance for accidental starts of passion and human infirmity than the English, for the simple reason that it was framed neither by time-servers nor by men in whom the study of technical details had, with every finer perception, extinguished every spark of common sense,[p] but by men whose minds were fortified by a generous learning, and who were deeply conversant with human nature. Our law of murder, for instance, includes offences of the most varied kinds in one general description. Men have been hanged for doing what the highest persons in the country had done, and were dishonoured if they did not do, at the very time of their execution. A man shoots another, after some outrageous insult, in a duel; or a man passionately attached to his wife, kills her in a sudden transport of passion: a girl, betrayed and insulted by some miscreant, and maddened by the smart of intolerable wrongs, kills him. These persons are, by our law, guilty of the same offence as a parricide who shoots an indulgent father from behind a hedge.[q] Papinian says, ' Ei qui uxorem suam in adulterio[r] deprehensam occidisse se non negat ultimum supplicium remitti potest, cum sit difficillimum justum dolorem temperare et quia plus fecerit, quam quia vindicare se non debuerit, puniendus sit.'[s] There is a redeeming law in the code, headed, ' Si quis imperatori maledixerit.' The words of him who had spoken disrespectfully of the ruler were

---

[p] See Lord Coke's *Institutes*, passim. The state trials, particularly the argument on the reversal of Walcot's sentence after he had been embowelled alive—the maxim that all acts of Parliament date from the first day of the session—the Norman-French of the reports, and the hideous idiom in which law proceedings were carried on, etc., etc., etc.—compared with all this, the very decisions on points of special pleading in Meeson and Welsby are almost rational.

[q] Nor let any one suppose that, in fact, a difference is always made ; it is no such thing. The law is often left to take its course from the best motives, as it used to be when men were hanged for stealing ten shillings in a dwelling-house, and in our own times for horse-stealing, when the fate of the sufferer, though no doubt deeply criminal, excites the strongest commiseration.

[r] By our law, homicide, if the adulterer was killed. 1 Hale, *P. C.*, 486.   [s] *Dig.* xlviii. 5. 38, *ad Leg. Juli.*

overlooked: 'Quoniam si id ex levitate processerit contemnendum est—si ex insaniâ, miseratione dignissimum—si ab injuriâ, remittendum.'[t] Papinian, we are told by Marcianus, was unwilling to execute the laws against suitors or their representatives, who made false charges which they afterwards retracted: 'Quæri possit si ita fuerit interlocutus,' i.e., the judge, 'Lucius Titius temere accusâsse videtur—an calumniatorem pronunciâsse videatur et Papinianus temeritatem facilitatis veniam continere, et inconsultum calorem calumniæ vitio carere, et ob id hunc nullam pænam subire oportere.'[u] By a foolish provision in a recent act of Parliament, 'advised and open speaking' was (in the true spirit of our legislation, for two years only!) put on a level with overt acts, and publishing any printing or writing.[v] 'Rien,' says Montesquieu,[x] 'ne rend encore le crime de lèse majesté plus arbitraire qui quand des paroles indiscrètes en deviennent la matière les discours sont si sujets à l'interprétation, il y'a tant de différence entre l'indiscrétion et la malice et il y en à si peu dans les expressions qu'elles emploient—que la loi ne peut guère soumettre les paroles à une peine capitale à moins qu'elle ne déclare expressément celles, qu'elle y soumet. Les paroles ne forment point un corps de délit elles ne restent que dans l'idée la plupart du temps elles ne signifient point par elles mêmes, mais par le ton dont ou les dit—souvent en redisant les mêmes paroles ou ne

---

[t] L. Si quis, *Unic. Cod.*

[u] Ad Senat. Turpillianum, *Dig.* xlviii.16.5; and, on the general subject, the *Rapport* of M. MONSEGNAT. 'En se conformant à la distinction adoptée par le Code de 1791, celui qui vous est présenté n'a pas soumis à la même peine et confondu l'assassinat et l'homicide qui n'ayant pas été commis avec préméditation et de guet-a-pens, est qualifié meurtre—celui-ci suppose l'action de la volonté, mais il écarte les combinaisons de la haine les projets de la vengeance, et les complots de la scéleratesse —presque toujours il est le produit d'un premier mouvement, l'effet un d'entrainement irréfléchi, le résultat de l'effervescence d'une grande passion et la passion ne voit que l'objet qui l'anime; elle ne calcule pas est chances qu'elle court.'—LOCRÉ, vol. xxx. p. 505.

[v] 11 and 12 Vict., c.12.

[x] *Esprit des Loix*, xii. c.12; BLACKSTONE, *Commentaries*, vol. iv. p. 137; GREAVES, *Russell*, On Crimes, vol. i. 579.

rend pas le même sens . . . il n'y à rien de si équivoque
que tout cela . . . partout ou cette loi [making words
treason] est établie non seulement la liberté n'est plus
mais son ombre même.' The illustrious writer then proceeds to shew that words are then important, when they
accompany and qualify an action, a truth which even
our judicial legislators have been obliged to recognise.

 ' Les paroles qui sont jointes à une action prennent la nature
de cette action—ainsi, un homme qui va dans la place publique
exhorter les sujets à la révolte devient coupable de lèse majesté;
parceque les paroles sont jointes à l'action et y participent—
ce ne sont les paroles que l'on punit mais une action commise
dans la quelle on emploie les paroles. *Elles ne deviennent* des
crimes que *lorsqu'elles preparent qu'elles accompagnent, ou qu'elles
suivent une action criminelle.'* [y]

If we compare this passage with the barbarous nonsense
uttered in cases of libel and treason by our judges, down to the
time of Lord Ellenborough *inclusive*, we may, perhaps, think
that the ' practical sense,' which we are talking about so perpetually, as an excuse for the utter want of all comprehensive
views, might be a little improved by the study of jurisprudence.[z]
Certainly, men trained in the studies which formed the writer
I have quoted, would never have convicted the Queen's waterman, for raising a mob who set fire to dissenting chapels, at
the time of Sacheverell's trial, with the cries of ' Church and

---

[y] *Esprit des Loix*, xii. 12.
[z] The expression applied by Lord Bacon to the schoolmen, that they
were 'fierce with dark keeping,' exactly describes the vast majority of
those who have held great judicial offices among us.   Lord Mansfield's
servile opinions in political matters, and his noble birth, atoned for his
love of justice, his elegant taste, his captivating eloquence, and his extensive knowledge ; and, above all, for his liberal, philosophical, and
deeply-meditated opinions on jurisprudence.   But if he had lived to
our day, and seen his great decisions reversed, his opinions ridiculed,
his efforts to humanise the studies and views of the English Bar overthrown by pettifoggers, who selected his political conduct for imitation,
he might have said, as another great man did, ' Je voyais à DES BÊTES
l'esprit qui me fuyait.'

Queen, and passive obedience!' of a design to compass the death of the sovereign; nor have framed a system of pleading which gave no information whatever to the suitor of the demand, or defence of his antagonist; nor have found that Charles II., when he was hid in the oak at Boscobel, or was a fugitive at Cologne, was ' de facto' King of England; nor have given almost every Act of Parliament a retrospective operation; proofs of practical wisdom, for which, in the history of the civilised part of the species, it would be difficult to find a parallel.[a]

Our history furnishes a noble instance of a ruler's acting in the spirit of this maxim, in the forgiveness extended by our great deliverer, William III., to the Duke of Shrewsbury, when that gifted but irresolute nobleman had allowed himself to be entangled in a Jacobite conspiracy. If our magnanimous Elizabeth had acted in the same manner towards Essex, she would have saved herself from sufferings which the vindictive ruler of both the Indies never could make her feel, and her sun would have been as serene in its setting as in its meridian it had been glorious.

And before I quit this maxim, I must advert—in illustration of it, and of the coarse and slovenly character of our law, even on the most important matters—to the punishment of women for destroying their new-born children. A woman, maddened by agony of body and shame of mind, takes away the life she has given to a being not capable of pain or terror. She is by our law liable to the same punishment as the most savage assassin. The consequence of this atrocious pedantry is, that judges, counsel, witnesses, and juries conspire to bring about her acquittal.

Thus, instead of suffering some punishment, which she has deserved, she escapes altogether. Every now and then, to be sure, a miserable wretch is hanged, to the horror of every one who considers the true character of the offence, and the

---

[a] Neither, indeed, would they call legal education ' humbug,' especially if they were invested with the highest judicial office in the country.

utterly disproportioned nature of the punishment. Surely, if ever the beautiful passage of Scripture, ' As I live, saith the Lord God, I have no pleasure in the death of a sinner, but rather that he should turn from his wickedness and live,' is applicable, it is to such a case. But a short time has passed since cutting a twig and parricide—murdering a family in their sleep and stealing a sheep—breaking the mound of a fish-pond and poisoning a wife—associating for a month with persons called Egyptians and blowing out the brains of a man from behind a hedge—were punishable alike by death. In spite of the rancorous efforts of Lord Eldon and Lord Ellenborough, this state of things has been altered; but the evil effects of judicial legislation—of the times when Englishmen quietly beheld their fellow-citizens quartered alive for constructive treason, and burnt alive for constructive heresy—are not all effaced. The injury still done to the public mind, in consequence of humane efforts to prevent the noxious effects of an absurd law by making it useless, is not inconsiderable. Juries acquire a habit of disregarding their oaths, and judges, of great learning and ability, set the example of ransacking their invention for arguments, which, in any other case, they would repudiate with disdain and indignation. The security and welfare of society alone justify the infliction of any punishment, much more of that terrible punishment where mistake is irretrievable. Can any man say that these objects are promoted by hanging a girl for an offence to which she has been driven, in some cases by the strongest instincts of her sex, the very power of which shows a mind not absolutely depraved, and committed when her faculties are confused by the tortures which every comfort and sympathy can hardly enable a woman to endure, and which she has often been obliged to suffer, without pity, without help, and with the prospect of disgrace and ruin before her eyes.[b]

---

[b] ὡς τρὶς ἂν παρ' ἀσπίδα
Στῆναι θέλοιμ' ἂν μᾶλλον—ἤ τεκεῖν ἅπαξ.

XLI.

NON capitur qui jus Publicum sequitur.—ULPIAN.
To insist on a rule of public law is not to overreach.

The acts of a minor, that were detrimental to him, might
be set aside. If, however, the act done was one which the
'jus Publicum,' that is, the public or constitutional law, as
opposed to the 'jus privatum,' required to be done, the rule
did not apply, for the reason alleged in this maxim. That it
could not be said that any one was 'captus,' deceived, injured,
or led into error, who had obeyed the dictates of such a law.
The same principle is asserted by Papinian: 'Non deceptus
videtur jure communi usus.' The instance given to illustrate
this example was that of a minor who chooses to sue sureties.
By the Roman law, all the sureties who had agreed to be responsible for the debt, 'pro virili et in solidum,' were liable for
it; and when the action began, every one was liable for an
equal share. The obligation was then distributed 'pro ratâ'
among all. Supposing, however, that after the minor began
his suit one of the sureties became insolvent, the minor could
not begin proceedings anew, after the debt had been appor-
tioned by the 'jus Publicum,' with the view of making the
other sureties liable for the share of the insolvent.[c]

Thus, even where the 'jus Publicum' did not apply, a minor
could not always succeed in setting aside his acts; it must be
shown that he was 'captus.' Ulpian has drawn the distinction
most clearly: 'Sciendum est,' he says, 'non passim minoribus
subveniri sed causâ cognitâ si capti esse proponantur.' So, he
says, the minor who has acted without imprudence, 'qui sobrie
rem gessit,' is not entitled to relief merely by reason of an
accident, 'occasione damni'; for it is not the loss itself, but the
cause of the loss—the 'inconsulta facilitas'—which is the crite-
rion of such a claim. So if a minor had purchased a slave, and
the slave died; or if he accepted an inheritance, and from some

---

[c] *Dig.* xlvi. 1. 51 : 'de fidejuss.'—PAPINIAN. 'Inter eos fidejussores
actio dividenda est qui solidum et partes viriles suâ fide esse jusserunt,'
κ.τ.λ.

sudden accident the inheritance became a burden to him (' puta prædia fuerunt quæ chasmate perierunt, insulæ exustæ sunt servi fugerunt aut decesserunt'), he could not claim to be released from his engagements. 'Neque enim ætatis lubrico captus est adeundo locupletem hæreditatem et quod facto contingit cuivis patrifamilias quamvis diligentissimo possit contingere.'

'But,' he adds, 'the minor may demand restitution, if he has imprudently accepted an inheritance, 'in quâ reserant multæ mortales vel prædia urbana, vel æs alienum grave'; because he did not anticipate the death of the slaves, the dilapidation of the buildings, etc.'

XLII.

NULLUS videtur dolo facere qui suo jure utitur.
No one is guilty of a fraud, because he exerts his right.

As an instance of this rule, may be cited the case of a creditor who obtains payment of the sum due to him from an insolvent debtor. So the man who chose to dam up the rainwater which fell on his land, instead of allowing it to descend to his neighbour's field, might defend himself on this principle (*Dig.* xxxix. 3. 11): 'Prodesse enim sibi unus quisque dum alii non nocet non prohibetur.'

XLIII.

DESINIT debitor esse is qui nactus est exceptionem justam nec ab æquitate naturali abhorrentem.—MARCELLUS.

He is no longer a debtor who has a defence that is righteous and consistent with natural equity.

The question, Who ceases to be a debtor? is answered in this sentence, in which a distinction is manifestly drawn between a righteous and an unrighteous plea. He ceases to be a debtor who has obtained the former, not he who insists upon the latter.

The law *De Verb.*, *Sign.* 55, corresponds with this rule: ' Creditor is est qui exceptione perpetuâ summoveri non potest.'

Suppose the bond of a debtor returned to him by his creditor; if after this, the debtor was sued either by the creditor, or the heirs of the creditor, he might oppose their demand successfully, ' exceptione doli mali.' Nay, farther, if he had paid the money after this bond had been given back to him, he might recover it again ' ex æquo et bono,' for the restoration was equivalent to a covenant not to sue (*Dig.* xxxix. J. 18).

Titia gave the bonds (chirographa) of her debtors to Ageria, ordering her, if she, Titia, died, to give them up to her debtors, but if she recovered, to give them back to her. Titia died, and Ageria gave the bonds up to the debtors. The heir of Titia wished to sue the debtors; and it was answered that she might be answered by an ' exceptio,' either ' pacti conventi,' or ' doli.' The same rule is laid down, *Dig.* ii. 14ᵃ: ' Si debitori meo reddiderim conventionem videtur inter nos convenisse ne peterem profuturumque ei conventionis exceptionem placuit.' So if a legacy were given on condition that the legatee should give up to his debtor the deed containing the obligation. This was tantamount to a condition that he should release the debt. ' Hujusmodi conditio hanc vim habet si hæredem meum debito liberaverit' (*Dig.* xxx. 1. 84, § 7). And here we may remark the difference between the re-delivery of the ' pignus' and the restoration of the bond. For the re-delivery of the " pignus' did not cancel the debt. A bequest to the debtor by the creditor, did not of necessity release his debt; it gave the legatee a right to that which he had pledged for its security. *Dig.* xxxiv. 3. 1, § 1: ' Julianus scripsit si

---

ᵃ Sc. ' tacito consensu.'—*Dig.* xxxii. 1. 59: ' Qui chirographum legat non tantum de tabulis cogitat sed etiam de actionibus quarum probatio tabulis continetur.'

res pignori data legetur debitori a creditore valere legatum habereque eum actionem ut pignus recipiat priusquam pecuniam solvat—sic autem loquitur Julianus quasi debitum non debeat lucrari sed si alia testantis voluntas fuit et ad hoc pervenietur exemplo luitionis.'

The word used is ' desinit,' or ' ceases to be,' which implies that he was really and *bonâ fide* a debtor. The rules, therefore, which relate to cases where a person imagining himself to be debtor, has paid or promised to pay money, do not touch this instance. Neither do the rules which illustrate cases where there was a good ' exceptio ' in the first instance, as where the ' senatus-consultum Velleianum,' or the ' senatus-consultum Macedonianum in odium ejus cui debetur ' might be pleaded, as this case turns upon an ' ex post facto' liberation.

Again, it must be a righteous defence, ' exceptionem justam,' such a defence as has been stated; a payment, or that arising from a ' pactum de non petendo;' or as the Greek commentators add, from prescription or the sentence of a judge. In all these cases the debt is obliterated; nor does even any natural obligation remain : 'Naturalem obligationem ut pecuniæ muneratione ita justo pacto vel jurejurando ipso jure tolli, quia vinculum æquitatis quo solo sustinebatur conventionis æquitati dissolvitur ' (*Dig. de Solut*, 95, § 4).

It is not, therefore, the man who has contrived by any means to get back his deed, or to obtain a ' pactum' that he shall not be sued, but he who has done so righteously, ' juste,' who can take advantage of this rule, and who in the words of it, ceases to owe the debt for which at one time he was liable.

XLIV.

VERUM est neque pacta neque stipulationes factum posse tollere, quod enim impossibile est neque pacto neque stipulatione potest comprehendi, ut utilem actionem aut factum facere possit. — ULPIAN.

No compact or stipulation can displace a fact, for what is impossible cannot be the subject of any compact or stipulation, so as to give rise to any equitable action or any result.

It is evident, from the first words of this rule, that it was intended as a concession, which the latter part of the sentence was used to qualify.

It relates to an impossibility in fact. How far is the contract of a person valid, binding himself that a fact, against which it is impossible that he can certainly guard, shall never happen? This question had arisen on the liability for 'noxæ servorum' and 'noxales actiones.' It was common for the seller of a slave to guarantee that he was not a thief, 'furem non esse;' that he was not a runaway, 'fugitivum non esse.' Such covenants were usually inserted in contracts for the sale of slaves. And hence came the words of the edict of the Ædile: 'Si adversus quod dictum promissumve fuerit cum veniret,' etc.

Now, as a general rule of law, an impossible condition was void. Admitting then, the doctrine 'Neque pactum neque stipulationem factum posse tollere, quod enim impossibile est neque pacto neque stipulatione posse comprehendi ut utilem actionem aut factum efficere possit,' admitting this, how can a condition declaring that a slave who has robbed is not a thief, or that he never will commit any given offence,[b] be valid. This argument had, it appears, to a certain degree prevailed; for it was said the condition is useless. If the slave be a thief: 'Si in hâc causâ sit,' the promise is of no value, 'quia impossibile est ut non sit quod est;' if he is not a thief it is unnecessary. To this Ulpian replies, that the contract 'furem servum non esse,' was not intended to make what had been done, undone—but to make up the difference to the buyer, if that had been done which it was the buyer's interest should have been undone. Therefore the seller contracted, not 'factum tollere,' but

---

[b] *De evictionibus,* l. 31.

'quanti interesset præstare,'[c] if it should appear that it had occurred.

The effect of this rule is to illustrate the ' auctoritas juris.'[d] No rule could change 'causa facti,' or 'factum.'[e] But by a fiction of law, what had happened was supposed not to have happened; in other words, was not taken into account by the judge.[f]

The children slain in battle were reckoned as living, for the purpose of exonerating their parent from particular duties and charges.[g]

XLV.

VI factum id videtur esse, quâ de re quis cum prohibetur fecit: clam quod quisque cum controversiam haberet, habiturumve se putaret fecit. — QUINTUS MUCIUS SCÆVOLA.

The word violence applies when a man has done what the law prohibits.—The word fraud when he has done something during a suit, or in expectation of one.

This sentence relates entirely to the explanation of the interdict, in which the Prætor declares: ' Quod vi aut clam factum est quâ de re agitur, id cum experiundi potestas est restituas.'

That was considered prohibited, which, even the slightest act, was done in order to resist; such as holding out the hand, or flinging a pebble in the direction of a work begun. ' Si quis factu vel minimi lapilli prohibitus facere perseveravit facere hunc quoque vi fecisse videri Pedius et Pomponius scribunt eoque jure utimur—sed et si contra testationem denuntiationemque fecerit idem esse Canellius et Trebatius putant —

---

[c] *Impossibile,* 50, ii., *de pactis.*

[d] Τὸ ἅπαξ γεγονὸς πρᾶγμα.

[e] L.20, ii., *Ex quib. caus. majores ;* L. 1, *Si vir,* ii., *de acquir. poss ;* L. 12, § *facti.*

[f] ALTASERRA, *de Fictionibus Juris. Postliminium.*

[g] *Instit. de excus. Tutorum vel curat.*

quod verum est.' (*Dig.* xxiv., 1, § 5, § 6.) Any decided intimation of an aggrieved person that he meant to appeal to the law, in order to prevent the act of which he thought himself entitled to complain, was sufficient to arrest its progress; so refined were the provisions of the Roman law, and so careful to guard against possible violence. Our law on this subject betrays the confused and inaccurate genius of the barbarous usages from which it springs. A man who imagines himself entitled to land held by another, forces his way over it; or, if he is a rich man, sends his servant to dig up and carry away a fence. If he were a direct and frontless trespasser, some few years back, he might very likely have succeeded in his attempt, and might be quite sure to ruin his antagonist, if the latter was of humble means. But even if such a person had the right to the land he seized upon, the Roman law considered the trespass an offence, for which it exacted redress, and it replaced the parties in their original position. Hawkins, the English text writer, says, that a party may enter by force into that to which he has a legal title: thereby making each man the judge in his own cause, if he is rich and powerful enough, to take immediate possession; thus exposing the public peace to constant jeopardy. And this in a country where, at the time he wrote, to cut down the bank of a pond, or a young tree worth a shilling, was a capital felony.

The word in the text is ' fecit;' this includes what was done by the command of the person concerned. ' Quod tu aut tuorum quis fecerit aut tuo jussu factum est.'

That is done clandestinely, ' clam,' which is done with a view to expected litigation. What a person did and kept concealed from his adversary, in order to escape his prohibition, was ' clam.'q So if a person induced a magistrate to summon

---

q ' I take it to be a settled rule, that where a man indirectly and by trick, does that which it would have been illegal for him to have done directly, he shall be considered as having done it directly.'—Kirkpatrick *v.* Kelly, 3 DOUGLAS, 30.

Turner *v.* Meymott, 1 BING. 158: ' It was held that a landlord might, in the absence of the tenant whose term had expired, break

his adversary, that he might be out of the way and unable to oppose his proceedings, this was ' clam,' and gave the Prætor a right of interference. ' Responsum est si magistratum ro-gâsses ut adversarium tuum adesse ad judicium juberet ne opus novum tibi nuntiaret, clam videri te opus fecisse quod interim feceris.' (*Dig.* xliii., 24. 18, § 1.)

He was said ' clam facere,' who had good reason to expect litigation, whether he expected it or not. For the opinion, or languid indolence of an individual, was not to obstruct the law. ' Quia non opinionem ejus et resupinam existimationem sequi oportet.' The reason he gives is one which will astound those who look around them in this country. ' Ne melioris conditionis sint stulti quam periti.'[r]

---

open the door and resume possession.' It never seemed to cross the mind of the judges, that a man ought to regain his own by the decision of others, and not his own.

[r] ' At Common Law . . . if a man had a right of entry upon lands and tenements, he was permitted to enter with force and arms, and to retain his possession by force where the entry was lawful . . . it is clear that in MANY CASES an indictment will lie for a forcible entry.'—RUSSELL, *Greaves*, vol. i. 305. In Newton *v.* Harland, 1 M. and GR. 144, The judges seem to have been of opinion, that the landlord who entered forcibly into the house of his tenant, after the term of his tenancy had expired, was guilty of a forcible entry—but the doubt was (observe the difference between the English law and the passage in the text) whether the possession gained was legal ; in other words, whether a man could turn his own wrong to profit—whether he could make himself judge in his own cause, and be a gainer by it.—The view taken by Parke B., and Coltman J, was that he could.

Lord Kenyon, after asserting, in conformity with all reason, one day, that no man should assert with force his own title, retracted what he had said the next day, in these words, which are truly characteristic of our jurisprudence—the question being one of constant occurrence, and in which the peace and order of society are concerned—' *Perhaps some doubt may* hereafter arise respecting what Mr. Hawkins says, etc. But *without giving any opinion on that subject one way or other*, etc.' One would have supposed that judges were appointed expressly that in a simple question of that nature, they might deliver an opinion one way or the other, and so put a stop to confusion, riot and bloodshed.

This principle about which Lord Kenyon declined to give an opinion, ' created great inconvenience by arming the tenants of the lords, and

XLVI.

SI in duabus actionibus alibi summa major, alibi in-
famia est, præponenda causa est existimationis.
Ubi autem æquiparant famosa judicia etsi summam
imparem pro paribus accipienda sunt.—ULPIAN.

*If there are two actions, one of which involves the
hazard of a large sum, and the other that of infamy,
the cause affecting character is to be preferred. Where
an adverse judgment in either inflicts equal infamy,
though the sum at issue may be different, the causes
are to be considered as equal.*

The true meaning of the rule probably is, that where two
actions are brought, the most important shall be tried first,
lest any prejudice should be excited by the trial of the other;
and that the action affecting reputation, the ' dignitatis illæsæ
statum,' is always to be considered the most important, whatever pecuniary interests may be put in jeopardy by the other:
' Per minorem causam majori cognitioni præjudicium fieri non
oportet, major enim quæstio minorem causam ad se trahit.'ˢ

This rule shews the value which the Roman law annexed to
a spotless reputation.   Infamy was the consequence of a judgment against the defendant in certain cases.   The question
here to be answered was, if two actions, one of which imported such a consequence, the other of which did not, were
pending at the same time and concerning the same object,

---

encouraging those in mischief, who were already too forward in rebellion in their neighbourhood ; also it gave opportunity to powerful men,
under pretence of title, to eject their weaker neighbours ;' as it may do
now,·where an employer, as in the mining districts, has many people at
his command. BACON, *Abrid.*, tit. Forcible Entry ; therefore, even in
early times, many statutes were passed :—2 Ed. iii. c. 3, Statute of North-
ampton ; 5 Rich. ii. c. 7 ;   15 Rich. ii. c. 2 ;   8 Hen. vi. c. 9 ;   31 Eliz. c. 11 ;
21 Jac. i. c. 19.

ˢ *Dig.* v. 1.54, *Cod. de Ordine Judiciorum,* 4 : 'Quoniam civili.'—
Imparitas rei debitæ non distinguit inter famosa judicia si sint paria.
—D'ANTOINE, *Droit Civil.*

which was to have the priority? The answer shews that the Roman law allowed no conceivable amount of pecuniary value to weigh in the balance with reputation. An instance of such concurrence may be found (*Dig.* xix., 5. 14,): ' Sed et si quis servum alienum spoliaverit isque frigore mortuus sit—de vestimentis quidem furti agi poterit, de servo vero in factum criminali pœnâ adversus eum servatâ.' So Ulpian says on the Aquilian law (*Dig.* ix. 2, 5. § 1), ' Interdum actio concurrit et legis Aquiliæ, et injuriarum, sed duæ erunt æstimationes alia damni, alia contumeliæ.' And the same writer under the head pro Socio. (*Dig.* xvii., 2. 45) ' Rei communis nomine cum socio furti agi potest si per fallaciam dolove malo amovit vel rem communem celandi animo contrectet—sed et pro socio actione obstrictus est—nec altera actio alteram tollet.'

So we find (*Dig.* xlviii. 12) ' Sepulchri violati actio infamiam irrogat;' and (9 *ib.*) ' De sepulchro violato actio quoque pecuniaria datur.'

This is the first part of the rule, which distinguishes between actions which involve infamy, and those which do not.

The second part of the rule applies to the case in which two actions were to be considered, an adverse decision in either of which equally inflicted infamy on the defendant, and it says that in this case the pecuniary result is not to be considered:—so careful was the law of Rome not to shock the moral sense. For instance: Suppose that Titius has embezzled a deposit. He is liable to an action ' furti,' or to an action ' depositi,' and if he is cast in either he is infamous. In the action ' depositi' his pecuniary interests are not as much in danger, as in the action 'furti,' in which he may be compelled to restore twofold or fourfold the value of what he has appropriated. ' This,' said the Roman jurist, 'is of no consequence in determining which action shall have priority.'[t]

---

[t] GOTHOFRED, *Reg.*

XLVII.

FERE in omnibus pœnalibus actionibus et ætati et imprudentiæ succurritur.

In almost every penal action indulgence is shewn to youth and inexperience.

This rule is taken from that part of the work of Paulus on the Edict, in which he interprets the portion of it, ' de in jus vocando,'[u] where the prætor imposes a fine of fifty aurei on the libertus, who, without permission, summons his patronus to appear in a court of justice.

Still, although the words of the edict do not allow any such mitigation,[x] if the ' libertus' had imprudently committed this offence, had repented of it, and abandoned the proceeding, or if the ' patronus' had refused to appear, or not been summoned against his will, the ' libertus' was relieved. The words, ' in pœnalibus judiciis,' apply to cases where the fact done, and not the intention, is considered. So, if a minor rashly impeached a will, he did not forfeit his legacy, 'ætati ignoscitur'[y] (*Dig.* xxxiv. 9. 5. 9). But in ' delicta,' cases where the intention qualified the act, no relief was given to minors: ' Placet in delictis minoribus non subveniri . . . nam et si furtum fecit et damnum injuriâ dedit ei non subvenietur' (*Dig.* iv. 9, § 2). So no relief was given to the minor who suffered the sixty days to elapse during which he might accuse, ' sine calumniâ,' his wife of adultery, ' denegatur ei in integrum restitutio,' for it is to claim a right, ' calumniam et cum neque in delictis neque in calumniatoribus prætorem succurrere certi juris est,' his claim to restitution in such a case was rejected (*ib.* 37). ' Quid habet commune delictum cum veniâ ætatis' (*Dig.* iv. 4. 20). And to the same purpose is the remarkable law, ' Si mulier cum culpâ divertisset velit sibi subveniri, vel

---

[u] FABER. GOTH. 108. ' Si libertus,' etc., ' in jus vocando.' *Dig.* ii. 4. 24 : ii. 4. 25. ' In eum qui adversus ea fecerit quinquaginta aureorum judicium datur.'

[x] GOTH. *Reg. R.* 104.

[y] ' De his quæ est indignis auferuntur.'

si maritus puto restitutionem non habendam, est enim delictum non modicum nam si adulterium minor comminit ei non subvenitur' (*Dig.* iv. 4. 9, § 3). The offences for which this rule might be pleaded to obtain impunity were offences against the civil law, not against the law of nature or of nations. If a woman, from ignorance of law, had made a marriage incestuous only by the civil law, she might allege this rule to escape punishment;[b] but a minor who had committed this offence with his mother-in-law, or with the daughter of his wife, was not protected by it. The maxim allows the defence of 'imprudentia.' By 'imprudentia' is meant what Ulpian calls 'rusticitas' (*Dig. de Jurisdictione*, vii. 4), where he says, persons who, 'propter simplicitatem,' destroy or mutilate what is authentically written 'in albo' or ' in charta,' he shall not be liable to the penalties of one who did so ' dolo malo.' Paulus uses the same expression (*Dig.* ii. 5. 1).

XLVIII.

NEMO ex suo delicto meliorem conditionem suam facere potest.[d]

No man can better his condition by his own wrongful act.

In the same sense, the law (*Dig.* xvii. 2, 7) says, ' Hoc quoque facere quis posse videtur quod dolo fecit quominus possit.'[e] Every one is supposed to be able to do that which

---

b ' Jus ignorare potest.'—*Dig.* xxiii. 6. 9, § 1.

c *Ad Legem Juliani*, 4854, 160 MERLIN, *Repertoire*.

d In Law French, ' Nul prendra advantage de son tort de mesme.'— 2 *Inst.* 713. COKE, *Littleton*, 148 6; BURROWS, *Reports*, vol. ii. 660; BROOM, *Legal Maxims*, p. 209 ; Hawkins *v.* Hall, MYLNE and CRAIG, vol. iv. 281. In Fennor's Case it was held that a fine fraudently levied by lessee would not bind lessor. 3 C. R., 77 ; Twyne's Case, 3 *Reports*, 80.

e So *Dig.* vi. 1. 69 : ' Is qui dolo fecit quominus possideret hoc quoque nomine punitur ;' and *ib.* 70, *ib.* : 'De donationibus inter virum et uxorem ;' xxiv. 1. 3 : ' Fas non est eas donationes ratas esse, ne melior sit conditio eorum qui deliquerunt ;' i. e., where the marriage was

he has by fraud made it impossible for himself to do: ' Nec enim æquum est dolum suum quemquam relevare.' So, if a debtor made a ' cessio bonorum' with a fraudulent reservation to himself, he could not afterwards insist on the privilege ' competentiæ quod et in cæteris qui in id quod facere possunt accipiendum est.'[f] If a husband, on his wife's death, was entitled to her fortune, he could not take the benefit of it if he murdered her.[g] If she was taken in adultery, and he put her to death, a question arose whether he was entitled to the benefit of the arrangement that the survivor should enjoy the other's fortune. In France it was decided that he could not; to which sentence, says Gothofred, I do not subscribe: ' Nam cum aliquid lege permittente factum est id pœnam non meretur' (see L. GRACCHUS, *Code de Adult.*); and he adds, in the case supposed the husband has committed an offence, and therefore the law cited in the digest does not apply.

Our law refuses to an executor ' de son tort' the protection it extends to a rightful executor.[h] ' Every one,' says Lord Abinger, ' who has been in a court of justice has heard the maxim, that a man cannot take advantage of his own wrong.'[i] The case of Hyde *v.* Watts,[k] in which the defendant was not

---

illegal.—2 *Instit.* 713 ; Lord Denman, worthy from his qualities to have sat in a Roman senate, or presided in a Roman court of justice ; Pickard *v.* Sears, 6 AD. and ELLIS, 469 ; Gregg *v.* Wells. 10 AD. and ELLIS. A person who assists in persuading another of a fact, cannot dispute that fact in an action against the person whom he has deceived.

[f] See *Dig.* iv. 8. 31 : ' Sub hâc conditione committitur stipulatio ne quis doli præmium ferat.' *Dig.* xlvii. 2. 12 : 'Furti actio malæ fidei possessori non datur, quamvis interest ejus rem non surripi—sed nemo de improbitate suâ consequitur actionem.' *Dig.* xlvii. 1. 2 : 'Nunquam plura delicta concurrentia faciunt ut ullius impunitas detur, neque enim delictum ob aliud delictum minuit pœnam.'

[g] *Dig.* xxiv. 3. 10, § 1 : 'Si vir uxorem suam occiderit, κ. τ. λ. Non enim æquum est virum ob *facinus* suum dotem lucrifacere.' The word ' facinus' shows that the husband had put her to death without adequate cause.

[h] Carmichael *v.* Carmichael, 2 PHILLIPS, 105.

[i] Findon *v.* Parker, 11 M. and W., 681.

[k] 12 M. and W. 254 ; Attorney-General *v.* Anstead, *ib.* 520.

allowed to take advantage of his own neglect to keep on foot an insurance, in which event the indenture of trust for his creditors was to be void, illustrates, as Mr. Broom remarks, the rule in a very striking manner.

XLIX.

IN omnibus causis pro facto accipitur id in quo per alium moræ sit quominus fiat.—POMPONIUS.

That is always to be considered as done, which the fault of another has prevented.

The very comprehensive and important doctrine which is summed up in this short sentence, is over and over again applied in the works of the Roman jurists, which have been transmitted to us. It is the dictate of common equity, and has not been the less on that account disregarded by those who have in England undertaken the task of legislation.[a] The principle is, that no one shall be a sufferer for the act or omission of another. Thus if the creditor refuses to accept the money that his debtor offers to him, or contrives that the debtor shall lose the money he was about to pay, this principle applied. In like manner it was enforced—if a bequest being left to me on condition that I pay you ten pounds, and you refused to receive it, or one of the heirs (for whose interest it is that I should lose the legacy), prevents me from giving it to you—or on condition that I ascend the Capitol and you prevent me from ascending it—on condition that I marry Seia, and Seia refuses to marry me—that I erect statues in a town, and the burgesses will not allow me. In all these cases I am entitled to the bequest, and may dispose of it as if I had fulfilled the condition on which it was given. So if I

---

[a] Principle applied by Lord Mansfield; BURROWS' *Reports*, 2; Michel *v.* Cue et uxor; *Doe dem* Murton *v.* Gladwin, 6 L. B., *Reports*; COKE, *Littleton*, 206, *b.*; Keys *v.* Harwood, 2 C. B., 905. Where the law requires personal service, if a man chooses deliberately not to look at the document served upon him, this is personal service. Emerson *v.* Brown, 8 SCOTT, *New Reps.*, 222.

make a will, declaring my son to be my heir, on condition
that he adopt Titius, otherwise that he be disinherited, and
Titius refuses to be adopted, my son has fulfilled the condition.
So in the case cited by Papinian, where a mother left to a
man a certain sum, on condition that he became the guardian
of her son; and the prætor, whose authority was requisite,
refused to sanction his appointment as guardian; it was answered that the legatee was entitled to his action: 'Non jure
tutori dato mater legavit si consentiat ut decreto prætoris confirmetur et prætor non idoneum existimet actio legati non
denegabitur' (*Dig.* xxx. 1. 76, § 6). This rule is so true, that
if the obstacle to the fulfilment of the condition arises not
from the person himself whose interest it is to prevent it, but
from his guardian, it is held as if it were accomplished. If a
bequest is given to a freedman, on condition that he shall not
depart from the sons of the testator, and the guardians will not
allow him to fulfil the condition, he is entitled to the legacy,
'for,' says Modestinus, 'it would be unjust that he who is
blameless should lose his legacy' (*Dig.* xxxi. 34, § 3). So
Papinian, whom our Equity Judges (as long as the barbarous
distinctions between Courts of Law and Equity are allowed to
be the scandal of our Jurisprudence) ought, if they wish to
become jurists and reasoners, to study day and night, says:
' Cum pupillus aut tutor ejus conditionem in personam pupilli
collatam impedit tam legati quam libertatis conditio *communi*
jure impleta esse videtur.'

Another instance may be quoted (*Dig.* xxx. 54, § 2). If
money be left on condition that you manumit a slave, and the
slave dies, you are entitled to the legacy. ' Sed et si servi
mors impedisset manumissionem cum tibi legatum esset si
eum manumisisses, nihilominus debetur tibi legatum—quia
per te non stetit quominus perveniat ad libertatem.'

A legacy left on condition that the testator's son should
attain the age of fourteen, ceased to be due if the son died
before that age. But if liberty had been granted to a slave
on the same condition, he would have been entitled to his
freedom in the same event—' favore libertatis' (*Dig.* xl. 7. 19).

The rule, it may be remarked, is universal—' In omnibus causis.' So if the different patrons of a freedman went on purpose into different countries, and at the same time imposed different tasks on their freedman, the freedman was not liable: ' Quia non per eum sed per patronos stet quominus operæ dentur' (*Dig.* xxxviii. 1. 23). ' Per alium;' the words include not only those who were interested in preventing an event from taking place, but strangers to the law. The Digest (xxxv. 1. 40) says, that a person prevented by a neighbour from travelling on the highway to fulfil a condition, is not to be considered as having forfeited his right by the delay: ' Quibus diebus vicinus tuus te viâ publicâ cum ad parendum conditioni ire velles, ire prohibuerit nec per te staret, quominus agendo ob calumnias eum summoveas—hi dies conditioni non imputabuntur.'

Finally—Where an act is to be done in performance of a contract, be he who he may whose interest it is to retard or prevent its performance, the delay caused by such person shall not be imputed to the person obstructed. But the act that was to be done, shall be taken as done for the purposes of the contract.

As illustrations of the rule in our law, the case put by Noy may be mentioned[b]—that if a man be bound to appear on a certain day, and before that day the obligee put him in prison, the bond is void.

A frightful instance of its disregard is the case of Sir Thomas Armstrong, who was embowelled alive for not doing what the state had made it impossible for him to do. The cases of Mrs. Gaunt and Lady Lisle are more cruel, but the case of Sir Thomas Armstrong is the most flagrant instance of open and insolent violation of the law to be found even in the long catalogue of judicial murders recorded in our state trials. The inquisition sanctioned no such open murder. The expulsion of Sir Robert Sawyer from the House of Commons, for his active share in this horrible transaction, was but an inade-

---

[b] Noy, *Maxims*, Ed. 9, p. 45.

quate punishment for wickedness, for any type of which we must go back to the worst days of Imperial Rome.

L.

Q UI dolo desierit possidere pro possidente damnatur quia pro possessione dolus est.—PAULUS.[b]

*He who fraudulently gets rid of his possession, is con-
demned as if he were in possession, because his fraud
is equivalent to possession.*

This particular law refers to the edict ' de noxalibus actionibus.' The master of a 'noxius' slave, the conduct of whom
had given rise to a 'noxalis actio,' was bound on interrogation
to admit or deny that the slave was in his possession. If he
admitted that the slave was his, he was bound either to produce him 'exhibere,'[c] or to defend him in his absence. If he
denied it, the adversary had his choice either of an action
against the master, or of obliging him to swear that the slave
' in potestate suâ non esse neque se dolo malo fecisse quominus
esset;' and in the action the plaintiff succeeded if he could
either prove the slave to be in the possession of the master, or
that he had ceased to be so by the master's fraud—' dolove
malo fecerit quominus haberet.'[d] On the same principle, the
' prædo'[e] of an inheritance, who got rid of his possession 'ante
litem contestatam,' was to be condemned as if he had kept it:
' Perinde condemnandum quasi possideret.'[f] So the law which
absolves the innocent owner of a fugitive slave, on his giving

---

[b] GOTHOFRED, *Reg. Juris.*

[c] *Dig.* xliii. 24. 15, § *eum autem* ; Daly v. Kelly, 4 Dow., *Reports*, 440 ;
Eq. Juris, 908 : Eckliff v. Baldwin, 16 VESEY, 267 ; Curtis v. Marquis of
Buckingham, 2 V. and B., 168, § 953, 406 ; Bishop of Winchester v.
Paine, 11 VESEY, 197 ; Metcalf v. Pulvertoft, 2 V. and B., 205.
' Dominus qui servum in suâ potestate esse confitetur aut exhibere
eum debet aut absentem defendere quod nisi faciat punitur atque si
præsentem non noxæ dederit.'—*Dig.* ix. 4. 22.

[d] *Dig.* ix. 4. 21, § 1.

[e] Prædones—'Qui cum scirent ad se non pertinere hæreditatem
invaserunt bona,' distinction of fact and law.—*Dig.* v. 3. 25, § 3.

[f] *Dig.* v. 3. 25, § 8.

security that the slave if found shall be given up, implies that if the owner has fraudulently contributed to the slave's flight, he shall be responsible. In short, the principle that the person who had fraudulently got rid of the possession of anything, was to be considered as the possessor, runs through all the Roman law. So the interdict, 'ne quid in loco publico' (*Dig.* xliii. 8. 42), lay against him 'Qui dolo malo fecit quominus possideret vel haberet, etiam parem esse conditionem oportet ejus qui quid possideat, vel habeat atque ejus cujus dolo malo factum sit quominus possideret.' So the interdict 'de tabulis exhibendis' was given (*Dig.* xlii. 5) against him 'penes' whom the 'tabulæ' were, or 'penes' whom they had ceased to be 'dolo malo suo.' So by the interdicts 'unde vi,' and 'de vi armatâ,' an action was given in 'heredem, bonorum possessorem, cæterosque successores,' for so much as had come to them, or but for their fraud would have come to them. 'In factum actio competit in id quod ad eos pervenit.' 'Dolove malo eorum factum est quominus perveniret' (*Dig.* xliii. 16. 48; *Ib.* ii.).

So the purchaser who did not restore the 'ruta cæsa,'[g] was liable to the claim of the vendor, 'ad exhibendum,' to the amount of value sworn to—'Si possideat aut dolo malo fecit quominus possideat.'[h]

LI.

IMPERITIA culpæ adnumeratur.—GAIUS.[i]
  Want of skill causes responsibility.

This was the rule established by Celsus and quoted by Ulpian, of which several instances are given; e. g., if any one

---

[g] The 'ruta cæsa' were articles separated from the soil or building sold, and reserved to the vendor.—ULPIAN, *Dig.* iv. 1, 17. 'Si ruta et cæsa excipiantur in venditione.'—See *Cicero De Or.*, ii. c. 55.

[h] *Dig.* x. 4. 5, § 2.

[i] Si quis fundum—ἡ ἀπειρία τῇ ἀμελείᾳ συναριθμεῖται.—CELSUS, xix. 2. 9. 5. GOTHOFRED, *Reg. Juris;* FABER, *Reg. Juris;* 1 MILES, *Reports*, 40; POTHIER, *Obs. Générale, Traité des Oblig.*, 142; TOULLIER, *Droit Civil Français*, iii. 3. 231; *Civil Code of Louisiana*, 3522; BOUVIER, *Law Dict.*, tit. *Fault.*

undertake to pasture calves, to mend or polish anything, and fulfil his task unskilfully, he is responsible for his fault, and therefore for his want of skill, 'quippe ut artifex conduxit,' and an action 'ex locato,' or 'lege Aquiliâ,' would lie against him. So, if a workman took a gem to cut, or a cup to perforate, and it was broken by his negligence, he was liable also 'ex locato' or 'lege Aquiliâ.' And if a physician, 'servum imperite secuerit' (*Dig.* ix. 2. 7, § 8), or administered drugs improperly, he was liable in the same way.[b] So, if the muleteer could not manage his mules, and in consequence a man was run over, it was no excuse that 'propter infirmitatem sustinere mularum impetum non potuerit.'[c] Nor can it be considered harsh that infirmity is imputed as a fault, since no one ought to undertake a task in which his infirmity may be the cause of misfortune to others: 'Nec videtur iniquum si infirmitas culpæ adnumeretur cum affectare quisque non debeat in quo vel intelligit vel intelligere debet infirmitatem suam alii periculosam futurum.'[d] So, if an architect undertook to build a house for £200, and I afterwards—finding it would cost me £300, and having advanced £100 to you—forbid you to proceed,[e] I may abandon the contract; and, if you persevere, recover what remains of the money in an action 'ex locato.' But if an accidental fire interrupted and destroyed the work, the contractor was allowed to begin his reckoning for the time within which he had engaged to complete the work anew after the fire, but the loss was his.[f] If, however, an earthquake, or any natural cause, destroyed or impeded the work, it was at the risk of the employer: 'Si vi naturali hoc acciderit Flacci [i. e., locatoris] esse periculum' (*Dig.* xix. 3. 59). Nor, if any acci-

---

[b] See the clause, which I suspect to be an interpolation of Tribonian, from its impure style, 'Sicut Medico,' in the law 'Illicitas,' *Dig.* lib. i. tit. 18. 6, § 7 ; see also *Dig.* ix. 2. 27, § 9.

[c] *Dig.* ix. 2. 8, § 1.

[d] A maxim our ministers should recollect.

[e] *Dig.* xix. ii. 60, § 4. Vitruvius Praem. £10, lib. x., complains that men are ruined by ignorant architects.

[f] *Dig.* xlv. 1. 15 : 'Verius est ut integrum ei detur.'

dent happened to a public work, was the contractor responsible[g] (*Dig.*l. 12. 1, § 6); but, by a law of Theodosius and Arcadius, if any public work gave way (unless from a ' vis major') within fifteen years after its erection, it was taken to be the fault of the architect, and he or his heirs were bound to repair it.

According to our law, every one who undertakes an office undertakes to fulfil its duties with reasonable skill and diligence. A carrier is to this extent responsible for the goods he has undertaken to carry; a tailor, for the proper cutting of cloth; a farrier, for the proper shoeing of his customer's horse; an attorney, for mismanagement of his client's affairs. ' That,' says Mr. Justice Cresswell,[h] ' cannot be considered gross negligence concerning which persons of competent skill entertain a doubt. . . . It was for the judge to say whether the construction of these orders of the House of Lords was so doubtful as to exonerate an attorney from gross negligence, who had put a construction upon them which turned out, according to the view taken by the committee of the house, not to be correct.' ' An attorney,' said Lord Ellenborough, in an action brought for negligence, because the attorney had failed to point out a flaw in the memorial of annuity deeds before the decision making the omission fatal had been pronounced, 'is only liable for crassa negligentia.'[i] An attorney employed by a vendor to settle on his part the assignment of a term, is responsible if he allow his client to execute an unusual covenant without explaining the liability thereby incurred. ' It may be assumed as a general principle, that an attorney, by reason of the emolument he derives from the business in which he is employed, undertakes, and is bound to take care, that his client does not enter into any covenant or stipulation that may expose him to a greater degree of responsibility than is ordinarily attached to

---

[g] Omnes, 7 *Cod. de Oper. Public.*

[h] Bulmer *v.* Gilman, 4 MANNING and GRANGER, 126 ; Pitt *v.* Yalden, 4 BURROW, 2060.

[i] Baikie *v.* Chandless, 3 CAMPBELL. On the general subject, see Dixon *v.* Bell, 5 M. and SEL. 198 ; Lynch *v.* Nardin, 1 *Q. B.* 35.

the business in hand, or, at all events, that he does not do so till the consequences have been explained to him.'[j]   Ordinary care, Lord Denman remarks, in Lynch v. Nardin,[k] means the care to be expected from a person in the situation in which the person suing or sued has placed himself.   An action on the case lies against a surgeon for want of skill and negligence. ‘ Every one,’ says C. J. Tindal,[l] ‘ undertakes to bring a reasonable degree of skill and care.   He does not, if he is an attorney, undertake at all events to win the cause; nor, if he is a surgeon, that he will perform a cure; nor does the latter undertake to use the highest possible degree of skill, as there may be persons of higher education and greater advantages than himself; but he undertakes to bring a fair, reasonable, and competent degree of skill.’   Another important class to which this rule is applicable, is that of the collision of vessels at sea.[m]

LII.

DOLO facit qui petit quod redditurus est.—Paulus.
It is fraudulent to claim what you must restore.[n]

This is the rule which Lord Mansfield endeavoured to establish, and which, after his death, was immediately overthrown by the narrow-minded men to whom the office of judge was confided. ‘ I never will allow,’ said that judge, who vainly tried to introduce something like order and principle in the chaos of our truly barbarous jurisprudence, ‘ the trustee to set up his right against the cestuique trust.’ This drew down upon him the denunciations of Lord Eldon, who

---

[j] Tindal, C. J., Stannard v. Whithorne, 10 Bingham, Reports, 304.

[k] Smith, Leading Cases, vol. i. 132, Ashby v. White ; Bridge v. Grand, Jun., R., 3 Meeson and Welsby, 244; Butterfield v. Forrester, 11 East, 60.

[l] Lampier v. Phipps, 8 Car and P. 475 ; Seare v. Prentice, 8 East, 348; Slater v. Baker, 2 Wilson, 359.

[m] 53 Geo. III., c. 109 ; Brown v. Wilkinson, 15 M. and W. 391 ; Pardessus, Droit, Commer., p. 3, tit. 2, c. 2 ; Abbott, On Shipping, ed. Shee, p. 198 ; Vennall v. Gardner, 1 C. and M. 21.

[n] Faber, Reg. Juris.

took care that the old system, so hideously favourable to the most odious pettifogging and extortion, so ruinous to all but the most opulent suitors, and so oppressive even to them, should be upheld in all its deformity.

The Roman law applied where the claimant would be compelled to give back what he claimed to the identical person from whom he claimed it, not where he would be compelled to give it back to another: 'Absurde dicitur dolo videri eum facere qui non ipsi quem convenit sed alii restituturus petit' (*Dig.* xxiv. 3. 44, § 1). Therefore, a husband might sue for a portion, which he might be obliged to repay to his wife. And, again, it did not apply where the claimant, though bound to give back what he claimed to the person from whom he claimed it, was entitled to an interval of possession (*Dig.* xxxvi. 3. 18, § 1). Again; the thing sought must be the same, and therefore the heir might sue for the possession, though he was bound to give up the property. So the interdict, 'quod legatorum,' lay 'ut quod quis legatorum nomine non ex voluntate hæredis occupavit id restituat hæredi' (*Dig.* xliii. 3. 2). And so in possessory judgments generally, where the salutary maxim, 'spoliatus ante omnia restituendus,' is enforced. Therefore, to give this rule effect, the person, the time, and the thing sought, must be the same.

LIII.

CULPA caret qui scit sed prohibere non potest.— PAULUS.[z]

He is guiltless who knows but cannot prevent.

By the Roman law, a master was liable for the crime of his slave, if it was in his power to have prevented it: 'Actione noxali tenetur dominus qui non prohibuit cum posset.'[a] It was presumed that he had ordered what he did not choose to prevent: 'Jussisse videtur qui non prohibuit.' This rule was introduced by the Aquilian law, and on the same principle it was held by

---

[z] GOTHOFRED, *Reg, Juris.*
[a] *Dig.* ix. 4. 2, § 1: 'De noxalibus actionibus.'

Ulpian, that a tenant was responsible, when his slaves had set
fire to the barns and dwellings of his landlord. Proculus,
indeed, had been of opinion, that in such a case it was enough
for the master to deliver up the culprits; but Ulpian goes
further, and says: 'Hæc ita si culpâ colonus careret—cæterum
si noxios servos habuit damni eum injuriâ teneri cur tales
habuit—idem servandum et circa inquilinorum insulæ personas
scribit—quæ sententia habet rationem.'[b] But he was not responsible for an accident which he could neither foresee nor
avert: 'Non tenetur de casu, quem prævidere et cui providere
non potuit.' It is true that we are not legally bound to assist
all persons, yet Papinian beautifully says: 'Hominis interest
hominem beneficio offici'; and a man who did not interfere to
prevent the perpetration of an open crime was, by the Roman
law, considered 'primâ facie' as an accomplice: 'Non caret
scrupulo societatis occultæ, qui manifesto facinori occurrere non
tentavit.'[c] Paulus says: 'Scientiam hic,' i.e., in the Aquilian
law, 'pro patientiâ accipimus ut qui prohibere potuit teneatur
si non fecerit.'[d]

To the same purpose is the law: 'Pupillus nec velle nec nolle
in eâ ætate nisi appositâ tutoris auctoritate creditur nam quod
animo judicio fit, in eo tutoris auctoritas—necessaria est.'[e]
He could not, therefore, be said 'pati' what he could not
prevent: 'Pupillus pati posse non intelligitur'[f]; and again,
'Furiosi vel ejus cui bonis interdictum sit nulla voluntas est.'[g]

---

[b] *Dig.* ix. 2. 27, § 11.

[c] *Dig.* xlviii. 10. 9, § 1.

[d] TACITUS, *Ann.* xiii. 32 ; xiv. 43. *Dig.* xxix. 5. 1 : 'De senatusconsulto Silaniano.' 'Cum aliter nulla domus tuta esse possit nisi periculo
capitis sui, custodiam dominis tam ab domesticis quam ab extraneis
præstare servi cognitur, ideo seu introducta sunt de publicâ quæstione
a familiâ necatorum habenda,' etc. . . . 'Magis est ne puniatur ob hoc
quod sub eodem tecto fuit nisi particeps sceleris fuerit.' 'Toties pu-
niendi sunt servi quia auxilium domino non tulerunt, quoties potuerunt
ei adversus vim opem fene et non tulerunt.' 'Cæterum quid potuerunt
facere adversus eos qui veneno vel quo alio more insidiantur.' Therefore, they were not held responsible in such a case.

[e] *De Reg. Juris.*, 189.

[f] *Id.* tit. 110.   [g] *Id.* tit. 40.

By the 117th novel of Justinian, any one privy to a design against the state was bound, under penalty of passing for an accomplice, to give immediate notice, of it; and the *Cod. ad Leg. Juliam Majestatis* lays it down: ' Subditus qui consilia adversus principem habita non detegit puniendus est.'

' Misprisions [h] are divided by our books into two sorts: negative, which consists in the concealment of something which ought to be revealed; and positive, which consists in the commission of something that ought not to be done. On the latter the maxim here considered has no bearing. Misprision of treason, of the bare knowledge and concealment of treason, without any assent thereto; for any assent makes the party a principal traitor, as, indeed, the concealment did at the common law. But by the statute 1 and 2 Philip and Mary, it is enacted, that a bare concealment of treason shall only be held a misprision. ' Under the second head,' says Livingstone, ' our law now calls for the punishment of acts which, if not strictly virtues, are certainly too nearly allied to them to be designated as crimes. The ferocious legislation, which first enacted this law, demands (and sometimes under the penalty of the most cruel death) the sacrifice of all the feelings of nature, of all the sentiments of humanity, breaks the ties of

---

[h] If the charge against Lord Russell had been proved by credible witnesses, instead of resting on the contradictory statements of the prostituted and abandoned wretch, who saved his life by enabling the Court to murder its enemies on that occasion, it would have amounted to no more than misprision of treason.

There is a memorable example of enforcing this law in French history. I allude to the execution of De Thou, the worthy son of the great historian, for not revealing the projects of his friend Montmorenci, in which the Duke of Orleans, the first prince of the blood, was an associate. Guy Patin, in his amusing and instructive letters, says that the real cause of De Thou's execution was the slur cast by his father in his history on an ancestor (I am not sure that it was not the grandfather) of Cardinal Richelieu.

' If thy brother, the son of thy father, or thy son, or thy daughter or the friend that is to thee as thine own soul, entice thee secretly, thou shalt not consent, neither shalt thine eye pity him, neither shalt thou conceal him ; thou shalt surely kill him.'

gratitude and honour, makes obedience to the law to consist in a dereliction of every principle that gives dignity to man, and leaves the unfortunate wretch, who has himself been guilty of no offence, to decide between a life of infamy and self-reproach, or a death of dishonour. Dreadful as this picture is, the original is found in the law of accessories after the fact. If the father commits treason, the son must abandon or deliver him up to the executioner. If the son be guilty of a crime, the stern dictates of our law require that his parent—that the very mother who bore him—that his sisters and brothers, the companions of his infancy, should expel nature from their hearts, and humanity from their feelings—that they should barbarously discover his retreat, or with inhuman apathy abandon him to his fate. The husband is even required to betray his wife, the mother of his children; every tie of nature or affection is to be broken; and men are required to be faithless, treacherous, unnatural, and cruel, in order to prove that they are good citizens and worthy members of society."[i]

LIV.

CONSILII non fraudulenti nulla obligatio est cæterum, si dolus et calliditas intercessit de dolo actio competit.—ULPIAN.[j]

No one is responsible for honest advice; but where fraud and cunning have intervened, there is ground for an action ' de dolo.'

This rule governs the case cited (*Dig.* xvi. 3. 14). If I wish to deposit my goods with you, and you recommend me to deposit them with your freedman, can I bring an action ' depositi ' or ' mandati' against you? The answer is, If I made the deposit with your freedman as if with you, and as if it would be under your custody, I have an action ' depositi ' against you; but if I have been persuaded by you to prefer the freedman as a depositary, I have no action ' depositi '

---

[i] *Report on the plan of a penal code*, p. 14.
[j] GOTHOFRED, *Reg. Juris.*

against you, neither are you liable to an action 'mandati,' 'quia rem meam gessi,' it was my own choice (*Dig.*xvi. 3. 1.14). The law says, 'nulla obligatio est,' in conformity with Cicero (16 *Epist. ad Attic.*), who asks: 'Quid enim debet qui consilium dat præstare præter fidem.' [k]

But if fraudulent advice is given, the giver is responsible. Thus, if knowing a man to be insolvent, you recommend me to trust him as solvent: 'Merito adversum te, cum mei decipiendi gratiâ alium falso laudasti de dolo judicium dandum est' (*Dig.* iv. 3. 8). So if you counsel me to abandon an inheritance, as insolvent, or to select a bad slave, Ulpian says. 'Dico de dolo dandum si callide hoc feceris' (*Dig.* iv. 3. 9. 1). The action 'de dolo,' which made the defendant, if judgment was against him, infamous, lay whenever there was no other specific remedy for the fraud. Therefore, if any one affirmed an inheritance to be almost of no value, and so bought it from the heir, who was deceived: 'Non est de dolo actio cum ex vendito sufficiat' (*Dig.* iv. 3. 9). The difference between 'mandatum' and 'consilium' is clearly and most elegantly drawn (*Dig.* xvii. 1. 2, § 6): 'Tuâ autem gratiâ intervenit mandatum.' If I advise you to invest your money in land, rather than put it out at interest, 'si mandem tibi ut pecunias tuas potius in emptiones prædiorum colloces quam fœneres; vel ex diverso ut fœneres potius quam colloces'; which is to be considered rather as advice than as a 'mandatum,' and, therefore, gives rise to no obligation: 'Et ob id non est obligatiorum, quid nemo ex consilio obligatur, etiamsi non expediat ei cui dabatur; quia liberum est cuique apud se explorare an expediat sibi consilium' (*Dig.* xvii. 1. 2, § 6).

The reason of the difference is, that the mandator takes the risk upon himself: *e. g.* It may happen, says Paulus (*Dig.* xvii. 1.22, § 1), that I may take care of my own interests, and yet while I do so, give myself a right to an action 'mandati' for what I do. Suppose my debtor desires me to sue his debtor 'periculo suo,' or suppose I sue a person liable to me, at the

---

[k] ἡ ἄδολος συμβουλὴ οὐκ ἐνοχοποιεῖ.—HARMEN., lib. vi.

request of that person's surety; in both cases, though I endeavour to recover my own debt, I am promoting the interests
of others, and therefore have a right to be saved harmless.
'Igitur quod minus servavero consequar mandati actione.' To
these cases may be added that (*Dig.* xvii., 1. 7), where I direct
my agent to follow the advice of Sempronius, if that advice
is followed, and my money is ill placed, Sempronius ' qui non
animo procuratoris inter venit sed affectionem amicalem promisit in monendis procuratoribus et actoribus et in regendis
consilio, mandati non teneri' is not liable in an action
' mandati.'

This principle, like many others, has been half adopted and
half rejected in our courts. The suitor, instead of referring
to a plain rule, is obliged to compare conflicting authorities
and cases that differ just enough to produce that obscurity
which Homer says is better than night itself for purposes of
fraud. The wretched decision pronounced in Cornefoot *v.*
Fowke,[d] notwithstanding an admirable judgment of Lord
Abinger's, did not tend to diminish the perplexities which
have found so congenial a soil in the Court of Exchequer, or
to remove the crotchets which swarm there on every subject, the maggots of corrupted texts in Norman French. In
Pasley *v.* Freeman,[e] it was held, that a false affirmation made

---

[d] Broom, *Legal Maxims*, p. 618 ; 6 M. and W. 358. This wretched
decision was overruled, and an opinion in conformity with Lord
Abinger's pronounced by the Court of Queen's Bench. Fuller *v.* Wilson,
32 B. Q. 58; and Evans *v.* Collins, 5 *ib.* 804; both of which cases, in spite
of Lord Abinger, were, as might be expected, overruled by the Court
of Error.

[e] 3 *Term Reports* 51. *Smith's Leading Cases*, ed. Keating and Willes,
vol. ii. p. 76. Pontifex *v.* Bignold, 3 M and Gr. 63 ; Story, *Equity Juris.*
191 ; Polhill *v.* Walter, 3 B. and Adol. 122 ; Fonblanque, B. i, c. 1, § 8 ;
Chandelor *v.* Lepus, 1 *Smith's Leading Cases*, ed. Keating and Willes, 79.
Langridge *v.* Levy, 2 M. and W. 519 ; in which a sound principle was
blundered into. Pidcock *v.* Bishop, 3 B. and C. 605 ; Moens *v.* Hey-
worth, 10 M. and W. 157 ; Stone *v.* Comptions (representations to creditors by sureties), 5 N. C. 142 ; Railton *v.* Mathews, 10 Cl. and Finn.
934 ; Hamilton *v.* Watson, 12 Cl. and Finn., 109.
Since the above note was written I perceive that the case of Corne-

by the defendant with a view to deceive the plaintiff, whereby
the plaintiff receives damage, was a sufficient cause of action;
and it was held that it was not necessary for the plaintiff to
shew that there was any profit accruing to the defendant, or
any collusion between him and the person in favour of whom
he made a false representation.' 'Fraud without damage,' said
Coke, quoted by Mr. Justice Buller, 'gives no cause of action;
but where these two concur, an action lies. This rule was
carried to some length in the case cited below of Hamilton v.
Watson. In that case Lord Campbell says: ' If it is essen-
tially necessary that everything should be disclosed by the
creditor which it is requisite for a surety to know, questions
must be particularly put by the surety to gain this information;
unless this be done, I hold it quite unnecessary for the creditor
to whom suretyship is given to make any such disclosure.'
The case of Lyde v. Barnard [f] turned upon whether the representation on which the action was brought should have been
in writing, to satisfy the statute of frauds, as altered by Lord
Tenterden's Act, 9 G. IV. c. 14. So much, however, seems to
be settled; that the plaintiff must at any rate shew that the
defendant's assertions were false within his, defendant's, own
knowledge, that he, plaintiff, relied upon those assertions, and
that damage was thereby occasioned to him. In the case of
Pilmore v. Hood,[g] Lord C. J. Tindal says, after stating the
averments in the declaration, ' This appears to me to contain
a substantive allegation that there was a fraud or deceit practised, by the allowance and consent of the defendant, upon the
plaintiff, through which the plaintiff has incurred certain
damage. In Haycroft v. Creasy,[h] Lord Kenyon said: ' Here

---

foot v. Fowke has been censured in America.—*Vermont Reports*, 21, by
REDFIELD, J. 2 KENT'S *Com.* 39, p. 482.

[f] 1 M. and W. 101. Ashlin v. White, HOLT 387.

[g] B. and C. 105. COMYN'S *Dig.* Action in the case for a deceit.

[h] EAST, *Reports*, vol. ii. 102. The words were, ' I can positively assure
you, of my own knowledge, you may credit Miss Robertson with perfect safety :' and see Lyde v. Barnard, cited before ; and 9 Geo. IV. c. 14.
Taylor v. Ashton, 11 M. and W. 465. As to character of a servant,

is a tradesman who has suffered loss to a large amount in consequence of his having been induced to give credit to a third person—and by this action he calls on the defendant, through whose misrepresentation the loss occurred, to make it good. . . It was enough to state this, that the defendant affirmed that to be true within his knowledge, which he did not know to be true—this is fraudulent. . . . The fraud consists, not in the defendant's saying that he believed the matter to be true or that he had reason so to believe, but in asserting positively his knowledge of what he did not know. . . If any one become an actor in deceiving another, if he lead him, by any misrepresentations to do things which are injurious to him . . . an action will lie against him to answer in damages for his acts.'

' It is a very old head[i] of Equity,' says Lord Eldon, ' that if a representation is made to another person going to deal in a matter of interest on the faith of that representation, the former shall make that representation good if he knows it to be false; and in that case,' he most characteristically adds, ' there *appears* a disposition to hold, that if there was relief to be administered in equity there ought to be relief in law, a proposition that seems to me extremely questionable, and I *doubt,'* etc.

LV.

EJUS est non velle qui potest velle.[k]
 He who can say Yes, can say No.

Velle non creditur qui obsequitur imperio patris vel domini.

An heir who repudiated an inheritance offered to him, could not claim it again, ' qui semel noluit . . . perdidit jus,' as the

---

Fountain *v.* Boodle, 3 Q. B. 11 ; LORD MANSFIELD in Buller, N. P. 8 ; Blagg *v.* Stuart, 16 L. J. Q. B. 39 ; Affleck *v.* Child, 9 B. and C. 405. On case of false representation generally, Small *v.* Atwood, 8 CL. and FINN.

i Evans *v.* Bicknell, 6 VESEY, 183 ; Wilde *v.* Gibson, 1 *House of Lords Cases,* 626 ; Lake *v.* Croker, 2 SWANSTON, 289.

k κατὰ ἐκείνου ἐστὶ τὸ μὴ θέλειν, τοῦ δυναμένου θέλειν.—*Greek Interpret.* Βασιλικῶν, lib. i. 3. Some of my readers will forgive me for re-

property straightway belonged to others. But unless it was offered 'delata' to him, it could not be said that he had repudiated it. 'Furiosi curator nequaquam poterit repudiare quid necdum delata est.' (*Dig.* xxxviii. 9. 5.) So the heir under a condition, if he repudiated the inheritance before the condition was accomplished, did an act that was wholly insignificant. 'Is qui hæres institutus est vel cui legitima hæreditas delata est, repudiatione hæreditatem amittit. Hoc ita verum est si in eâ causâ erat hæreditas ut et adiri posset—ceterum hæres institutus sub conditione si ante conditionem existentem repudiavit, nihil egit.' (*Dig.*xxix. 2. 13; so xxix. 2. 23.)

'In repudiandâ hæreditate vel legato certus esse debet de suo jure is qui repudiat.' Therefore the heir who doubted whether the testator was alive or not, or who doubted whether the testator had the power to make a will, could not, while he was in that state of uncertainty, repudiate the inheritance. He was not 'certus de suo jure.' (*Dig.*xxix. 2, 13, § 1 and 2.) So he who has not the power to enter upon an inheritance cannot be said not to will to enter upon it. 'Nolle adire hæreditatem non videtur, qui non potest adire.' So in the famous law, 'Pater Severianam' (*Dig.*xxxv. 1. 101) Papinian applies the rule thus: A father, by his will, desired his daughter to marry Ælius Philippus, and after leaving her an estate if she did marry him, left it to Ælius Philippus if she did not. She died before she had reached a marriageable age. The question was, whether Ælius Philippus was entitled to the estate; which Papinian answered in the negative—because the condition on which the estate was to go to Ælius Philippus had not taken place; it could not be said that the daughter had refused to marry him, as it had never been in her power to do

---

minding them of a beautiful passage in Euripides ἑκαβή. Polyxena bids Ulysses not fear her supplications :

> θάρσει—πέφευγας τὸν ἐμὸν Ἱκέσιον Δία
> ὥς ἕψομαί γε—τοῦ τ'ἀναγκαίου χάριν
> θανεῖν τεχρήζους—εἰδε μὴ βουλήσομαι
> κακὴ φανοῦμαι καὶ φιλόψυχος γυνή.

so. ' Respondi cum in conditionibus testamentorum voluntatem potius quam verba considerari oporteat, Ælio Philippo
fideicommissum ita datum videri, si ei Proculâ defuncti filia
nubere noluisset—quare cum ea prius quam viripotens fieret,
vitâ decesserit conditionem extitisse non videri.'

And if any one ' metu verberum aut a justo timore coactus'
entered upon an inheritance ' fallens adierit hereditatem,' he
did not, if he was free, become heir himself, nor if he was a
slave, give his master the inheritance. (*Dig.* xxix. 2. 6, § 7;
but see *ib.* iv. 2. 21, 6.)

But if a son married ' patre cogente' a woman, whom if he
had been left to the exercise of his own will, he would not
have married, ' quam non duceret si sui arbitrii esset,' the
marriage was valid, ' contraxit matrimonium,' for ' maluisse
hoc videtur.' (*Dig.* xxiii. 2. 22.) The gradual shades by which
the will of a free agent disappears, are as hard to define as it is
to settle the precise moment at which day becomes night.
The sagacity, however, is wonderful, with which the Roman
jurists,[m] avoiding all metaphysical dissertations and scholastic
refinements, from which it was difficult to extricate such a
subject, have adjusted their rules to the exigencies of social
intercourse and the comfort of human life—' coactus volui' is
their concise expression, where a dozen pages of Meeson and
Welsby would hardly contain the mock subtilties of a pleading
judge—and it is taken from Homer, the fountain of all that is
wise and great.

ἑκὼν ἀέκοντί γε θυμῷ.

LVI.

FILIUSFAMILIAS neque retinere neque recupe-
rare neque adipisci possessionem rei peculiaris
videtur.—MARCIANUS.

---

[m] See the beautiful law, *Dig.* xlvi. 2. 91. 'Et hoc modo patronus quoque liberto et is cujus magna verecundia ei quem in præsentiâ pudor
ad resistendum impedit, furtum facere solet.'

An unemancipated son has no kind of possessory action for his 'peculium.'

Under the old Roman Jurisprudence, whatever was acquired by the unemancipated son, was at once the property of the father. 'Quicquid filius peculiari nomine apprehendit id statim ejus pater possidet,'[a] are the words of Ulpian. 'Ejus quod in patriâ potestate agens habuisti dominium ad patrem tuum pertineat,'[b] says Antoninus. 'Placet ut quidquid filiusfamilias acquirit ne momento quidem penes ipsum remaneat,'[c] are the expressions of Ulpian on the same subject, in another part of the *Pandects.* Nevertheless, there were three kinds of 'peculium:'

1. The 'peculium castrense,' or 'quasi castrense';[d] that is, money required by military service, or by any kind of public service, or from the bounty of the prince; over this the father had no kind of power.

2. The 'peculium profectitium,' which the son gained by the capital entrusted to him by his father. This was divided between the father and son, but the father enjoyed the 'usufruct' of the son's portion.

3. The 'peculium adventitium'; that the son acquired entirely by his own industry; by gift or inheritance; the property in this belonged to him, but the 'usufruct' to the father; unless, according to the later legislation, the father had refused to sanction his son in accepting the property,[e] or it had been expressly declared[f] in the gift that the father should not have the 'usufruct,'[g] or that it was the succession of a brother or sister of the son.

Besides these beneficial and profitable rights, the father had others, which the son could not violate without exposing him-

---

[a] *Analyse du Code Civil,* vol. i. p. 382 ; *Dig.* xli. 2. 4.
[b] *Cod. de Pati. Pot.*—MALEVILLE.
[c] *Dig.* xxix. 2. 79.
[d] *Cod. de Castr. pec.* iii.
[e] *Cod. de bonis quæ,* lib. vi.
[f] *Nov.,* 117. 1.
[g] *Nov.,* 118. 2.

self to the treatment of a criminal—and the utter absence
of any allusion to which in any part of our legislation, as it
is the effect is no doubt also the cause of that want of tenderness in some of the most sacred relations of private
life, that hardness and want of reverence towards age, when
unaccompanied with rank or money, for which men and women
in the higher, middle, and lower classes of England are un-
fortunately notorious. The son, without the permission of the
magistrate, could not summon the father before any tribunal.[h]

He could not bring against him any action that involved
loss of character, e.g., any question of fraud.[i]

The father could only be obliged by a court of law to make
compensation to the extent of his abilities[k]—'in id quod facere
potest.' These rights extended not to the son only, but to all
the male descendants. The ' patria potestas,' as far as the ' jus
vitæ et necis' was concerned, ceased with the Republic. Before
the father could execute, he was obliged to have recourse to
the magistrates, who were bound to fulfil his wishes; but,
nevertheless, it was a salutary delay against the sudden trans-
ports of even legitimate indignation. On this subject we have
an excellent law of the Emperor Alexander.

' Si filius tuus pietatem patri debitam non agnoscit, castigare
eum jure patriæ potestatis non prohiberis—acriore remedio
usurus, si in pari materiâ perseveraverit, eumque præsidi provinciæ oblaturus, dicturo sententiam quum tu quoque dici
volueris' (Cod. iii. de patriâ potest).

The ' filiusfamilias' could only leave by will the ' peculium
castrense,' but the paternal authority was confined to the relations of father and son. He might buy and sell, be surety,
be defendant, carry on commerce, fulfil the duties of a magistrate, and be named tutor.[l] The barbarians who invaded Gaul

---

h *Dig. De in jus vocando,* iv. and v.
i *Dig. de Obsequiis parentum et patr. præst.* xxxvii. 15. 2 and 5.
k *Id.* tit. 7. 3. *Inst. de pat. pot.*
l *Dig. de act. empti,* vi. 7 ; *Cod. cum eo qui,* l. 5, *Dig. de oblig. et act.*
39 ; *Dig. de his qui sui vel alieni juris sunt,* ix.

swept away these maxims in most of the provinces,[1] where their customs were established. Their rule, as Tacitus has told us, was, that till the son could wield the javelin he belonged to his home, and after that time to the Republic— 'Ante hoc domûs pars videntur, mox reipublicæ.'

The 'garde noble,' or 'bourgeoise,'[m] which existed in Paris, and generally throughout the 'pays de coutûme,' gave the father, or in default of him, the mother, then the grandfather, and then the grandmother, the management of the person and fortunes of the children, and the profits of their estates, so long as they defrayed the charges incident to their support. The 'garde noble' lasted till twenty years for the males, and fifteen years for the females. The 'garde bourgeoise' to fourteen for the first, and twelve for the second.[n] Both ceased on a second marriage of the guardian.

As to the 'Pays de droit écrit,' the law continued as it had been modelled by Justinian, with two exceptions. The first, that if a son had been ten years separated from his father, and carrying on his own affairs, he was to be considered as emancipated from the date of the separation. The other, that the father on the marriage of his children, was obliged to surrender the 'usufruct' of their property, reserving what was necessary for his support, and that of his other children. It is remarkable that St. Louis, in his 'établissemens,' obliges the father, on the marriage of his son, to give him up the third part of his land. I may observe, that though the Roman law invested the father only with authority, it enjoined an equal share of veneration to the mother: 'Pietas parentibus etsi inæqualis sit eorum potestas, æqua debetur.'[o] Montesquieu[p]

---

[1] Not in all. In Bretagne, Poitou, Auvergne, La Manche, Châlons, Rheims, Sedan, Laon, Valenciennes, they were upheld.—CÆSAR, lib. vi.

[m] *Régles du Droit Français:* 'De la garde noble ou bourgeoise.'— Tit. 7, c. 1, p. 160.

[n] *Coutûme de Paris,* 265.

[o] *Dig.* xxvii. 10. 4; 'L'enfant à tout âge doit honneur et respect à son père et mère.'—*Code.*

[p] *Régles du Droit Français:* 'De la puissance paternelle.'—POCQUET de Livonnière, p. 30, etc.

complains that so precious a support of morality as the 'patria potestas' of the Romans should not have been more enforced in France. In another place he says: 'La puissance paternelle se perdit à Rome avec la république, parceque dans *les monarchies où l'on n'a que faire de mœurs si pures,* on veut que chacun vive sous la puissance des magistrats.'

LVII.

QUOD quis ex culpâ sua damnum sentit non intelligitur damnum sentire.

No man is injured by what he suffers through his own fault.

The consequences of this rule are twofold. First, that the risk of anything falls on him whose fault has caused the loss; e. g., if, through the fault of the buyer, he is evicted from the possession of the thing bought, he cannot bring his action for the eviction, or on the express 'stipulatio dupli,' against the seller. *Dig.* xxi. 2. 29 § 1: ' Si duplæ stipulator ex possessore petita factus et victus sit quam rem si possideret retinere potuerit peti autem utiliter non poterit—vel ipso jure, promissa duplæ tutus erit—vel certe doli mali exceptione se tueri poterit—vel ita si culpâ vel sponte duplæ possessoris possessio amissa fuerit.'

The second consequence is, that he who suffers loss by his own fault cannot call upon another to share the burden. An heir who is responsible for anything he has done, cannot call upon his co-heir for contribution: ' Quod ex facto suo unus ex cohæredibus ex stipulatione hæreditariâ præstat a cohærede non repetet' (*Dig.* x. 2. 44 § 5).

So Titius, the joint-master of a slave, could not call upon the other proprietor to share the loss occasioned by the injury which the slave had caused at his (Titius's) command: ' Iniquum est eum qui jussit servum facere consequi aliquid a socio cum ex suo delicto damnum patiatur' (*Dig.* ix. 4. 17). So, although a partner might call upon his colleague to contribute to the loss which he had sustained 'injuriâ judicis,' he could not oblige him to bear any share in that which he had brought upon himself ' ob maleficium suum.' So, if a ' socius' made default, he must bear the loss himself: ' Aufidius refert si socii bonorum fuerint deinde unus cum ad judicium non adesset, damnatus sit, non debere eum de communi id consequi.'

By a parity of reason, if I lend you a horse for a journey to a particular place, and the horse, without any fault of yours, and because he is unequal to the work, is injured, I have no action against you; for it was my fault to lend my horse for a service which he was too weak to perform (*Dig.* xiii. 6. 23): ' Si commodavero tibi equum quo utereris usque ad certum locum. Si nullâ culpâ tuâ interveniente in ipso itinere deterior equus factus sit, non teneris commodati—nam ego in culpâ ero qui in tam longum iter commodari qui eum laborem sustinere non potuit.'

To these instances I will add another, taken from the edict ' De damno infecto.' This most valuable edict applied only to mischief that was apprehended, not to that actually done: ' De damno vero facto nihil edicto cavetur.' If, therefore, before any application under it had been made, the house of Titius, not by any act of his, but from old age and want of repair, fell upon his neighbour's property and injured it, his neighbour must bear the loss, and could not apply for compensation, since the delay in asking security under the edict was the cause of it; nor, if the owner chose to abandon his right to the materials that had fallen, could the neighbour oblige him to take them away. Therefore it may happen, says Caius, that, though we have suffered loss, we have no action: ' Veluti si vicini ædes in meas ædes inciderint adeo ut plerisque placuerit nec cogi posse eum ut rudera tollat—si modo omnia quæ jaceant pro derelicto habeat' (*Dig.* xxxix. 2. 6).

But if the neighbour was prevented from applying for the edict by any reasonable cause—e. g., if he were absent on the public service—or if the prætor had granted his application for security, but the security had not been given, he was entitled to compensation (*Dig.* xxxix. 2. 8). And, again, Julianus: ' Inquit si quis propter angustias temporis aut quia reipublicæ

causâ aberat non potuerit damni infecti stipulari non inique
prætorem curaturum ut dominus vitiosarum ædium aut damnum sarciat aut ædibus careat.' Ulpian adds, ' sententiam
Juliani utilitas comprobat' (*ib.* 9).

Among many instances in our law may be mentioned, the
lapse of the presentation to a benefice if the patron do not
present within a certain time. Laches generally does not prejudice an infant; e. g., if for non-payment of rent it is stipulated that it shall be double, if the infant does not pay, he
shall not be bound by it; but lapse incurs if he does not present to a church within six months (COMYNS, *Digest*, Enfant,
d. 4). The laches of the husband may prejudice the wife
(COM., *Dig.*, Baron and Feme [L.]). There can be no laches
in the sovereign: but see 9 Geo. III., c. 16; 32 Geo. III., c. 58;
7 Will. IV.; and 1 Vict., c. 78, § 23, 217, 1, 14; Goodwin *v.*
Baldwin, 11 EAST, 493; Doe *v.* Morris, 3 and 4 Will. IV., c. 27;
2 SCOTT, 276.

LVIII.

CREDITOR qui permittit rem venire pignus
dimittit.—GAIUS.[p]

*A creditor who permits the sale of the thing pledged
loses his security.*

This rule declares that if a creditor has allowed his debtor
to dispose of [for the word ' venire' is used in that sense
here] anything that he holds as a pledge or mortgage, he loses
his right as mortgagee. Modestinus (*Dig.* xx. 6. 9) supposes
the case of Titius, who has mortgaged his farm first to Sempronius and then to Gaius, and afterwards sold it to them as
joint owners. The question he puts is, whether the ' jus

---

[p] ' Non videtur consensisse creditor si sciente eo debitor rem vendiderit sed si subscripserit forte in tabulis emptionis consensisse videtur
nisi manifeste apparet deceptum esse.' — *Dig., Quibus modis pignus
vel hypotheca solvitur*, xx. 6. 8, § 15. *Règles du Droit Français*, p. 341,
c. 4, POCQUET DE LIVONNIÈRE.

pignoris' is extinguished? or, whether Sempronius and Gaius have any right but the 'jus emptionis'? And the answer is, that 'cum consensum mutuo venditioni dedisse proponantur,' the 'jus emptionis' alone remains, and that they have not the 'actio pigneratitia.' And if the creditor allowed the debtor to sell the pledge, and it was sold by the debtor's heir, the right was lost: 'Recte venisse dicendum est hæ enim subtilitates a judicibus non admittuntur' (*Dig.* xx. 6. 8. § 16); 'Si consensit venditioni creditor, liberatur hypotheca' (*Dig.* xx. 6. 7). If the creditor was a minor, the consent of his guardian, or the sanction of a judge, was requisite: 'Sed in his pupilli consensus non debet aliter ratus haberi quam si præsente tutore consenserit, aut etiam ipse tutor, scilicet si commodum aliquid vel satis ei fieri ex eo judex æstimaverit.'

The word 'venditionis' was taken in a wide sense, and included gifts or legacies: 'Venditionis appellationem generaliter accipere debemus ut ei si legare permisit, valeat quod concessit' (*Dig.* xx. 6. 8. § 11). So the rule extended to him 'qui permutaverit vel insolutum accepit, item in similibus qui vicem emptorum continent' (*Dig.* xliv. 6. 4. § 31).

The creditor might, however, by an express stipulation, reserve his right (*Dig.* xx. 6. 4. § 1): 'Si in venditione pignoris consenserit creditor vel ut debitor hanc rem permutet vel donet vel in dotem det dicendum erit pignus liberari, nisi salva causâ pignoris sui consensit (vel venditioni vel cæteris) nam solent multi salvâ causâ pignoris sui consentire, sed et si ipse vendiderit creditor sic tamen venditionem fecit, ne discederit a pignore nisi ei satisfiat dicendum erit exceptionem ei non nocere.' Thus the furniture of a town-house always, of a country-house by agreement, was pledged for the rent; but if the owner allowed the tenant to sell the furniture, an interdict lay if he prevented him from removing them.[q]

---

[q] *Dig., de Migrando,* xliii. 32.

LIX.

CULPA est immiscere se rei ad se non pertinenti.
—POMPONIUS.

*To meddle with affairs in which a man has no concern,
makes him a wrong doer.*

Ulpian cites from Julianus a striking illustration of this rule
in the following case: ' If I buy from Titius a slave who belongs to Mævius, and after Mævius has claimed the slave from
me I sell him to another person who kills him, I am bound to
pay the value of the slave to Mævius. For though the death
of the slave was not owing to any fault of mine, yet it was my
fault that I put the slave in the power of the person to whom
I sold him, and made myself a party to the dispute' (*Dig.* vi.
1. 17).

So, if being the bonâ fide purchaser of land, I find out that
it belongs to another, and then build upon it, I cannot claim
the expense I have incurred in building from the owner (*Dig.*
vi. 1. 37): 'Nec enim deberi jam alienam certus ædificium
ponere.' All I can do is, to remove the building I have
erected: ' Sine dispendio domini areæ;' according to the rule
(*Dig.* l. 17. 203), 'Quod quis ex culpâ suâ damnum sentit
non intelligitur damnum sentire.' So any one was liable to
an action, 'negotiorum gestorum,' who even under some
fancied necessity 'immiscuit se negotiis alienis et ea gessit
(*Dig.* iii. 4. 3. § 10). The law says, ' culpa est.' So, if the seller
of an inheritance after the sale exacts the debts due to the inheritance, and then is robbed of the money he has collected,
he is liable for the amount to the purchaser; though, if the
debts had been collected before the sale, he would have been
safe (*Dig.* xviii. 4. 3): ' Si venditor hæreditatis exactam pecuniam sine dolo malo et culpâ perdidisset non placet eum
emptori teneri.'

LX.

The Law of Inheritance.

QUAMDIU potest valere testamentum, tamdiu legitimus non admittitur.—Paulus.

No successor, pointed out by law only, shall take the inheritance, so long as it is possible for the will to operate.

To the same effect are the words of Ulpian: 'Quamdiu potest ex testamento adiri hæreditas ab intestato non defertur' (*Dig.* xxix. 2. 39); and those of the *Code*: 'Provisio hominis facit cessare legis provisionem.' Scævola puts an exceptional case, that of a testator appointing an heir, in case the legitimate successor should refuse to take 'ab intestato.'[a] In this case, says Scævola, if the relation should accept, the heir is, no doubt, excluded: 'Puto deficere conditionem testamenti si legitimus hæres vindicet hæreditatem' (*Dig.* xxviii. 5. 82).

The Law of Inheritance is discussed in the thirty-eighth chapter of the Pandects, under the sixth and following titles, under several heads of the sixth title of the Code, in the 118th and 127th Novels, and the first thirteen titles of the third book of the Institutes.

In every code of laws there are, as Monsieur de Maleville observes, four important subjects, which cannot be governed, and which never have been governed, exclusively by the principles of municipal justice. I mean, that the form of the government which prevails in each country must be the foundation of the rules by which they are determined. These are —the paternal authority, the contract of marriage, the law of inheritance, and the law of wills. There are two other subjects, also, of vast importance, and, as the history of our legislation shows, materially affected by political considerations, but which have a scope far less extensive, and which are con-

---

[a] In which case, says Gothofred : 'Ex voluntate testatoris potest causa intestati præcedere causam testati.' Pocquet de Livonnière, *Règles du Droit Français*, l. iii. c. 1, p.191: 'En pays coutumier, institution d'héritier n'a lieu,' etc.

centrated almost wholly on commercial purposes; I mean the law of loans and of mortgage.[b]

For the general questions which the laws are called upon to settle, the rules of plain and simple equity are the only guides which the lawgiver should follow; but in considering the questions I have enumerated, it is necessary that he should lift himself above the common view, and fix his eyes on the genius of the constitution and the people for whom he is about to legislate. In the twenty-seventh book, Montesquieu has explained the mysteries which hang over the Roman law of inheritance, and the causes of the vicissitudes which they have undergone, until they were invested with the shape in which they have been transmitted to us. He says that the object of the first Roman law was to preserve equality in the original distribution of land, and that their changes are to be ascribed to the changes which were brought about in their constitution. According to the law of the twelve tables, the class of heirs was that of ' hæredes sui '; that is to say, of those who were under the power of their father at the moment of his death. Emancipated children were not called to the succession, if they had been emancipated by the formal sale, which transferred them to another stock; to that stock they would have carried their hereditary portion. If the emancipation had left them simply their own masters, the father, it was supposed, had given them a ' peculium ' to provide for their subsistence, or they had found other means to establish their independence.

Daughters were called with males to an equal share in the succession of their father; nor did this break in upon the scheme for the equal division of land. Nothing more than an usufruct was in reality granted to them; for as the children did not succeed to the mother, nor the husband (if any other heir could be found) to the wife, the estate of the wife returned to the family from which she had been separated.

If there were no ' hæredes sui,' the ' agnati,' *i.e.*, the relations on the male side, were called to the inheritance; and in default

---

[b] POCQUET DE LIVONNIÈRE, l. iv. c. 4, *des Hypothèques.*

of the 'agnati,' the succession was transferred to the relations on the female side, 'cognati.'

According to the law of the twelve tables, daughters shared in the inheritance with sons; but the evils to which such a state of things led were so considerable, the corruption, luxury, and insolence of the women thus endowed occasioned such alarm among the Romans,[b] who thought the purity of the mother the best guarantee for the qualities which made a valuable citizen of the son, that the Voconian law prevented all women from inheriting property above a certain value, even that of their father, when he had no other child.

Such was the course of successions 'ab intestato.' But the absolute right of disposing of their property by will, of which the Romans were most tenacious, rendered all these precautions unavailing, and soon put an end to the original equality of the shares, into which the soil of the republic had been divided among the citizens; and as the original harshness and severity of that 'antique age' yielded to more refined influences and humaner views, it was thought hard that emancipated children should be deprived of all share in their father's property; and the prætor, acting on the maxims of natural equity, admitted them to a share in his estate.

The 'senatusconsultum Tertullianum'[c] allowed mothers to inherit from their children, and the 'senatusconsultum orphilianum'[d] allowed children to inherit from their mothers. The prætor, meanwhile, had divided the succession 'ab intestato' into four degrees: first of the children, then of the 'legitimi hæredes,' then of the 'cognati,' then 'viri et uxoris.'[e] The first, 'bonorum possessio,' was called 'unde liberi'[f]—the grand-

---

[b] 'Intolerabilius nihil est quam fœmina dives.'

[c] *Cod.* vi. 56. *Dig.* xxxviii. 17, A.D. 158. GAII *Inst.* iii. 14.

[d] *Cod.* vi. 56, A.D. 178. *Dig.* xxxviii. 17. *Inst.* iii. 4. These privileges were extended to grandchildren (1 *Inst.* iii. 4, l. 4; *Cod. Theod.* v. 1; 9 *Cod.* vi. 55), and to the mother who had not the 'jus liberorum' (*Cod.* ii. 8, 59). At last the mother always shared with her children in the inheritance of a deceased intestate child (l. *Ult. Cod.* viii. 59).

[e] *Dig.* xxxviii. 6.

[f] *Dig.* xxxvii. 4, de b.p.c., tab. 1, § 1; 11, § 1. *Cod.* h.f. vi. 14. 1.

children took the share of their deceased parent under it; the second was called 'unde legitimi'[g]; the third, 'unde cognati'[h]; the fourth, 'undevir et uxor';[i] to sanction which a 'justum matrimonium' must have existed at the time of the death when the succession arose. At last Justinian, by the 118th and 127th novels, abolished all distinction between the 'cognati' and the 'agnati,' and admitted indiscriminately the descendants of sons, and of daughter relations by the male and the female side, to the succession. His remarks show his usual presumption, and his utter ignorance of, and inability to comprehend, the political reasons by which the Roman law of inheritance had been modified and controuled at different periods of its history.

In the 'pays de droit écrit' in France, the laws of Justinian were implicitly followed; and the heirs 'ab intestato' were, first, the descendants, male and female, 'à l'infini,' the grandchildren, according to the better opinion, taking 'par souches,' and not 'par tête.' 2ndly. 'Les ascendans,' according to proximity of degree and without representation, so that the father, or mother, or either of them, excluded the grandfather, etc. The 'édit des mères' of Charles IX., as it was called, excluding mothers from all share in that part of their children's estate which came from the father, never prevailed in the 'pays de droit écrit,' and was repealed for the rest of France, 1729.

The exception to this rule was, that the brothers or sisters of the deceased shared with the 'ascendans par tête.'

3rdly. The collaterals, among whom the right of representation prevailed. The whole blood excluded the half blood altogether in this class. The right of representation did not extend beyond the children of brothers and sisters.

The Roman Law relatively to succession, made no distinction between different kinds of property; it did not conceive the possibility of a double patrimony. Property real and personal, paternal and maternal, moveable and immoveable,

---

[g] *i. e.*, 'Quem hæredem esse oporteret si intestatus mortuus esset.' —*Dig.* xxxviii. 7. 1—4, 'unde legitimi.'

[h] *Dig.* xxxviii. 8. *Inst.* iii. 8. GAIUS *Inst.* iii. 28. 27—31.

[i] *Dig.* xxxviii. 11. 11.

corporeal and incorporeal, by descent or by purchase, belonged to the same heir.

The genius of the feudal lawyers was different; every sort of scholastic distinction was substituted for the plain and simple rules of equity and convenience. In some countries the most remote excluded the nearer relation; sometimes the eldest son took all; sometimes he had only a 'préciput;' sometimes the 'droit d'aînesse' was extended to women; sometimes it was limited to the direct line; sometimes it was extended to collateral heirs. In France, before the Revolution, the Law of Descent varied with every 'coutûme'; property was divided into 'meubles' and 'immeubles,' 'propres'[a] and 'acquêts,' 'nobles' and 'roturiers.'

The same property might in certain cases fall under the head of 'meubles,' in others, under that of 'immeubles.' The 'acquêts' were what the deceased had acquired otherwise than by descent. They followed usually the same line with the 'meubles.' The 'propres,' that is the 'immeubles inherited' were divided into 'propres réels,' land, etc.; 'propres fictifs,' property that by a fiction of law was treated as 'immeubles,' 'propres conventionnels,' heir-looms, moveables, to which by a particular arrangement the quality and effect of 'propres' had been annexed. Moreover into 'propres naissans,' and 'propres anciens,' 'propres paternels' and 'propres maternels,' 'propres de ligne' and 'propres sans ligne.'[b] The maxim with regard to all was, that they never went in the ascending

---

[a] The idea denoted by the word 'propres,' will be found in the *Pandects, de jure dotium*, xxiii. 3. 6: 'Jure succursum est patri, ut filiâ amissâ solatii loco cederet si redderetur ei dos ab ipso profecta, ne et filiæ amissæ et pecuniæ damnum sentiret,' *i.e.*, that the property should return to the estate from which it had been taken.

[b] I trust that no member of the Court of Exchequer, 'solatii loco,' will, as a consolation for the decay of special pleading, take it into his head to use his influence with the Lord Chancellor to introduce a law for the regulation of landed estates in England, founded on these distinctions. Judging from the ideas of legislation propounded in that quarter, the success of such of a scheme might be not altogether improbable.—(*Written Dec.* 1855).

line. ' Propres ne remontent point.' In this disorder, however, it is easy to mark the ascendancy of two leading principles. The first, that of giving estates to males. The second, that of restoring them to the family from which they had been taken. The first principle founded on the law of military service, and therefore limited to ' propres nobles,' was by an irresistible tendency extended to the estates of ' roturiers.' The second cannot be vindicated by any similar argument, but proceeds from a feeling liable no doubt to superstitious exaggeration, but implanted for wise purposes in our nature, which makes men cling to ancient possessions. ' The Lord forbid I should sell the inheritance of my fathers unto thee.'

The Roman system did not obtain a complete triumph in the French code[c]—though it prevailed so far as to deliver the ' pays coutumiers ' from a mass of contradictory rules, which fomented an incessant litigation. The difference established by the customs between different kinds of property was abolished. But property that fell to collaterals, or ascendants, was divided into two equal parts; the one for those of the paternal, the other for those of the maternal line.[d] Instead of this, it was proposed that the rule ' paterna paternis,' ' materna maternis,' be limited to cousin-germans; but this principle, because it was thought that it would lead to litigation, and that the affections of the actual owner were alone to be considered, was abandoned in favour of the rule as it now stands.

By our Common Law, in the time of Henry II., a man's goods were divided into three equal parts; one of which went to his heirs, or lineal descendants, another to his wife, and a third was at his own disposal. The law altered without leaving any visible traces of its changes, and the deceased was allowed to bequeath all his goods and chattels. The idea of an administrator appointed by the bishop, as described in the passage cited below,[e] is among the peculiar freaks of our law;

---

[c] *Cod.*, lib. iii. c. 3 ; POCQUET DE LIVONNIÈRE, *Règles*, liv. iii. c. 1.

[d] *C. C.*, 733, with regard to the law of those who perish by the same accident. See art. 720, and *Dig.* xxxiv. 5 ; *Ib.*, ' de rebus dubiis,' *si inter.*

[e] ' Where a man dies intestate,' says Finch, p. 410, ' the ordinary shall

and, as Godolphin surmises, this gross usurpation of the church, which it must have turned at one time to very considerable profit, was probably built on a canon of the Emperor Leo: ‘ That the bishop shall take care to see such legacies duly performed as are for the redemption of captives, in case the testator appoint not one to execute his will in that particular.’[f]

‘ At Common Law,’ says Lord Holt, ‘ the ordinary appointed committees of the personal estate, and in those times it was the practice to compel such committees to distribute, but afterwards, when the ordinary granted administration . . . it was adjudged that he was not compellable to make any distribution, which being thought hard! as to those of kin to the intestate in equal degree the statute of distribution was made.’[g] The Common Law Courts, in their usual spirit, declared that the bond given by an administrator to the Ecclesiastical Court,[h] for the honest discharge of his duty,[i] was void, thereby giving impunity to the plunderer. These evils caused the Statute of Distributions, 22 and 23, C. II., c. 10, to be passed, the object of which was to take care that the property should not be embezzled, and that it should be properly distributed. This statute has the infallible stamp of English Legislation, in excepting the province of York and city of London from

---

have the disposition of all his chattles to pious uses. For he that had the care of his soul during life, is presumed to be the fittest person to have the care and disposal of his goods to pious uses after his death.’ This is a very different style of reasoning from that of Papinian. ‘And therefore the ordinary may seize the goods and keep them without waste and may alien, or sell them at his will, and dispose of the money that he hath for them to pious uses ; and if he doth not, he breaketh the trust and confidence the law reposes in him, but yet his gift or alienation remaineth good in law. But he, being a spiritual governor, shall not be liable to temporal suits;’ i. e., although he took all the money belonging to other people!—FINCH’S Law Book, iv. c. 7.

[f] GODOLPHIN’S Abridgment Eccl. Law, c. 10, § 9 ; lib. xxviii., C. de Episc. et Cler., ‘ nulli licere.’

[g] Petit v. Smith, 1 PEERE WILLIAMS ; BACON’S Abridgment, 7, Exors(1),

[h] By virtue of, 31 Ed. iii. c. 11.

[i] Hughes v. Hughes, LEVINZ, 233.

its operation;[k] it is founded on the 118th *Novell* of Justinian, it provides that ' One-third shall go to the widow of the intestate, and the residue in equal proportions to his children; or if dead to their representatives, that is, their lineal descendants; if there are no children or legal representatives subsisting, then a moiety shall go to the widow, and a moiety to the next of kindred in equal degree, and their representatives; if no widow, the whole shall go to the children; if neither widow nor children, the whole shall be distributed among the next of kin in equal degree, and their representatives; but no representatives are admitted among collaterals farther than the children of the intestate's brothers and sisters.'[l] By the statute of 1 James II., c. 17, it is provided, that if the father be dead, and any of the children die childless and intestate, and without a wife, during the life of the mother, she and each of the remaining children, or their representatives, shall divide his effects in equal portions.'[m]

The history of the power of alienation, as it applies to landed property, flings, as might be expected, great light upon the genius of the English people.[n] The contrivances em-

---

[k] Archbishop of Canterbury *v.* Robertson, 1 CR. and M., 705.

[l] ' Person,' in § 5, means ' judge,' 8 B. and C., 158 ; Archbishop of Canterbury *v.* Tappen,

In Stanley *v.* Stanley, 1 ATKYNS, 457, Lord Hardwicke says : ' The first question,' *i.e.*, whether the nephew and nieces of the intestate shall share with the intestate's mother, there being a widow, ' depends on the construction of the statute of James, which is very incorrectly penned, and so is the statute of distributions.'

[m] ' Requiritur,' says Struvius, Syntagma juris feudalis, p. 197, c. 9, *de successione in feudum*, ' itaque in his successoribus feudalibus ut ex sanguine primi acquirentes per lineam masculinam legitime sint procreati.' Unde sequitur quod non succedant in feudo (1) ascendentes, (2) adoptivi, (3) cognati, (4) illegitime nati. And he proceeds to discuss the effect of the words—' Für sich und seine ehelich geborene, leibes-, leben-erben ' (p. 302, etc.).

' Leges Angliæ plenæ sunt tricarum ambiguitatum et sibi contrariæ— fuerunt quidem excogitatæ atque sancitæ a Normannis quibus nulla gens magis litigiosa atque in controversis machinandiis fallacior reperiri potest.'—PHILIP HORA, Barrington, 51.

[n] Serjeant Runnington has very well expressed the evils of the cir-

ployed to turn form into substance; the technical learning growing out of those contrivances; the importance annexed to them, and their continuance long after the danger they had been intended to overcome had ceased; the contented way in which the English gentry allowed the possession and inheritance of their estates to depend upon forms, and a process of reasoning grounded upon those forms, which must to them have been utterly unintelligible, without making one serious and persevering effort for its alteration (just as they acquiesced in the Norman-French), simply because they were told by persons in authority, and acquiring honours and opulence by their knowledge of this queer assemblage of almost incredible quirks and devices, that everything was as it should be—illustrate in the clearest manner, that antipathy to change, that ignorance of method, and that suspicion of theory, which if they have saved us from much evil, have undoubtedly perpetuated much that is deplorably foolish and unjust in our institutions. The real cause of the progress of Uses among us, and of the power of the court by which the law of Uses was administered, is beyond all doubt to be found, not only in the cunning and rapacity of ecclesiastics, by whom they were introduced, but in the means which they furnished of evading the Common Law, according to which land was not devisable. In other countries the old system would have been altered—in ours it was allowed to subsist side by side with that which in diameter was opposed to it.[o] The conflict of systems led to the conflict of jurisdictions; phrases were invented which, without conveying any distinct or settled meaning, gradually grew up into a regular language, and answered

---

cuitous remedy: 'The ostensible reason, from the fictitious recompense hampered succeeding times, how to distinguish cases within the false reason, but not within the real policy of the invention.'—HALE, *Hist. of the Law*, note, p. 208.

[o] So when the absurdity of 'wager of law' was seen, it was not abolished, but new forms of action were invented, in which the defendant could not wage his law, allowing the old one in which it could be waged still to exist. This continued till 1830.

all the purposes of litigation.[p] Things were moulded to suit these phrases, and as Mr. Justice Blackstone said, in words which appear to me to convey as bitter a reproach on a system that everybody is supposed to know, and the part of that system to which every citizen may have occasion to appeal, for the security of those most dear to him, as words can utter: ' The law of real property in this country is now formed into a fine artificial system, full of unseen connections and nice dependencies, and he that breaks one link of the chain endangers the dissolution of the whole.'[q]

Can there be a more serious objection to that which is requisite for the common course of ordinary life, which should be of a texture tough and strong enough to withstand the convulsive struggles of passion and of interest, of fierce excitement and disappointed hope, than excessive subtilty. True refinement consists not in the waste of power, but in the simplicity with which the means are adapted to the end. Do we make the sails which are to render the impetuosity of sweeping winds and sudden tempests subservient to the wants of man, of lace and fine linen? Do we wantonly make the path slippery along which we, and the helpless and infirm old men and women must tread every day, that we may shew our strength and dexterity in traversing it without a stumble? Do we plough with race horses, or give the edge of a razor to the axe which is to clear away the forest?

It may be worth while to give an outline of the manner in which this system, full of unseen connections and nice dependencies, was created. ' It was enacted, by Magna Charta,[r]

---

[p] For the history of this part of the subject, I refer to the admirable preface to GILBERT on *Uses and Trusts*, by LORD ST. LEONARDS, a work hardly more valuable to the technical lawyer than to the philosophical historian.

[q] Perrin *v.* Blake ; ' Will it be said that where the testator's intent is manifest, the law will supply the means of carrying it into execution ?' The Roman Law said ' Yes.' Blackstone answers, ' This would be turning every devise into an executor's trust.'—COKE, *Litt.,* 376. 6, n. 1, BUTLER Ed.

[r] REEVES, vol. i. 293 ; *Magna Charta,* 32, ' Liceat unicuique libero

that no freeman should give or sell any more of his land, but so that the lord of the fee might have the service due to him.' The statute ' de donis conditionalibus' proves that the jealousy of the great aristocracy was awakened, and that they began already to dread that union of the crown and people which would be fatal to their influence. They succeeded in enacting this statute, which destroyed the right of alienation, that before had only been suspended till the birth of issue—on the birth of issue, *i.e.* on the fulfilment of a condition, which once fulfilled was gone for ever, the holder of a fief in fee simple conditional limited to him and his descendants, had the same power over it as if it had been a fee simple. The statute took away this power from the holder of such an estate, leaving him still an estate of inheritance.[b] This was followed by the 18 Ed. I., commonly called ' Quia emptores,' which provided that the person enfeoffed thenceforth of lands should hold them of the superior lord of the fee in the same manner as he by whom he had been enfeoffed of them. This statute removed, except as to the king's tenants in capite, the general restraint on alienation introduced at the conquest. It enacts that it shall be lawful for every freeman to sell his lands and tenements or part thereof, so nevertheless that the feoffee shall hold the same lands of the same chief lord and by the same services as before. And at the same time artifices were employed to elude the statute ' de donis.' Though the statute ' de donis' took away the power of alienation, it did not suspend the fee, therefore during the life of the alienor the alienation could not be attacked—after his death the heir could only assert his title by a formedon, a tedious, intricate and expensive process; another mode was by warranty; another by the operation

---

homini terras suas seu tenement a sua seu partem inde ad voluntatem suam vendere ita quod feoffatus teneat se de capitali domino.' WRIGHT'S *Tenures*, 162, COKE *Litt.*, iii., 6 ; Butler note 1.

[b] 'The will of the giver, according to the form in the deed of gift manifestly expressed, shall be observed.'—13 Ed. I. *Coke Litt.*, BUTLER, note page 191 *a*. REEVES, *History of the English Law*, vol. ii., c. 10, p. 164.

of fines and recoveries, which, by a proceeding that was fictitious and a compromise that was fictitious (much at the expense of public morality) evaded the grasp of the law; meanwhile feoffments to uses came into fashion, and last wills as declarations of uses were enforced in the Court of Chancery. But this system was destroyed by 27 Hen. VIII., which by transferring the legal possession to the use, made them inseparable. The proof how widely the power of devising had been employed through the medium of uses is, that very soon after the passing of this last statute it became necessary to pass the 32 and 34 Hen. VIII.,[c] which enables all having

---

[c] Preamble to 27 Hen. VIII., c. 10. ‘Whereby the common laws of this realm, lands, tenements, and hereditaments be not devisable by testament, nor ought to be transferred from one to another but by solemn livery and seisin, matter of record, writing sufficient made bona fide without covin or fraud; yet nevertheless divers and sundry imaginations, subtle inventions and practices, have been used, whereby the hereditaments of this realm have been conveyed from one to another by fraudulent feoffments, fines, recoveries, and other assurances, craftily made to secret uses, intents and trusts, and also by wills and testaments sometime made by nude parolx and words, sometime by signs and tokens, and sometime by writing, and for the most part made by such persons as be visited with sickness in their extreme agonies and pains or at such time as they have scantly had any good memory or remembrance, at which times, they being provoked by greedy and covetous persons lying in wait about them, do many times dispose indiscreetly and unadvisedly their lands and inheritances, by reason whereof and by occasion of which, fraudulent feoffments, fines, recoveries, and other like assurances, to uses, confidences and trusts, divers and many heirs have been unjustly at sundry times disinherited, the lords have lost their wards, marriages, reliefs, harriots, escheats, aids pur fair fitz chevalier and pur file marier, and scantly any person can be certainly assured of any lands by them purchased, nor know surely against whom they shall use their actions or executions for their rights titles and duties; also men married have lost their tenances by the curtesy, women their dowers, manifest perjuries by trial of such secret wills and uses, have been committed, the King's Highness hath lost the profits and advantages of the lands of persons attainted, and of the lands craftily put in feoffments to the uses of aliens born, and also the profits of waste for a year and a day of lands of felons attainted, and the lords their escheats thereof, and many other inconveniences have happened and daily do increase among the king's subjects, to their

estates in fee simple, except as joint tenants, to devise the whole of their socage land and two-thirds of that held by knight's service; and the 12 C. II., c. 2, converting all land held by knight's service into socage, completed the downfall of the feudal system, of which the practice of subinfeudation marked the first decline. Uses, however, in spite of the clear intention of the legislature to destroy them, were still preserved under the name of trusts—and as the chancellors maintained the analogy between feuds and trusts, as to the order of descent, entails, duration of estates, the mode of barring them, and the estates into which they may be moulded, the consequence is, that a large proportion of the landed property of the kingdom belongs to some one whom a Court of Common Law would refuse to recognise as the owner, being charged in the name of the legal tenant with a trust for some other person. The beneficial and legal ownership are now as distinct as they were when the statute of Henry VIII. was passed expressly to[d] consolidate them.[e] The object of the legislature was to prevent the transfers ' craftily made to secret uses, intents, and trusts,' and to take care that ' there should be no transfer but by public act or matter of record'; and yet, so completely and

---

great trouble and inquietness, and to the utter subversion of the ancient common laws of this realm,' etc.

Who would imagine, after this, that fines and recoveries were ever heard of again in our legal history ; there however they remained, until Dec. 31, 1833.

BARRINGTON on Statutes, ed. 1st, p. 133. ' Can the sergeants who mutter such a jargon, or the judges who preside, explain (to the suitor) what is going on ? . . . it is high time there should be an end of such unintelligible trumpery.' 'One objection,' says the learned judge, 'to the proceeding is, that it is in direct opposition to the express words of a subsisting law.' Sir Robert Berkeley might have quoted this glaring defiance of the law to illustrate his doctrine, laid down to a grand jury in Yorkshire, 'That judges were above an Act of Parliament.'— RUSHWORTH, vol. i. 364.

[d] 1 Collect. Jurid, 235, LORD MANSFIELD. Coke Litt., 191 a, ed. BUTLER, note. Juridical Tracts, by A. HAYWARD, Q. C., on the Law of Real Property. Preamble to statute Hen. VIII.

[e] 27 Hen. VIII. c. 16, declares that no land shall pass by bargain and sale unless indented and enrolled.

utterly technical was the view taken by our judges, that the statute might as well never have been passed, and the invention of Sergeant Moore added another instance to the long catalogue of the triumphs of form over substance in the curious history of our judicial legislation. To prevent all possibility of evading the statute of uses, an act was passed shortly afterwards, requiring bargains and sale of freehold interests to be enrolled. But this statute did not apply to terms of years—now the necessity of entry for obtaining possession was destroyed by the statute of uses, which transferred possession to the use—so that it was only necessary, in order to baffle the statute, first to make a bargain and sale to the use of a man for a year, which gave him the possession without livery of seisin on actual entry, and then he, so being in possession, was capable of having his estate enlarged by a release, to a fee; and by this childish trifling the Act of Parliament was set aside. ‘ *Fraus enim legi fit* ubi quid, *quod fieri noluit,* fieri autem non vetuit id fit ’[f]—however our judges, as usual, adhered to the letter and violated the spirit of the law—the bargain and sale was allowed to operate, the bargainee was in possession by the statute. Three words were added to a statute, and Lord Coke wrote panegyrics on the transcendant wisdom of the English law and its interpreters. A more striking example is hardly to be found of the profound remark, ‘ Credunt homines rationem suam verbis imperare sed fit etiam ut verba vim suam super intellectum retorqueant et reflectant.’[g]

LXI.

IN omnibus quidem maxime tamen in jure æquitas spectanda sit.—PAULUS.

Equity is to be kept in view in all things, but especially in the administration of the law.

This rule was laid down to inform the conscience and to guide the decisions of the judge, by the Roman jurist, as to

---

[f] *Dig.* i. 4. 30. ULPIAN.　　　[g] *Novum Organum,* 59.

that paramount and universal principle, which was indeed, as it was emphatically called, ' viva vox juris civilis.' Without it law is what the greatest of our poets says hypocrisy makes religion, ' a rhapsody of words;' and it may be reckoned among the misfortunes peculiar to our country, that the decisions of so many of our equity judges, down to comparatively modern times, from a date very soon after that when the various and grotesque absurdities of the common law established their authority, betray an utter ignorance of this salutary maxim, and rival in miserable narrowness, and perverse indifference to its precepts, those of their brethren in Westminster Hall. Indeed, the evil thus inflicted on society made, for a time, the remedy worse than the disease. If all the attornies in England had been ordered to take counsel together to devise a system which should make litigation as ruinous and incessant as was compatible with the existence of property, their combined efforts could have produced no system more perfectly and effectually corresponding to such a description than the Court of Chancery in the days of Lord Eldon. If the souls of Jeffreys, Scroggs, and Page had been blended together to devise a system which, without actual mutilation or certain death, should inflict the utmost possible amount of agony on the suitor, the result of such an effort could have produced no system better calculated to make the soul sick in its contemplation, and in the contemplation of its effects, as exemplified in famine, despair, and madness, than the system of the Court of Chancery as it was under the administration of Lord Eldon. And if the souls of Cervantes, Rabelais, and Swift, had been united to digest human folly into one system of complete absurdity, it may be doubted whether such a creation would surpass in absurdity the procedure of the Courts of Equity and the transactions in the Masters' Office[a]—the commission of

---

[a] ' If a man commences a suit in equity, the first process is by a proceeding introduced in the time of Richard II.' (A.D. 1822 ! Ed.).— COMYN's *Dig.*, vol. ii. p. 393, tit. *Chancery.*

' If the defendant does not appear, the plaintiff shall have attachment with proclamation.'—*Ib.* 408.

rebellion, the law of fines and recoveries, the exemption of landed estates from simple contract debts, and the interpretation of wills—during the time that every attempt at legal improvement was successfully resisted, and the Court of Chancery year after year consigned the fate of widows and orphans to the cavils,[b] doubts, and scruples of Lord Eldon;[c] for, by a delay which Shakespeare never imagined, and which would have added terror to the scenes described by Dante, by encouraging every attempt at extortion from the miserable suitors (of which some notion may be formed from the report of the Chancery Commissioners as to the proceedings before Masters in Chancery), he actually made the very word 'equity,'[d] in every

---

' If the defendant does not appear upon the proclamation, the plaintiff shall have—a commission of rebellion!'—*Ib.* 409.

' If the defendant be not taken on the commission, a serjeant-at-arms shall be sent for him.'—*Ib.* 410.

This was the simple, cheap, and expeditious means of compelling a suitor to appear in the Court of Chancery, endured by this practical nation till about twenty years ago. Of course, Lord Eldon never suggested its alteration.

[b] It was not for such conduct that Cicero praised his friend Sulpicius (*Philipp.* 9) : ' Admirabilem Servii Sulpicii in legibus æquitate interpretandis scientiam fuisse ait, cum non magis juris quam justitiæ consultus esset, et jus civile æquitatem referret.'

[c] It is curious that a judge who, when cavilling and delay were fatal to the interests of others, split hairs and stumbled at straws, and was always talking of his conscience, should have been so unscrupulous a politician as, when George III. was actually under personal restraint, to put the great seal to acts which could not be legal without the full and complete acquiescence of the sovereign, and declare in his place in Parliament that there was no necessary suspension of the royal functions. If an attorney had made a client in the mental state of George III. when Lord Eldon declared his assent to acts of Parliament, sign a deed or will, he would have been struck off the rolls by an honest judge.

' It is not my practice, nor is it in my disposition, to make charges or urge accusations upon light grounds. In performing what I conceive to be my duty to my country, I am bound to arraign the noble lord for an offence little short of high treason.'—LORD GREY, *Parliamentary Debates*, vol. xviii. p. 1052, Jan., 1811.

[d] A very striking proof of the terror and dismay with which the word ' equity' freezes the blood of English gentlemen was exhibited last year in the House of Commons. A measure, long looked for and loudly

other country a word of grace and healing, a word in which almost every idea of torture, vexation and absurdity, was abridged to the English nation. A singular proof, certainly, of the practical talent, the imagined possession of which consoles us for so many deficiencies.

There are many passages in the *Digest* in which ' æquitas' is opposed to 'jus.' So Ulpian (*Dig.* xv. 1. 32) says, ' Licet hoc jure contingat' (i. e., that there should be no right of action) ' tamen æquitas dictat judicium in eos dari, qui occasione juris liberantur;' and, in the chapter ' De aquâ et aquæ pluviæ arcendæ' (*Dig.* xxxix. 3. 2, § 5), Paulus, speaking of a case in which, owing to the destruction of a mound in a man's field, the water has run down upon a lower field to the injury of his neighbour, says, ' Quamquam tamen deficiat pluviæ arcendæ actio, attamen opinor utilem actionem mihi competere contra vicinum,' if I choose to repair the mound in his field, ' qui factus mihi quidem prodesse potest ipsi vero nihil nociturus est;' and adds, ' hæc æquitas suggerit et si jure deficiamur;' and ' Celsus adolescens scribit eum qui moram fecit insolvendo Sticho quem promiserat posse emendare eam moram' (might purge his delay), for it was a question of equity, ' esse enim hanc quæstionem de bono et æquo—IN QUO GENERE PLERUMQUE SUB AUCTORITATE JURIS SCIENTIÆ PERNICIOSE ERRATUR.' So it is distinguished from the ' *scriptum jus*' in an excellent law (*Dig.* xxxv. 1. 16): ' In his quæ extra testamentum incurrerent possunt res *ex æquo et bono* interpretationem capere, ea vero quæ ex ipso testamento orirentur necesse est secundum *scripti juris* rationem expediri.' So ' Qui operas suas ut cum bestiis pugnaret, locavit, quive rei capitalis damnatus neque restitutus est ex senatusconsulto Orphiliano ad matris hæreditatem non admittebatur—sed humanâ interpretatione placuit eum admitti' (*Dig.* xxxviii. 17. 1. § 6).

So, even if the words of a law are general, it may be taken in

___

called for, was condemned at once and irrevocably, because the words ' Court of Equity' were so used as to lead to the notion that, if the measure was carried, the jurisdiction of those courts would be enlarged.

a restricted sense (*Dig.* xxxvii. 14. 6, §2); 'Quamvis nulla persona lege excipiatur tamen intelligendum est de his legem sentire qui liberos tollere possunt.'[e] So a law is modified (*Dig.* ii. 4. 11): 'Licet edicti verba non patiantur.' So Papinian (*De Testibus*) says, 'Quod legibus omissum est non omittendum religione judicantis.' So the law (*Dig.* xlv. 1. 36), shews the extent to which the Roman lawyers carried the principle of equity. If a man was induced to make one kind of stipulation when he thought he had made another, he might defend himself by the 'exceptio doli'—this if he had been circumvented by his antagonist. But even if he had not been circumvented, 'si nullus dolus intercessit stipulantis,' he might defend himself in the same way; for to attempt to take advantage of such a mistake was fraudulent: ' Hoc ipse dolo facit quod petit.'

As an instance of indulgent construction, the law (*Dig.* l. 16. 135) may be cited, the question whether, if a woman had brought forth ' portentosum vel monstrosum vel debilem vel non humanæ figuræ alterius magis animalis quam hominis partum,' the parents were entitled to the privileges conferred on parents by the Roman law. Ulpian says they were: ' Nec enim est quod eis imputetur quæ qualiter potuerunt statutis obtemperaverunt, neque id quod fataliter accessit matri damnum injungere debet.' But the Roman jurist's notion of equity was

---

e 'Licet autem prætor districte edicat sententiam se arbitrum dicere coacturum, attamen interdum rationem ejus habere debet et excusationem accipere causâ cognitâ.'—*Dig.* iv. 8. 15 ; AULUS GELLIUS, xx. c. 1. On the other hand, see the law 'Prospexit,' *Dig.* xlvi. 9. 12, § 1 : ' Quod quidem perquam durum est sed ita lex scripta est.' This severe law was modified, 1. adulterii Cod. de Adult.'—QUINTILIAN, lib. vii. c. 6.

' Æquitatem ante oculos habere debet judex qui huic actioni (i. e., arbitrariæ) addictus est.' *Dig.* xiii. 5. 4, § 1. · Ubicunque judicem æquitas moverit æque oportere fieri interrogationem, dubium non est. *Dig.* ix. 1. 21. *Dig. de in Integrum Restitutione*, iv. 2. 23 : 'Si justo metu perterritus . . . id quod habere licebat compulsus vendidit res suæ æquitati per præsidem provinciæ restituitur.' *Ib.* 2, 3. *Dig.* xvi. 1, 2 : 'Æquum autem visum est ita mulieri succurri,' κ. τ. λ. *Dig.* xxxix. 1. 5 : 'Æquissimum est omnes filios matri præferri.' κ. τ. λ. *Dig.* xliii. 16. 1 : ' Hoc interdictum proponitur ei qui vi dejectus et enim fuit æquissimum vi dejecto subvenire.'

to carry into effect the true meaning and spirit of the law, and not to allow a quibble or 'cavillatio' (such as the decision of our judges on the Statute of Uses) to overrule its plain intention and policy.[f] 'Scire leges,' he said, 'non est verba legis tenere sed vim ac potestatem;' therefore the judge's notion of equity was not allowed to prevail over the words and spirit of a law: 'Perquam durum est sed ita lex scripta est;'[g] and again, Modestinus (*Dig.* xlix. 1. 19), 'si expressim sententia contra rigorem juris data fuerit valere non debet, et ideo et sine appellatione causa denuo induci potest, non jure profertur sententia si specialiter contra leges vel senatusconsultum vel constitutionem fuerit prolata.' κ. τ. λ.

The construction of wills, of course, affords the greatest scope for the display of that luminous wisdom which equity inculcates. The great object of the Roman jurist was to ascertain the meaning of the testator, and to carry it into effect. Questions also arose, independently of the construction of wills, as to their effect, of which the following example may be cited, to illustrate the meaning of the word equity in the language of Roman jurisprudence. The birth of a posthumous child or grandchild, who was unnoticed in a will, revoked it.[g] A posthumous grandchild, unnoticed in the will, died during the life of the testator: the testator died, leaving his will unaltered. Strictly speaking, 'juris scrupulositate et nimia subtilitate,' the will was cancelled; but it was decided (by the writers, to be

---

[f] De constit Pec., *Dig.* xiii. 5. 1 : 'Hoc edicto prætor favet naturali æquitati qui constituta ex consensu facta custodit—quoniam grave est fidem fallere.' *Dig.* iv. 4. 1 : Hoc edictum prætor naturalem æquitatem secutus proposuit quo tutelam minorum suscepit.' *Dig.* iii. 3. 33 : 'Æquum prætori visum est eum qui alicujus nomine procurator experitur eundem etiam defensionem susciperet.' So, if the slave ordered to be free by the will of his master, after the death of his master, and before the heir had accepted the inheritance, stole or injured anything belonging to it, an action 'dupli' was given him against the letter of the civil law, according to which a master could not have an action against his slave. *Dig.* xlvi. 4. 1 : 'Hoc autem actio naturalem potius habet in se quam civilem æquitatem.' 'Sed naturâ æquum est non esse impunitum eum qui hâc spe audacior factus est.'

[g] Vide the famous law, 'Gallus,' *Dig.* ii. 28. 2, § 29.

sure, who formed Lord Mansfield, and not Lord Eldon) that, supposing it in all other respects to be regular, and that the child died during the life, and not after the death of the testator, that the designated heir, 'scriptus hæres,' was equitably entitled to the estate, and should be put in possession of it, ' bonorum possessionem secundum tabulas accipere hæres scriptus potest, remque obtinebit.' ' Idcirco legatarii et fidei commissarii habebunt ea quæ sibi relicta sunt, securi' (*Dig.* xxviii. 3. 12); see *Lex Paula*, ' placuit humanius interpretari:' and Paulus gives us as a reason for his decision, that the one proposed seemed to him altogether inconsistent with every particle of the testator's will: ' Mihi ab omni voluntate recessum videbatur.' So the prætor enlarged the narrow rule of inheritance laid down in the Twelve Tables. So, where possession was given ' contra tabulas,' it was said that natural equity obliged the son to pay the legacies and execute the trusts of the will in favour of certain persons: ' Hoc est liberis et parentibus et uxori numique dotis nomine legatum.'

In short, to borrow the words of Faber, ' Æquitas per totum jus civile omnesque ejus partes fusa est.[g]

' Les conventions,' says the French code, ' obligent non seulement à ce qui est exprimé, mais encore à toutes les suites que l'equité, l'usage, ou la loi donnent à l'obligation d'après sa nature," 1158.

The true reason why Equity is the soul and spirit of all law is, the impossibility for any human foresight to anticipate or provide for every circumstance to which the endless combinations and infinite variety of human affairs may give occasion. Equity is the return to natural reason, where positive law is silent, ambiguous, or contradictory. If the subject were not too sad, and, for an Englishman, too humiliating, it might make the reader smile to observe the absurdities, follies, and inconsistencies which a disregard of this plain and simple principle has entailed upon our legislation. The most ex-

---

[g] DOMAT., tit. 1, § 2, p. 86: ' Ce n'est donc pas assez,' etc. *Dig. de reb. dub.* 9. 1 ; *de lib. et Port.* 13.

pensive machinery has been employed, with the least result; words have been multiplied, and in proportion to their number has been the ease with which the law, that it was their object to enforce, has been evaded; at the same time, as if to set an example of every variety of error, our judges, in many instances, of which Taltarum's case and the decision on the statute of uses are signal instances, while they rendered municipal laws useless by a servile adherence to the letter, repealed laws, founded on motives of great national policy, by the most daring hostility to their object.

Thus any one who seeks instances, either of the evils which arise from superstitious timidity, or of the errors which arise from presumptuous indifference, may find both in the reports which transmit the decisions of our judges as precedents to future ages. Our judges have been alternately slaves and rebels to the law. Their disobedience to it has often been servile, and their submission to it rebellious; and it is hard to say which error has inflicted the greater amount of evil on society. Ignorance of this maxim, which Portalis has so admirably stated—'Il faut une jurisprudence parcequ'il est impossible de régler tous les objets civils par les lois'—has led to that prolixity which multiplies opportunities for captious objections. The attempt to enumerate everything, to guard against every doubt, as in the case of the Statute of Uses— where the omission of bargain and sale for years overthrew the statute—has furnished a strong argument for those who wished to take advantage of the case not enumerated, and of the doubt not provided for.[a] An appeal to the spirit and purpose of the legislator was rejected, where he had affected such minute caution; and the judges, carrying with them to the bench the habits they have formed at the bar, had brought our law to its actual condition, in spite of Ulpian's admonition, which ought to be read over to every member of the House of Commons (in the language most agreeable to him) when he takes

---

[a] I include the subsequent statute for the enrolment of bargain and sale in the Statute of Uses, as in ' pari materiâ.'

his seat: ' *Non possunt omnes articuli singillatim aut legibus aut senatusconsultis comprehendi* sed cum in aliquâ causâ sententia eorum manifesta est, is qui juris dictioni præest ad similia procedere, et ita jus dicere debet.'[b] Otherwise, a failure in a single instance defeats the whole; and in the words of a really great and patriotic statesman, on a great occasion, in which his advice, unhappily for his country, was disregarded: ' If any one channel of escape remains unclosed, the whole dyke, with all its difficulty, and cost, and labour, becomes a useless burden to the earth.'[c] ' Aliud est legem aut probabili aut etiam urgente causâ tollere—aliud declarare factum ab initio mente legis non fuisse comprehensum.'[d] To quote the words of D'Aguesseau: ' Le premier objet du legislateur, dépositaire de son esprit, compagne inséparable de la loi, l'equité ne peut jamais être contraire à la loi même. Tout ce qui blesse cette equité veritable source de toutes les lois ne résiste pas moins à la justice, le législateur l'auroit condamné s'il l'avait pu prévoir.'[e] Equity means, as Grotius says elsewhere, ' Partem illam justitiæ quæ legis sonum generalem ex mente auctoris adductius interpretatur.'[f]

To enter upon any examination of the notion of Equity, as it is applied in the Court of Chancery, would, of course, be quite beyond the purpose of this undertaking. Some references, however, to the inconsistent language of the judges may be not altogether inappropriate. In Davis *v.* the Duke of Marlborough,[g] Lord Eldon said, ' The question whether the duke can alien Blenheim House must be the same at Law and in Equity. . . . The construction of the acts must be the same in Courts of Law and of Equity; but there may be a peculiar principle, which this court will apply to the acts, though it

---

[b] *Dig.* i. 3.

[c] LORD GRENVILLE, East Indian Affairs, *Parliamentary Debates,* vol. xxv. p. 742.

[d] GROTIUS, *De Jure Belli et Pacis,* lib. ii. c. 2, § 27.

[e] D'AGUESSEAU, vol. i. p. 139.

[f] GROTIUS, *De Jure Belli et Pacis,* iii. 20. 47.

[g] 2 SWANSTON, 132.

T

agrees in the construction with a Court of Law.' 'It has been argued, that the plaintiff could not support this bill if he had a legal defence. I cannot accede to that doctrine. It has always been held here, that time given to the principal releases the surety. The *recent* adoption of that doctrine by Courts of Law will not exclude the concurrent jurisdiction of this court.'[b]

'If the plaintiff,' says Chief Baron Eyre, 'is non-suited at law for want of evidence, which the defendant has in his power, and withholds from him, I take it to be clear that he may come to a Court of Equity, and he shall not only have discovery but relief, and the defendant shall be made to pay the costs of the non-suit.'[c] In an old case, reported 1st *Modern Reports*, p. 307, VAUGHAN, C. J., a most excellent magistrate said: 'I wonder to hear of citing of precedents in matters of equity; for if there be equity in a case, that equity is a universal truth, and there can be no precedent in it. So that in any precedent that can be produced, if it be the same with this case, the reason and equity is the same in itself; and if it be not, it is not to be cited, as not to the purpose.'[d]

In the case of Mutter v. Chauvel, Lord Eldon said: 'It was not for him to settle the law which he was bound to follow.'[e] 'Whoever,' says Lord Mansfield, 'has attended the Court of Chancery, knows that if an injunction, in the nature of an injunction, to stay waste, is granted upon motion, or continued after answer, it is in vain to go to hearing. For such an injunction never is granted upon motion, unless the legal property of the plaintiff be made out, nor continued after answer, unless it remains clear, allowing all the defendant has said.'[f] In Stockdale v. Onwhyn, Abbott, C. J., says: 'As to cases in

---

[b] Hawkshaw *v.* Perkins, 2 SWANSTON, 347.

[c] Wilmot *v.* Lennard, 3 SWANSTON, 682.

[d] Fry *v.* Porter, 1 *Mod. Reports*. This seems to have served Lord Keeper Bridgman a good deal. 'Certainly, precedents are very necessary to us,' etc.

[e] Mutter *v.* Chauvel, 1 MERIVALE, 494.

[f] Millar *v.* Taylor, 4 BURROW, 2399. Hogg *v.* Kirby, 8 VESEY, 224.

Equity, it is admitted they are no authority for us. One person of great authority may think the publication of such a work will be most effectually restrained by granting an injunction; another may think the same object may be best effected by holding there can be no property in the work. Each would act on the rules of common law.'[g] Bayley, J., cites the Chancellor's opinions, and founds his own upon it. Lord Kenyon says, in Farr v. Newman[h]: ' I am *not* prepared to exclude from our consideration the decisions in Courts of Equity. When the Law is ineffectual, Equity steps in to give redress, following, however, the rules of Law.'[i] On the other hand, he says elsewhere: ' A Court of Equity knows its own province; it will examine into cases of this kind. But if this court,' etc.[k] ' The liabilities of sureties are governed by principles which have been long settled in Equity, and are now adopted in Courts of Law. I say now, because the Court of Common Pleas formerly held a different doctrine.' In the case of Tabor v. Tabor, reported by Mr. Swanston, vol. iii. p. 637, Lord Nottingham says: ' Though by the Law of Chancery, an equity of redemption does still subsist after forfeiture, the question is, in what manner it shall subsist, and upon what terms? And it were most unreasonable in the Chancellor to give the mortgagor an election, to pay the heir or executor; for though there be no great inconvenience in such an election, at the Common Law seeing it is to be executed and determined at a precise and certain day, yet it were intolerable to allow the mortgagor such an election in Equity, where there is no certain time of redemption fixed; and it were yet worse to leave such a power of election in the court itself, for that were to make every redemption of a mortgage ' casus pro amico,' and is too great a latitude to trust a Chancellor with.' In another case, where the opinion of a Court of

---

[g] 5 B. and C., 876.

[h] *T. Reports*, 650.

[i] Especially in cases of mortgagee *v.* mortgagor.

[k] See the case of The Mayor of Southampton *v.* Graves, 8 *Terin Reports*, 592.

Law as to a 'modus' had been asked for, Lord Eldon said:
'To ask the Court of King's Bench a question of law which
this court could answer in the first instance, is not the best
way of disposing of a suit in Equity.'[m]   The same judge says,
when an application was made for an injunction to prevent
piracy: 'A Court of Equity takes upon itself to determine, as
well as it can, the right in this period, with a conviction, that
if, then, the cause was hearing, they would act upon the same
rule.   The court takes upon itself that which may involve it
in a mistake to determine the legal question.'[n]   Nor is the
perplexity less with regard to the value of equitable authorities in Courts of Common Law—in Farr v. Newman,[o] in
Browning v. Wright,[p] in Millar v. Taylor,[q] in Doe v.
Waterton,[r] in Bodenham v. Purchas,[s] in Brooke v. En-
derby,[t] in Mason v. Hill,[u] the decisions of Courts of
Equity were held binding authorities in law; and it has
been said, that it is 'absurd and pernicious to the public,
that different rules should prevail in different courts on the
same subject.'[v]   Lord Eldon went even so far as to recommend Courts of Law, to enquire of Courts of Equity, not
about points merely equitable, but for 'legal judgments proceeding upon legal grounds, such as the Courts of Equity have
been for many years in the habit of pronouncing as the foun-

---

[m] Goodenough v. Powell, 2 RUSSELL, 229.

[n] Hogg v. Kirby, 8 VESEY, *Reports*.

[o] 4 *Term Reports*, 641.

[p] 2 Bos. and PULLEN, 26.

[q] 4 BURROW, 2350. 'I think this case is decided by Clayton's case,
which was very fully argued. All the decisions were there before the
Master of the Rolls, and he pronounced judgment against Clayton.'—
ABBOTT, C. J.

[r] 3 BARN. and ALD., 149.

[s] 2 B. and ALD., 39.

[t] 2 BROD. and BING.

[u] 3 B. and ADOLP.

[v] Mason v. Hill, 3 B. and AD., 312. The only decision upon a judgment like that in the present case is the judgment of the Vice-Chancellor in Wright v. Howard, 1 SIM. and STU., 190.

dation of their decrees.'[w]   On the other hand, we are told that
'no authorities in a Court of Equity are of the least avail in a
Court of Law, because the two courts go upon different principles'[x]; and that 'cases which have been decided by the Lord
Chancellor on principles of general equity, must not give the
rules for decisions in Courts of Law.'[y]   Lord Mansfield has
been severely censured 'for endeavouring to administer equity
in a Court of Law'[z]; we are told that the man 'will deserve ill
of his country who shall endeavour to confound the rules by
which Courts of Law and Equity are severally guided'[a]; and
that the interference of the Chancellors was occasioned by the
'adherence of our legal judges to technical rules, subversive of
substantial justice,' whence, it would seem to follow, that it is
desirable that there should be two sets of courts in the same
country acting upon opposite rules, one set of rules being subversive of substantial justice.   Equity is no longer to be considered as intended to correct the harsh operation of the law;
it is a jurisdiction most irregularly formed, incapable of any
precise definition, abused often to purposes of the most vexatious litigation, and requiring the efforts of a luminous and
powerful intellect, fortified by long and deep study of the
Roman law, raised above vulgar prejudices by extensive observation, conversant with the past, and, therefore, anticipating
the future, to regenerate our Courts of Equity, and to make
them a blessing to the people, for whose welfare they were
designed, but to whose misery and ruin, in too many instances,
they have unquestionably contributed.

---

[w] Smith *v.* Doe d. Jersey, 2 BRODERIP and BING., 599.

[x] BULLER, J.; Farr *v.* Newman.

[y] 3 Bos. and PULLEN, 492; Houghton *v.* Mathews.

[z] SUGDEN, *Letters*, p. 5.

[a] *Ib.*, p. 4, ib. 'If one is bound to J. S., to the use of W. N., and then
J.S. releases the debt, W.N. shall have equitable remedy in Chancery.'
—C. PURTON COOPER'S *Cases in Chancery*, p. 515.

LXII.

ID quod nostrum est sine facto nostro ad alium transferri non potest.[a]

What is ours cannot, without an act of ours, be transferred to another.

Neither the will of the owner without his act, nor his act without his will, can transfer the possession of his property. It does not literally belong to the discussion of this law, to consider what the act should be by which the transfer of property is complete. Pomponius says: ' Sine facto nostro non potest ad alium transferri quod nostrum est.' This rule is not intended merely for the protection of the owner, by the Roman jurists, for they laid it down, that the owner could not, whatever his wishes might be, transfer his property to another but by delivery. This, says Ulpian, is the difference between property and possession—property remains in the owner, even against his will—but when a man is unwilling to possess, possession withdraws. ' Differentia enim inter dominium et possessionem hæc est—quod dominium nihilominus ejus manet qui dominus esse non vult, possessio autem recedit ut quisque constituit nolle possidere.' (*Dig.* xli. 2. 17, § 2.)

The word used is ' transferri.' Another may acquire what is ours ' jure gentium' or ' jure civili' without any act of ours; ' jure gentium,' for instance, by occupation or alluvion—' jure civili' by ususcapio, by the operation of law, or the sentence of a court of justice, or the authority of the magistrate. A man is held to deliver himself, when another delivers by his command, either express or implied; ' Nihil enim tam conveniens est naturali æquitati quam voluntatem domini volentis rem suam in alium transferre ratam haberi' (*Dig.* xli. 1. 9, § 3); and a man is held to receive himself when another receives by his command, ' Nihil interest utrum mihi an et cuilibet jusserim custodia tradatur.' (*Dig.* xli. 2. 51.) So we have the rule

---

[a] ' Cessions de biens.'—*Maximes du Droit Français,* chap. vi. art. 1, p. 511.

'Quod jussu alterius solvitur pro eo est quasi ipsi solutum esset.'
So if the article which has been placed in the possession for
one purpose, is allowed to remain in it for another, the change
of destination may be tantamount to a delivery.—As, if I buy
a thing that has been lent to me or deposited with me, no
farther delivery is requisite. 'Si quis rem apud se depositam
vel sibi commodatam emerit vel pignori sibi datam pro traditâ
erit accipienda si post emptionem apud enim remansit.' (*Dig.* vi.
2. 9, § 1.) 'Interdum etiam sine traditione nuda voluntas
domini sufficit ad rem transferendam.' (*Dig.* xli. 1. 9, § 5). To
the same effect is the very singular case (put in the *Dig.* vi. 1.
77) of a woman living on an estate, and giving it away in a
letter.—She became the tenant of this estate from the donee—
it was held that her possession was the possession of the donee,
and that delivery was not requisite. 'Proponebatur quod
etiam in eo agro qui donabatur fuisset cum epistola emitteretur,
quæ res sufficiebat ad traditam possessionem licet conductio
non intervenisset.' (*Dig.* vi. 1. 77.) Nor was it necessary
that bodily possession of the thing delivered should be taken;
if the thing sold is in my sight, and I bid the seller deliver it
to my agent, it is enough. 'Si jusserim procuratori venditorem rem tradere cum ea in præsentiâ sit, videri mihi traditam
Priscus ait idemque esse si nummos debitorem jusserim alii
dare—non est enim corpore et actu necesse apprehendere possessionem sed etiam oculis et affectu—et argumento esse eas
res quæ propter magnitudinem ponderis moveri non possunt ut
columnas, nam pro traditis eas haberi si in re præsenti consen-
serint et vina tradita videri cum claves cellæ vindicæ emptori
traditæ fuerint.' So if the seller of goods in a barn gives the
keys of the barn to the purchaser, it is a delivery of the goods:
'Item si quis merces in horreo repositas vendiderit simul atque
claves horrei tradiderit emptori transfert proprietatem mercium
ad emptorem.' (*Dig.* xli. 1. 9, § 6.) But the keys must be
delivered near the barn: 'Ita . . . si claves apud horrea traditæ sint' (*Dig.* xviii. 1. 74). There must be the intention to transfer the property, imaginary contracts were not
binding: 'Cum fides facti simulatur non intercedente veritate.'

(*Dig.* xliv. 7. 54.)   Not only was a delivery invalid where
'vis' or 'metus,' but where error could be proved: 'Nemo
enim errans rem suam amittit.' (*Dig.* xli. 1. 35.)   He who errs
has no will: 'Nulla voluntas errantis est' (*Dig.* xxxix. 3. 19);
hence it follows that a madman and a minor, without the consent of his guardian, can transfer no property, for they have
no will.   Neither could property be transferred by mere
delivery, unless that delivery had been preceded by a sufficient
cause: 'Numquam nuda traditio transfert dominium—sed ita
si venditio aut aliqua justa causa præcesserit' (*Dig.* xli. 1. 31).
But if the persons concerned agreed as to the thing to be
delivered, though they differed as to the causes of its delivery
one delivering land as given by will, the other receiving it as
the effect of a stipulation, the delivery was not therefore invalid: 'Cum in corpus quidem quod traditur consentiamus, in
causis vero dissentiamus, non animadverto cur inefficax sit
traditio.'   The general rule, however, was; that delivery was
always construed according to the intention of the parties:
'In traditionibus rerum quodcunque pactum est, id valere
manifestissimum est' (*Dig.* ii. 14, 48).   The property of the
thing delivered was transferred as it was possessed by the
deliverer; if an estate liable to servitudes, with its servitudes;
if free, as it was: 'Quoties dominium transfertur ad eum qui
accipit tale transfertur quale fuit apud eum qui tradit; si servus fuit fundus cum servitutibus transit, si liber uti fuit; et si
forte servitutes debebantur fundo qui traditus est cum jure
servitutum debitarum transfertur' (*Dig.* xli. 1. 20).   This rule,
Pomponius says, in the absence of any express stipulation,
pervades every part of the civil law.   'Alienatio cum fit cum
suâ causâ dominium ad alium transferimus quæ esset futura
si apud nos res ea mansisset, idque toto civili jure ita se
habet — præterquam si aliquid nominatim sit constitutum.'
(*Dig.* xviii. 1. 67.)

Therefore what did not exist could not, be taken away.   This
rule as to legacies is laid down with great elegance, *Dig. de
anni leg.* xxxiii. 1. 4: . 'Si in singulos annos alicui legatum
sit, Sabinus cujus sententia vera est, plura legata esse ait et

primi anni purum sequentium conditionale—videri enim hanc inesse conditionem si vivat ideo mortuo eo ad hæredem legatum non transire.' The rule that in stipulations the time of the contract is to be considered, is to be taken with reference to the principal contract, and not with reference to its accessory. For if the accessory precedes the principal contract, as in the case of a surety, the time to be considered is the time when the principal obligation and not when the obligation of the surety, was contracted. (*Dig. de fidejuss.*, xlvi. 1. 50; *Dig. de judiciis*, v. 1. 35): 'Non quemadmodum fidejussoris obligatio in pendenti potest esse . . . ita judicium in pendenti potest . . . nam neminem puto dubitaturum quin fidejussor ante obligationem rei accipi possit.' So if the 'filiusfamilias' before he was emancipated, took a surety for the money lent to Titius—and after he was emancipated lent the money—the surety was liable to him and not to his father, as the time of lending the money was the time to be considered in adjusting the obligation (*Dig.* xlv. 1. 132, § 1).

Another effect of this distinction applies to acts fraudulent towards creditors. A stipulation to pay a certain sum every year fraudulent against creditors might be cancelled, because the stipulation was entire and one. (*Dig.* xlii. 8. 10, § 15): 'Per hanc actionem et ususfructus et hujusmodi stipulatio. In annos singulos dena dare spondes, exigi potest—quæ in fraudum creditorum.' But a legacy of a certain sum, to be paid annually, was considered as absolute for the first year, and conditional for the rest of the time. ' Stipulatio ejusmodi in annos singulos una est et incerta et perpetua—non quemadmodum simile legatum morte legatarii finitur(*Dig.* xlv. 1. 16, § 1, *de verborum oblig.*). So the 'mortis causâ donatio' was distinguished from the legacy and placed on the same ground with the 'stipulatio,' for a reason which illustrates this topic. ' Qui mortis causâ in annos singulos pecuniam stipulatus est, non est similis ei cui in annos singulos legatum est, nam licet multa cessent legata stipulatio tamen una est—*et conditio ejus cui expromissum relinquit*' (*Dig.* xxxix. 6. 35, § 7). So the promise of a certain sum ' si Titius consul factus erit,' if he dies before the event, leaves his heir under the obligation (*Dig.* xlv. 1. 57).

The reason of the difference between the effect produced by the death of the legatee before the happening of the condition and the death of the creditor, of the destruction of the right in the former case and its continuance in the latter, was, that in the case of the legatee, the motive was personal, arising from the regard of the testator for the legatee; whereas, in the case of the creditor, the motive was some benefit actually received or expected by the party binding himself. So the conditional creditor might claim to be sent into possession of the goods of the deceased, without an heir, or of an undefended debtor, on account of the lien on the estate, though the condition had not happened. ' In possessionem mitti solet creditor, etsi sub conditione ei pecunia promissa sit ' (*Dig.* xlii. 4. 6).[a]

If, as Savigny remarks,[b] it were possible to make property and possession legally inseparable, and to consider the possessor alone as the proprietor, the theory of possession would be very simple. It happens, however, that such a state of things is not compatible with the artificial habits and exigencies of social life. The separation of possession and property is an infallible consequence of advancing refinement.[c] Possession, the external sign of property, ceases to be an infallible guide to the real owner; and yet as there are many cases in which it indicates the real owner, it cannot be stripped of all the ad-

---

[a] See *Dig.* 1. 16. 55.

[b] SAVIGNY, *Recht des Besitzes*; *American Jurist*, vol. xix. p. 27; *Thémis*, tom. iii. p. 233 (WARNKÖNIG) ; *Dig.* xli. 2, *de acq. vel ret. possessione*; *Cod.* vii. 32 ; MÜHLENBRUCH, *Doct. Pand.*, p. 224; POTHIER, *Traité de la possession et de la prescription.*

[c] *Dig. uti possidetis*, xliii. 17. 1, § 2 : ' Hujus autem interdicti proponendi causa hæc fuit, quod separata debet esse possessio et proprietate fieri enim potest ut alter possessor sit dominus non sit, alter dominus quidem sit possessor vero non sit—fieri potest ut et possessor idem et dominus sit.'

See, however, MURATORI, *Difetti della Giurisprudenza*, p. 150 : 'Un altro lodévol fréno all, esorbitante licenza de fideicommissi,' etc.

vantages which seem naturally to belong to it. Here arises a
fertile cause of difficulties, which have been solved by different countries in different ways—by none in a manner so
deficient in all that contributes to the cheap and easy defence
of property, and to the maintenance of substantial justice, as
by the legislature of England. The Roman Law conferred
two rights upon the possessor, the one that of ' usucapio,' the
other that of the ' interdicts.' ' Usucapio ' was the consequence of a possession in virtue of the Civil Law, *i.e.*, the law
of the twelve tables; ' interdicts ' were remedies granted by
the prætor for the provisional maintenance of every possession
not proved to have been obtained by fraud or violence. Savigny distinguishes three kinds of possession—' civil possession,'[d] which may ripen into a complete title by ' usucapio,'
' possession,' properly so called, which gives a right to the
' interdicts,' and ' natural possession,' which consists in a
physical act, without any intention to make the thing on
which the act operates our own.

The whole effect of possession, as an active legal principle,
is comprised in the two rights that I have mentioned. It
should not be confounded with the ' usucapio,' to which the
' Publiciana in rem actio, and the ' fructuum perceptio' must
be referred. These two passages in the *Digest,* which, carefully considered, do not contradict but explain each other, are
quite sufficient to clear up the difficulties that have been
wantonly multiplied about its real nature—' Ofilius possessionem rem facti, non juris esse ait ' (*Dig.* iv. 6. 19); and
' Possessio plurimum ex jure mutuatur' (*Dig.* xli. 2. 47). It is
a question of fact, if considered as a cause—of law, if considered as to the effects which flow from it—' Omnis de
possessione controversia aut eo pertinet ut quod non possidemus nobis restituatur, aut ad hoc ut retinere nobis liceat
quod possidemus—restituendæ possessionis ordo, aut interdicto
experitur, aut per actionem. Retinendæ itaque possessionis

---

[d] The common opinion is, that there are only two kinds of possession,
civil and natural.—SAVIGNY, p. 39—81.

duplex via est, aut exceptio aut interdictum exceptio datur
multis ex causis ei qui possidet.'ᵉ The interdicta ' uti possidetis' and ' utrubi,' were given by the prætor, ' retinendæ
possessionis causâ,' the first for immoveable property, ' interdicto uti possidetis de fundi vel edium possessione contenditur,'
the second for moveable things, ' utrubi vero de rerum immo-
bilium possessione.'ᶠ There were several ' interdicts' for giving
back possession, the chief being the ' interdictum de vi.'ᵍ I
will only add, that the Romans did not consider ' actual
contact' necessary to constitute possession.

' La délivrance est le transport de la chose vendue en la
puissance et possession de l'acheteur.'ʰ The French Law ⁱ
deviates from the Roman maxim — ' Traditiönibus et non
pactis dominia rerum transferuntur.' It considers the delivery
of the thing sold, and the payment of the price as consequences
of the contract, not as the contract itself. The moment the
promise is given the engagement is complete. After the
engagement is made, the will of the parties to a contract is no
longer free—he is bound to deliver, and bound to pay the
price of the thing delivered. The contract gives a civil
delivery—a transfer of legal right—and enables the will of
those who entered into it, to surmount all obstacles, and to be
like the law itself present to enforce its execution, wherever
the object of it can be found. This doctrine, however, applies
only to simple contracts, not to those which are conditional,
or subordinate to any particular event.ᵏ

ᵉ *Dig.* xliii. 17. 1, § 4.

ᶠ *Dig.* xlvii. *de interdictis* ; xliii. 31.

ᵍ *Dig.* xliii. 16, *de vi et vi armatâ ; Cod.* viii. 4, *unde vi.* See the
discussion of the question—' An plures eandem rem in solidum possidere possunt ?' Sabinus, Trebatius, and Julianus answered ' no ;' Labeo,
Paulus, Celsus, and Ulpian, ' yes ' Tribonian inserted the opinions of
both schools in his *Pandects,* without pronouncing in favour of either.
Savigny adheres to Paulus, pp. 136—163 ; *Dig.* xli. 2. 3, § 5.

ʰ *Cod.,* 1604, etc.   ⁱ Locré, vol. viii. p. 140.

ᵏ In Ward *v.* Turner, 2 Vesey, Jun., the Lord Chancellor said : ' It is
dangerous to support parol declarations on gifts of this kind not accompanied with a visible act to give notice to all the world. It is

The rules of our law which correspond with this doctrine is this: 'Quod meum est sine facto vel defectu meo in alium transferri non potest;' where 'factum' means alienation, and 'defectus,' forfeiture;' and the meaning is, that where property has been once acquired, some act on the part of the owner, or of his representatives, equivalent to alienation, or entailing forfeiture, is the only means by which it can be transferred.[a]

The general rule of English law is, that, except by sale in market overt, no one can acquire a title to a personal chattel from any one but the owner. The celebrated case of Miller v. Race,[b] reported and commented upon by John William Smith in that admirable work, the publication of which forms an epoch in the history of English law, has established an exception in the case of negotiable instruments. The general rule was established in the case of Pen v. Humphrey,[c] in which it was held that the person who had been robbed might recover his goods from a person by whom the things had been honestly purchased, but not in market overt. It had been held before,

---

said, if this is not allowed it will be impossible to make a donation 'mortis causâ' of stock or annuities, because in their nature they are not capable of actual delivery. I am of opinion it cannot without a transfer, or something amounting to it.'

Palmer v. Hind, 13 JOHNSON, Reports, 435 : 'If goods are actually delivered to the vendee where no credit is stipulated for, and the vendee refuses pay, the property is not changed.'

PLATT, J., New York ; Hill v. Chapman, 2 B. C. C., 612 ; 14 JOHNSON, Reports, 167 ; 4 MASS., 661 ; 8 MASS., 287 ; BOUVIER, Law Dict.

[a] Bromage v. Lloyd, 1 Ex. Rep. 32. Though it be a rule of law applicable to legal estates, that 'quod meum est,' etc., yet an equitable estate may be lost by the alienation of a trustee to a purchaser for a valuable consideration and without notice ; and it may be lost by escheat from the trustee as a consequence of his attainder, vol.i. p. 147. PRESTON, Ab., p. 318 : 'Quod semel meum est amplius meum esse non potest. 1 Inst., 49 : 'Hence a conveyance to the owner must operate as a release or confirmation ; it may improve, but cannot change the title.'

[b] Smith's Leading Cases, vol. i., ed. KEATING and WILLIS.

[c] 2 AD. and ELLIS, 495.

that no property in stock passed by a transfer made under a forged power-of-attorney[d]—the owner having done his duty by prosecuting the felon to conviction. If the seller retains his lien over the goods for the price, the delivery is not complete,[e] even though the goods still remaining in the custody of the seller are placed in boxes belonging to the purchaser, and marked with his name.[f] Without delivery, or what is tantamount to it, property in goods is not altered, nor can an action be maintained for the price of them. Where Smith sold Chance a haystack, which Smith's landlord prevented Chance from carrying away, it was held that Smith could not recover from Chance the price of the haystack, as it was incumbent on him to have removed the obstacle to the carrying away of the haystack by Chance before he could sue him for the price.[g] The English law allows of symbolical as well as actual delivery; but the anomalous rule of stoppage ' in transitu,' which operates in favour of the creditor who is least entitled to indulgence at the expense of all other creditors, qualifies the general principle, and gives rise to much litigation. The question of delivery being one of the most critical questions of law, and especially requiring a mind trained to the consideration of legal topics, is held to be a question of facts for a jury, and is decided half-a-dozen different ways at every Guildhall sitting and Liverpool assizes.

With regard to negotiable instruments, the law has undergone considerable change. It was held by Lord Mansfield, ' that when money or notes were paid ' bonâ fide,' and for a

---

[d] Davis v. Bank of England, 2 BINGHAM, 393.

[e] Simmons v. Swift, 5 B. and C., 865 ; Holderness v. Shackels, 8 B. and C., 612.

[f] Dixon v. Yates, 5 B. and AD., 313.

[g] Smith v. Chance, 2 B. and ALD., 755. ' It appears to me that the separation of the oil of a particular part owner from the residue, and putting his initials on the cask, was not an absolute appropriation of the cask and its contents to that part owner.'—LORD TENTERDEN. Transfer of stock in the public funds, 11 Geo. IV., and 1 Will. IV., c. 13, § 13 ; Stewart v. Cauty, 8 M. and W., 160 ; Stephens v. Medina, 4 Q. B., 428 ; Fletcher v. Marshall.

valuable consideration, they never shall be brought back by the true owner; but where they come ' malâ fide' into a person's hands, they are in the nature of specific property, and if their identity can be traced, the party has a right to recover.'[h] In Gill v. Cubitt,[i] the principle was applied by the Chief Justice, who asked ' whether the plaintiff had taken the bill under circumstances that ought to have excited the suspicion of a prudent man?' This case overruled Lawson v. Weston,[k] and was itself overruled by Backhouse v. Harrison,[l] in which a different doctrine was laid down, which has been since maintained by various decisions.[m]

LXIII.

RES judicata pro veritate accipitur.—ULPIAN.

The judgment of a competent tribunal is taken for truth.

Modestinus defines the ' res judicata' to be that state of things when an end is put to controversy by the decision of the judge: ' Res judicata dicitur quæ finem controversiarum pronuntiatione judicis accipit quod vel condemnatione vel absolutione contingit.'[n] Ulpian, writing on the ' Lex Julia et Papia,' says, that a ' libertinus' was to be considered as free as if a sentence had been pronounced to that effect: ' Ingenuum accipere debemus eum de quo sententia lata est, quamvis fuerit libertinus, quid res judicata pro veritate accipitur.'[o] If an inquiry took place as to the person by whom a woman was with child, and the judge decided that Titius was the father, Titius was bound to support the child: ' Quæ causa si fuerit acta apud judicem, et pronuntiaverit cum de hoc agetur quod ex eo prægnans fuerit, in eâ causâ est ut agnosci debeat, sive filius

---

[h] Clarke v. Shee, COWPER, 197.   [i] 3 B. and C. 466.

[k] 4 ESP., 56.   [l] 5 B. and AD., 1098.

[m] Uther v. Rich, 4 AD. and ELL., 780 ; Arboin v. Henderson, 1 Q. B., 498.

[n] *Dig.* xlii. 1. 1, *de re Judicatâ.*   [o] *Dig.* xii. 6. 28.

non fuerit, sive fuerit esse suum.'[p] On which law Godefroy remarks: 'Sententia lata in causâ filiationis inter patrem et filium facit fidem *quoad eos* et nulli præjudicat præter quam patri et filio.' What would that profound jurist have said to such cruel decisions as those of the Privy Council in Meadowbank *v.* Meadowbank? Ulpian says, that if any one, under the erroneous belief that a judgment adverse to him had been pronounced, enters into a compromise with his adversary, he may recover the money paid in consequence of that compromise: 'Si post rem judicatam quis transegerit et solverit repetere poterit, idcirco quia placuit nullius esse momenti;'[q] because, he says, an ignorant man can give no consent: 'Ignorantis nullus est consensus.' If, however, with full knowledge, I renounce a judgment in my favour, my renunciation is valid: 'Si paciscar ne judicati agatur hoc pactum valet.'[r] The rule holds only 'Quando sententia est indubitata nulloque remedio attentari potest.'[s] For instance: if, in the belief that Titius was my co-heir, I had sued him and obtained a sentence, and it afterwards appeared that my belief was erroneous, the sentence was of no effect: 'Cum putarem te cohæredem meum esse idque verum non esset egi tecum familiæ erciscundæ judicio, et a judice invicem adjudicationes et condemnationes factæ sunt—detectâ veritate, sententia est nulla.'[t] And the rule does not hold where the sentence was collusive.[u] Posterity will be surprised to find that the chief part of the system of the transfer of real property among us originated in open defiance of this obvious principle of natural justice.[x]

This maxim applied not only to the litigant parties, but to those who derived their title from them. If, for instance, it had been improperly determined by the judge that a particular jewel did not belong to Titius, and Titius afterwards pledged that jewel, the sentence was conclusive against the creditor.

---

p *Dig.* xxv. 3. 1, § 16. q *Dig.* xii. 6. 23, § 1. r *Dig.* ii. 14. 7, § 13.

s *Dig.* xii. 6. 23, § 1. t *Dig.* (*Familiæ Erciscundæ*) x. 2. 36.

u *Dig.* (*de Collusione Detegendâ*) xl. 16.

x Even a special pleading judge, in a lucid interval, would hardly, I should imagine, vindicate such immoral folly; which, however, continued to be the law till 1831.

This is the case put by Papinian: ' Per injuriam victus apud judicium rem quam petierat postea pignori obligavit, non plus habere creditor potest quam habebat qui pignus dedit.'ʸ If, however, the debtor should have submitted to the judgment without giving any notice to the creditor with whom the property was then pledged, Papinian judiciously remarks that the rule ceases to apply: ' Si superatus sit debitor qui rem suam vindicabat quod suam non probaret, æque servanda erit creditori actio Serviana, probanti rem in bonis eo tempore quo pignus contrahebatur ejus fuisse ;'ᶻ e. g., in that case the transaction would be ' res inter alio acta,' and therefore of no effect as far as the creditor was concerned.

It is the knowledge of the person compromised that makes the sentence pronounced between other parties binding, e. g., the case of the creditor, put above; the case of the husband, who allows his father-in-law to defend an action for the jointure land of his wife; or the possessor of a purchased article, who allows the seller of it to defend an action which puts the property of what has been sold to him in issue. ' Sæpe constitutum est res inter alios judicatas aliis non præjudicare—quod tamen quandam distinctionem habet nam sententia inter alios dicta, aliis quibusdam etiam scientibus obest — quibusdam vero etiam si contra ipsos judicatum sit nihil nocet.ᵃ . . . Sed scientibus sententia quæ inter alios dicta est obest, cum quis de eâ re cujus actio vel defensio primum sibi competit, sequentem agere patiatur—veluti si creditorem experiri passus sit debitor de proprietate pignoris, aut maritus socerum vel uxorem de proprietate rei in dotem acceptæ, aut possessor venditorem de proprietate rei emptæ.'ᵇ The sentence of a judge cancelling a will as inofficious was of no value, unless it had been opposed

---

ʸ *Dig.* xx. 1. 3, § 1.   ᶻ *Dig.* xx. 1. 3.
ᵃ *Dig.* xlii. 1. 63.
' A judgment is evidence against one who might have been a party, for he cannot complain of the want of those advantages which he has voluntarily renounced.'—BACON'S *Abridgment, Ev.* F. ; STARKIE, *on Ev.*, 331.
ᵇ *Dig.* v. 2. 8, § 17, compare with *Ib.* v. 2. 17.

'justo contradictore'; and if the legatees suspected the heir of collusion, they might support the will: ' Si suspecta collusio sit legatariis inter scriptos hæredes et eum qui de inofficioso testamento agit adesse etiam legatarios et voluntatem defuncti tueri necesse est.'[c] The words are 'res judicata,' which, so long as an appeal could be brought against a sentence, were not applicable.[d] 'Quod pendet non est pro eo quasi *sit*'; *e. g.*, if a man was cast in a judgment involving infamy, so long as he could appeal, he was not reckoned infamous: ' Si furti vel aliis famosis actionibus quis condemnatus provocavit pendente judicio, non dum inter famosos habetur.'[e] The sentence of the court of final appeal, though erroneous, was conclusive: ' Si quæratur judicatum sit necne et hujus quæstionis judex non esse judicatum pronuntiaverit licet fuerit judicatum rescinditur etsi provocatum non fuerit.'[f] To be binding, judgments must bear immediately on the points at issue. The decision of a collateral matter, from which a particular state of things might be inferred, was not conclusive as to the existence of that state of things. Subtle and delicate questions often arose on this point; and this is what Ulpian means when he says, in words that might seem to contradict the maxim I am remarking upon, that the sentence ' Veritati non facit præjudicium.'[g] He expresses himself in this manner with reference to a case in which the judge had ordered a child to be supported at the expense of a particular person.[h] This order, Ulpian says, is

---

[c] *Dig.* v. 2. 29.

[d] MEERMAN, *Thesaurus Juris,* vol. vii. p. 115. *Treatise of* FRANCISCO RAMOS DEL MANZANO, *ad tit. de re judicata.* 'Deinde hoc etiam sensu apparet non posse proprie dici rem judicatam quando appellatum est aut appellari potest, sed solum quando lis ita judicata est ut non unius controversiæ aut judicii sed controversiarum ut Modestinus loquitur omnium scilicet finem accipiat . . . quod quia non evenit nisi postquam appellari jam non potest, tunc transire sententia dicitur in rem judicatam.'—CUJACIUS, *Quæst. Papin.,* lib. viii.

[e] *Dig.* iii. 2. 6 : 'De iis qui notantur infamiâ.'

[f] *Dig.* xlix. 8. 1.

[g] *Dig.* i. 6. 10.

[h] 'Ce ne sont pas les motifs d'un jugement qui constituent le jugement même, le dispositif seul en forme l'essence.' So where the 'Præ-

not to conclude or prejudice the question as to the 'status' of the child, for the law ordered a summary decision: 'Si vel parens neget filium idcircoque alere se non debere contendat, vel filius neget parentem, summatim judices oportet super eâ recognoscere, et si constiterit filium vel parentem esse tunc ali jubebunt, cæterum si non constiterit nec decernent alimenta — meminisse autem oportet et si pronuntiaverint ali oportere, attamen eam rem præjudicium non facere veritati.'[i]   For the decision only was that the person should be supported: 'Nec enim hoc pronuntiatur filium esse—sed ali debere.'   So the oath of the mother, 'Ex quo venter in possessionem mittitur,' could not affect her offspring for good or evil.   'Marcellus ait veritatem esse quærendam quia jusjurandum alteri neque nocet neque prodest, matris igitur jusjurandum partui non proficiet, nec nocebit, si mater detulerit et juretur ex eo prægnans non esse.'[k]   The great exceptions to this rule are—fraud, collusion, the corruption of the judge, or his overstepping the bounds of his authority.   Not only is the 'res judicata' taken for the truth, but the 'rerum perpetuo similiter judicatarum auctoritas' had the effect of law; and Cicero enumerates the 'res judicatas' among the integral parts of the Roman law.[l]

In order to give the authority of the 'chose jugée,' the French code requires that the thing demanded shall be the same, that the demand shall rest upon the same ground, shall be between the same parties in the same capacity[m]: 'Idem

---

fectus annonæ' condemned an individual to pay a debt said to be guaranteed by his slave, and rested his decision on grounds altogether untenable, the judgment was upheld for reasons that he had not alleged, after saying that there was no reason for assuming a guarantee. 'Sed quia videbatur in omnibus eum suo nomine substituisse, sententiam conservavit imperator.'—*Dig.* xiv. 5. 8.

    [i] *Dig.* xxv. 4. 5, § 8, § 9.

    [k] *Dig.* xii. 2. 3, § 3.

    [l] *Cod.*, l. 4: 'De judiciis.'   *Cod.*, l. 2: 'Sententiam rescindi non posse.'

    [m] LOCRÉ, vol. xii. p. 410, *Cod.* 1351. *Ibid*, p. 532. MERLIN, *Chose Jugée*: 'Il s'en faut de beaucoup que fonder une demande sur un nou-

corpus, eadem causa petendi, eadem conditio personarum.'[n] So the Roman law did not allow a change of the form of action, to evade the rule: 'Generaliter ut Julianus definit exceptio rei judicatæ obstat quoties inter easdem personas eadem quæstio revocatur, vel alio genere judicii,' because the change of action does not necessarily prevent an identity of object: 'Cum quis actionem mutat et experitur, dummodo de eâdem re experiatur etsi diverso genere actionis quam instituit, videtur de eâdem re agere.'[o]

'From the variety of cases,' says Lord Chief Justice De Grey, in his admirable judgment on the Duchess of Kingston's case—when a collusive sentence in the Ecclesiastical Court had been set up as a bar to further proceedings—'relative to judgments being given in evidence in civil suits, these two deductions seem to follow as generally true: first, that the judgment of a court of concurrent jurisdiction directly upon the point is, as a plea, a bar, or as evidence conclusive between the same parties upon the same matter, directly in question in another court; secondly that the judgment of a court of exclusive jurisdiction directly upon the point is, in like manner, conclusive upon the same matter, coming incidentally in question in another court between the same parties for a different purpose. But neither the judgment of a concurrent or exclusive jurisdiction is evidence of any matter which came collaterally in question, though within their jurisdiction, or of any matter incidentally cognisable, nor of any matter to be inferred by argument from the judgment.' In Moses v. Macfarlane,[p] Lord

---

veau moyen ce soit la fonder sur une nouvelle cause, dans le cas sur lequel porte notre question, la *cause* de la demande était la nullité de l'acte attaqué. Cette *cause* le demandeur pouvait la déduire de tels moyens qu'il jugeait expédient d'employer, mais il devait les employer tous à la fois.' 'Ces verités elementaires ont été solennellement consacrées dans l'espèce suivante,' etc.

[n] *Dig.* xliv. 2. 12, § 13, 14.

[o] *Dig.* xliv. 2. 5. and 7, § 4.

[p] Moses v. Macfarlane, 2 BURROWS, *Reports*, 1010; COMYN'S *Dig.*, tit. *Estoppel*; BACON'S *Abridgment*, tit. *Evidence*, letter F; STARKIE, *On Evidence*, vol.i. p. 317.

Mansfield said, ' It is most clear that the merits of a judgment can never be overhaled by an original suit, either at law or in equity. Till the judgment is set aside or reversed, it is conclusive as to the subject matter of it to all intents and purposes. It is enough for us, that the commissioners adjudged they had no cognizance of such collateral matter,' on which the case brought before Lord Mansfield turned. ' We cannot correct an error in their proceedings, and ought to suppose what is done by a final jurisdiction to be right.'[b] ' Although regularly no recovery or judgment is to be admitted in evidence but against parties or privies, yet under some circumstances they may, as in an information in nature of a ' quo warranto,' a judgment of ' ouster' was allowed to be given in evidence, to prove the ' ouster' of a third person, the mayor, by whom the defendant was admitted; and such evidence is conclusive, unless judgment can be impeached as obtained by fraud.'[c]

Where the suit does not relate to a transaction merely private, the decree or judgment may be evidence against a person who was neither party nor privy to the cause in which

[b] Here, as everywhere, we stumble upon the evils arising from the sacrifice of substance to form in the English law. ' A judgment in one action of ejectment is not conclusive in another'—Why ? because it would be unjust, inequitable, oppressive ? No such thing—'in consequence of the fictitious nature of the proceedings.'—3 EAST, 354, Outram *v.* Morewood ; Purcell *v.* Macnamara, 9 EAST ; COMYN's *Dig., ubi supr.;* SALKELD, 276 ; COKE, *Littleton,* 352 *a* ; BULLER, *N.P.,* 14 ; 2 B. and ALD., 662. ' A man shall not be estopped by a record coram non judice.'— 1 ROLLE, 863, l. 50. See, on this subject, Mayor of York *v.* Pilkington, *Rep. Temp.,* HARDWICKE, p. 296.

[c] BACON's *Abridgment, Evidence,* F ; COMYN's, *Dig., Ev.,* A 5. Where our law is in the main right, care is taken that the reason for its doctrine shall be as opposite to any rational or enlarged view of jurisprudence as possible ; e. g., a verdict, to be conclusive, must be between the same parties, speaking generally. Why ? Because a person not a party cannot have a writ of attaint; i. e., a proceeding from which, if the jury impeached were convicted under it, it followed that their houses were to be razed to the ground, their fields ploughed up and left fallow for a year, etc. Again, printed statutes are evidence, as hints of what is in every man's mind already. Such is the grand, solid, luminous and dignified reasoning familiar to the oracles of our law.

it was pronounced. The decisions of the Court of Admiralty in questions of prize, and of a Court of Quarter Sessions on settlement cases, are binding upon all the world. Judgments of this nature are technically termed ' in rem.'[d] Where a person has not had the power of cross-examining witnesses or controverting evidence, the judgment founded on that evidence is only so far available against him, as it is ' in rem,' or as it is a simple fact, justifying no inference as to the reasons upon which it was founded.

It is a general rule, that a verdict shall not be evidence against a man unless, if it had been found the other way, it would have been in his favour.[e] And it is held, on technical grounds (of course) inasmuch as according to our laws the parties can never be the same, that a conviction upon an indictment is not evidence in a civil action, and that a verdict in a civil case is not evidence in criminal proceedings. But this point cannot be considered as finally settled. The argument as to the privilege of proceding against the jury by attaint, is, we may hope, for the sake of reason and the respect due to courts of justice, at an end.[f] To lay down an inflexible rule of exclusion would be in many cases an obstacle to justice: it would be safer to say that such a judgment shall not operate conclusively, but may be disputed by him who seeks to set aside its consequences when the scene is shifted from the atmosphere of a court of civil to that of a court of criminal justice.[g]

The well-known case of Marriott v. Hampton is as flagrant

---

[d] Garnett v. Ferrand, 6 B. and C., 611 ; Davies v. Lowndes, 1 B., N. C., 606 ; Pritchard v. Hitchcock, 6 M. and G., 151 ; King v. Norman, 4, C. B., 884.

[e] B. N. P., 232 ; GILBERT, Law of Evidence; Gaunt v. Wainman, 3 B. N. C., 70 ; Doe v. Errington, 6 B. N. C., 83.

[f] Gibson v. Macarthy, Cases Temp. Hard., 311 ; PHILLIPS, Law of Evidence ; Jones v. White, 1 STRANGE, 6, 8 ; Richardson v. Williams, 12 MODERN, 319 ; Brownsword v. Edwards, 2 VESEY, 246 ; Bartlett v. Pickersgill, 33 BURR., 2255 ; Smith v. Rummons, 1 CAMPBELL, 9 ; Hathaway v. Barrow, 1 CAMPBELL, 151.

[g] Blakemore v. Glam. C. Cy., 2 C. M. and R., 139 ; 11 State Trials, 222 ; STARKIE, Ev., vol. i. p. 332.

an instance of gross unintentional injustice as any contained in the reports of civil cases among us. It is founded on a misapplication of the doctrine that I have endeavoured to illustrate. The language of the judge, in the utter ignorance which it displays of all law but that of England, in the narrow view which it exhibits of the wants and interests of society, and in the indifference to substantial justice (springing from the most honest convictions and rooted habits) on which it rests, gives but too faithful a notion of the tone of thought and habit of study predominant among those who have made the common law of England what it has been, what it is, and what, if left exclusively to the same influences, it will still continue to be. The absurd doctrine which has led to such repeated acts of oppression and injustice, and is dwelt upon by Lord Coke with such emphasis of approbation, that ' a record imports such absolute verity, that no person against whom it is admissible shall be allowed to aver against it,'[h] springs from the same confused and inaccurate view of a principle sound in itself, and mischievous only from the preposterous pedantry of its enforcers; e. g., in the case of the King v. Carlisle, a fact was alleged which, if true, it was admitted vitiated all the proceedings against the defendant, making them irregular, unjust, and unconstitutional. The complaint was, that the record stated what was not true; and it was gravely held that an averment contrary to the record could not be received, though the falsity and corruption of the record was the very thing complained of. Observe the practical wisdom of this decision. Titius complains that he has been tried by a wrong judge, by a judge to whom the constitution has given no power to try him; and he is answered by being told, not that he was tried by the right judge, but that as the record—made by the officer of the court of whose corruption he is actually complaining—

---

[h] 1 *Inst.*, 260 ; Rex v. Carlisle, 2 B. and AD., 367 ; Barrs v. Jackson, 1 PHILLIPS, 582 ; 1 YOUNG and COLLIER, 595 ; BACON'S *Abridgment*, tit. *Error ;* Molins v. Wesby, 1 SIDERFIN. Error assigned, that the wrong judge had tried the case. 'This was held not assignable, being contrary to the record.'—Cole v. Green, CROKE, *Jac.*, 244 ; 2 PHILL., *Ev.*, 9, ed. 26.

states the contrary, he cannot be allowed to contradict it, or to prove the record false. And this is the law of a civilised country, promulgated with the utmost solemnity, as if it were a solid principle of jurisprudence, from the bench; i.e., that that the very act complained of shall be a bar against an inquiry into it for ever![1]

LXIV.

IN ambiguis orationibus maxime sententia spectanda est ejus qui eas protulisset.—MÆCIANUS.

In doubtful phrases, the chief point is the purpose of the person using them.

This rule, taken from the rules of Volusius Mæcianus, might seem to contradict other rules incorporated with the Pandects, and especially the law (*Dig.* xlv. 1. 99): ' Quicquid astringendæ obligationis est id nisi palam verbis exprimatur omissum intelligendum est,' and the law (*Dig.* l. 172): ' In ambiguo pacto contractu stipulatione adversus paciscentem locantem stipulantem ambiguæ orationis interpretationem faciendam esse,' to which the reason is annexed: ' Quia in potestate eorum fuit re integrâ apertius dicere.' But the solution of the difficulty will be apparent to any one who asks this question—Who is the person by the intention of whom the interpretation of an ambiguous expression is to be decided? a question that perpetually recurs when wills, laws, and judicial determinations are to be explained. The distinction, then, is between cases where the will of one person is conclusive, and cases where the consent

---

[1] To make the whole doctrine complete, the judgment is no bar because it is just, but because it is pleaded. A judgment is no estoppel unless it be *pleaded ;* as if the mistake of a man's pleader could affect his right if the judgment existed, or as if a great principle of jurisprudence could in any way be affected by such an accident. The pleading in no way affects the *existence* of the judgment, which is the only thing to be considered. — PARKE, B., Doe *v.* Huddart, 2 CR. M. and R., 316 ; Doe and Strode *v.* Seaton, 2 CR. M. and R., 731 ; Williams *v.* Thacker, 1 B. and B., 524 ; Ricardo *v.* Garwas, 12 CL. and FINN., 368 ; Stewart *v.* Todd, 16 L. J., *Q. B.*, 327 ; R. *v.* Hoare, 13 M. and W., 494.

of two or more persons must be established to give validity to
the transaction—a distinction with which Paulus furnishes us
(*Dig.* xliv. 1. 83, § 1): ' Si Stichum stipulatus de alio sentiam
tu de alio nihil actum erit . . . sed hic magis est ut is petitus
videatur de quo actor sensit nam stipulatio ex utriusque consensu
valet judicium autem in invitum redditur et ideo actori potius
credendum est alioquin semper negabit reus se consensisse';
and again (*Dig.* l. 17. 172, § 1): 'Ambigua intentio ita accipienda est ut res salva actori sit.' The rule cited in the text
holds incontrovertibly, therefore, when the meaning of one
person is alone to be considered, as when the purpose of the
legislator or of the sovereign is to be ascertained. So the
'ambigua intentio' of the plaintiff in his 'libellus' was construed, not after the fashion which has prevailed in other
countries, but in a spirit directly the reverse; that is, in such
a way as to promote (instead of baffling) his object, and to
facilitate (instead of obstructing) the attainment of substantial
justice, as the laws, above quoted, show. To these we may
add *Dig. de reb. dubiis* xxxiv. 5. 12, and the law, *Dig. de judiciis* v. 1. 66: ' Si quis intentione vel oratione ambigua usus
sit id quod utilius ei est accipiendum est.' See, too, *Dig. de
appell.* xlix. 1. 4, § 1, the memorable law (*Dig.* xxxiv. 5. 22):
' Semper in dubiis id agendum est ut quam tutissimo loco res
sit bonâ fide contracta nisi cum aperte contra leges scriptum
est '; as to the will of the testator (*Dig. de Cond. et Dem.* xxxv.
1. 19): 'In conditionibus primum locum voluntas defuncti
obtinet eaque regit conditiones'; and *Dig. de Hæred. Inst.*
xxviii. 5. 35, § 3: 'Rerum autem Italicarum vel provincialium
significatione quæ res accipiendæ sunt? Et facit quidem
totum voluntas defuncti, nam quid senserit spectandum est.'
Dig. xxxiii. 2. 26, *lex Sempronius*: 'His casibus de sententiâ
testatoris quærendum est.'

But in those cases which rest on agreement and compact
ἐκ συναλλάγματος, doubtful phrases are to be decided for the
buyer against the seller, for the person bound by the promise
against the person enforcing it, and for the debtor against the
creditor.

This particular rule, though it applies to the cases above stated, belongs especially to the 'stipulatio fideicommissorum causâ'—a strictly prætorian stipulation—the formula of which was propounded by the prætor himself (*Instıt. de Divis. Stip.* § 2; *Dig.* xlvi. 5), and therefore where there was ambiguity, it was to be settled by the intention of the prætor: (*Ibid.* 9) ' In prætoriis stipulationibus si ambiguus sermo acciderit prætoris erit æstimatio ejus enim meus æstimanda est.' The word 'protulisset' shews that the rule is not intended for cases where the will of more than one person is in question, but solely where the intention of one person is to be considered and propounded. The sentence of a judge is said emphatically ' proferri;' compacts, ' componi' and ' conscribi.'

This rule may be compared also with that cited (*Dig.* l. 17. 168, § 1): ' Quod factum est cum in obscuro sit ex affectione cujusque capit interpretationem:' an act, if doubtful, is to be explained by the affections of the agent; though it should be remembered; first, that our rule relates to ambiguous words, and this to ambiguous acts; secondly, that in the text the purpose is to be considered of him who has exercised his authority to propound, and in the other rule the affection of any individual.

LXV.

A LTERIUS circumventio alii non præbet actionem.—ULPIAN.

The fraud of one man gives no right of action to another.

The question which this sentence answers, is, can a guardian, by circumventing a third person on behalf of his ward, give a ward a valuable right of action; and the answer is, that he cannot. To this effect is the law (*Dig.* xliv. 4) which says, that if any one, without the authority of his guardian, has paid his debt to the ward, ' ex eâque solutione locupletio factus sit pupillus,' that an attempt to make him pay the debt a second time, might be repelled by the ' exceptio'; therefore

where the ward had derived benefit from the fraud of the
guardian, in spite of the favour with which the law considered
the ward with reference to the acts of his guardian; ' et si per
eas personas pupillo favetur,' the ' dolus ' of the tutor was,
except in cases of collusion (plane si mihi proponas collusisse
aliquem cum tutore factum suum ei nocebit) a valid bar to his
demand (*Ibid.* 23. 24).

The tutor stood, with reference to his ward's property, in
the light of an owner; and he was bound to exercise the same
diligence in managing it, as a careful ' paterfamilias ' acting
' bonâ fide' would do in the management of his own: ' A
tutoribus et curatoribus pupillorum eadem diligentia exigenda
est circa administrationem rerum pupillarium quam paterfamilias rebus suis ex bonâ fide præbere debet' (*Dig.* xxvi.7.33).

It may be asked whether, as the action would always lie by
the person circumvented against the tutor, that is, the person
who had deceived him, it would not be better to give him
that remedy, than to furnish him with a defence against the
ward.   But the ' utilitas,' or equity, which the civilians always
had in view, puts an end to this subtilty or futility (I beg
pardon of Mr. Baron Parke, but they are the very words of
Gothofred [a]) at once; for no one is obliged to pay one man,
because he may recover what he has paid from another; and
therefore Papinian lays down the broad rule: ' Dolus tutorum
pupillo neque nocere neque prodesse debet.'   As illustrations
of this principle may be cited (*Dig.* xli. 2. 24) ' Quod servus
tuus ignorante te vi possidet id tu non possides quoniam is qui
in tuâ potestate est ignoranti tibi non corporalem possessionem
sed justam potest acquirere.'   (*Ibid.* xvii. 2. 53) ' Quod autem
ex furto vel ex alio maleficio quæsitum est in societatem non
oportere conferri palam est quia delictorum turpis atque fœda
communis est.'   And this law, which ought to govern so many
cases that are brought into our Courts of Equity (*Ibid.* xix. 1.

---

[a] ἄλλου περιγράφοντος ἄλλος ἀγωγὴν οὐκ ἔχει.—*Basilica.*

I say valuable, because strictly speaking, there would be an action
which would be repelled by the 'doli exceptio.'   Ranger *v.* Gt.Western
Railway Company, CLARK, *House of Lords' Cases,* p. 72.

37) ' Sicut æquum est bonæ fidei emptori alterius dolum non nocere, ita non est æquum eidem personæ venditoris sui dolum prodesse.'

LXVI.

SEMPER in obscuris quod minimum est sequimur.
—ULPIAN.

There are seventeen rules on this subject collected in the last chapter of the *Digest*: all full of admirable sense; all disregarded almost universally by our ancient judges, with the exception of one or two, borrowed at second hand, and disfigured in their application, and quoted probably as dicta of Lord Coke, it would be no exaggeration to say that no allusion whatever to them is to be found in our reports, abounding as they do in cases which cry out for their application.[a]

The obsurity to which they refer, arises from indistinct phraseology, e. g., *Dig.* l. 17. 34.

From silence, to which relate—*Dig.* l. 17. 41, § 1; 114; 179; 191; 192, § 1; 200.

From the use of equivocal words (*Dig.* l. 17. 67): ' Quoties idem sermo duas sententias exprimit, ea potissimum excipiatur quæ rei gerendæ aptior est.' (A rule, the reverse of which has guided our Courts in the construction of wills.)

From the use of phrases that are unintelligible(73, § 3).

From the ignorance of the motive and intention with which an act was done, to which relate the 114th: ' In obscuris inspici solet quod verisimilius est aut quod plerumque fieri solet;' and 168, § 1: ' Quod factum est cum in obscuro sit ex affectione cujusque capit interpretationem;' and, lastly, the interpretation to be put on events (56).

The matters in which such obscurity must be dispelled, are, as enumerated in the *Digest*, wills and legacies, contracts and stipulations, ' pacta dotalia,' acts of persons, penal laws and sentences, ' actiones,' ' manumissions,' the rescripts of the

---

[a] *De Rebus Dubiis, Dig.* xxxiv. 5; HARMENOPULUS, περὶ ἀσαφοῦς καὶ ἀμφιβολίας, i. 15 ; ' Cum species, 9 ff. de supell. legata.'

prince. The means of escape from such difficulties are fourteen:—

1. To choose the least.

2. To choose that which operates least harshly: ' Quod minimum habet iniquitatis.' There are too many of our decisions which seem as if ' maximum ' had been written for ' minimum ' in the copies of the *Digest* studied by our judges.

3. To follow the custom of the country: ' Quod in regione frequentatur sequendum.'

4. To favour the person who desires to save himself from loss, rather than the person whose object it is to gain: ' Repetitioni potius quam lucro favendum.'

5. To adopt the most benevolent construction. This is repeated in every possible shape: ' Benigniora preferenda,' ' benignius responsum rapiendum,' ' benignior interpretatio sequenda.'

6. To adopt that construction whieh is best suited to the object.

7. To adopt that construction which is in favour of the ' dos.'

8. To consider especially the purpose of the person using the expression (191).

9. To consider on which side is the greatest probability.

10. And what is most usual.

11. To consider the affection of the author of the phrase to be interpreted.

12. To give the interpretation which is against the seller ' contra venditorem.'

13. To decide in favour of the suitor.

14. To decide in favour of liberty.

The rule, it may be observed, is universal, ' semper.' It may seem from the law, ' si ita sit' (*Dig.* xxx. 1. 14), that the rule was Papinian's, and inserted by Ulpian in his work, *De vitiis testamentorum et legatorum,*' addressed to Sabinus.

In the case of the law ' si ita,' the testator had bequeathed several times legacies of different value to the same person, but he added, that only one of them should be paid.

Papinian says, ' posse dici,' that is, that on the whole it was most equitable to consider the legatee entitled to the smallest only. See for cases of doubt, *Dig.* xxx. 1. 39, *cum servus*, especially *Ib.* xxx. 1. 50, § 3;[b] xxxi. 1. 43; xxxii. 75. 1, *nummis indistincte legatis.* In penal matters, *Ib.* xliii. 1, 38; xlviii. 19. 32, *mitior lex erit sequenda.*[c]

It must be recollected, however, that this rule applies to cases only where there is obscurity,[d] ' si non pareat;' in Ulpian's words, ' quod actum est,' and that where from the use of the word, the meaning of the testator can be fairly conjectured, there is no room for its application, as instances where the intention, though doubtful at first, was explained; there are the laws ' si lancem' (*Dig.* xxxiv. 2. 31) where the testator who had left three a greater, a smaller, and a least, desired that the legatee should have the smaller. ' Si is qui ducenta' *Ib.* xxxiv. 5. 13; vii. 1. 43, ' etiam.'

' Standum,' says a great authority on the law of nature,[e] ' omnino est iis quæ verbis expressis quorum manifesta est significatio indicata fuerunt nisi omnem a rebus humanis certitudinem removere volueris.'

' In a science,' says Mr. Troplong,[f] ' words must be taken in the sense generally attributed to them; and it would be to expose persons to mistakes, if we were to make words bend to a meaning more conformable to etymology.'

For instance, the Aquilian law consisted of several chapters. In the first chapter, the person who killed an animal belonging to another, was obliged to pay the highest value it had borne

---

b ' Si numerus nummorum legatus sit neque apparet quales sint legati, ante omnia ipsius patrisfamilias consuetudo, deinde regionis in quâ versatus est, exquirenda est, sed et meus patrisfamilias et legatarii dignitas vel caritas et necessitudo.'

c ' Inter pares numero judices.'

d And if there be any obscurity not to be explained, it ought to be to the disadvantage of him ' in cujus potestate fuit legem apertius conscribere.'

e WOLF, *Jus Naturæ*, p. 7, § 822 ; VATTEL, 262.

f TROPLONG, *Du Louage*, 1709, § 29, vol. i. 128.

within a year to the proprietor: 'Quanti id in eo aurei plurimi fuit.'[a] The second chapter related to the case where there had been inflicted injuries not followed by death, and in that case compensation was fixed at the price the animal would have borne within the thirty days following the injury: 'Quanti ea res erit in diebus triginta proximis.'[b] The word 'quanti' was used, but the word 'plurimi' was omitted. The question was, whether it should be considered as if it had been used, and it was answered in the affirmative: 'At nec plurimi —verbum adjicitur sed Sabino recte placuit perinde habendam æstimationem ac si etiam hâc parte plurimi verbum adjectum fuisset —nam plebem Romanam quæ Aquilio tribuno interrogante hanc legem tulit contentam fuisse quod primâ parte eo verbo usa esset.'[c]

Lucius Titius Octavius Felix was a banker, and trusted the management of his bank to his freedman, Octavius Terminalis. This manager gave Gaius Seius a note, drawn up to this effect: 'Octavius Terminalis rem agens Octavii Felicis, Domitio Felici salutem. Habes penès mensam patroni mei denarios mille, quos denarios vobis numerare debebo pridie Calendas Maias.'[d] The question was, whether the manager was himself bound to pay the sum mentioned in the note, the principal having died insolvent, and it was held that he was not; for that the word 'debebo' must be held to refer to the words 'rem agens Octavii Felicis' 'nec jure his verbis obligatum nec æquitatem conveniendi eum superesse, cum in institoris officio ad fidem mensæ præstandam, scripsisset.' Attia left a trust that her heirs should pay to the priest and hierophylax of a chapel ten 'denaria' on a particular day, when a market she had set up was held: 'Quisquis mihi hæres erit fidei ejus committo uti det ex reditu cænaculi mei et horrei post obitum sacerdoti et hierophylaco et libertis quo in illo templo erunt, denaria decem die nundinarum quas ibi posui.' The question, whether the

---

[a] *Dig.* ix. 2. 2; ix. 2. 51, § 2. DE LISLE, *Interpretation des Lois*, vol. ii. p. 13.
[b] *Dig.* ix. 2. 27, § 5.
[c] *Instit. de Lege Aquiliâ*, iv. 3.
[d] *Dig. de Instit. Act.* xx. 14. 3.

money was to be paid always, or only so long as the persons mentioned in the will were alive—whether it was a bequest to them or the chapel; the answer, that the bequest was intended for the chapel, and that the persons were only mentioned to denote those who served it: 'Ministerium nominatorum designatum cæterum datum templo.'[e] The third paragraph of the 317th Art. of the French penal code inflicted certain penalties on physicians and other 'officiers de santé,' in cases where they had procured abortion. The question was, whether midwives were included under the words 'officiers de santé,' and it was. held that they were[f]: 'Auberge ou l'hôtellerie dans laquelle le le voleur était reçu,' were held to include a 'maison garnie.'[g]

A punishment was inflicted (*Cod. penal.*) on any one who should offer to certain functionaries 'quelque outrage par paroles.' It was held, after much deliberation, by the Cour de Cassation, that the word 'paroles' did not extend to 'lettres missives.'[h] Dumoulin held that a law which forbad all conversation with a condemned person, did not necessarily import the prohibition of writing or sending messages. Relying upon the law (*Dig.* xxxi. 1. 75), which makes a distinction between letters and conversation, and on the law (*Dig.* iv. 8. 17, § 7) which, where reference has been made to three arbiters, declares the sentence of two to one valid, if all have met, but not otherwise, because the arguments of the third might have altered the views of the other two: 'Poterit præsentia absentis trahere alios arbitros in ejus sententiam.' He concludes that the end of the legislator, and the circumstances of the case, ought to be considered: 'Ideo circumstantiæ considerandæ— quod si constet litteras nihil continere mali prorsus cessat statutum—cui nec verbis nec mente contraventum fuit.'[i]

---

[e] *Dig.* xxxiii. 1. 20, § 1.   [f] DE LISLE, vol. ii. p. 78.

[g] 'Ainsi si les mots de *maison* ou *hôtel garni*, ne se trouvent pas littéralement répétés on ne peut douter qu'ils n'y soient implicitement compris sous les expressions génériques *auberge* ou *hôtellerie.*'

[h] DE LISLE, vol. ii. p. 89.

[i] DUMOULIN on the law 'stipulatio,' *Dig.* xlv. 1, § 1. *De Lisle*, vol. ii. p. 100 ; vol. iii. p. 22.

Dumoulin answers the question, whether, if it is agreed that the stakes of a race shall be given to that one among several who shall first reach the goal, if two reach it at the same moment before the rest, they can claim it; and he answers it in the negative: ' Cum præmium uni soli et omnes præcedenti sit propositum et certo constet *nullum* hoc fecisse—*nullum* cæteros omnes post se reliquisse apparet conditionem modo esse impletam et nullum victorem nullum victum esse, nulli jus bravii quæritum et sic nihil et cæteris obstare.'[k]

RULES FOR THE INTERPRETATION OF LAW.

EVERY law consists of the words used to express the meaning of the legislator, and of the meaning which they are employed to convey.   The Romans called the latter, ' mens legis '; so they said—' Verba legis captanda non esse sed quâ mente quid diceretur animadvertendum ' (*Dig.* ix. 1. 19).

So Donellus[a] says the meaning of the law is everything. The law does not consist of black strokes on white paper, but of the intention which they denote, and which the legislative authority of the country has judged it expedient to ratify.

---

[k] DUMOULIN, vol. i. p. 231.   8 *Art. Cout. de Paris ancienne.*   13 *De la nouvelle in verb. le fils ainé.*

[a] DONELLUS, L. i. c. 13 ; VATTEL, ii. 17, § 285 ; DWARRIS *on Statutes,* p. 558 ; BROOM, *Legal Maxims,* 440 ; Reg. v. Millis, 10 CL. and FINN., 749 ; Sussex Peerage Case, 11 CL. and FINN., 607 ; Heydon's Case, 3 *Reps.* ; VIN., *Abridg. Stat.,* 137 ; Hatton v. Cave, 1 B. and AD., 538 ; COKE, *Littleton,* 79 a ; Crespigny v. Wittenoom, *T. Reps.,* 723 ; Stockton and Darlington Railway v. Barrett, 11 CL. and FINN., 590 ; 11 *Reports,* 34 ; Borradaile v. Hunter, 5 M. and GRAINGER, 653 ; Everett v. Mills, 4 SCOTT, Q. C., 531 ; R. v. Burrell, 12 AD. and ELLIS, 468 ; In re Scott 4 M. and W., 291 ; East v. Pell, 4 M. and W., 665.

Where the words and meaning coincide, therefore, no question can arise—where there is any discrepancy, as the words are not the law, we must not cleave to them in a servile spirit, but adhere to the ' mens ' and purpose of the legislator.

So the Roman jurist Celsus laid it down—' Scire leges non est verba earum tenere sed vim ac potestatem ' (*Ib.* xvii., *de legib.*).

Now it may happen that words employed by the legislator are too narrow or too comprehensive for his purpose.[b] Suppose general words are used comprising a whole class, and there are certain numbers of that class which it was not the wish of the legislator to comprehend.[c] Here the words are too compre-

---

[b] 'I agree with Lord Tenterden, that the want of a satisfactory reason is not a sufficient ground for overturning a practice long established,' says a Judge, on whose wisdom, love of justice, candour and fairness, it is unnecessary to pronounce an opinion, in Mirehouse *v.* Rennell, 7 BINGHAM, 537 ; Hall *v.* Smith, 2 VESEY, Jun., 427.

Lord Mansfield, however, says : 'It is argued, and rightly, that notwithstanding it is not prohibited by any positive law, nor adjudged illegal by any precedents, it may be decided to be so upon principles, and the law of England would be a strange science indeed (!) if it were decided upon precedents only. Precedents serve to illustrate principles, and to give them a fixed certainty ; but the law of England which is exclusive of positive law enacted by statute depends on principles (alas !).' COWPER, 39.   On the contrary, Best, C.J., said, unhappily with more truth, after the overthrow of all Lord Mansfield had done— 'Judgments of Westminster Hall are the only authority we have for by far the greatest part of the law of England.' 3 BINGHAM, 588 ; Hincksman *v.* Smith, 3 RUSSELL, 435.

[c] R. *v.* Manchester Water Works, 1 B. and C., 680 ; 'Hereditaments' applied in a limited sense ; R. *v.* Mosley, 2 B. and C., 226.

Though the words be general, they are to be reduced to a particularity by exposition made according to the intent of the act.   Those statutes which comprehend all things in the letter the sages of the law have expounded, to extend, but to some things those which generally prohibit all people from doing such an act, they have interpreted to permit some persons to do it ; and those which include every person in the letter, they have adjudged to reach some persons only, all founded upon the intent collected by considering the cause and necessity of the act, and comparing one part with another, and sometimes by foreign circumstances.' Eyston *v.* Studd, PLOWDEN, 621 ; DWARRIS *on Statutes,* p. 621, 2nd ed. ; BACON, *Reg.* 10.

hensive. On the other hand, suppose the legislator has used words confined to particular places, times, and persons, and it is clear that he must have intended to comprehend others who are not mentioned—or to say that to them a contrary rule must be applied. Here the words are too narrow. Let us take each of them in their order; and first, let us take the case where the words are too wide for the manifest intention. Here there is a certain rule—the meaning of the legislator is never to be stretched, the words are never to prevail over the meaning, but the meaning is always to limit the words. To none of those things, causes, or persons, to whom the legislator did not intend that his words should apply, are they to be extended. This is the restrictive interpretation.[d] Now there are according to the most eminent jurists, four things, from which we may infer that a restrictive interpretation ought to be used. We may be guided to this result by considering—

First. Other portions of the law to be interpreted;

Secondly. The object of the law;

Thirdly. The principles of equity;

Fourthly. Other laws.

All these are elements which are to be considered, sifted, and examined, to enable us to arrive at the meaning and spirit of the law.

---

[d] Zouch v. Stowell, PLOWDEN, 385 ; Martin v. Ford, 5 *Term Rep.*, 501 ; Eyston v. Studd, *Ibid.*, 465 ; Proctor v. Mainwaring, 3 B. and ALD., 115 ; Henderson v. Sherborn, 2 M. and W., 236 ; Fletcher v. Calthrop, 6 Q. B., 887 ; Murray v. Reg., 7, 2 B., 707 : United States v. Wittberger, 5 WHEATON's *Reps.*, 96 : Ash v. Abdy, 2 SWANSTON's *Reps.*, p. 664 ; 'Acts which restrain the Common Law, ought themselves to be restrained by exposition.'—LORD NOTTINGHAM ; Ex parte Clayton, 1 R. and M., 372 ; Rex. v. Hall, 1 B. and C., 237 ; Rex. v. Wallis, 5 *T. Reps.*, 375 ; 2 *Inst.*, 301 ; PLOWDEN, 365, Stowell v. Zouch ; Case of Leases, 5 *Reps.*, 6 ; 11 *Reps.*, 34 ; 10 *Reps.*, 105 ; 'Enumeration weakens in cases, not enumerated.'—BACON. Mention of coal mines, 43 Eliz. c. 2, excludes other mines. R, v. Manchester Water Works, 2 B. and C., 680 ; R. v. Mosely, 2 B. and C., 226 ; 'Equity must take place in the exposition of statutes,' HOBART, C.J., JONES, 39 ; 'e contra,' see the narrow construction, Robinson v. Allsop, 5 B. and ALD., 142 ; KENT's *Commentaries*, vol. i., 450.

Now we arrive at this result,[e] from a comparison of the clause to be interpreted with Other Portions of the same law, when that which is stated as if for the sake of argument, in one part of the law, is when the precise question at issue is to be determined altogether or partially denied.

So in the ' Senatusconsultum de petitione hæreditatis,' it was ordained that the bonâ fide possessor should restore the price of the inheritance which he had received. By another clause, it was provided that he should only pay so much as he had added thereby to his estate—' quatenus locupletior factus est.' ' Puto sequentem clausulam sequendam etsi prior generalis et ambigua est.'—ULPIAN.

Hence the doctrine, that the whole law ought to be considered before any part of it is interpreted: ' Incivile est nisi totâ lege perspectâ unâ aliquâ particulâ ejus propositâ judicare vel respondere.' ' Incivile,' that is, ' iniquum,' and ' contra jus.'

Secondly. We come to the Object of the Law[f] which is the

---

[e] ' A person ought not to think if he have the letter on his side, that he hath the law in all cases on his side ; words are only verberations of the air.'—PLOWDEN, *ubi supra*.

Instances of narrow decisions, 14 Geo. II. c. 1, 15 Geo. II. c. 34, 3 BINGHAM, 581 ; Salkeld *v.* Johnson, 1 HARE, 196 ; General terms in Stockjobbing Acts restrained, Henderson *v.* Bix, 3 STARKIE, 158 ; Wells *v.* Porter, 3 B., Q.C., 722 ; Elsworth *v.* Cole, 2 M. and W., 31.

[f] COMYN's *Digest*, tit. *Parl.* ; 'Every statute ought to be expounded, not according to the letter but according to the intent,' PL. c. x.

' The end of the statute ought to be considered.' 3 M. and S., 510 ; 2 *T. Reps.*, 161.

' A case out of the mischief shall be judged out of the Purview, though within the letter.' 2 *Inst.*, 386.

' Such exposition of the statute ought to be favoured or prevent it from being eluded.' 2 ROLL., 1. 27.

3 Wm. IV., c. 15, Remedy confined to cases where debt lies. 7 EAST, Wilson *v.* Knubley, 134.

' Where the not restraining the enacting part by the preamble will be attended with inconvenience, the preamble shall restrain it.'—BACON's *Abridg.*, vol. vii.

7 B. and C., 660 ; ' The reason and spirit of cases make law, not the language of particular precedents.'—3 BURROW, 1364.

surest guide to its spirit and intention—that to effect which the law was passed, and without which it would not have passed—that in short, which in enacting the law, it was the purpose of the legislator to accomplish.

Hence, if that purpose was not so wide as the words employed, it follows that a restrictive interpretation must be used and that the words must be qualified and limited. For instance, the Ædilitian edict required that the seller of a slave or an animal to specify the vices, or diseases, or defects of what they sold; and if they did not, an action 'ad redhibendum' lay against them. But this action did not lie against the seller of a blind or lame horse for his silence. The words of the edict were general; but the object for which it was promulgated was, to prevent frauds on buyers. But if the vice or defect of the thing purchased was patent, it could not be said that the buyer was imposed upon (*Dig.* vi. 1. 6, c. 2). So by the 'senatusconsultum Velleianum,' no woman could be responsible for another person. But it was held that this law did not apply to the case of a woman who had deceived the creditor, by assuring him that the transaction was her own (*Dig.* xvi. 7. 8, § 3,).

Hence the rule, that a law established for the benefit or protection of a particular class is not to be interpreted against them. It may often happen that the words admit such a construction; but the principle of the law forbids it. So the prætor declared, that ' pacta dolo malo facto facta' were not to be enforced; but if the party defrauded held the deceiver to his bargain—though the words of the edict were clear and unqualified—it was agreed that he might enforce the compact, since the rule was established not for the deceiver but for the deceived. So an action could not be brought against a minor, ' sine tutore'; but if an action was so brought, and judgment was given in favour of the minor, the judgment was valid. ' Minoribus enim,' says the code, ' ætas in damnis subvenire non in rebus prospere gestis obesse consuevit.'[a]

---

[a] 14 *de Procur.*

I come to the third head—the Principles of Equity; that is, where manifest injustice would be the consequence of a literal interpretation, or of an interpretation comprehending as much as the words used might include. Such cases are taken out of the law, against its words, but in conformity with its intention. This proceeding is sanctioned by two passages in the Digest:—

' In omnibus quidem maxime tamen in jure æquitas spectanda est;'[b] and

' Benignius leges interpretandæ sunt quo earum voluntas conservetur.'[c]

For instance, the senatusconsultum (*De Hæred. Pet.*) required the possessor, ' hæredes,' after judgment given against him, to restore every thing of which he had taken possession, ' quasi et nunc possideret.'[d] Thus if, in the course of the suit, the cattle or flocks had perished by some inevitable accident, he would be bound, if the law was strictly taken, to replace them. But this, says Paulus, shall not be, although against ' verba divi Hadriani,' simply because it would be inequitable, that is, unjust: ' Nec enim debet possessor aut mortalitatem præstare aut propter metum hujus periculi temere indefensum jus suum relinquere.'[e]

So it was the law that if the debtor delayed to give to his creditor the thing he was bound to deliver, and after the proper time had elapsed for its delivery the thing perished, the loss fell upon the debtor. Now, according to the strict interpretation of this law, if the debtor had failed the thing due at the proper time, and then offered it to the creditor, who refused unreasonably to accept it, and afterwards the thing perished, the loss should fall upon the debtor. This consequence, however, was denied by Celsus, on account of its hardship. He says that the original fault was extinguished.[f] His words are worth quoting as they lay especial stress on

---

b *De Reg. Juris,* 90.   c *De L. L.,* 18.
d *De Hæred. Pet.* xxv. 5. 7, § 40.   e VINER's *Ab.,* tit. *Stat.,* p. 523.
f *Dig.* xlv. 1. *de Verb. Ob.,* 91, § 3; ii. 4. 11. *de in Jus Vocando.*

the principles of equity, so it is said. ' Jus simpliciter scriptum est sed ex causâ moderandum—ex magnâ et idoneâ causâ aliud servandum.'[g]

Lastly we come to the consideration of Other Laws, in which the legislator has declared his views on the same subject matter. Not only are former laws modified by later, but later laws are modified and interpreted with a view to earlier.[h] So much of the former as is not repealed by the later law indicates the intention of the legislator to qualify and restrain the latter. By making new enactments an exception to the former ones, the legislator sufficiently declares his wish that where the exception does not apply the former enactment should prevail. This is laid down in the *Digest* viii. 1. 3. § 26. 27. 28.[i]

This shews that the construction of later may be narrowed by the meaning of former laws; otherwise, to what purpose would it be to institute a comparison between them. It is manifest that the object of this comparison is that they shall be embodied into a single law. Here we apply the rules ' in toto jure per speciem generi derogatur,' and ' id potissimum habetur quod ad speciem directum est.'[k]

---

[g] GAIUS, *qui et a quibus manumittuntur*, § 12.

[h] 2 *Inst.*, 200; 1 *Inst.*, 111, 115. Statute made in the affirmative does not take away the common law.—COKE, *Litt.*, 115.

43 Ed. III., c. 11 : 'The panel of assize shall be arrayed four days before the day of assize : two days are good, because they were sufficient at the common law.'

Statute of Marlbridge, 2 *Westminster*, § 39 : 'After complaint made to the sheriff, he may take the posse comitatus, and make replevin. . . . Notwithstanding this, the sheriff may take the posse comitatus to serve any process with, as he could before.'

Enumeration weakens in cases not enumerated.

[i] R. *v.* Loxdale, 1 BURROW, 447; BACON, *Ab.*, tit. *Statute*, 1, 3; Gale *v.* Lawrie, 5 B. and C., 162.

[k] *De B. S.*, 181 ; *De Reg. J.*, 80 ; Morris *v.* Mellin, 6 BAB., 446.

Statutes in ' Pari materiâ ' are to be construed as one law. DOUGLAS, 30 ; 1 *T. Reports*, 53 ; 3 *T. Reports*, 135. 18 Eliz., c. 11, recites only 14 Eliz., c. 11, held to include 13 Eliz. 10, which the last enlarges. B. *Ab.* 455.

General words do not take away a particular privilege or benefit.

If then the first law is general, and the law contains exceptions to its enactment, it is apparent that the class excepted is taken out of the operation of the first law, and also that which is not excepted continues subject to its enactments. If, on the contrary, the first deals with certain particular classes, and the words of the second law are general, it must be taken as a general rule that it was the intention of the legislator to leave the first law as it stood—that the specific cases it contains are exceptions to the general rule promulgated afterwards. The last ought to be read as if it contained the first. (*Dig.* xlviii. 12. 41, PAPINIAN, *de Pœnis*). In short, it is only in the case where the latter law altogether contradicts the former that the former is altogether abrogated.

That the law means a wider signification to be given to its expressions than the words literally taken would impute may be inferred from four circumstances:—[1]

W. II., c. 18, gives an ' elegit,' but does not take away the privilege an infant has that he shall not be sued during his nonage, if an ' elegit ' be against the heir of a common, being an infant. 2 *Inst.*, 395.

Remedies given by statute are cumulative. 1 *T. Reports*, 103 ; 7 *T. Reports*, 620. Affirmative statutes do not take away a prior exemption. DOUGLAS, 188 ; BARNARDISTON, *Ch. Reports*, 276 ; Wallis *v.* Hodson ; 22 and 23 C. II., c. 10, to be construed with 1 J. II., c. 17.

[1] Lord Abinger says, ' I never doubted that Lord Coke was right when he says of the statute, *West.* 2, ' Here be five kinds of improvements, and these five kinds be put for examples ; and besides these enumerated there may be others.' Patrick *v.* Stubbs, 9 M. and W. 830.

' Sometimes,' says Lord Coke, ' makers of a statute put the strongest case, and by construction the lesser shall be included.'—*Statute of Gloucester*, c. 11 ; COKE, 2 *Inst.*, 25, 84 ; Reniger *v.* Fogassa, PLOWDEN, 13 ; Simpson *v.* Unwin, 3 B. and AL., 143 ; R. *v.* Upper Papworth, 2 EAST, 413—'tried' means ' preferred '; R. *v.* Pembridge, 2 *L. J.*, 1842 ; Thompson *v.* Gibson, 8 M. and W., 228—'immediately'; Winter *v.* Winter, 5 HARE ; Rule of Cyprès, in a ' casus omissus ;' Smith *v.* Wedderburne, *L. J. Ex.*, vol. xvi. p. 14.

9 Rich. II.. c. 3, gives a writ of error to him in reversion, held to include remainder-man. Winchester's Case, 3 *Reports*, 4 : ' Circumspecte agatis,' names only the Bishop of Norwich, but extends to all bishops. Platt's Case, PLOWDEN 36, 9 Ed. III., c. 3, against executors, has always been extended to administrators. Statute giving action of waste against tenant for life or years, held to include tenant for half-a-

1st. From a comparison with different parts of the same law.

2ndly. ' Ex contrariis.'

3rdly. ' Ex consequentibus.'

4thly. From the wider object of the law.

1st. From the comparison with other portions of the same law of which an example may be found (*Dig.* xxiii. 1. 9, § 5).

2nd. ' Ex contrariis' in this manner: if the law makes a specific provision in one class of circumstances, it must be supposed in opposite circumstances to intend the reverse. The Julian Law, ' de vi,' provided, for instance, that a person entrusted with the functions of judge on public questions might, if he travelled, delegate his functions. Hence, it must be understood that if he staid in the province where they were to be exercised the privilege did not exist (*Dig.* i. 21, § 1). On this ground is supported the rule 'Cum lex in præteritum aliquid indulget in futurum vetat.' ' Indulgentia' says Antonius Faber, ' ad ea tantum pertinet quæ prohibita vult legislator nisi quatenus indulget.   Ergo indulgentia restricta ad tempus præteritum includit tacitam prohibitionem in futurum.'[m]   Such laws, as they are retroactive, must be fortunately for civilization uncommon, for the province of the law is the future and not

---

year.   Eyston *v.* Studd, PLOWDEN, 467; Chudleigh's Case, 1 *Reports,* 131 ; Wembish *v.* Tallboys, PLOWDEN, 59; Doe *v.* Routledge, COWPER, 712.   ' Equity says, if the party knew of the unregistered deed, his registered deed shall not set it aside ; because he had that notice which the act of Parliament intended he should have.'   Nash *v.* Allen, 4 *Q. B. R.,* 784; Copeman *v.* Gallant, 1 *P. W.,* 320 ; R. *v.* Pierce, 3 M. and S., 66.

[m] 3 *T. Reports,* 442 ; R. *v.* Cunningham, 5 EAST, 478 ; 2 *Inst.* 256 ; *Stat. West.* 1, c. 46': extracts to others become declaratory of the common law.

3 ATKYNS, 203, Basset *v.* Basset ; 10 and 11 Wm. III., c. 16, enabling posthumous children to take : 'If the enacting words can take it in, they shall be extended for that purpose, though the preamble does not warrant it ; and innumerable instances of this kind are in the books.' Dean and Chapter of York, *v.* Middleburgh, 2 YOUNG and JARVIS, 215 ; 13 Eliz. c.10, § 3 ; Doe dem Robinson *v.* Allsop, 5 B. and ALD., 142 ; DWARRIS, *On Statutes,* p. 574.

the past. But in another sense, such laws are not uncommon: for instance, the Julian gave the right of prosecuting an adulterer for five years after the offence. Thus it prohibited such an accusation after that time. The law continues the 'restitutio in integrum' for minors during four years after they have attained majority. Therefore, it withholds the right after that period. The same may be said of our statutes, which require that penalties should be sued for, or a prosecution instituted, within a certain period after the commission of the offence.[n]

3rdly. The meaning of the law is extended 'ex consequentibus'; when what the law prohibits will happen, if certain things are done, it must be taken that the legislator who forbids the end forbids the means—that the prohibition of the consequence implies the prohibition of its antecedents. Therefore, it was established as a rule of Roman jurisprudence, that he violated the law who transgressed its meaning, though he kept within its letter: 'Contra legem facit qui id facit quod lex prohibet—in fraudem vero legis qui salvis verbis legis, sententiam ejus circumvenit.' The Canon law, with its usual sagacity, has laid it down: 'Cum quid unâ viâ prohibetur alicui ad id eum non debere aliâ admitti.' The Ælian law prohibited the emancipation of slaves by minors, except with certain sanctions. The minor gave his slave to a person, by whom the slave was emancipated; this was held a fraud upon

---

[n] 2 *Inst.*, 572 ; 2 *Inst.*, 394, c. 40, on *Stat. West.* 2, c. 18 : 'Sheriff' is applied to every other officer of a court of record. Gale *v.* Lawrie, 5 B. and C., 162 ; Forster's Case, 11 *Reports*, 78. 'No statute law,' says C. J. Hobart, 'shall exclude all equity.' Dean and Chapter of Norwich, 3 *Reports*, 75 ; BACON, *Reg.*, 10 ; Case of Leases, 5 *Reports*, 6 ; Perry *v.* Skinner, 2 M. and W., 472 ; 7 B. and C., 643, Doe *v.* Brandling : 'It is our duty to give effect to larger expressions,' etc.—LORD TENTERDEN. Forth *v.* Chapman, 1 PEERE WILLIAMS, 667 ; recognised, 2 VESEY Sen., 611 : Green *v.* Wood, 7 *Q. B. Reports*, 178 ; Simpson *v.* Unwin, 3 B. and ALD. 134 : 'Although this case be within the literal meaning of the words taken by themselves, we must not give them a construction which will not only be contrary to the general intention of the legislature, but lead to this absurd consequence,' etc.

the law, and, therefore, the emancipation was of no avail (*Dig.* xl. 9. 7, § 1).[a]

The law forbad donations between husband and wife. The husband gave the donation intended for his wife to Titius, that he might give to her: it was held that the gift was invalid.

The senatusconsultum Macedonianum forbad loans of money to young heirs. Instead of money, the creditor had given goods, which the heir was to sell: it was held a fraud on the senatusconsultum, because that was done which it was the object of the senatusconsultum to prevent. It was held the same thing as if the money had been placed at once and directly in his hands (*Dig.* xiv. 6. 7, § 3, ' mutui,' etc.).

4thly. The ' ratio legis ' justifies an interpretation beyond the letter, on the same grounds that it justifies a limited one.[b]

---

[a] Kinaston *v.* Clarke, 2 ATKINS' *Reports*, 205. Many cases, where the enacting part of a statute extends farther than the preamble, as in 33 Hen. VIII. c. 23, for trying treasons and murders where the words, ' within the king's dominion,' have been extended to the West Indies, and persons have been tried and executed under it. Decision, which overthrew the Statute of Uses. 3 M. and S., 66. Roe *v.* Pierce, 1 B. and C., 660. Doe dem Bywater *v.* Brandling. Preamble enlarged, 32 Hen. VIII. c. 37. BACON'S *Abridgment, Rent*, 48.

Wembish *v.* Tallboys, PLOWDEN, 59. Ratcliffe's Case, 3 *Reports*, 39. Eyston *v.* Studd, PLOWDEN : ' When the words of a statute enact one thing, they enact whatever is in the same degree.' Hool *v.* Bell, LORD RAYMOND, 172. BACON'S *Abridgment, Rent*, vol. vii. p. 48. 8 Anne, c. 14.

' It is a rule in the construction of statutes, that all which relate to the same subject, notwithstanding some of them have expired, or are not referred to, must be taken to be one system.' Rex *v.* Loxdale, 1 BURR., 447, Lord Mansfield. BACON'S *Abridgment*, tit. *Statutes*. So the 13 Eliz. c. 10, though unmentioned in it, was held to be comprised in 18 Eliz. c. 11. Bailey *v.* Hart, 1 VENT., 244. The first Statute of Distributions was held to be recited in the second (1 James II. c. 17) by Lord Hardwicke, Wallis *v.* Hodson, BARN. *Chan. Reports*, 276.

[b] Every statute ought to be construed according to the intent of Parliament ; and, therefore, if a corporation be misnamed, if it appears that it was intended, it is sufficient, 10 c. 57 b COMYN'S *Dig.*, tit. *Parl. R.* 10 b.

2 *Instit.* 256. *Stat. West.* i. c. 46. The King's Bench only mentioned, but the provision extends to other Courts. ' Every statute ought to be expounded, not according to the letter, but the intent.'—COMYN'S *Dig.*

The meaning of the law is the law. So we are told: 'Cum lege certi aliqui casus comprehensi sunt si in aliquâ causâ sententia eorum manifesta est ea ad similia produci et secundum hoc in his jus dici debet' (*De Legibus non possunt*). So, again: 'In casibus et rebus omissis verba cessant, sed sententia eo porrigenda est' (*De Jurisd.*, π. *si id.*). So, again: 'Verba deficiunt sed lex plenius interpretanda ut suppleatur quod legi deest' (*De fundis dot. Lex Julia*, π.). That the meaning of the law is to govern its interpretation all will, I suppose, agree. But how is this meaning to be ascertained? From its reason? 'Valeat æquitas,' says Cicero, 'quæ paribus in causis paria jura desiderat' (*Dig.* ix. 2. 32, Gaius).

So the rule established against the possessor who wrongfully, *i.e.*, 'mente prædonis,' took possession of a patrimony, applies to him who, having on justifiable grounds taken possession, and afterwards becoming conscious that he had no title, remained in possession nevertheless (*sed etsi de eo, L.: de pet. hæred. Dig.*).[c] So when one thing or one person is mentioned, it is to be understood as an example, and to apply to all things and persons of a similar class (π. 5. 3. 20. 17; π. 43. 16. 25). 'Quod vulgo dicitur æstivorum hibernorumque saltuum possessionem nos animo retinere, id exempli causâ didici Proculum dicere nam ex omnibus prædiis ex quibus non hâc mente recedimus ut omisisse possessionem velimus idem est.' 'Licet municipum mentio in hâc persona fiet tamen et in quâlibet personâ idem

---

ubi supra. 13 Ed. I. 'Circumspecte agatis' names only the Bishop of Norwich, but extends to all bishops. Platt's Case, PLOWDEN, 36. 1 Rich. II. c. 12, names the warden of the Fleet only, but the rule extends to all gaolers. Uses taken in the Equity of the Statute, etc., DOMIN, 1 *Reports*, 88. Chudleigh's Case, 1 *Reports*, 131. Remedy given (9 Ed. III. c. 3) against executors extends to administrators.

[c] 'When the end of the act is wider than the meaning of the words.' VAUGHAN, 179. HEB., 298. Copeman *v.* Gallant, LORD C. COWPER. 1 P. W., 320. R. *v.* Pierce, *cit.* Doe *v.* Bundling, *cit.* Bellaris *v.* Burbrych, 1 ROY. *Reports.* Mason *v.* Armitage, 13 VESEY, 36.

'A statute may be repealed by express words, or by implication. So if a subsequent statute, contrary to the former, has negative words, it shall be a repeal of the former.'—COMYN's *Dig. Parl. R.* 9 a.

observabitur' (*Dig.* xxi. 1. 9. 5). So, it is said, the word 'si quis' includes women as well as men (*De Verb. Sign.*, π. *de neg. gestis* iii. 5. 3. 1).

All that has been said with reference to a liberal interpretation relates exclusively to the 'jus commune,' or the law which applied generally, and not to the 'jus singulare,' or exceptional law, which had been introduced for the protection of particular persons, or to guard against a special inconvenience. Such, for instance, were the 'restitutiones in integrum' of minors; the 'senatusconsultum Velleianum,' by which the responsibility of women was taken away; the 'senatusconsultum Macedonianum,' by which money lent to an heir could not be recovered.[d] So certain privileges were conferred on soldiers. With regard to all such cases, it is expressly laid down: 'Quod contra rationem juris receptum est non est producendum ad consequentias'; in other words, that the argument, from parity of reason, did not apply.[e] Take, for instance, the 'restitutio in integrum' of minors.[f] By this edict, if a minor had lost anything that he possessed, or failed to gain anything that he might have acquired, or contracted any obligation from which it was for his interest to be exonerated, he might be placed in the same condition as he was in before the event to his disadvantage had taken place (*Dig.* iv. 5. 44).[g] The

---

[d] 'Quæ propter necessitatem recepta sunt non debent in argumentum trahi. Propter necessitatem recepta hic dicuntur quæ ad tempus constituta sunt et tempore commutato, mutantur et ipsa.'—122 *De Reg. Juris.*

'Multa jure civili contra rationem disputandi pro utilitate communi recepta esse innumerabilibus rebus probari potest. Unum interim proposuisse contentus ero. Cum plures trabem alienam furandi causâ sustulerint quam singuli ferre non possent—furti actione omnes teneri existimantur quamvis subtili ratione dici possit neminem earum teneri —quia neminem verum sit eam sustulisse.'—*Dig. Ad leg. Aquiliam,* 51.

[e] CUJACIUS, vol. iv. p. 725. τὸ κοινῶς λεγόμενον. 'Titulus omnis de regulis jure est de jure ordinario et summo non de extraordinario et mitiori.' SAVIGNY, *System,* vol. vii. p. 123. *Zeitschrift,* vol. x., § 232-297.

[f] 'Jus commune.'—*Dig.* xxviii. 6. 15 'Vulgatum.'—*Ibid,* xxi. 1. 32, § 24.

[g] On the general question of the construction of statutes, I may refer to the valuable treatise of DWARRIS, ed. 2; COMYN'S *Dig.,* tit.

reason of the edict is founded on the want of experience of such persons, and the dangers to which they would otherwise be exposed. The same reason, it is clear, would often apply to persons of full age; but it is not extended to such cases, because the privilege is 'contra rationem juris' (*Ibid.* xvi.).

The same limitation applies for the same reason to the 'senatusconsultum Velleianus.'

And here we may observe the illustration of the maxim so often misapplied, that the exception proves the rule. The very exception of minors and women from the law shows the will of the legislator that it should be binding upon other classes of the community, and thus corroborates its efficacy. In the same category we may include the exoneration of certain persons from the office of guardian; the priority of particular classes of creditors; the law resting upon inveterate tradition, which forbad gifts between the husband and wife. Sometimes the exception is in favour of particular persons, then it is called 'beneficium'; sometimes it is adverse to them, of which instances may be found in the laws enacted against Jews and heretics by the Greek emperors.

ARGUMENT FROM ANALOGY.

'Semper hoc legibus inesse credi oportet ut ad eas quoque personas et ad eas res pertineant quæ quandoque similes erunt' (*Dig. de Legibus*).

Ibid. xxxii.: 'De quibus causis scriptis legibus non utimur id custodiri oportet quod moribus et consuetudine introductum est. Et si quâ in re hoc defecerit tunc quod proximum et consequens est.'

So the law, 'Qui servum alienum recepisse, persuasisseve quid ei dicetur dolo malo, quo eum deteriorem faceret, in eum quanti ea res erit in duplum judicium dabo' (1 *Dig.*, de servo corrupto'), was extended to the 'filiusfamilias' (*Ib. ut tantum*,

---

Parliament; VINER'S *Abridgment*, tit. *Statutes;* BACON'S *Abridgment*, tit. *Statute;* COKE, 2 *Instit.;* RAM'S *Science of Legal Judgments;* BROOM'S *Legal Maxims*.

§ 12): ' De filio filiâve familias corrupto huic edicto locus non est quia servi corrupti constituta hæc actio est, qui in patrimonio nostro esset et pauperiorem se factum esse dominus probare potest dignitate et famâ domus integrâ ei manente. Sed utilis competit officio judicis æstimanda quoniam interest nostra animum liberorum nostrorum non commissi.' So Julianus, arguing that inveterate custom is law, argues from the ' ratio legis,' ' cum ipsæ leges nullâ aliâ ex causâ nos teneant quam quia judicio populi receptæ sunt, merito et ea quæ sine scripto populus probavit tenebunt omnes—nam quid interest suffragio populus voluntatem suam declaret, non rebus ipsis et factis' (*De Legibus* xxx., *inveterata* π)?

Still more remarkable (*Ad Legem Aquiliam* 32): ' Illud quæsitum est an quod proconsul in facto observat quod a familiâ factum sit id est, ut non in singulos detur pœnæ persecutio, sed sufficiat id præstari quod præstandum foret, si id furtum unus liber fecisset, debeat et in actione damni injuriæ observari.   Sed magis visum est idem esse observandum et merito—cum enim circa furti actionem hoc idem sit, ne ex uno delicto totâ familiâ dominus careat.   Eaque ratio similiter et in actione damni injuriæ interveniat—sequitur ut idem debeat æstimari.'—*De Adulteriis*, l. ' si postulavit, 27, § ratio autem.' *De bonorum possess. ex testamento militis.   De edendo*, l. ' quædam, 9, § numularios.'   *De verborum obligationibus*, 108, a Titio. *Dig.*

' Quamquam tamen deficiat pluviæ arcendæ actio attamen opinos utilem actionem vel interdictum mihi competere adversus vicinum si velim aggerem restituere in agro ejus, qui factus mihi quidem prodesse potest ipsi vero nihil nociturus est hæc æquitas suggerit etsi jure deficiamur.'—*Dig.* xxxix. 3. 2, § 5.

We have hitherto been considering a case in which there is a difference between the words and meaning of the legislator —a difference obtruded upon us for the different reasons that have been mentioned.   But where no such reasons exist, it may happen that the words of the legislator are ambiguous and obscure.   Here the first rule is to keep to the letter of the law: ' In re dubiâ melius verbis edicti servire.'   It is not to be supposed that the legislator has said what he does not mean (*Dig.* xxxiii. 10. 7, *de supell. leg*). It is clear that the legislator or testator, using ambiguous words, annexes a particular signification to them; and in order to ascertain his meaning, certain rules have been laid down by the Roman jurists, which I propose to enumerate: 'Differentia autem est inter obscurum et ambiguum. Obscurum quod nullam interpretationem facile recipit seu quod perspicuum sensum habet nullum. Ambiguum quod duas aut plures facile recipit—obscure loquitur qui quid senserit ambigue qui utrum senserit dubitatur' (CUJACIUS, *Lex de Pactis,* xxxix.). The first rule is, that the proper sense is then only to be changed when it is manifest that it does not express the purpose of the writer: 'Non aliter a significatione verborum recedi oportet quam cum manifestum sit alium sensisse testatorem' (*Dig.* xxxii. 1. 69). The rule is of much more force when applied to legislation. An examination of a precedent, or a subsequent passage, often removes an apparent ambiguity: 'De bonis eorum, etc., sanguinem' (*Dig. de pet. hæred.* v. 3. 23, *Utrum*).[h]

If we can gain no light by this, we are next to consider whether one of these senses is not tainted with some error, and in that case, of course, to prefer the other: 'In ambiguâ voce legis ea potius accipienda est significatio quæ vitio caret. Præsertim cum etiam voluntas legis ex hoc colligi potest.' Such will be the case if the reading proposed makes the law altogether useless (*Dig.* xlix. 15. 19. 5, *de captivis*).

So a law enabled a testator to bequeath to his wife the donations he had made to her during the marriage. By the Roman law, however, such donations, ' inter vivos,' were altogether null. A testator leaves to his wife all his donations: does he mean to include the gifts made during the marriage,

---

[h] Doe dem Perrin *v.* White. Coles *v.* Hulme, 8 B. and C., 572. Word 'pounds' supplied. 10 *Modern,* 40. The word 'grantor' supplied in a bargain and sale to the words 'hath granted.' Subsidiary rules. STORY, *Conflict of Laws,* 226. 9 EAST, 101, in case R. *v.* Everdon. Bank of England *v.* Anderson. 'We should, by adopting such a meaning, guard against a danger which by no possibility could exist.'

which gifts were null, and, therefore, no gifts?[i]   Undoubtedly it shall be supposed that he does, as otherwise the bequest would be unmeaning (*Dig.* xxx. 1. 109).[j]   Hence the rule of law: ' Quoties idem sermo duas sententias accepit eam potissimum accipiendam quæ rei gerendæ aptior est' (*Dig.* xliii. 19. 3, § 4; *id.* 5, § 3).[k]

In the third place we must have recourse to custom,[l] and to the language of former laws.

Therefore, if in times past a particular construction has been put upon the law, unless it involve manifest injustice, we should abide by it, on the principle ' optima legum interpres consuetudo;' and it is so because it implies the tacit consent of those with whom the legislative authority resides.   After custom we have recourse to the language of former laws, and if they refer the signification to particular persons, or particular things, that signification should be preserved, since it is for the interest of the public that legal language should not vacillate, and that the particular meaning stamped on words by public authority should not be altered.   Hence the rule of the civilians (*Dig.* 27, *de Leg.*), ' Semper quasi hoc legibus inesse credi oportere, ut ad eas quoque personas et ad eas res pertineant quæ quandoque similes erunt.'   Certain privileges were given by the Roman law to the sons of consuls and decuriones.   Was he to be considered the son of a consul or of a decurio who was born of a father actually consul or decurio, or he whose father had obtained that situation; either construction is reasonable; and it is to usage, or to the language of former laws, that we must appeal for that by which the question will be determined.   After these guides we come to the general rules, ' in dubiis benigniora preferenda sunt.'   'In re dubiâ benigniorem

---

[i] '*Cod. De don. inter virum et uxorem*, 16. 25. 'Donationes quas parentes,' etc.

[j] Doe dem. Burdett *v.* Spilsbury, 10 CL. and F., 402.

[k] HOBBES, vol. iii. 254, 264, Ed. MOLESWORTH.

[l] ' A custom which has obtained the force of a law . . . being only matter of fact, and consisting in use and practice, it can be recorded and registered nowhere but in the memory of the people.'—SIR JOHN DAVY's *Reports*, Preface.

interpretationem sequi debemus.' 'Rapienda occasio est quæ præbeat benignius responsum;' and of this the answer given in the cases last proposed affords an illustration; for it was held on these grounds, not only that he was to be considered a decurio's son whose father afterwards obtained that dignity, but he whose father had ever held that office, although his crimes had afterwards forfeited it. That humane interpretation was adopted which rescued, as much as possible, the innocent members of a family from the disgrace which one among them had incurred; for, as Papinian said with equal wisdom and benevolence, *De servis export. Dig.* xviii. 7. 7: 'beneficio affici hominem, intersit hominis.'[a]

A person accused of 'vis' had been condemned by the præses of a province. There were two laws, the 'Lex Julia de vi publicâ,' and the 'Lex Julia de vi privatâ.' The former inflicting much severer penalties than the latter. The question was, which of the two (for the sentence of the magistrate had left the matter uncertain) should be applied; and it was decided, that the 'Lex Julia de vi privatâ' should be enforced, because the punishment it inflicted was less severe (*Dig. de Pœnis.* xlviii. 19. 32. 'Si Præses').

The French laws of different dates inflicted a certain penalty on persons exercising the medical profession without a certificate; a question arose as to the amount of the penalty, and it was held by the Cour de Cassation, that 'il suit sans doute du silence de la loi, que l'amende encourue doit être la plus faible des peines pécuniaires déterminées par le Code Pénal,' 761. If the judges were equally divided, the Romans held, without any distinction of civil or criminal cases, that the more humane opinion ought to prevail. 'Inter pares numero judices si dissonæ sententiæ proferantur in liberalibus quidem causis— pro libertate statutum obtinuit, in alium autem causis pro reo, quod et in judiciis publicis obtinere oportet. (*De re judicatâ, Dig.* xlii. 1. 38.)

By the ordonnance of 1670, art. 12, tit. 25, it was provided,

---

[a] 'Odia restringi favores convenit ampliari,' says the Canon law.— 15 *Tit. de regulis Juris.*

that unless the severer opinion prevailed by a majority of one, the milder opinion should be adopted: ' les jugements passeront à l'avis le plus doux si l'autre ne prévaut d'une voix dans les procès qui se jugeront à la charge de l'appel et de deux en ceux qui se jugeront en dernier ressort.'ᵃ

USAGE.

WRITTEN LAW CAN NEVER BE A SUBSTITUTE FOR USAGE.

MORIBUS inter nos receptum est ne inter virum et uxorem, donatio valeret (*Dig. de Donationibus,* xxxix. 5).

So if my money be lent in your name to a third person, the right of action is with you, and the reason is founded on custom.

' Cum quotidie credituri pecuniam ab alio poscamus, ut nostro nomine creditor numeret futuro debitori nostro' (*Dig.* xiii. 3, *Si certum petatur* 9, § *si nummos*). So the word 'Rome' included the suburbs. ' Romam non muro tenus existimari ex consuetudine quotidianâ posse intelligi, cum diceremus. Romam nos ire etiamsi extra urbem habitaremus, (π. *de verb.sign.* 87.— ALFENUS). So the right is proved by law, ' Quæ interpretationem certam semper habuerunt.' If, for instance, the clause was omitted in the sale of a slave, which contained the penalty of restoring double the price, if he should be vicious or diseased or should run away, it was considered as if inserted because general usage had established it. ' Quia assidua est duplæ stipulatio idcirco placuit etiam ex empto agi posse si duplum venditor mancipii non caveat ea enim quæ sunt moris et consuetudinis in bonæ fidei judiciis, debent venire' (*Dig. Ædilitio edicto,* 1. 31, § 20).ᵇ

ᵃ PLINY, book viii. 14.—*a.* death ; *b.* banishment ; *c.* acquittal.

In the law, *Dig.* iv. 8. 27, § 3 ; 15. aurei ; 10. aurei ; 5. aurei. So, 'inter pares,' *Dig.* xlii. 1. 38, § 1 ; 'de re jud.' ' Si extribus 1. de arbitris in sexto, i. 22. 1.

ᵇ So 'Ovibus legatis non continentur agni quamdiu autem agnorum, loco sint ex usu cujusque loci sumendum est, nam in quibusdam locis

There is a difference between custom and prescription—prescription is acquired by the act of many, custom by that of all: custom is the right of all; prescription, of an individual. The proofs which establish prescription are, acquiescence after knowledge—in the part of persons interested—' bona fides' and title. It confers a right only on him who can establish it. Custom, on the other hand, springs from a series of uniform acts, and becomes a rule for those who have not contributed to establish it. It overrules and modifies the law; it binds those to whom it is unknown, and makes a law for all alike. D'Argentre, the writer on the custom of Bretagne, compares custom to a fountain in the market-place, whence every one may draw the water he requires; and prescription, to a spring on the estate of a private man, to which none but those who have acquired a right to it by possession can have recourse.[b]

Custom binds because it implies the assent of those who have the power to make the law. This assent can only be proved by facts; and it has been laid down that these facts must unite these six qualities. They must be—

> Uniform,
> Public,
> Multiplied,
> Observed by the people,
> Spread over a long space of time,
> Acquiesced in by the legislature.

(*Dig. de legibus*, xxxvii. xxxviii. 38. 32, § 1, *Tacito consensu*).

D'Aguesseau (xxvi. 1736), says all laws are liable to fall into desuetude, and when this is the case, no argument can be

---

ovium numero esse videntur cum ad tonsuram venerint.' *Dig.* xxxii. 63, § *fin.* 'Flumen a rivo magnitudine discernendum est aut existimatione circumcolentium.'—ii. *de flum.* 1, § 1. 'Non mirum est moribus civitatis et usu rerum appellationem supellectilis mutatam esse.'—*Dig. de sup. leg.* 7.

[b] Law of the Particular Place. 'Quod in regione in quâ actum est frequentatur.'

'Ratio non scriptura.' 2 H. BL., 393 ; 9 AD. and ELLIS, Tyson *v.* Smith. 'Consuetudo ex certa causa rationabili usitata privata communem legem.'—*Coll. Litt.* 113 *a.* 3 BURROW 1692.

drawn from a law which has been tacitly abrogated by a custom opposite to it.[c]

As originally custom preceded law, in modern Europe law preceded custom. When the barbarians overran the Roman empire, they found the use of writing and written law among its inhabitants, and in imitation of the Romans they drew up their customs in writing, and formed them into codes. The miserable times which followed the reign of Charlemagne, and which ended in the complete supremacy of the feudal system, the invasions of the Normans, the internal wars, replunged the victorious nations into the gloom from which they were just emerging, and obliterated in France and Germany the memory of the Roman law, of their own written customs, and even of the capitularies. Customs grew up out of the broken traditions and shattered fragments of former law, which gradually established themselves.

As to the effect of precedent in the construction of statutes, it is singular enough, in a country where courts are established to administer justice not only on different but hostile principles, to hear judges gravely dwell on 'the great importance that there should be an uniformity of decision in the Courts of Westminster Hall (6 B and C, 533), as an excuse for the most servile adherence to the most mischievous precedents. In some cases we find judges condemning the case to which they adhere, and in others, praising the authority which they overrule. Gabay v. Lloyd, 3 B. and C., 698; the King v. Deptford, 13 EAST, 321; Fayle v. Bird, 6 B. and C., 931; Williams v. Germaine, 7 B. and C., 468; Townley v. Beddell, 14 VESEY, 591; Gee v. Pritchard, 2 SWANSTON, 414; are instances of the first of these propositions;—Aldrich v. Cooper, 8 VESEY, 390; Wallroyn v. Lee, 9 VESEY, 34; 'ex parte' Young, 2 VESEY and BEAMES, 245; 'ex parte' Harrison, 2 ROSE, 78; are examples of the second. Sometimes we are told that the doctrine must be upheld, though it is 'not founded in good

---

[c] 634 *Coutume de Bret.* False coiners first boiled then hanged.— D'AGUESSEAU, 2 Sess., 1742.

sense,' not 'bottomed on reason.' 'A shocking decision' (the word was never better applied), says the judge in Morgan *v.* Surman, 1 TAUNTON, 292, 'has produced considerable mischief;' 'ex parte' Hooper, Lord Eldon says, 19 VESEY, 477, 'is an extraordinary case;' Brummell *v.* Macpherson, 14 VESEY, 174; and 'never ought to have been established,' MERIVALE 9, though the series of cases on which it rests were recently decided, though 'one would wish that such a rule had never been adopted,' or though the 'Court's private opinion is the other way,' that 'Stare decisis is a first principle in the administration of justice,' that 'the errors of great judges should be adhered to,' that the 'Court may regret but cannot overthrow;' that 'though the whole doctrine has arisen by contrivance of courts of law [these are the words of Tindal, C. J., 7 BINGHAM, 443], rather than on the language of Acts of Parliament, it is too late to alter it.' Sometimes we are told on the contrary, and often by the lips of the same judge, 'that the case decided has no weight with me,' 'that the case referred to *had had* its day, and it was time it should cease,' (Lord Ellenborough, Kightly *v.* Birch, 2 M. and SELW., 533); that the judge 'feels it his duty to understand a case before he confirms it,' and that 'it cannot be supported on point of principle;' that 'if a judgment be decided on a mistaken view of the law, it is our duty to decide contrary to it;' 'that the Court ought to have come to a contrary conclusion;' 'that the decision outrages all reason;' 'that the Court has not adopted the true construction, nor one warranted by the ordinary rules of construction.' There are the two sets of phrases which a judge may adopt, as he judges it meet, to overrule or to uphold the absurdities of past ages. And then it is gravely said that the objection to a code is its uncertainty.[d] 'Certainty is the mother of repose, and therefore the

---

[d] RAM, *Science of Legal Judgment,* 116, *etc.*; DWARRIS, *On Statutes,* 550, *etc.*; BROOM, *Legal Maxims,* 110; WILLES, *Reports,* Topner de Peckham *v.* Merlott, 182; Welles *v.* Trahern, 240. Williams *v.* Bosanquet overrules Eaton *v.* Jaques, DOUGLAS, 438; 1 BROD. and B. 238; The King *v.* Brewers' Company, cited 3 B. and ALD, 172, overrules R. *v.* Bennett, 2 *T'*

law aims at certainty,' said Lord Hardwicke.[e] How far it has succeeded let the pages of MEESON and WELSBY, and of VESEY tell.

What is called with us unwritten, or common, or customary law,[f] is, in truth, to be collected from a vast and increasing

Reports, 197; Lewis *v.* Sapio, 1 M. and M., overrules Powell *v.* Ford, 2 STARKIE,164; Binnington *v.* Wallis, 4 B. and ALD., overrules 3 M. and SEL., 463. Other cases on this subject are : Lees *v.* Somergill, 17 VESEY, 508, overruled by Emanuel *v.* Constable, 3 RUSSELL, 436 ; Milner *v.* Horton M'CLEL., 647 ; Smith *v.* Compton, 3 BARN. and ADOL., 189, 199, 200 ; the King *v.* Rennett, 2 DURN and EAST, 197, overruled by the King *v.* the Brewers' Com., 3 BARN. and CR., 172, 4 DOWL. and RYL., 492, cited 3 BARN. and CRES., 175 ; Golding *v.* Dias, 10 EAST, 2 ; by Ricketts *v.* Lewis, 1 BARN. and ADOL., 197 ; Bishop *v.* Champtre, 1 DAVIS and IL., 83 ; by Jardine *v.* Payne, 1 BARN. and ADOL., 671 ; Milner *v.* Horton, M'CLEL., 647, by Smith *v.* Compton, 3 BARN. and ADOL., 189, 199, 200; Eaton *v.* Jaques, DOUGLAS, 439, ED. 1783, 455, 4 ED. ; by Williams *v.* Bosanquet, 1 BROD. and B. 238, 3 MOORE, 500 ; Dickenson *v.* Shaw, by Dyer *v.* Dyer, 2 Cox, 92 ; Strode *v.* Blackburn, 3 VESEY, 222, by Wallwyn *v.* Lee, 9 VESEY, 24 ; Doddington *v.* Hallett, 1 VESEY, 497, by 'ex parte' Young, 2 VESEY, and B., 242 ; 2 ROSE, 78 ; Lees *v.* Somergill, 17 VESEY, 508, by Emanuel *v.* Constable, 3 RUSSELL, 436 ; and in Bankruptcy 'ex parte' Ogilby *v.* Ogilvy, 3 VESEY and B., 133, 2 ROSE, 177, by 'ex parte' MOORE, 2 GLYNN and J. 166, cited ibid 315 ; Hankey *v.* Hammond, 1 COOKE BANK, L., 67, Ed. 78, by 'ex parte' Garland, 10 VESEY, 110, 1 SMITH, 220 ; and stated from Reg. B., 3 MADD., 148, in BUCK., 210. VAUGH, 383 ; HARDR., 52 ; WILLES, 182. 240; 2 BARN and ALD., 337; 2 Cox, 98 ; 8 VESEY, 388 ; 9 VESEY, 30, 34; 11 VESEY, 529, 530; 19 VESEY, 314 ; 2 CROMPT and M. 64. Most are cited, RAM, *ubi supra.*

[e] From the speech of Mr. Hakewill, *State Trials*, vol. ii., Bates's Case.

[f] The legislature has often been obliged to interfere in order to avert the evils of judicial legislation ; e. g. 1 Wm. IV. c. 40, on the undisposed of residue of testators ; and 1 Wm. IV. c. 46, on illusory appointments. The law of limited liability. The statute of frauds was 'pro tanto' repealed ; 1 B. C. C. 269 ; Russel *v.* Russel, as to which, see ex parte Comyng, 9 VESEY, 117 ; Edge *v.* Worthington, 1 Cox, 212. 'The statute of frauds must not be repealed by me, further than it has been repealed my predecessors,' ex parte Whitbread, 19 VESEY, 212 ; ex parte Kensington, 2 VESEY and BEAMES, 83. 'Stock,' says Lord Eldon, cited Franklin *v.* the Bank of England, 7 RUSSELL *Reports*, 589, 'cannot be given by will except with two witnesses, yet this Court often considers it given without witnesses.'

As to what Lord Kenyon calls, judges assisting to repeal an Act of Parliament (the upholding of which is their sworn duty), see Smith *v.*

number of written volumes. Fortescue said, that in his time they required the lucubrations of twenty years. Whether the life of an antediluvian patriarch would now suffice to attain a perfect knowledge of it, may perhaps be a question. All this is not really left to oral tradition, nor to the recollection of individuals; neither is there the plain text of a comprehensive ordinance, to which, in doubt, any man may have recourse, not indeed for minute and accurate knowledge, but for some outline of the existing law. The law not promulgated reposes in the breasts of the judges, who are its oracles and interpreters. In this circumstance, according to some, consists the superiority of the common law over written; one disadvantage seems indeed to belong to it, a disadvantage sometimes attended with rather serious consequences to the suitor, that it is inaccessible; nay, it seems even doubtful whether, before promulgation, it is always known that it is clearly and certainly known to the judges themselves;[b] for there are many cases in

---

Armourers' Company, 7 PEAKE, W. 192. Statute de Donis, Statute of Uses, Statute of Frauds, all set aside in part or altogether by the judges; sometimes, as in the case of common recoveries, by sanctioning an outrage on common sense and common probity; sometimes, as in the statute of uses, by miserable narrowness; sometimes, as in the last cases, by an evasion. As to illusory appointments, see the cases cited WHITE and TUDOR, *Leading Cases in Equity*, Aleyn *v.* Belchier, note p. 267.

[b] The extent to which judicial legislation has been carried among us is almost incredible. In the case of Tanner *v.* Smart, 6 B. and C. 604; the received law of a hundred years was overruled by Lord Tenterden: any one who reads that decision carefully, and refers to the authorities it enumerates, will judge of the security afforded to ordinary men by unwritten law, as the decisions of the judges are called. Judicial legislation, in such a case, is retrospective legislation, and retrospective legislation of a most mischievous kind. Nothing can be more important than to keep the functions of the judge, quite arduous and important and dignified enough, if fulfilled in a proper spirit and with a singleminded elevation of purpose, to satisfy the most generous ambition and to employ the most active industry, as separate as human affairs will allow from those of the legislator. Judges, when they put on their ermine, should say, in the language of the church, 'sursum corda'; and if they execute their high and holy duties with firmness and

which the law deposited in the bosom of one judge has differed from the law deposited in the bosom of another. I may mention as instances, the Braintree case, and the Bridgewater Peerage; the latter involving a question as simple as it was important, so simple that a variety of opinions would appear almost impossible, as there were no fine riddles to be read, no subtle analogies to be explained, nothing like an obscure point of law to be discovered; so important as immediately to affect the principles of the constitution; yet in this case, the law deposited in the bosoms of two equity, and the great majority of the common law judges, was not written in the same characters as the law deposited in the bosoms of two of the common law judges and those lawyers who had obtained the peerage. And this will appear less surprising to those who reflect that, though Numa had recourse to Egeria, and Sertorius to a Fawn, our judges, when a difficult case is brought before them, do not withdraw to consult some code of which they are the sole possessors, and from the instruction contained in which, they can reveal an unerring decision to those who call for their interference; it often happens that they call loudly for information. When the rule is once pronounced, the custom is fixed; it is sufficient, says Blackstone, that there be nothing in it flatly contradictory to reason, and then the law will be taken to be well founded. It is indeed true, that in some cases custom, when absurd, has been superseded; but it is also true, that customs quite unreasonable and indeed shocking to every idea of natural jurisprudence, have been allowed to remain part of our jurisprudence till swept away

---

simplicity, if they keep their ermine unsoiled by the stains (which, if carried about among coxcombs and demagogues, among the great vulgar, and the small, it will inevitably contract), though they die poor and technically unennobled, unknown to courts and courtiers, to fine ladies and fine gentlemen, their memories will live in the recollection of a grateful country, and though the prerogative is not strained to gratify their trivial vanity, they will transmit to their descendants, a name prouder than any which accident, or caprice, or party favour, can bestow.

by a special interference of the legislature, provoked by
so intolerable an evil. By the law of England, until the
legislature actually interfered to alter it, every statute, as I
have said, had a retrospective operation to the first day of
the session when it was passed; therefore, a man who did, in
March, an act perfectly lawful, might be punished for it by a
law passed in July; or a man who committed an offence in
March punishable by imprisonment, might be hanged for it by
a statute passed in August. I do not know that I could produce a stronger instance to shew that the words, 'perfection of
reason and common sense,' cannot always be applied to the
common law; and that lovely as it may be as a whole, there
are some specks and blemishes to be discovered in it.

GENERAL RULES FOR THE INTERPRETATION
OF CONTRACTS.

I.

UBI est verborum ambiguitas valet quod acti
est.

*Where words are ambiguous, that interpretation ought
to prevail which is most in conformity with the purpose of the parties.*[c]

---

[c] Locré, *Leg.* tom. xii. p. 336, etc., art. 1116; 'On doit dans les conventions rechercher quelle a été la commune intention des parties con-
tractantes plutôt que de s'arrêter au sens littéral des termes.'

Pordage *v.* Cole, 1 Wm. Saunders, 319, notes; Lloyd *v.* Lloyd,
2 Mylne and Craig, 202. To the intention, when discovered, all technical forms must give way. Stavers *v.* Curling, 3 B. and C. 368; Giles
v. Giles, 15 L. T. Q. B. 387; Macintosh *v.* Mid. C. R. C., 14 M. and W.,
548; Broom's *Legal Maxims,* p. 420; Noy, 50; Com. *Dig. Pleader* C.
25; Furze *v.* Sharwood, 2 Q. B. 415; Glahollen *v.* Hays, 2 Scott *N. Reports*; Ritchie *v.* Atkinson, 10 East, 306.

' In conventionibus, contrahentium voluntatem potius quam verba spectari placuit cum igitur eâ lege fundum vectigalem municipes locaverunt ut ad hæredum ejus qui suscepit pertineret—jus hæredum ad legatarium quoque transferri placuit.' PAPINIAN, *Dig. de Verb. Sign.* 219.[d]

In agreements, the intention of the parties rather than their words is to be considered. Therefore, when a corporation made a lease of land on condition that it should go to the heir of the tenant at his death, it was held that the right of the heir might be transferred to the legatee.

II.

IN emptis venditis potius id quod actum est quam id quod dictum sit sequendum est (*Dig., de Contract. Emptione,* 6, § 1).

In sales we are to consider, not so much what the parties said, as what it was their intention to do.

---

[d] ' If the parties have furnished a key to the meaning of the word used, it is not material by what expression they convey their intention.'—LORD COTTENHAM. 2 MYLNE and CRAIG, 202 ; BACON'S *Abrid. Grant T.*; FINCH *Law*, 58 ; SHEPH. *Touchstone*, 83, pl. 14 ; PLOWDEN, 154 ; 2 VENT. 278 ; Jackson *v.* Wilkinson, 17 JOHNSON'S *Reports*, 153 ; ADDISON, *On Contracts*, vol. ii., 959 ; Napier *v.* Bruce, 8 CL. and FINN., 470 ; HOBART, 275.

[e] ' Quand le contrat est clair il faut en respecter la lettre, s'il y a de l'obscurité et du doute, il faut opter pour ce qui paraît le plus conforme à l'intention des contractans, les parties dans lesquels cette intention n'est pas facile à découvrir, doivent être interprétées contre le vendeur, parcequ'il dépendait de lui d'exprimer plus clairement sa volonté.' —PORTALIS, vol. viii. ; LOCRÉ, *Leg.*, p. 158.

' Words shall have a reasonable intendment and construction.'— COMYN'S *Dig.* xxv. Parkhurst *v.* Smith, WILLES, 332 ; COKE, *Litt.*, 217 *b* ; 15 EAST, 541 ; 6 M. and SEL., 12 ; 1 *T. Reports*, 703 ; Doe *v.* Walker, 2 Sc., *N. R.*, 334 ; Robertson *v.* French, 7 EAST, 137 ; Doe *v.* Guest, 15 M. and W., 160.

' Where an averment admits of two intendments, that shall be preferred which will support the pleading.'—6 *T. Reports*, 134. ' The court will make any intendment *against* a mere captious objection.'—1 *T. Reports*, 117, sed v. MEESON and WELSBY — as to accuracy of word ' against ;' whether it should not rather be ' in favour of' ?

III.

QUOTIES in stipulationibus ambigua oratio est commodissimum est id accipi quo res de quâ agitur in tuto sit (*Dig. de Verb. Sign.* 80).

Whenever there is ambiguity in the words of a stipulation, it is best to adopt the sense which places the thing in question out of danger.

'Semper in dubiis id agendum est ut quam tutissimo loco res sit bonâ fide contracta nisi cum aperte contra leges scriptum est.'[b]

'Quoties idem sermo duas sententias accipit ea potissimum accipitur quæ rei gerendæ aptior sit.'[c]

'Semper in stipulationibus et in cæteris contractibus id sequimur quod actum est.[d] Si hoc non appareat, erit conse-

---

[b] Halliwell *v.* Morrell, 1 Scott, *N. R.*, 309; Hill *v.* Grange, 2 *Q. B.*, 509. As an instance of the injustice flowing from the distinction maintained by the English law between deeds and other writings, see the case of West *v.* Blakeway, 3 Scott, *N. R.*, 199.

'Where the condition of a bond was that it should be void if the obligor did not pay, a performance being pleaded on the ground of literal expression, the court held the palpable mistake of a word should not defeat the intention of the parties.'—Buller, J.; Douglas, *Reports*, p. 383; see, too, Jarvis *v.* Wilkins, 7 M. and W., 410.

[c] Sampson *v.* Easterby, 9 B. and C.; Saltoun *v.* Houston, 1 Bing., 433; Bache *v.* Proctor, 1 Douglas, 383.

[d] It has been held that the scope of general words may be limited on the ground of error. This was decided in the case of Davis *v.* Davis, 1 Dickens, *Reports*, 301, which was a bill to rectify a mistake in a conveyance; and in a recovery, to have a reconveyance of an estate which had passed under general words by a mistake, and to stay proceedings on an ejectment brought for it, Sir Thomas Clarke said, 'I admit this evidence [parol evidence of counsel and attorney, accompanied with circumstances] to constrain and controul the general words.' See the absurd case of Pippin *v.* Ekins, *cit.* 2 Vesey, 195. See also Browning *v.* Wright, 2 Bos and Pullen, 26 Lord Eldon; Hesse *v.* Stevenson, 3 Bos and Pullen, 575. As to the equity administered to correct errors, see Sugden, *Vendors and Purchasers*, p. 182, etc.

Lord St. Leonards, in his *Concise View*, lays down a rule directly opposite to that in the text as the rule of English jurisprudence: 'It is clearly settled that, in the construction of an agreement or deed, the

quens quod sequamur quod in regione in quâ actum est fre-

---

acts of the parties cannot be taken into consideration' (p. 116, § 9, 10) ; that is to say, that the surest of all guides to a safe and just construction is wantonly rejected by English jurisprudence, which, reversing the principle of common reason, ' Quid verba audiam, cum facta videam ?' says, ' Quid facta videam, cum verba audiam ?' In conformity with this wholesome principle, a gross fraud was upheld in Clifton *v.* Walmesly, 5 *Term Reports*, 567, in defiance of plain facts, to which the judges shut their eyes ; Lord Kenyon charitably suggesting that ' perhaps a Court of Equity [in the nadir gloom of Eldon] might afford the plaintiff some relief.' Lord Denman, indeed, held that a judge might look at ' surrounding circumstances,' but that the conduct and correspondence of the persons could not justify a particular construction. Simpson *v.* Margetson, 11 AD. and ELLIS, 23 ; see also Iggulden *v.* May, 7 EAST, 243 ; PLOWDEN, 239. Why are not the acts of the parties surrounding circumstances ? and what possible construction of an instrument can be more likely to give its real meaning than that which the makers have themselves annexed to it ? Lord St. Leonards states, but does not approve the rule, which it is hoped will not long be suffered to disfigure our jurisprudence. I am, however, bound to add, with the utmost deference to so great an authority as that of Lord St. Leonards, that in the case of Bourne *v.* Gatliffe, decided by the House of Lords, 11 CLARK and FINNELY, p. 67, it was stated that evidence of this kind was held to be admissible by Lord Lyndhurst. ' There is no foundation,' he said, ' for the objection to the direction of the judge respecting the admissibility of the evidence. . . . It is said that the evidence offered was that of instances of individual contracts. Be it so ; that does not render the evidence less admissible : it was to explain the meaning of the contract, by showing what had been the meaning of the parties.' This was acquiesced in by Lords Brougham and Campbell. Smith *v.* Wilson, 3 B. and AD., 728 ; Clayton *v.* Gregson ; Hutchison *v.* Bowker, 5 M. and W., 535 ; 5 D. and E., 302. This seems to shake the decision of C. J. Gibbs, in Yates *v.* Pym, 6 TAUNTON, 446, if the rule laid down in Altham's Case, COKE, *Reports*, as relating to deeds (Smith *v.* Wilson was the case of a deed), is untouched: ' If a man make a feoffment to one and his heirs, no averment can be taken that the intent of the feoffor was that the feoffee should have but an estate to him and the heirs of his body, for such an averment would be against the judgment of the law, which appears to the judges on the view of the deed. So, in the case at bar, if the general word ' demanda' had . . . barred ·her of her dower, no foreign or collateral averments 'dehors' could qualify the force or operation of the said word, but it ought to be qualified by apt words contained in the said deed'—contradicting the principle of Davis *v.* Davis. See, too, Doe d. Peters *v.* Hopkinson, 1 YOUNGE and COLL., *Ex. Reps.*, 407. As usual there are precedents on both sides.

quentatur.[e] Quod si neque mos regionis apparuit quia varius fuit, ad id quod minimum est redigenda summa est' (*Dig*.xlv.3 *.*

In stipulations, and in other contracts, the thing to be accomplished by the parties is our guide. If this be not evident, we must follow the custom of the country in which what has happened took place. If here, too, there is room for doubt, because it is various, we must take the interpretation which gives the smallest sum.

IV.

CUM quæritur in stipulatione quid acti sit, ambiguitas contra stipulatorem est'[f] (*Dig. de Reb. Dub.* xxxiv. 5. 26).

When the question is, What was the purpose of the stipulation? ambiguous words are to be construed against the person to whom the other is obliged.

' In contrahendâ venditione ambiguum factum contra venditorem interpretanda est' (*Dig.* l. 172).

In sales, an ambiguous phrase is to be construed against the seller.[g]

---

e Wiggleworth *v.* Dallison, 1 SMITH's *Leading Cases;* Wilkins *v.* Wood, 17 *L. J.*, *Q. B.*, 319 ; Dalby *v.* Hirst, 1 BR. and B., 244 ; LITT., § 212 ; Doe *v.* Burt, 1 *T. Reports*, 703 : ' It may be necessary to put a different construction on leases made in London, from that on those made in the country. We know that in London different persons have different freeholds over the same spot,' etc.—ASHURST, J. 4 *Inst.*, 274 ; Hilton *v.* Earl Granville, 5 *Q. B.*, 701 ; Lewis *v.* Lane, 2 MYLNE and KEEN ; Gibbs *v.* Flight, 3 *C. B.*, 581. Three days grace allowed to payees of bills of Exchange and notes, Mallan *v.* May, 13 M. and W., 511. Six score herrings go to the hundred, and sixty score to the thousand, in the herring trade, 3 Ed. III., *Year-book*, ii. c. 2. A thousand rabbits mean twelve hundred. Smith *v.* Wilson, 3 B. and AD., 728 ; Wade *v.* Waters, 3 CAMPBELL, 16 ; Anderson *v.* Pitcher, 2 Bos. and PULL., 168, word 'level ;' Clayton *v.* Gregson, 4 NEVILLE and MANNING, 602. But custom cannot overrule express words. Boraston *v.* Green, 16 EAST, 71.

f BACON'S *Maxims, Reg.* 3 : 'Verba fortius accipiuntur contra proferentem.' 'A man's deeds and words shall be taken strongliest against himself.'

g Art. 1602, 'Tout pacte obscur ou ambigu s'interprète contre le ven-

' Venditoribus placuit pactionem obscuram vel ambiguam, venditori et qui locavit nocere—in quorum fuit potestate legem apertius conscribere' (*Dig.* ii. 14. 39).

' Quicquid astringendæ obligationis est id nisi palam verbis exprimitur omissum intelligendum est; ac fere secundum promissorem interpretamur, quia stipulatori liberum fuit verba late concipere—nec rursus ferendus promissor, si ejus intererit de certis potius vasis aut hominibus actum.'

Unless a binding obligation be clearly expressed, it is not taken as if it were expressed at all, and the interpretation is to be made in favour of the promiser,—because, if the plaintiff had chosen, more comprehensive words might have been employed; —on the other hand, the defendant would not be allowed to limit comprehensive words by confining them to particular articles.

v.

UBI de obligando quæritur propensiores esse debemus si occasionem habeamus ad negandum ubi de liberando ex diverso ut facilior sic ad liberationem (*Dig.* xliv. 7. 47).

---

deur.'—Locré, *Leg.* vol. xiv. p. 242. As to latent ambiguity, Miller *v.* Travers, 1 M. and Sc., 345 ; Bacon's *Maxims,* 23.

' Doubt created by parol evidence may be removed by parol evidence.' Cheyney's Case, 5 Coke, 68 ; Doe *v.* Needs, 2 M. and W., 140 ; Wigram, *On Extrinsic Evidence,* 86, 88 ; Addison, *On Contracts,* 968 ; Altham's Case, 8 Coke, 155 *a*; Jones *v.* Newman, 1 W. Bl., 60 ; Shore *v.* Wilson, 9 Cl. and Finn., p. 566. Lord C. J. Tindal remarks, ' Where any doubt arises upon the true sense and meaning of the words themselves, or any difficulty as to their application under the surrounding circumstances, language may be investigated and ascertained by evidence, dehors the instrument itself; for both reason and common sense agree that by no other means can the language of the instrument be made to speak the real mind of the party.'

' Parol evidence is inadmissible to remove a patent ambiguity, as if a blank be left for a name.' 2 Atkyns, 239 ; 3 Atkyns, 257 ; Richardson *v.* Watson, 4 B. and Adol., 787 ; Shore *v.* Wilson, *ubi supra,* 13 M. and W., 200 ; 8 Viner, *Abridg.,* 188, 5. See, however, Jarvis *v.* Wilkins, 7 M. and W., 410 ; and Bache *v.* Proctor, 1 Douglas, 383.

Where it is a question of obligation we ought to lean to a negative—where it is a question whether a debtor shall be liberated, to an affirmative decision.

'Plerumque in stipulationibus verba ex quibus stipulatio oritur inspicienda sunt.—Raro inesse tempus vel conditionem ex eo quod agi apparebit intelligendum est, nunquam personam nisi expressa sit.'—*Dig.* xlv. 1. 126, § 2.ᵃ

In stipulations, as a general rule, the words which give rise to the obligation are to be examined.

Time, or a condition not expressed, should rarely be inferred—a person never, unless specifically mentioned.

VI.

UNIUSCUJUSQUE enim contractus initium spectandum est et causa.—*Dig.* xvii. 1. 8.ᵇ

ᵃ In the case of Coles *v.* Hulme, 8 B. & C. 573, one of our most narrow-minded judges supplied the word 'pounds' in a bond. 'In every deed there must be such a degree of moral certainty as to leave in the mind of a reasonable man no doubt of the intent of the parties. The question in this case is, whether there is in this bond that degree of moral certainty as to the species of money in which the party intended to become bound. I thought at the trial there was. The obligatory part of the bond purposes, that the obligor is to become bound for 7700. No species of money is mentioned. It must have been intended that he should become bound for some species of money. The question is, whether from the other parts of the instrument we can collect what was the species of money which the party intended to bind himself to pay.'—See note *a. Ib.* 534. Simpson *v.* Margitson, 11 *Q. B. N. R.* 71 ; HOBART, 275 ; Doe *v.* Guest, 15 M and W., 160; Napier *v.* Bruce, 8 CL. and FINN., 470 ; the name of the bargainor supplied in the operative part of a bargain and sale upheld. Lloyd *v.* Lord Say and Sele, 10 *Modern.*, 1 B. *P.C.* 379 ; Langdon *v.* Goole, 3 LEV. 21, name of obligor supplied. Uvedale *v.* Halfpenny, 2 P. WM., 151 ; Ex parte Symonds, 1 Cox, 200 ; Bishop *v.* Church, 2 VESEY, *Sen.* 100 ; SHEPHERD'S *Touchstone*, 88 ; Targus *v.* Paget, 2 VESEY. 194 ; Cholmondeley *v.* Clinton, 2 Jac. and W. 1 ; 1 MARSHALL, 214 ; Waugh *v.* Russell ; COKE, *Litt.* 217 *b* ; Parkhurst *v.* Smith, WILLES, *Reps.* 332 ; 3 ATKYNS, 136 ; Mills *v.* Wright, 1 FREEMAN, 247.

ᵇ COKE, *Institut.* ii. 173 ; Doe *v.* Godwin, 4 M. and S. 265 ; Cage *v.* Paxton, 1 SEA., 116 ; PLOWDEN, 329; Jowett *v.* Spencer, 15 M. and W.

The beginning and cause of every contract are to be considered.

' Quæ dubitationis tollendæ causâ contractibus inseruntur, jus commune non lædunt.'

When in a contract a particular has been taken as an example, it is not to be construed as if it was thereby meant to take away from the legal effect of the engagement in cases not enumerated. (*Vide supra.*)

These rules are as invariable as the equity from which they emanated.[b] They were the basis and ornament of Roman legislation, and ought to be incorporated with that of all countries.[c]

RULES FOR THE INTERPRETATION OF WILLS.

IN testamentis plenius voluntates testantium interpretantur.

In testaments the will of the testator is very liberally expounded.

This rule relates to the principle in conformity with which wills, as they are emphatically termed in our Saxon dialect, should be interpreted. It is a rule, the importance of which increases with advancing civility, and which to any one who

---

662 ; Hesse *v.* Stevenson, 2 B. and P. 365. As to the rule 'Noscitur a sociis.' See BROOM. *Legal Maxims*, p. 450 ; Cullen *v.* Butler, 5 M. and S. 465 ; Borradaile *v.* Hunter, 5 SCOTT, *Q. R.* applied by C. J. Tindall. Phillips *v.* Barber, 5 B. and ALD. 161 ; Devaux *v.* Janson, 5 B. and C. 619.

[b] They have 'l'empire que donne la raison sur tous les peuples.'— *Discours de Bigot Préameneu*, LOCRÉ, vol. xii. p.312.

[c] For general rules in English law on this subject, and a magazine of opposite arguments—CRUISE *Dig.* tit. *Deed* ; COMYN's *Dig.* tit. *Fait*; VINER's *Abrid.* tit. *Deeds, Faits, Grants* ; SHEPHERD's *Touchstone*, c. 5 ; BACON, *Abrid.* tit. *Grant* ; BROOM's *Legal Maxims;* DWARRIS *On Statutes;* RAM, *Science of Legal Judgment.*

studies the history of our law, it will almost seem that our judges set aside every consideration of reason and humanity to violate. So uncouth and preposterous are the rules which they established, and the decisions which in conformity with those rules they repeatedly pronounced.

'Plenius' is the word on which the accent should be laid. By 'plenius' it is meant, that every help should be sought which can lead to a sound and correct knowledge of the testator's will, that no means should be rejected by which his intention can fairly be ascertained ' interpretatione extrinsecus extra testamentum assumptâ,' says Gothofred, that is, in matters 'extra testamentum.' It is not meant that the plain meaning of the words used should be neglected for any fanciful conjecture, but that where the intention of the testator is manifest they should receive a liberal interpretation. 'Non aliter a significatione verborum recedi oportet quam cum manifestum est aliud sensisse testatorem,'[d] says Marcellus. On the other hand, he adds, that in expounding wills we are not to have recourse to pettifogging and minute cavils. ' In causâ testamentorum non ad definitionem utique descendendum esse ;' and he proceeds to give the reason, ' Quia testatores plerumque abusive loquuntur nec propriis nominibus ac vocabulis semper utuntur.' What would these lights of jurisprudence have thought if they had been told, that in a country calling itself civilized, and arrogating to itself exclusively the title of practical wisdom, the expounders should invent for words in common use a set of meanings totally different from those usually annexed to them; and should interpret wills on the principle, that the meaning which they had invented, and which the testator in nine cases out of ten had never heard of, was the meaning which the testator had intended to employ in spite of obvious and clearly expressed intentions, the condition of his family, and the avowed purpose of his bequest, and that this wild absurdity should be a ' præsumptio juris et de jure,' which no evidence was allowed to contradict. But the word ' ple-

---

[d] *Dig.* xxxii. 1. 69.

nius' in the rule we are considering shews, that it was matter not of equitable indulgence but of strict right, that by a reasonable latitude of construction the matter of the bequest, and the object of the testator considered, care should be taken to carry his wishes into effect.[e] So, if the ' usus' of a house was left to Titius, it was asked, as the Roman law confined the ' usus with great strictness to the usuarius, whether his wife (during his life) might live in it, and it was answered that she might. *Dig.* vii. 5; vii. 8, 9; vii. 8. 15. So, where a father left his daughter a right of way through a particular house, it was held to extend to her husband.[f] *Dig.* xxxiii. 3. 6.

The meaning of this rule is not that a will should be supported which might otherwise fail by a strained interpretation, but that the lawful intention of the testator should by law be fully expounded by every solid and reasonable conjecture. It applies to legacies as well as to successions, and it may recreate the mind that has wandered over the barren waste of our reports, in which dulness, poverty of language, and absence of all sentiment, even when its display is most called for, seems to be considered the test of superior reason and learning, to observe the arguments and motives to which Papinian, and Ulpian, and Modestinus, are not ashamed to appeal. Besides the beautiful passage *Dig.* xxx. 50; there is the law *De Liberat. Legat.* xxxiv. 3. 28, § 3, where the question was as to the extent of the bequest of a son to his father. The answer was in favour of the legatee, ' præsumptio enim propter naturalem affectum facit omnia patri videri concessa;' so *Dig.* xxxiv. 1. 14, § 1. The decision is given ' pietatis intuitu,' and this reason, it is added, ' non est incivile,' xxxv. 1. 72, § 1; after the opinion the text runs ' fuit enim periculosum et tuiti libertum conjunctum patroni liberis eorum mortem expectare;' and in the first part of the same law are

---

[e] As an instance of this liberal construction, see the sixth clause of the law *Gallus, Dig.* xxviii. 2. 6 ; and *Ib.* xxviii. 2. 4. and 5.

[f] Pater filiæ domum legavit eique per domus hereditarias jus transeundi præstari voluit, si filia domum suam habitet viro quoque jus transeundi præstabitur alioquin filiæ præstari non videbitur.

the words; ' Non enim voto matris opponi tam ominosa—interpretatio debuit.' See too, xxxv. 1. 102, the remarkable law, ' Cum doces.'

RULES WITH REGARD TO LEGACIES.

L EGATUM est donatio testamento relicta.—Mo-
DESTINUS.[z]

A legacy is a gift bequeathed by the will.

Justinian, in the *Institutes*, altered this definition, as he allowed a legacy to be given by an intestate.

' Legatum est donatio quædam a *defuncto* relicta.'

After the Falcidian law which circumscribed the testator's right of bequest, the definition given, *Dig.* xxx. 116, was—

' Legatum est delibatio hæreditatis quâ testator ex eo quod hæredis universum foret alicui quid collatum velit.'

Ulpian has mentioned four kinds of legacies:—

1. ' Per vindicationem;'
2. ' Per damnationem;'
3. ' Sinendi modi;'
4. ' Per præceptionem.'

These distinctions were swept away by Justinian — ' Per omnia exæquata sunt legata fideicommissis.' The only trace remaining of difference was, that a direct bequest was a legacy —an indirect request or expression of a wish was a fideicommissum—' ea quæ precario modo relinquuntur fideicommissa vocantur.

An error as to the thing itself vitiated the bequest—' Si in re quis erraverit, ut puta dum vult larcem relinquere—vertem leget—neutrum debebitur.'[a]

An error as to the name, if the thing was certain, did not impair the bequest.[b]

---

[z] MURATORI, *Difetti della Giurisprudenza*, c. 19, p. 161.

[a] *Dig.* xxviii. 5. 9, § 1.

[b] *Cod. de leg.* vii. § 1 ; LORD BACON'S *Maxims, reg.* 25 ; 2 VESEY, Jun.,

If it was clear that the testator meant to leave one of his estates, but it was uncertain which, the heir might give which he pleased to the devisee.

' Si de certo fundo sensit testator nec apparet de quo electio hæredis erit quem velit dare.'[c]

If a bequest was made to two Titiuses separately, and afterwards cancelled as to one, and it could not be ascertained as to which of them, the bequest was cancelled as to both.

' Si duobus Titiis separatim legaverit et uni ademerit nec appareat cui ademptum sit, neutri debetur—quemadmodum et in dando si non appareat cui datum sit, neutri debetur;'[d] because a legacy was incomplete until its proper object was ascertained.

' Legatum perfectum non videtur non existente cui datum intelligi possit.'[e]

' A trust might be declared in any language.'

' Fideicommissa quocunque sermone relinqui possunt'[f]—by a sign of the head.

' Motu relinquitur fideicommissum.'[g] The question was not with whom the dying man had spoken, but whom he intended to benefit—' Non quæri oportet cum quo de supremis quis loquatur sed in quem voluntatis intentis dirigatur.[h]

Words that rather expressed a recommendation than a command to give were sufficient to create a trust—' Verba licet non satis exprimunt fideicommissum, sed magis consilium quam necessitatem relinquendi tamen vim fideicommissi videntur continere.'[i] So these words—' Cupio des—credo te daturum—fideicommissum est.'[k]

589; AMBLER, 75 ; 4 VESEY, 808 ; PLOWDEN, 344 ; 19 VESEY, 400, Smith v. Campbell ; 1 MERIVALE, 184 ; 1 VESEY.

It is perfectly settled, that the addition of a mistaken description will not vitiate a gift to persons otherwise sufficiently ascertained.

[c] *Dig.* xxx. 37. 1.

[d] *Dig.* xxxiv. 4. 3, § 7 : ' De adimendis vel transferendis legatis.'

[e] 7 VESEY, 508, Trimmer v. Bayne ; 6 *T. Reps.*, 671. Christian name of legatee may be supplied by extrinsic evidence. 4 VESEY, 680. Aliter as to the entire name. 2 *Ch. C.*, 61 ; 2 ATKYNS, 239 ; 3 *B. C. C.*, 311.

[f] *Dig.* xxxii. 11.   [g] *Dig.* xxxii. 21.   [h] *Dig.* xxxi. 77. 26.

[i] *Dig.* xxxii. 11. 9.   [k] *Dig.* xxx. 115.

In cases of trust, conjectures were admissible. ' In causâ
fideicommissi utcunque precaria voluntas quæreretur conjec-
tura potest admitti. '[1]

A mistaken statement by the testator, that he had bequeathed
what he had not in fact bequeathed, is no legacy.

' Falsam legati demonstrationem non facere legatum Sabinus
respondit.'[m]

To recommend a person to one's heir, was not tantamount
to a bequest in his favour.

' Aliud est personam commendare aliud voluntatem suam
fideicommittendi hæredibus insinuare.'[n]

Every one who had the right to make a will, might create
a trust.

' Sciendum est eos posse fideicommissum relinquere qui
testandi jus habent.'[o]

Legacies might be left to corporate bodies—' Hodie civitatibus legari potest.'

' Nulla dubitatio est quod si corpori cui licet coire legatum
sit debeatur.'[p]

A testator might charge any one with a trust, who derived
any advantage positive or negative from his will—even an
unborn heir—' Sciendum est eorum fideicommittere quem
posse ad quos aliquid perventurum est morte ejus vel dum eis
datur vel dum eis non adimitur.'[q]

' Et ejus qui nondum natus est fideicommissum relinqui
potest, si modo natus nobis successumus sit.'[r]

All things in commercial rights and servitudes might be
bequeathed.

' Corpora legari omnia, et jura et servitutes possunt.'[s]

---

[1] *Dig.* xxxi. 64.   [m] *Dig.* xxxv. 1. 72, § *fin. de cond. et deni.*

[n] *Dig.* xxxii. 11. 2.   [o] *Dig.* xxx. 12.

[p] *Dig.* xxx. 122 ; *ib.* xxxiv. 5. 10, *de rebus dubiis.*

[q] *Dig.* xxxii. 5. 6.   [r] *Dig.* xxx. 77.

[s] *Dig.* xxx. 41.

' Si talis res sit cujus commercium non est nec æstimatio ejus debetur.' *Institut.* ii. 20, § 4, *de legatis.*

Even things not actually existing—'Etiam quæ futura sunt legari possunt.'[t]

Things annexed to buildings could not be bequeathed.

'Senatus ea quæ sunt ædium legari non permisit.'[x]

A man redeemed from the enemy may be bequeathed to himself.

'Qui ab hostibus redemptus est legari sibi potest.'[y]

What was in the power of enemies might be bequeathed 'jure postliminii.'

'Quod apud hostes legari potest et postliminii jure constitit.'[z]

Things may be bequeathed which are not the property of the testator.

'Consistat res alienas legari posse.'[a]

If a thing was bequeathed in trust for Titius which actually belonged to him, the bequest was to no purpose unless it appeared to be the testator's wish that Titius should receive its value.[b]

'Fideicommissum relictum et apud eum cui relictum est ex causâ lucrativâ inventum extingui placuit, nisi defunctus æstimationem præstari voluit.'[c]

'Si quis scripserit testamento fieri quod contra jus est et bonos mores non valet.'[d]

'Fideicommissum quo quis rogatur est adoptet, ratum non est.'[e]

No man can be bound to give the same thing more than

---

[t] *Dig.* xxx. 7.

'Servitus prædium habenti recte legatur.' *Dig.* xxxii. 17.

[x] These were taken out of commerce to prevent injury to the appearance of streets; therefore, where the house was pulled down, the rule did not apply. *Dig.* xxx. 43.

[y] *Dig.* xxx. 43.   [z] *Dig.* xxx. 9.

[a] *Dig.* xxxi. 39. 7.   [b] *Dig.* xxxii. 21, § 1.

[c] The bequest in such a case was only unavailing on the supposition that the legatee had the full benefit of the thing bequeathed already—'Non quocunque modo legatarii res facta fuerit legatum extinguitur, sed ita si eo modo fuerit ejus quo avelli non potest.'

[d] *Dig.* xxx. 112, § 7.   [e] *Dig.* xxx. 41. 8.

once. He may be obliged, however, to pay its value more frequently if such be the will of the testator.

' Eadem res sæpius præstari non potest, eadem summa volente testatore, multiplicari potest.'[f]

' Sæpius idem legando non multiplicat testator legatum, re autem legatâ etiam æstimationem ejus legando, amplicare legatum possumus.'[g]

' Si eadem res sæpius legatur in ejusdem testamento amplius quam semel peti non potest.'[h]

So if two people left me the same thing, I have a right to the thing and the value of it.[i]

' Si duorum testamento mihi eadem res legata sit bis petere potero, ut ex altero testamento rem consequar ex altero æstimationem.

An unconditional legacy was due at the testator's death.

' Si purum legatum est ex die mortis dies ejus cedit.'[k]

A conditional legacy was not due till the condition happened.

' Si sub conditione sit legatum relictum non prius dies legati cedit quam conditio fuerit impleta.'[l]

If the condition was void, the legacy was payable immediately.

' Si ea conditio fuit quam prætor remittit statim dies cedit.'[m]

The legacy of an ' usufruct' or of an ' usage' is not due till the succession has been accepted.

' Dies ususfructus item usus non prius cedit quam hæreditas adeatur.'[o]

If the legatee died after the legacy was due, it went to his heir.

' Si post diem legati cedentem legatarius decesserit ad hæredem suum transfert legatum.'[p]

---

[f] *Dig.* xxx. 34. 3.
[h] *Dig.* xxx. 34. 1.
[k] *Dig.* xxxvi. 2. 5, § 1, *Quando dies legatorum.*
[l] *Dig.* xxxvi. 2. 5, § 2.
[o] *Dig.* vii. 3, 1.

[g] *Dig.* xxxiii. 2. 42, § 1.
[i] *Dig.* xxx. 34. 2.
[m] *Dig.* xxxvi. 5, § 2, 3.
[p] *Dig.* xxxvi. 2. 5.

The bequest transferred at once the property to the legatee, if he accepted it without any act on the part of the heir.

' Si pure res relicta sit et legatarius non repudiaverit rectâ via dominium quod hæreditatis fuit ad legatarium transit nunquam factum hæredis.'[q]

The Prætor gave the legatees security for the legacies, or put them in possession of the inheritance.[r]

' Legatorum nomine satis dari oportere prætor putavit aut si satis non datur in possessionem venire voluit.'[s]

And this right held whatever was the nature of the bequest: ' Sive pure sit relictum sive ex die certo vel sub conditione, sive res aliqua, sive hæreditas sive jus aliquod relictum est.'[t]

But the heir was only liable for his proportion of the inheritance: ' Non ex majore parte quis ex stipulatu tenetur quam ex quâ hæres est.'[u]

On the other hand, the interdict, ' quod legatorum,' was given to the heir against the legatees, who had taken possession of the things bequeathed without his consent.[x]   Any addition to the legacy after the will was made, accrued for the benefit of the legatee.[y]

The thing bequeathed in the absence of any express direction on the part of the testator, was to be delivered on the spot where it was at the time of the bequest.[z]

A fugitive slave was to be brought back at the expense of the heir, if he ran away after the death of the testator;—if he ran away during his life, at the expense of the legatee.[a]

---

[q] *Dig.* xxxi. 80.

[r] But the person so placed in possession was never looked upon in the light of the owner, *Dig.* xxxvi. 4. 5, ' Nunquam quo domino,' nor could he eject the heir, *ib.*

[s] *Dig.* xxxvi. 3. 1, § 14 : ' Ut leg. vel. fid. causâ caveatur.'

[t] *Dig.* viii. and ix.   [u] *Dig.* i. 19.

[x] *Dig.* xliii. 3. 1, § 3 ; ' Ut quod quis legatorum nomine non ex voluntate hæredis occupavit, restituat hæredi.' So careful was the Roman legislator never to allow the citizen to take the law into his own hands.

[y] *Dig.* xxxi. 10.

[z] *Dig.* xxx. 47.

[a] *Dig.* xxxi. 8 : But ' quod pondere aut numero aut mensurâ constat ibi dari debet ubi petitur.' *Dig.* v. 1. 38.

Every simple bequest was due from the day when the inheritance was entered upon.[b]

If the heir did not dispute the legacy, and it was of money, a reasonable time was allowed him to pay it: ' In pecuniâ legatâ modicum tempus confidenti hæredi ad solutionem datum est.'[c]

The person burdened with a trust after delay, is responsible not only for the fruits of it, but for any damage that the person intended to benefit by the trust may have sustained.

' Is qui fideicommissum debet post moram non tantum fructus sed etiam omne damnum quo affectus est fideicommissarius præstare cogitur;'[d] and he was responsible not only for the profits he had actually derived, but for those which the legatee might have derived from it.[e]

If the thing bequeathed was not to be found, without any misconduct on the part of the heir, the legatee could not sue for them.[f]

If one, ordered by the testator himself to do a particular work, offered money in its stead, he was not to be heard.

If the will was invalid, the trusts were inoperative, unless the will of the testator could be so proved as to make it binding on those who succeeded ' ab intestato.'[g]

The prayers of an ardent and settled will were held to affect every species of succession: ' Enixæ voluntatis preces ad omnem successionis speciem porrectæ, videntur.'[h]

The decision of the judge against the heir, either not defending himself, or defending himself carelessly, did not prejudice the legatees.[i]

The heir might, if he chose, renounce the succession, though, by so doing, he destroyed the legacies of the will: ' Liberum

---

[b] Dig. xxxi. 32.

[c] Dig. xxx. 71, § 2.

[d] Dig. xxxii. 26.

[e] Dig. xxx. 39, § 1.

[f] Dig. xxxi. 32, § 5.

[g] Cod. de fid. xix.

[h] Dig. xxxi. 77, § 23.

[i] Dig. xxx. 50. 1: 'Si hæreditatis judex contra hæredem pronuntiavit, non agentem causam vel lusorie agentem nihil hoc nocebit legatariis.'

cuique esse debet etiam lucrosam hæreditatem omittere licet
eo modo legata libertatesque intercidant.'[g]

He who did not possess the inheritance, but had fraudulently
contrived not to possess it, might be treated as if he had
entered thereupon.

' Etsi non possideat quis hæreditatem dolo autem malo fecerit
quominus possideat eveniet ut perinde teneatur ac si rediisset.'

ADEMPTION OF LEGACIES AND TRUSTS.

Trusts are revocable by a simple act of the will.[h]

It matters not whether the revocation be direct or indirect.[i]

' Inimicitiis interpositis—si quidem capitales vel gravissimæ
intercesserint ademptum videtur quod relictum est—sin levis
offensa manet fideicommissum.'[k]

The first testament is only cancelled when the later is valid.[l]

' Ita demum a priore testamento velim recedit si posterius
valiturum est.'

If a testator take away more than he gave, the ademption
is valid.[m]

The same causes which invalidate a bequest invalidate an
ademption.[n]

' Pars adimi potest,' where the thing left was divisible.[o]

As a legacy may be taken away, it may be transferred.[p]

Though the person, to whom it was originally left, be dead.[q]

A conditional legacy, transferred to another, is transferred
with the condition, unless the condition be personal to the first
legatee.[r]

---

[g] *Dig.* xxix. 4. 17.   [h] *Dig.* xxxiv. 4. 3, § 11.

[i] *Dig.* xxxiv. 4. 16 : ' Nihil interest inducatur quod scriptum est, an
expresse adimatur.'

[k] *Dig.* xxxiv. 4. 3, § 11 ; xxxiv. 4. 1. 1, § 2.

[l] *Dig.* xxxii. 18.   [m] *Dig.* xxxiv. 4. 3, § 5.

[n] *Dig.* xxxiv. 4. 14, § 1.   [o] *Dig.* xxxiv. 4. 2, § 2.

[p] *Dig. id.,* tit. 5.   [q] *Dig. id.,* tit.

[r] ' Legatum sub conditione relictum et ad alium translatum si non
conditio personæ cohæreat, sub eadem conditione translatum videtur.'
—*Dig.* xxxv. 1. 95.

If a legacy be transferred to a second person, it is no longer due to the first, although the second cannot profit by it.[s]

If that is bequeathed conditionally to Titius which has been already left, without any condition, to Mævius, the bequest to Mævius is not taken away, if the condition does not happen.[t]

If I bequeath ten gold pieces instead of an estate (as proved by circumstances, without express words), the estate is taken away.[u]

A legacy lapses by the death of the person to whom the bequest is made.[x]

'Intercidit legatum si persona deceperit cui legatum est.'

If the heir be commanded to give a specific thing, and that thing perishes, without the fraud or fault of the heir, the loss falls on the legatee.[y]

How can a specific thing be done when the species of it is altered?[z]

The accessories are lost when the principal things perish: 'Quæ accessiorum locum obtinent, extinguuntur cum res principales peremptæ fuerunt.'[a]

OBLIGATION OF THE HEIR.

If the heir be burdened with a trust, in favour of any one of a certain number whom he shall select, and he make no selection, he shall be bound to execute it in favour of all.[b]

---

[s] 'Ubi transferre voluit legatum in novissimum, priore non debetur tam etsi novissimus talis sit in cujus personâ non constitit.'—*Dig.* xxx. 34.

[t] *Dig.* xxxiv. 4. 7 : 'Si alii legetur sub conditione quod pure alii datum est. Non plene recessum videtur a primo—sed ita demum si conditio sequentis extiterit.'

[u] *Dig.* xxxiv. 4. 6, § 12.   [x] *Dig.* xxxv. 1. 54.

[y] *Dig.* xxx. 26. 1.

[z] Again : 'Mortuo bove qui legatus est neque corium neque caro debetur.'—*Dig.* xxxi. 49.

'Qui fieri potest ut legatum vel fideicommissum durare existimetur cum id quod testamento dabatur in suâ specie non permanserit.'—*Dig.* xxx. 35.

[a] *Dig. de pecul. legat.* ii.   [b] *Dig. de statu,* 21, § 1.

The necessity of choice excludes the notion of a bounty in the person obliged to make it.[c]

A prohibition to alienate is of no effect, unless a particular person can be found to whom it applies.[d]

The bequest of an annuity is absolute for the first year, and conditional for every other.[e]

A certain sum is left to Titia, until she marries; the words 'every year' are not added; the sum is due every year.[f]

When 'alimenta' are bequeathed, without the statement of any specific quantity: 'Ante omnia inspiciendum quid defunctus solitus fuerit ei præstare deinde quid cæteris ejusdem ordinis reliquerit—si neutrum appareat tum ex facultatibus defuncti et casitate ejus cui relictum est modus statui debet.'[g]

'Alimenta,' if the testator has not explained himself, are supposed to be left for life.[h]

USUFRUCT.

There is nothing of which the 'usufruct' may not be left: 'Nulla res quæ non cadit in usumfructum.'[i]

If the 'usufruct' of a house be left 'habitandi causâ,' the right of inhabiting it only is bequeathed.[k]

The bequest of a rent is the bequest of a yearly payment of the rent usually received by the testator from the farm, therefore the heir might sell the farm.[l]

RELEASE.

A debtor may, by a bequest, be exonerated from his debt.[m]

So may not only the debtor of the testator, but the debtor of any other person.[n]

---

[c] *Dig.* xxx. 21, § 1.

[d] 'Qui testamento vetant quid alienari nisi invenitur persona cujus respectu, hoc a testatore dispositum est nullius est momenti.'—*Dig.* xxx. 114, § 14.

[e] 'Primi anni purum, sequentium conditionale.'—*Dig.* xxxiii. 1. 4.

[f] *Dig.* xxxiii. 1. 17. [g] *Dig.* xxxiv. 1. 22.

[h] *Dig. id.* tit. xiv. [i] *Dig. de Leg. Fal.* xxxv. 2. 69.

[k] *Dig.* xxxiii. 2. 10, § 2. [l] *Dig. id.* tit. 38.

[m] *Dig.* xxxiv. 3. 3. [n] *Ibid.* 8.

If the discharge of my debt is bequeathed to me, and I am sued for it, I may oppose the exception. If I am not sued, I may bring an action for my formal release.[o]

A man excused from giving any account is still bound to pay up what is in his possession, only he is exempt from the consequences of negligence.[p]

OPTION.

The bequest of an option implied a condition, and if the legatee did not make it, could not be transmitted to his heir.[q]

We can only choose once.[r]

If the legatee make his option before he has seen all the objects from which he is to choose, his option still remains.[s]

If an option is made out of the testator's property, it is not exhausted.[t]

If the heir is to choose which of two things he will give, after he has once said which he cannot change.[u]

If one of two slaves be left, and one die, the other must undoubtedly be given.[x]

' Falsa causa adjecta non nocet;' a false reason for the legacy did not extinguish it. ' Quod juris est in falsâ demonstratione hoc vel magis est in falsâ causâ. Veluti ita Titio fundum do quia negotia mea curavit. Fundum Titius filius meus præcipito quia frater ejus ex arcâ tot aureos sumpsit, licet enim frater hujus ex arcâ pecuniam non sumpserit, utile tamen legatum est.' (*Dig. de cond. et demonst.* 17, § *quod autem, Inst. de Legatis, Longe magis.*)

But if the event was stated as a condition, it was different. ' At si conditionaliter concepta sit causa veluti hoc modo Titio si mea negotia curavit fundum do. Titius filius si frater ejus

---

[o] *Ibid,* 3, § 3.

[p] *Dig.* xxx. 1. 19 : ' Vetitus rationes reddere non hoc consequitur ut ne quod apud eum sit reddat sed . . . ut negligentiæ ratio non habeatur.'

[q] *Instit. tit. de legat.*

[r] 'Semel duntaxat optare possumus.'—*Dig.* xxx. 5.

[s] *Dig.* xxxiii. 5. 4.　　　　　　　[t] *Dig.* xxxiii. 5. 2, § 2.

[u] *Dig.* xxxi. 11.　　　　　　　[x] *Dig.* xxx. 47, § 3.

centum ex arcâ sumpsit fundum præcipito—ita utile erit legatum si et ille negotia mea curavit et frater ejus centum ex arcâ
sumpsit.' (*Ibid.*) If, however, it could be proved that but for
the false reason the legacy would not have been bequeathed,
it was otherwise, and the ' doli exceptio ' would bar the legatee's claim. ' Falsam causam legato non obesse verius est, quia
ratio legandi legato non cohæret sed plenumque doli exceptio
locum habebit, si probetur alias legaturum non fuisse.' (*Dig.*
xxxv. 1. 70.)

By the word 'supellex' in a will,[a] was understood: ' domes-
ticum patrisfamilias instrumentum, quod neque auro, argen-
tove facto, neque vesti adnumeratur ' (*Dig.* xxxiii. 10. 1. *de sup.
legatâ*). ' Quod in aliam speciem non cadit,' a most valuable
definition (*Ibid.* 7. § 1), ' et est res mobilis.' (see 3, 4, 5, *Ibid.*)

' De alimentis vel cibariis legatis.' [b]—*Dig.* xxxiv. 1, 6.

By this bequest ' cibaria et vestitus et habitatio debebitur,
quia sine his ali corpus non potest, cætera quæ ad disciplinam
pertinent hoc legato non continentur.' 6.

' Nisi aliud testatorem sensisse probetur.' 7.

I am glad to quote the admirable law which follows: ' Cum
alimenta per fideicommissum relicta, non adjectâ quantitate,
inspiciendum est quid defunctus præstare sit solitus (extrinsic
evidence to remove an ' ambiguitas patens,' instead of making
the bequest void) deinde quid cæteris ejusdem ordinis reliquit—
si neutrum appareat ex facultatibus defuncti, et caritate ejus
cui fideicommissum datum est, modus statui debet.'[c]

---

[a] ROPER, *On Legacies*, c. 4, § 1; Grandison *v.* Pitt, 2 VERNON, 740, ed.
RAITHBY, note ; Duke of Beaufort *v.* Lord Dundonald, *ib.* ; Heseltine *v.*
Heseltine, 3 MADDOX, 376; Pratt *v.* Jackson, 1 B. P. C., 222, cited 1
VESEY, sen. 97 : Nicolls *v.* Osborne, 2 P. WILLIAMS, 419; Le Farrant *v.*
Spencer, SWINBURNE, part vii. c. 10 ; Snelson *v.* Corbet, 3 ATKYNS, 270 ;
Flay *v.* Flay, 2 FREEMAN, 64; Cornewall *v.* Cornewall, 12 SIMON, 298;
Franklyn *v.* Earl of Burlington, PREC. CH. 251 ; Paton *v.* Shepherd, 10
SIMON, 186.

[b] Cole *v.* Fitzgerald, 3 RUSSELL, 301 ; Slanning *v.* Style, 3 P. W. 344;
Porter *v.* Soumay, 3 VESEY, 313 ; Andrew *v.* Andrew, 1 COLL. (C.) 690.

[c] Term of years, severed from the rest of the personal estate. Sy-
mons *v.* James, 2 Yo. and COLL. 307 ; Creed *v.* Creed, 11 CL. and F., 491 ;

De auro, argento, mundo, etc., legatis.' —*Dig.* xxxiv. 2.

' Auro vel argento legato omne factum vel infectum continetur.'

' Aurum factum est quod certam speciem recepit ut vasa aurea—Infectum quod certam speciem non recepit sed est in massâ, ut lamina—signatum est quod publicâ formâ percussum inter pecunias numeratas refertur.' 19.

'Mundus muliebris est quo mulier fit mundior et elegantior.'[d] (25. § 10.)

' Ornamenta muliebria sunt quæ ad nullam aliam rem, quam ornandi corporis causâ parantur.' (25. § 10, 11.)

' De instructo vel instrumento legato.'[e]—*Dig.* xxxiii. 7.

The ' instrumentum fundi '[f] was ' apparatus rerum mansuramur sine quibus exerceri possessio nequit.' 12.

There were the ' instrumentum agri,' 12, § 12; ' villæ,' 16, § 21; ' vinea,' 16, § 1; ' domus,' 12, § 16; ' pictoris,' *ib.* § 17; ' pistoris,' 18, § 1; ' piscatoris,' 17, § 1.

' General legacies do not become specific, because they are payable out of the proceeds of real estate.' Page v. Leapingwell, 18 VESEY, 463. *Roper*, ch. iv., § 1, *money*, p. 282, ed. WHITE. An intention to bequeath identical stock, makes the bequest specific. ROPER, i., 219, and cases cited.

[d] Crichton v. Symes, 3 ATKYNS, 61; Willes v. Curtois, 1 BEAVAN, 189; Duke of Leeds v. Lord Amherst, 13 SIMON, 459; Hunt v. Hort (linen), 3 BRO. C. C. 311.

[e] Stock, live and dead stock; Porter v. Tournay, 3 VESEY, 311. Stock of cattle; Randall v. Russell, 3 MERIVALE, 190. Stock upon a farm, not only all moveable property (the Roman definition included more), but standing crops; Cox v. Godsalve, cited 6 EAST, 604, decided by HOLT. West v. Moore, 8 EAST, 339; questioned, indeed contradicted, by Vaisey v. Reynolds, 5 RUSS. 12, SIR J. LEACH. Lord Hardwicke, in Brooksbank v. Wentworth, held that a malt house passed under the word, 3 ATKYNS, 64.

[f] Utensils. Dame Latimer's case, DYER 59, pl. 15; Hotham v. Sutton, 15 VESEY, 319, where the exception was held to shew that everything not excepted, was comprised under the word 'effects.' Fitzgerald v. Field, 1 RUSS. 427; utensils ' in and about my mansion house,' held not to pass farming utensils. Plantation: held to pass stock, implements, and utensils, sed? Lushington v. Sewell, 1 SIMON, 455.

There was a considerable difference between the bequests,[g] 'Fundum cum instrumento,' and 'Instructum fundum,' or 'Fundum et instrumentum.'

'Fundo cum instrumento legato, ea tantum continentur quæ ad fundi apparatum pertinent.'

'Fundo instructo legato ea præterea quæ ad patrisfamiliæ usum ibi sunt—ut supellex.' (12, § 27, 28; *Lex*. 1, 2, *Cod. de Verb. Signific.*)

In the 'legatum fundi instructi' (see Gower *v.* Gower, 2 EDEN, 201) were included 'servi, cibaria, vinum paratum, frumentum serendi causâ sepositum' (18, § 11. 12) 'pecus omne quod in fundo inspicitur.'

'In omnibus istius modi legatis non propria verborum significatio sed quod testator demonstrare voluit—conservandum.'[h] (18, § 2.)

'De liberatione legatâ.'—*Dig.* xxxiv. 3.

'Valet legatum liberationis debitori factum.' (1, 3, *Ibid.*)

This might be done in several ways. 'Si vel nominis liberatio expresse, vel chirographum legetur, vel damnetur hæres ne agat' (1, 3, 8; § *peri. velut debitorem liberet*, 19).

A thing pledged might be left to the debtor, but that did not release the debt.[h]

---

[g] Meaning of farm : Goodtitle *v.* Southern, 1 M. and T. 299. As a general rule, it may be inferred from the cases, that the words 'goods,' 'moveables,' 'chattels,' unless restrained by the context, will pass the personal estate. JARMAN, *On Wills*, p. 652, 2nd ed. by WOLSTENHOLME and VINCENT, vol. i.

[h] SHEP. *Touchstone*, 433. As to parol evidence to explain testator's meaning, see Hall *v.* Hill, 1 DRUV. and W., 94; questioning Wallace *v.* Pomfret, 11 VESEY, 542, LORD ST. LEONARD'S. 'Courts of Law have been jealous of admitting extrinsic evidence to explain the intention of a testator (being the only conceivable way in many cases, as the Digest would have taught them, to understand his meaning), and I only know of one case in which it is permitted ; that is, where an ambiguity is introduced by extrinsic circumstances.'—LORD ELDON. Doe *v.* Chichester, 4 Dow., 92 ; JARMAN, vol. i., c. 13, 2nd ed. ; Earl of Newburgh *v.* Countess of Newburgh, 5 MADD. 364 ; Hippisley *v.* Homer, T. and R., 482.

' Res oppignorata debitori legari potest, quo casu jus pignoris remissum non debiti liberatio legata videtur.' (1, § 1.)[i]

The release might be ' in totum,' or 'pro parte' (*Dig.* xxxii. 7, 37, § *nuptura*), or 'ad tempus,' or ' in perpetuum.'

There are annexed to legacies, as Cujacius tells us, ' Demonstratio, causa, modus.'

' Demonstratio ' is, as he defines it, ' significatio accommodata rei legatæ.'

It differs from a condition, because it relates to the present, and not to the future or the past.

' Stichum qui meus est do lego.'   ' Stichum quem a Titio emi lego.'

Although erroneous, it does not vitiate the bequest.[k]   ' Si de testatoris voluntate constat.' (*Dig.* xxxv. 1. 17, § 1.)

The ' causa' is that which has swayed the mind of the testator in making the legacy.

' Hæc licet falsa sit non vitiat legatum' (*Dig.* xxxiv. 72. 6); because it is no part of the legacy, ' legato non cohæret,' unless it be expressed conditionally (*ib.* 17, § 2, 3), or it can be proved that the testator would not, but for that error, have made his bequest.[l]

---

[i] Hamilton *v.* Lloyd, 2 VESEY, Junior, 416 ; a bequest of arrears of debt does not pass the principal, and vice versâ ; Roberts *v.* Kuffin, 2 ATKYNS, 112.

[k] SHEP. *Touchstone,* 433 ; white horse bequeathed as black horse, good. Selwood *v.* Mildmay, 3 VESEY, 306 ; 1 BRO. *C. C.* 477 ; 13 VESEY, 174 ; ROPER, book ii., c. 17, p. 166, etc. ; Goodtitle *v.* Southern, 1 M. and S. 299 ; Trimmer *v.* Bayne, 7 VESEY, 508 ; Roe *v.* Vernon, 5 EAST, 51 ; Thomas *v.* Thomas, 6 *T. Reports,* 671 ; Doe *v.* Greathed, 8 EAST, 91 ; Goodright *v.* Peers, 11 EAST, 58 ; Doe *v.* Earl of Jersey, 1 B. and ALD. 550 ; Down *v.* Down, 7 TAUNTON, 343 ; LORD BACON, *Maxim* 23 ; Standen *v.* Standen, 2 VESEY, 589 ; Brett *v.* Rigden, PLOWDEN 344 ; Schloss *v.* Stiebel, 6 SIMON, 1 ; Smith *v.* Campbell, 19 VESEY, 400 ; Bristow *v.* Bristow, 5 BEAVAN, 289 ; Beaumont *v.* Fell, 2 P. WMS., 140 ; Smith *v.* Coney, 6 VESEY, 42 ; Rivers' case, 1 ATKYNS ; Doe *v.* Danvers, 7 EAST, 302 ; Dowset *v.* Sweet, AMBL. 175 ; Lee *v.* Pain, 4 HARE, 251 ; Still *v.* Hoste, 6 MADDOX, 192 ; Masters *v.* Masters, 1 P. WMS., 421, 425.

[l] A very striking instance of this rule in our courts will be found in the case of Kennell *v.* Abbott. A woman left a sum of money to a man

The modus shows what the testator means the legatee to do with his legacy (17 *id.*; CUJAC., in *par. hic.*): ' Ut si testator dicat se ideo legare ut aliquid fiat veluti monumentum aliudve' (17, § *fin.* ' pro conditione observatur,' 1. 2 *Cod., id.*).

The Roman law allowed conditional legacies.[b]

' Possunt non tantum legata pure relinqui sed iis et dies certus aut incertus aut conditio tacita vel expressa ascribi' (1 *id.*).

If the day was uncertain, and the legatee died before the day happened, the legacy lapsed.

If the condition was tacit, and the legatee died before he was entitled to the bequest, the legacy went to the heir[c] (*Dig.* xxx. 4. 2, § 4; 65, § 2; 25, § 2). It must be literally fulfilled (*Dig.* xxxiv. 8. 6; *id.* 71, § 3; xl. 27), unless it be impossible or immoral,[d] or its accomplishment be prevented by the heir,[e]

---

whom she supposed to be her husband. It turned out that he was the husband of another woman, and the bequest was therefore set aside. 4 VESEY, 802. See ex parte Wallop, 4 BRO., *C. C.* 90 ; Giles *v.* Giles, 1 KEEN, 685.

[b] Tattersall *v.* Howell, 2 MERIVALE, 26 ; a case which marks the latitude allowed for conditions in a devise, as distinguished from a deed.

Where the happening of an event, or the performance of an act, is to precede the vesting of a bequest, unless the event happens, or the thing is done, the bequest fails. Sprigg *v.* Sprigg, 2 VERNON, 394.

Where courts of justice consider the executory devises as limitations, not as conditions. Mackinnon *v.* Sewell, 2 M. and K., 202 ; Hemmings *v.* Munckley, 1 BRO., *C. C.*, 303 ; Stackpole *v.* Beaumont, 3 VESEY, 89 ; Clifford *v.* Beaumont, 4 RUSSELL, 325 ; Lloyd *v.* Branton, 3 MERIVALE, 116 ; Clarke *v.* Parker, 19 VESEY, 15.

[c] Mayott *v.* Mayott, 2 BRO., *C. C.*, 125.

[d] POTHIER, *Pandects*, lib. xxxv. tit. 1, § 21—26, instances : COKE, *Litt.*, 206 ; Brown *v.* Peek, 1 EDEN, 140 ; Ughried's Case, 7 *Reports*, 10 *a* : Poor *v.* Mial, 6 Maddox, 32 ; Gath *v.* Burton, 1 BEAVAN, 478.

[e] Darley *v.* Langworthy, 3 BRO., *P. C.*, 359. As to subsequent conditions—where an estate vests at once, subject to be devested on the happening of some further event, Nicolls *v.* Osborne, 2 P. WILLIAMS, 240 ; 3 MERIVALE, 340 ; Deane *v.* Test, 9 VESEY, 147 ; Davidson *v.* Dallas, 14 VESEY, 576 ; Bland *v.* Williams, 3 MYLNE and KEEN, 411 ; Elwin *v.* Elwin, 8 VESEY, 547 ; Law *v.* Thompson, 4 RUSSELL, 42.

or any one who has an interest in its non-performance (*Dig. id.* 3. § 20, 24, 57), or by him on whom its fulfilment depends (71, § *fin. id.* 27, 28).

Antoninus Pius cancelled legacies left in the shape of a penalty, 'pœnæ nomine,' but they were restored by Justinian (*Dig.* xxxiv. 6. 1, § 2; xxviii. 7. 9, § 14, 15; xxxv. 1. 20).

With regard to land, it was a rule of the common law, that none shall take advantage of a condition but the party from whom the condition moves;[f] i.e., the grantor and his heirs. The rule with regard to dispositions by devise is different; there the apparent intent of the testator is to be considered.

To enter upon the rules which have governed the construction put by the judges on the wills of men in England would be a work far beyond the limits of this undertaking.[g] Into that 'Serbonian bog,' therefore, where whole estates have been swallowed up in the discussion of matters compared with which the discussions of the schoolmen were really solid and valuable, as they were undoubtedly embellished by far more acuteness (for after referring to a chapter in Thomas Aquinas, Smiglecius, or Zabarella, the reader will often find a certain clumsiness and ponderosity about the texture of our legal arguments), I shall not invite the reader to follow me. All I shall attempt will be to make a few general observations, which the study of this most important

---

[f] FEARNE, *Contingent Remainders,* 261 ; PLOWDEN, 296 : JARMAN, *On Devises,* vol. i. p. 558, c. 20.

[g] The admirers of Lord Eldon (whose profound knowledge of the learning which is learning nowhere but in England is as indisputable as the narrowness of his mind) talk of him as if, like the youthful lover,

> ' He could bestride the gossamers
> That idle in the wanton summer's air,
> And yet not fall ;'

but I confess that I never read one of his barbarously-written judgments without thinking of Burke's spider, that was as large as an ox, and spun cobwebs with threads as thick as cart-ropes.

(but in a national point of view, this most humiliating and oppressive one) topic in our jurisprudence has suggested. As the object of the rules laid down by our judges (on this point, our legislators) has been often stated to be that of preventing litigation[h] (the great evil which it is supposed a code would bring down upon us), the reader will judge by comparison how far that object has been obtained, and how far the country has reason to congratulate itself on that ignorance of, and antipathy to, the Roman law, which, as it has been an unquestionable attribute of the judicial mind in England, has furnished so fruitful a theme of patriotic exultation in a country which was the home of fines and recoveries, trial by battle, wager of law, writs of right, and special pleading (a concise expression for the most various absurdities), in *this* century; and where statutes had a retrospective operation, men forfeited their lives for cutting down a sapling, and women were burnt alive for petty treason, down to the close of the last.

It is a first principle, that the same words are construed in a different sense;[i] i. e., they are taken to indicate a different wish on the part of the testator, as they are applied to real, and as they are applied to personal property.[k] The wit of man

---

[h] The simplicity of our common law, which scarcely allowed a mere substitution, was overthrown by estates tail. Entails were overthrown by judicial fictions. 'Uses evaded the rigours of tenure. . . . Trusts supplied the narrowness of the judges, and silently transferred the jurisdiction over property to Courts of Equity.'—HUMPHREYS, *Letter to E. Sugden, Esq.*, p. 4.

[i] FEARNE, *Contin. Rem.*, vol. i. p. 462, § 463, chap. 3, 113 : 'That the limitation of a personal estate to one in tail vests the whole in him, is proved by many cases.'

'If personal estate be given by testament to A and the heirs of his body, as such words would create an express estate in freehold lands if applied to them, so, in personal estate, if applied to it, such words will vest the absolute interest.'—ROPER, *On Legacies.* The history of the the rule is traced, and the cases are cited, in chap. 22.

[k] It should be recollected, that our system rests on the feudal law ; but under the feudal system, as STRUVIUS shews in his *Syntagma*, land was not considered a thing of exchangeable value, but as a bond to knit the vassal to the lord. It was looked upon in a political, not in a commercial light. So tenures grew up ; the stubborn genius of the feudal

may be challenged to lay down a rule more likely to work injustice, to overthrow the purpose of the testator, and to foment the most odious litigation. If the judges had chosen to lay down a rule that the words in a will should receive a different construction as the land to which they referred had borne wheat or turnips, it would not have been more irrational.

Lord Eldon, in Chandless v. Price (3 VESEY, 101), says ' I have understood the rule that has for a long time prevailed to be, to try it by this: would the words give an estate tail in real estate? If so [what does the reader imagine?], they give the absolute property in personalty !'[1] Not, observe, because the testator might not legally have tied up his personal property as he wished, but because the judge chooses to apply a technical rule to his words, which gives them an opposite signification to that which he intended them to have.[m] And this, though the Lord Chief Justice said from the judgment-seat where he administered *his* law,[n] ' It would be very strange if words *had* a different meaning when applied to real and personal property.'[o]

---

yielded to the 'trusts' imported from Roman jurisprudence, which 'ferum victorem cepit,' at the very moment when he thought himself most guarded against all danger of its influence. The word 'seised' changed the aspect of society : the lawyers refused to hold that it could apply to the possession of a grantee for years, or a chattel interest. Thus terms of years were used for purposes of mortgages, etc., which were utterly repugnant to the genius of the feudal system.

[1] I have read somewhere of an abbot who took great liberties with the rules of his order. He ordered all his monks to dress in black. On his death the original copy of the rules was found, with this note in his handwriting : ' Blanc c'est à dire noir.' It may be doubted whether, if every decision on a disputed passage in wills pronounced in our courts of justice had been exactly the reverse of what it is, the intentions of the testators would not, in the majority of cases, have been better fulfilled.

[m] Forth v. Chapman, 1 P. WILLIAMS, 667 ; Jermy and Agar v. Agar, 12 EAST, 255 ; Doe d. Cadogan v. Ewart, 7 AD. and ELLIS, 657 : Doe v. Simpson, 3 SCOTT, *N. R.*, 774 ; Lees v. Mosley, 1 YOUNGE and COLLIER, 589 ; Elton v. Eason, 19 VESEY, 77 ; Andrew v. Andrew, 1 COLLIER, 690.

[n] Porter v. Bradley, 3 *T. R.*, 143.

[o] ' I allude to cases in which, from the application of technical rules,

'*If* such a distinction existed in the law, it certainly would not agree with the rule, ' Lex plus laudatur quando ratione probatur,' in which opinion of my Lord Kenyon's, in spite of the truly barbarous way in which it is expressed, most men not expecting to be put on commissions for improving the law will be ready to concur.   Lord Kenyon repeated the same observation some years afterwards, in Roe *v.* Jeffrey, 7 *Term Reports*, 589: ' That the very same words in the same clause in a will should receive one construction, as applied to one species of property, and another, as applied to another, is not reconcileable to reason,' and all this because ' none but estates of inheritance[p] are within the statute ' de donis,' and therefore, chattels, real and other personal estate, cannot be *entailed* but by executory devise, or through the medium of trusts, they may be *limited so as to answer the* purposes of entail,' applied in the case of a testator who never heard of the statute ' de donis' in his life.[q]   ' Intention is to be sought for in the construction of a will, but that the testator is to be so far indulged as to break through all rules of construction is a position to which I cannot assent.'   Why not, if the testator's intention be clear, nay, conspicuous as the sun at noon day, and the will of the legislature is that it should be fulfilled ?   Why adopt rules for the construction of his language which, in ninety cases out of every hundred must pervert their meaning ?   If an estate be limited to one for life, remainder to his heirs, it is a fee in the first taker, and this, whether by will or deed.   The intention is clearly the other

---

the reasons for which have long been obsolete, the lawful intentions of penalties are avowedly thwarted. The most striking instance of this sort is what is called the rule in Shelley's Case, a rule by which testators and others . . . are made to confer an absolute power of disposing of real estate *on persons to whom they had, by the same instrument, declared in the most explicit terms that they intended to give a life estate only.'*—CHRISTIE, J. H., *Letter to Sir Robert Peel*, p. 251. This rule is so far from being founded on any known reason, that lawyers dispute as to what the reason upon which it was originally founded could have been—and this we call practical wisdom !

[p] ROPER, *On Legacies*, c. 22, p. 1519.

[q] DUNNING, *Arguendo, Coll. Jurid.,* p. 292.

way, and yet the legal sense of the words must not yield to
that intention.   Why not?   How is it for the good of society
that the main purpose for which judges are appointed to
interpret wills should be overthrown ?   Is not this to do by
means of judicial legislation, ' quod nulla in barbariâ quisquam
tyrannus'?   This was what Lord Mansfield, in Blake *v.* Perrin,
refused to do.   ' It should be considered,' said that great man,
' that the different temper of the times may have occasioned
considerable difference, and the want of due attention to this
has caused the courts *to run into many absurd distinctions which
had now better be forgotten.*   The chancellors have, in their
decrees, made many distinctions particularly between the trust
and legal estate, and indeed even in the trusts, between trusts
executed and executory; neither of these distinctions are
founded in sense.'

In the case of Chester *v.* Chester, 3 P. W., 56, it was
decided that, under a general devise, a remote reversion in fee
of other lands was passed.   C. J. Mansfield, in Morgan *v.*
Surman, 1 TAUNTON, 292, called this a shocking decision.
It was overruled by Sir W. Grant, and upheld by Lord Eldon,
who reversed Sir W. Grant's judgment in Church *v.* Mundy,
15 VESEY, 508, ' collecting the intention of the testator
according to legal rules of interpretation.'   Such is the really
indescribable folly of our law.   It says, ' Now, you, the
testator, have communicated your intention so that every one
knows perfectly what you mean, I will thwart it, and put a
meaning on your words which I know to be reverse of what
you intended, not because your intention is cruel, unjust (to
support such an intention might show my power, and supported
it would be), or illegal, but because you have not expressed
yourself as a lawyer.'

Wisely does Lord St. Leonard, in his letters, page 105,
addressed to an educated gentleman, say, ' If you wish to tie
up your property in your own family, you really must not
make your will;[r] it were better to die without one, than to

---

[r] The learned writer's sense of justice betrays him into two or
three admissions dangerous to the system of which he is the advocate,

make one which will waste your estate in litigation to discover its meaning.[a]   Such is the state to which the fatal bias to chicane has brought the English law. ' The words, ' children,' ' issue,' ' heirs,' ' heirs of the body,' are *seldom used* by a *man who makes his own will*, without leading to a law suit'! and not only was this state of things acquiesced in, but all interference with it was resented as a crime by the gentlemen of England.

To enter into any detailed examination of the meaning put on particular words in wills by our courts of justice is, of course, impossible.   The decisions will be found in the useful work of Mr. Roper.[b]   Some of them I will shortly notice. The word, ' goods,' has been held to include running horses.[c] Lord Hardwicke held that it passed property in possession only, not ' choses in action,' except bank notes, which the court considers as cash.[d]   This was confirmed in Moore *v.* Moore, by Lord Thurlow.[e]   In the case of Stuart *v.* Lord Bute,[f] a very

---

e.g., 'We are all agreed that we should arrive at the substance by a cheap and direct road, instead of an expensive and crooked way.' He talks of 'forms at once useless and mischievous, expensive in their nature and dangerous in their application;' all which is owing to the judges.

[a] *Ibid.* p. 105.   As an illustration, the writer says, 'You have now both land and money.   I will suppose that you have by your will given your estate to your eldest son and the money among the younger children. You then grant a lease of the land to Thompson, and give him an option to purchase the estate for £20,000, any time within ten years. You would think, no doubt, that you had secured the estate to the eldest son. But on the contrary, if you die before the end of the ten years, and Thompson, after your death, elect to purchase the estate, the money would go to your younger children, and your eldest son be stripped of all his fortune.'   I ask if Caligula would decide otherwise.   Such a decision might shock Baron Parke himself.   Yet this picture is drawn by an admirer.

[b] Vol. i. 250, Ed., 4, WHITE.

[c] 2 ED., 201, Gower *v.* Gower, 3 VESEY, 313.

[d] Chapman *v.* Hunt, 1 VESEY, sen,, 271.   Not bonds, for instance, as they have no locality.   Popham *v.* Aylesbury, AMB. 68 ; Lord Eldon, 11 VESEY, 662 ; Green *v.* Symonds, 1 B. CL., 129, notes.

[e] 1 B. C. C., 127.

[f] 3 VESEY, 212 ; Lord Rosslyn, confirmed by Lord Eldon, 657.

wide construction was given to the word 'things,' which it is difficult to reconcile with Trafford v. Berridge,[g] and with the rule enforced by the cases mentioned above, that a legacy of all goods at such a place, does not comprise bonds and choses in action that may be there. If the testator use general words, and then enumerate specific chattels, the general words are in the absence of contrary intention restrained to chattels 'ejusdem generis' with those enumerated, because enumeration weakens in the cases not enumerated. Of this there is a remarkable instance in Boon v. Comforth,[h] and in Timewell v. Perkins,[i] where the words were as general as could be used, 'Whatever I have and shall have at my death,' and were followed by an enumeration of particular things. Lord Hardwicke said, 'I am of opinion that bank notes and goldsmiths' bills did not pass; for though there is no doubt the general words would have passed them, yet the particular words which follow confine and restrain them to things of the same nature.' Wine and books are not included in a legacy of furniture.[k] The word 'money' does not include promissary notes not payable to the bearer, Government stock, long annuities, Columbian bonds.[l] Not only moneys due on mortgage, but the legal estate in the mortgaged premises will pass under the words, ' securities for money.'[m]

---

[g] 1 *Eq. Cases Abridged*, 201, pl. 14 ; Cook v. Oakley, in P. W.

[h] 2 VESEY, 278 ; Lord Hardwicke.

[i] 2 ATKYNS, 103 ; Chrichton v. Symes, 3 ATKYNS, 61 ; Roberts v. Kuffin, 2 ATKYNS, 113 ; Porter v. Iournay, 3 VESEY, 311 ; Wrench v. Sutling, 3 BEAVAN, 521 ; Cavendish v. Cavendish, 1 BRO. C. C.; Lamphier v. Despard, Lord St. Leonards, 2 DRURY and W., 59 ; Ferguson v. Ogilby, 2 DRURY and W., 548.

[k] ROPER *on Leg.*, 272.

[l] ROPER, 282 ; Ommaney v. Butcher, 1 TUR. and R., 266 ; Gosden v. Dotterill, 1 MY. and K., 56 ; Douglas v. Congreve, 1 KEEN, 410 ; Willis v. Plaskett, 4 BEAVAN, 298 ; Smith v. Butler, 1 JONES and LAT., 692 ; Marquis of Hertford v. Lord Lowther, 7 BEAVAN, 1 ; see, however, Legge v. Asgill, 1 TURN. and R., 265 ; Kendall v. Kendall, 4 RUSSELL, 360.

[m] Gallien v. Moss, 9 B. and C., 267, decided the contrary. It was overruled by Mather v. Thomas, 10 BING., 44, and *ex parte* Barber, 5 SIMON, 451.

I conclude these observations with the following rules, extracted, with the cases supporting them, from JARMAN *On Wills* :—[n]

GENERAL RULES OF CONSTRUCTION.

1. That a will of real estate, wheresoever made, and in whatever language written, is construed according to the law of England, in which the property is situate,[a] but a will of personality is governed by the 'lex domicilii.'[b]

2. That technical words are not necessary to give effect to any species of disposition in a will.[c]

3. That the construction of a will is the same at law and in equity,[d] the jurisdiction of each being governed by the nature of the subject:[e] though the consequences may differ, as in the instance of a contingent remainder, which is destructible in the one case and not in the other.

4. That a will speaks, for some purposes, from the period of execution, and for others from the death of the testator; but never operates until the latter period.[f]

5. That the heir is not to be disinherited without an express devise, or necessary implication;[g] such implication importing, not natural necessity, but so strong a probability, that an intention to the contrary cannot be supposed.[h]

6. That merely negative words are not sufficient to exclude the title of the heir or next of kin.[i] There must be an actual gift to some other definite object.

---

[n] 1460, 4 Ed., WHITE.

[a] *Pre. Ch.*, 577. [b] JARMAN *on Wills*, vol. i. p. 2.

[c] 3 DURN. and E., 86 ; 11 EAST, 246 ; 16 Id., 222.

[d] 3 P. W., 259 ; 2 VES., Sen., 74.

[e] 1 VES., Jun., 16 ; 2 *Ib.*, 417 ; 4 VES., 329.

[f] *Vide* JARMAN *on Wills*, chap. 10, vol. i. p. 277.

[g] *Br. Devise*, 52 ; DYER, 330 *b* ; 2 STRA., 969 ; *Ca. t.*, HARDW., 142 ; 1 WILS., 105 ; WILLES, 303 ; 2 D. and E., 209 ; 2 MAU. and S., 448. See also 3 *B. P. C.* TOML. ed., 45.

[h] 1 VES. and BEA., 466 ; 5 DURN. and E., 558 ; 7 EAST, 97 ; 1 *New. Rep.*, 118 ; 18 VES., 40.

[i] JARMAN, *on Wills*, vol. i. p. 294 ; 4 BEA., 318.

7. That all the parts of a will are to be construed in relation to each other, and so as, if possible, to form one consistent whole; but, where several parts are absolutely irreconcilable, the latter must prevail.[k]

8. That extrinsic evidence is not admissible to alter, detract from, or add to, the terms of a will[l] (though it may be used to rebut a resulting trust attaching to a legal title created by it,[m] or to remove a latent ambiguity).

9. Nor to vary the meaning of the words;[n] and, therefore, in order to attach a strained and extraordinary sense to a particular word, an instrument executed by the testator, in which the same word occurs in that sense, is not admissible;[o] but the

10. Courts will look at the circumstance under which the devisor makes his will—as the state of his property,[p] of his family,[q] and the like.[r]

11. That, in general, implication is admissible only in the absence of, and not to control, an express disposition.[s]

12. That an express and positive devise cannot be controlled by the reason assigned,[t] or by subsequent ambiguous words,[u] or by inference and argument from other parts of the will;[x] and, accordingly, such a devise is not affected by a subsequent

---

[k] 9 Mod., 154 ; 2 Bl., 979 ; 1 Durn. and E., 630 ; 6 Ves., 100 ; 16 Ves., 314 ; 3 Mau. and S., 158 ; Swanst., 28 ; 2 Atk., 372 ; 6 Durn. and E., 314 ; 2 Taunt., 109 ; 18 Ves., 421 ; 6 Moore, 214. But see Barnard, C. C., 261.

[l] See judgment in 16 Ves., 486 ; 5 *Rep.*, 68 ; *Cas. temp.*, Talb., 240 ; 3 B. P. C., Toml. ed., 607 ; 2 *Ch. Cas.*, 231 ; 7 Durn. and E., 138.

[m] *Cas. temp.*, Talb., 78.

[n] 4 Taunt., 176 ; 4 Dow, 65 ; 3 Mau. and S., 171.   But see 2 P. W., 135.   [o] 11 East, 441.

[p] 1 Mer., 646 ; 7 Taunt., 105 ; 1 Barn. and Ald., 550 ; 3 Barn. and Cress., 870 ; 1 B. C. C., 472.

[q] 3 B. P. C., Toml. ed., 257 ; 4 Burr., 2165 ; 4 B. C. C., 441 ; 3 Barn. and Ald., 657 ; 3 Dow, 72 ; 3 Barn. and Ald., 632 ; 2 Moore, 302.

[r] 1 Black., 60 ; 1 Mer, 384.

[s] 8 *Rep.*, 94 ; 2 Vern., 60 ; 1 P. W., 54.

[t] 16 Ves., 36.   [u] 8 Bligh, N. S., 88.

[x] 1 Ves., Jun., 268 ; 8 Ves., 42 ; Cowp., 99.

inaccurate recital of, or reference to, its contents;[y] though recourse may be had to such reference to assist the construction, in case of ambiguity or doubt.

13. That the inconvenience or absurdity of a devise is no ground for varying the construction, where the terms of it are unambiguous;[z] nor is the fact, that the testator did not foresee all the consequences of his disposition, a reason for varying it:[a] but, where the intention is obscured by conflicting expressions, it is to be sought rather in a rational and consistent, than an irrational and inconsistent purpose.[b]

14. That the rules of construction cannot be strained to bring a devise within the rules of law;[c] but it seems, that where the will admits of two constructions, that is to be preferred which will render it valid; and therefore the court, in one instance, adhered to the literal language of the testator, though it was highly probable that he had written a word, by mistake, for one which would have rendered the devise void.[d]

15. That favour or disfavour to the object ought not to influence the construction.[e]

16. That words, in general, are to be taken in their ordinary and grammatical sense, unless a clear intention to use them in another can be collected,[f] and that other can be ascertained; and they are, in all cases, to receive a construction which will give to every expression some effect, rather than one that will render any of the expressions inoperative;[g] and of two modes of construction, that is to be preferred which will prevent a total intestacy.[h]

---

[y] Moore, 13, pl. 50 ; 1 And., 8 ; Cowp., 83.

[z] 1 Mer., 417 ; 2 Sim. and Stu., 295.

[a] 3 Mau. and S., 37 ; 1 Mer., 358.

[b] 4 Madd., 67.   See also 3 B. C. C., 401.

[c] 1 Cox, 324 ; 2 Mer, 389 ; 1 Jac. and Walk., 31.   But see 2 Russ. and M., 306 ; 2 Kee., 756 ; 2 Beav., 352.

[d] 3 Burr., 1626 ; 3 B. P. C., Toml. ed., 209.

[e] 4 See Ves., 574.   But see 2 Ves. and Bea., 269.

[f] 18 Ves., 466.

[g] 3 Ves., 450 ; 7 Id., 455 ; 7 East, 272 ; 2 Barn. and Ald., 441.

[h] *Cas. temp.*, Talb., 161 ; 8 Ves., 204 ; 2 Mer., 386.

17. That, where a testator uses technical words, he is presumed to employ them in their legal sense,[i] unless the context clearly indicates the contrary.[k]

18. That words, occurring more than once in a will, shall be presumed to be used always in the same sense,[l] unless a contrary intention appear by the context,[m] or unless the words be applied to a different subject.[n] And, on the same principle, where a testator uses an additional word or phrase, he must be presumed to have an additional meaning.[o]

19. That words and limitations may be transposed,[p] supplied,[q] or rejected,[r] where warranted by the immediate context, or the general scheme of the will; but not merely on a conjectural hypothesis of the testator's intention, however reasonable, in opposition to the plain and obvious sense of the language of the instrument.[s]

20. That words which it is obvious are mis-written (as dying *with* issue, for dying *without* issue), may be corrected.[t]

---

[i] DOUGLAS, 340 ; 6 DURNFORD and ELLIS, 352 ; 4 VESEY, 329 ; 5 VESEY, 401.

[k] DOUG., 341 ; 3 B. C. C., 68 ; 5 EAST, 51 ; 2 BALL and BE., 204 ; 3 Dow, 71.

[l] 2 *Ch. Cas.*, 169.

[m] DOUG., 269.

[n] 1 P. W., 663 ; 2 VES., Sen., 616 ; 5 MAU. and S., 126 ; 1 VES. and BEA., 260, But see 14 VES., 488.

[o] 4 B. C. C., 15 ; 13 VES., 39 ; 7 TAUNT., 85. The writer has heard Lord Eldon lay down the rule in these words. But see AMB., 122 ; 6 VES., 300 ; 10 VES., 166 ; 13 EAST, 559 ; 13 VES., 476 ; 19 VES., 545 ; 1 MER., 120 ; 3 MER., 316 ;—where the argument that the testator, notwithstanding some variation of expression, had the same intention in several instances, prevailed.

[p] 2 *Ch. Ca.*, 10 ; HOB., 75 ; 2 VES., Sen., 34 ; AMB., 374 ; 8 EAST, 149 ; 15 EAST, 309 ; 1 B. and A., 137. But see 2 VES., Sen., 248.

[q] *Cro. Car.*, 185 ; 7 DURN. and E., 437 ; 6 EAST, 486 ; 3 DOWL. and RYL., 398. See also 2 BL., 1014.

[r] 2 VES., Sen., 276 ; 3 DURN. and E., 87, n. ; 3 ID., 484 ; 4 VES., 51 ; 5 VES., 243 ; 6 VES., 129 ; 12 EAST, 515 ; 9 VES., 566.

[s] 18 VES., 368 ; 19 ID., 652 ; 2 MER., 25.

[t] 8 *Mod. Reps.*, 59 ; 5 BARNWELL and ADOLPHUS, 621 ; 3 ADOLPHUS and ELLIS, 340.

21. That the construction is not to be varied by events subsequent to the execution;[u] but the courts, in determining the meaning of particular expressions, will look to possible circumstances, in which they *might* have been called upon to affix a signification to them.[x]

22. That several independent devises, not grammatically connected, or united by the expression of a common purpose, must be construed separately, and without relation to each other; although it may be conjectured, from similarity of relationship, or other such circumstances, that the testator had the same intention in regard to both.[y] There must be an apparent design to connect them.[z]

23. That where a testator's intention cannot operate to its full extent, it shall take effect as far as possible.[a]

24. That a testator is rather to be presumed to calculate on the dispositions in his will taking effect, than the contrary; and, accordingly, a provision for the death of devisees will not be considered as intended to provide exclusively for lapse, if it admits of any other construction.[b]

---

[u] *Cases temp.*, TALB., 21 ; 3 P. W., 259 ; 11 EAST, 558, n. ; 1 COX, 324 ; 1 VES., Jun., 475.

[x] 11 VES., 457.

[y] *Cro. Car.*, 368 ; DOUG., 759; 8 DURN. and E., 64 ; 1 *N. R.*, 335 ; 9 EAST, 267 ; 11 Id., 220 ; 14 VES., 304 ; 4 MAU. and S., 58 ; 1 Pri., 353 ; 4 BARN. and CRESS., 667. See also GODB., 146.

[z] LEON., 57 ; *Cas. temp.*, HARDW., 143 ; 10 EAST, 503. This and the former class of cases chiefly relate to a question of frequent occurrence ; whether words of limitation, preceded by several devises, relate to more than one of those devises.

[a] FINCH, 139 ; 3 P. W., 250. See also 4 VES., 325 ; 13 VES., 486.

[b] 2 ATK., 375 ; 4 VES., 418 ; 4 VES., 554 ; 7 VES., 586 ; 1 VES. and BEA., 422 ; 1 Pri., 264. See also 1 SWANST., 161 ; 2 VES., Jun., 501 ; and 1 M'CLELAND, 168.

ARGUMENTS USED IN THE PANDECTS.[z]

I.

FROM THE NATURE OF THE PROPOSITION.

IN facto quod finitum et certum est—nullus est conjecturæ locus.' — VENULEIUS, *De Verb. Obligation.* xlv. 1. 137, § 2.

There is no room for conjecture where the fact is definite and ascertained.

That is certain which all may understand. ' Lata culpa,' says Ulpian, 'nimia negligentia est id non intelligere quod omnes intelligunt.' With regard to the precepts of natural law they require no argument. A father arguing that he was not bound to support his child; a son that he might drag his mother into a court of justice—a husband parading his grief at the seduction of his wife as a means of obtaining money, would have appeared to a Roman jurist horrible outrages against all that magistrates and tribunals are established to uphold. They would have said with Aristotle, ' Contra negantem principia non est disputandum,' to any one who attempted to sully the precincts of a court of justice by such topics, familiar to those magistrates who calmly witnessed fellow-creatures writhing on the rack, and adjudged prisoners to be pressed to death and embowelled alive [a] without being heard in their defence. Modestinus says, after laying down an equitable rule, ' Hujus fidem sufficit firmare ex ipsâ naturali justitiâ.' [b] ' Præter hæc omnia,' says Callistratus, ' natura nos quoque docet parentes pios, qui liberorum procreandorum animo et voto uxores ducunt, filiorum appellatione omnes qui ex nobis descendunt contineri, nec enim dulciore nomine pos-

---

[z] *Vigelius de Dreisa.*

[a] Sir Thomas Armstrong's Case.

[b] *Dig.* xxvii. 1, 13, § 6: ' De ex. tutorium.'

sumus nepotes nostros quam filii appellare.'[c] 'Ratio naturalis quasi lex quædam tacita liberis parentum hæreditatem addicit,' etc.[d] With regard to fact it was 'lata culpa' to be ignorant of what was notorious, as for a master not to know 'noxium servum fuisse.'[e]

II.

SUBTILTY TO BE AVOIDED.

BONÆ fidei non convenit de apicibus juris disputare.—ULPIAN (*Dig.* xvii. 1. 29).

To insist on extreme subtilties of law is an encouragement to fraud.

'Multa,' says Julianus, 'contra rationem disputandi jure civili pro utilitate communi recepta esse innumerabilibus, rebus probari potest;' and then he proceeds to give this instance, 'Cum plures[f] trabem alienam furandi causâ sustulerint, quam singuli ferre non possent furti actione omnes teneri existimantur—quamvis subtili ratione dici possit[g] ne-

---

[c] *De Verb. Signifi.* 2. 50 ; xvi. 220.

[d] *De Bonis Damnatorum, Dig.* xlviii. 20. The whole law is beautiful, it adjudges to the children a share in the property of the condemned parent ; 'Ne ... graviorem pœnam luerent quos nulla contingeret culpa interdum in summam egestatem devoluti.' Thus did the Roman lawyers, nourished by illustrious traditions and associations very different from those inspired by the names of Coke, Gaudy, Popham, Sanders, Shower, and Trevor, mitigate the horrors of despotism among a degenerate and irreclaimable, because a corrupt people—compare the language of our lawyers on the law of forfeiture for treason. Lord Coke, especially with his parallels from the Old Testament, justifying in detail every abomination that the genius of the feudal age had established as part of the 'common law of England.'

[e] *Dig.* xix. 1. 12. JUVENAL :—

'dabitur mora parvula, dum res

Nota urbi, et populo, contingat principis aures.

Dedecus ille domus sciet ultimus.'

[f] *Dig.* ix. 2. 51. *Ad Legem Aquiliam.*

[g] Julianus had never read the decision in Moffatt's Case. It was not from ignorance, but deep knowledge, that the Roman lawyers rejected useless subtilty. They were as well acquainted with all the 'nice sharp

B B

minem eorum teneri, quia neminem verum sit eam sustulisse.'
Again, 'Si debitori concessum est et hæres ejus vendiderit
potest facti quæstio esse quid intellexerit creditor,' but he says
the sale is valid; 'sed recte venisse dicitur—hæ enim subtilitates a judicibus non admittuntur.'[h] The same principle is
applied 'de jure dotium,' *Dig.* xxiii. 3. 9, § 'si res,' ending
with 'benignius est favore dotium necessitatem imponi hæredi
consentire,' and the code preserved this principle; the same
argument is used there l. vii. *C. de Institut. vel substitut.* ' ne
dum 'nimiâ subtilitate utimur circa hujusmodi sensus judicia
testantium defraudentur.' Again, vii. *De Senatusconsul. Tre-
bell.* 'Ne dum nimiâ subtilitate utimur circa res pupillares
ipsa subtilitas ad perniciem eorum revertatur.' Again, *De
Jure Dotium*, ' Quod satis scrupulosum et per nimiam subtili-
tatem perniciosum est.' In the *Institutes* it is said, 'Nobis in
legibus magis simplicitas quam difficultas placet.'

III.

EVERY THING CONTRA BONOS MORES IS INVALID.

QUÆ facta lædunt pietatem, existimationem vere-
cundiam nostram et ut generaliter dixerim contra
bonos mores fiunt nec facere nos posse credendum
est.

Dig. xxviii. 7. 15; PAPINIAN, *De conditionibus Institu-
tionem.* So it was a rule of the Roman law, unknown of course
to ours, that where certain relations existed between suitors bearing the stamp of the charities and sympathies which raise man

---

quillets of the law' as if they could have repeated Baron Parke's judgments by heart, but they were too profound to value them. A little
knowledge of medicine makes men quacks—a little knowledge of philosophy, atheists—a little knowledge of theology, sectarians—a little
knowledge of military science, martinets—a little knowledge of the
learned languages, pedants. So, a narrow and superficial view of
jurisprudence infallibly makes them, 'syllabarum ancipes, formularum
cantores; and always disposed to value what is merely technical, above
the object for which it is only tolerable so far as it preserves.

[h] *Dig.* xx. 6. 8, § 10. Debitori. 'Fortunati ambo,' judge and suitor.

above the brutes that perish, the defendant should not be ruined by his adversary, but only condemned 'in id quod facere posset.'   A husband had agreed to waive the benefit of this rule, and the question was, if the agreement could be upheld; the answer was in the negative, 'Negat servari oportere quod quidem et mihi videtur verum namque contra bonos mores id pactum esse melius est dicere.'—*Dig.* xxiv. 3. 14.

'Observandum est ne is judex detur quem altera pars nominatim petat—id enim iniqui exempli esse—Divus Hadrianus rescripsit.'—*Dig.* v. 1. 47.

IV.

ARGUMENTS FROM THE DEFINITION.

'Morbus sonticus æstimandus est qui cuique rei agendæ impedimento est litiganti—pono quid magis impedimento est, quam motus corporis contra naturam quem febrem appellant.' [i] A similar argument is used in the *Institutes*: 'Fur est qui alienam rem invito domino contrectat. Quis autem magis alienam rem invito domino contrectat, quam qui vi rapit?' See the argument of Ulpian as to the definition of 'dolus malus;' [k] as to the definition of the word 'exhibet.' [l]

On the question whether 'frumentum' was comprised under the word 'instrumentum,' it is said, 'plurimis non placet, quia consumeretur quippe instrumentum est apparatus rerum diutius mansurarum sine quibus exerceri possessio nequiret.' *De Instrumento Legato, Dig.* xxxiii. 7. 12. Ulpian, however, thinks that it was 'sed ego puto.'   Again, 'Quoniam defendere est eandem vicem quam reus subire defensor mariti amplius quam maritus facere possit non est condemnandus.' [m]

---

[i] *Dig.* xlii. 1. 60.
[l] *Dig.* l. 16. 246.
[k] *Dig.* iv. 3. 1.
[m] *Dig.* iii. 3. 51.

V.

ARGUMENT FROM THE GENUS TO THE SPECIES.

SEMPER specialia generalibus insunt. — GAIUS, *De Reg. Juris*, 189.

General words always include the species.

So the grandfather and grandchild were comprehended under the words 'parentes et liberos.' 'Generaliter," says Ulpian, 'parentes et liberos Prætor excepit, nec gradus liberorum parentumve enumeravit—in infinitum igitur eis præstabitur.'[n] Again, 'Generaliter vetuit Prætor ad infamiam alicujus quid fieri—Proinde quodcunque quis fecerit vel dixerit, ut aliquem infamaret—erit actio injuriarum :'[o] so the word 'lumina' was held to include not only those actually existing but those which might be hereafter. 'Si ita sit cautum ne luminibus officiatur, ambigua est scriptura, utrum ne his luminibus officiatur quæ nunc sunt, an etiam his quæ postea quoque fuerint, et humanius est verbo generali omne lumen significari sive quod in præsenti, sive quod post tempus conventionis contigerit.'[p] Where the law made no distinction the Roman judge made none; 'Facti quidem quæstio est in auctoritate judicantium, juris autem auctoritas non est;'[q] a rule which would have saved us from most of the absurdities by which our law is disfigured. The exception to this rule will be found in a maxim already commented upon.[r]

VI.

ARGUMENT A DIFFERENTIA.[s]

This topic is used by Labeo when arguing that the

---

[n] *Dig.* xxxvii. 5. 1.

[o] *Dig.* xlvii. 10. 15.

[p] *Dig.* viii. 2. 22.

[q] *Dig.* l. 1. 15.

[r] 'In toto jure generi per speciem derogatur,' etc.

[s] SMIGLECIUS, *Logica*, Disput. 5. Quæst. 7.—'Dicendum est omnem differentiam constituentem esse etiam distinguentem.' This is well illustrated by the distinction which Ulpian draws as between the 'transactio,' and the 'pactum de non petendo.' 'Qui transigit,' he says, 'quasi de re dubiâ et lite incestâ neque finitâ transigit. Qui vero paciscitur donationis causâ rem certam et indubitatam liberalitate

'scapha navis' is not included in the 'instrumentum navis.'[s] Scapha navis non est instrumentum navis—et enim mediocritate non genere ab eâ differt. Instrumentum autem cujusque rei necesse est alterius generis esse atque ea cujus sit;" and Paulus proving in the chapter *De Contrahendâ Emptione*,[t] that 'permutatio' was not a species of 'emptio,' says, 'Nam ut aliud est vendere aliud emere—alius emptor, alius venditor, sic aliud est pretium, aliud est merx, quod in permutatione discerni non potest uter emptor et uter venditor sit.' Another specimen of this reasoning is given on the same chapter, on the question, whether a particular contract fell under the head of hiring 'emptio locatio,' or of buying and selling 'emptio venditio.' 'Convenit mihi tecum ut certum numerum tegularum mihi dares certo pretio, quas tu faceres— utrum emptio sit an locatio. Respondi si ex meo fundo tegulas tibi factas ut darem, convenit, emptionem puto esse non conductionem. Toties enim conductio alicujus rei est, quoties materia in quâ aliquid præstatur in eodem statu ejus manet, quoties vero et immutatur et alienatur, emptio magis quam locatio intelligi debet.'[u] Another in the code 'Non codicillum sed testamentum aviam vestram facere voluisse, institutio et exhæredatio facta probant evidenter.'[v] Such is the argument

dimittit. Sic etiam servus et filiusfamilias quamvis sub eodem genere contineantur—ambo enim in potestate sunt alterius tamen inter alia in hoc quoque differunt, quod filiusfamilias civiliter alii obligari possit, servus non possit.'—*Dig.* ii. 15. 1. In illustration, I hope I may be excused for adding this passage from DEMOSTHENES—'Καί τοι καὶ τοῦτο ὦ ἄνδρες Ἀθηναῖοι ἐγὼ λοιδορίαν κατηγορίας, τούτῳ διαφέρειν ἡγοῦμαι, τῷ τὴν μὲν κατηγορίαν ἀδικήματ' ἔχειν ὧν ἐν τοῖς νόμοις εἰσιν αἱ τιμωρίαι τὴν δε λοιδορίαν, βλασφημίας ἃς κατὰ τὴν αὐτῶν φύσιν τοῖς ἐχθροις περὶ ἀλλήλων συμβαίνει λέγειν : π. σ. § 123.' And in a still more striking passage of the same marvellous and unequalled effort—'Ὁ γὰρ σύμβουλος καὶ ὁ συκοφάντος, οὐδὲ, τῶν ἄλλων οὐδὲν ἐοικότες ἐν τούτῳ πλεῖστον ἀλλήλων διαφέρουσιν—ὁ μέν γε πρὸ τῶν πραγμάτων, γνώμην ἀποφαίνεται καὶ δίδωσιν ἑαυτὸν ὑπευθυνοι, τοῖς πεισθεῖσι τῇ τύχῃ τοῖς καιροῖς τῷ βουλομένῳ—ὁ δὲ σιγήσας ἡνίκ' ἔδει λέγειν ἄν τι δύσκολον συμβῇ τοῦτο βασκαίνει.'

[s] *Dig.* xxxiii. 7. 29.

[t] *Dig.* xvii. 2. 1.   [u] *Dig.* xvii. 2. 65.

[v] *Cod.* xiv. *De Testamentis.*

' suum cuique tribuit,' therefore he is just—' de apicibus juris disputat,' therefore he is not a great judge—he is fond of the most irrational subtilties, therefore he has the mind of a pettifogger—he is an attorney's son, therefore he is at the bar, etc.

VII.

ARGUMENT FROM THE WHOLE TO THE PART.

' What has been said as to the recovery of the whole, is to be understood of the part.' ' Quæ de tota re vindicandâ dicta sunt—eadem et de parte intelligenda sunt'[a]—Gaius. So Ulpian: ' Sive tota res evincatur sive pars habet regressum emptor ad venditorem.'[b] And Paulus: ' Cujus effectus omnibus prodest, ejus et partes ad omnes pertinent.'[c] So with regard to the tutor, if he attempted to act out of his district, he had no more authority than if the affairs of the ' pupillus ' had never been entrusted to him. ' Atque si ei administratio tutelæ permissa non esset—quantum enim facit in totum denegata tantundem valet si in eâ re, de quâ agitur denegata sit.'[d] Ulpian uses the same argument in the chapter ' de pactis ': ' Constat in emptione cæterisque bonæ fidei judiciis, re nondum secutâ posse abiri ab emptione—si igitur in totum potest cui non et pars ejus pactione mutari possit?'[e] In the same chapter Paulus says: ' Si pactus ne hæreditatem peterem singulas res ut hæres petam, ex eo quod pactum erit, pacti conventi exceptio aptanda erit.'[f] And he gives these illustrations: ' Quemadmodum si convenerit ne fundum peterem —et usum fructum petam—aut ne navim ædificiumve peterem, et dissolutis iis singulas res petam.'

So Julianus says, that as none of the produce of land can be claimed by the ' malâ fide possessor,' so the possessor of common property can claim only a portion of its produce:

---

a *Dig.* i. 75, *De rei vindic.*   b *Dig.* xxi. 2. 1, *De evict.*

c *De reg. Juris,* 190.

d *Dig.* xxvi. 7. 50, *De admin. et per tutorum.*

e *Dig.* ii. 14. 7.   f *Id.* tit. 27.

' Quemadmodum si totum fundum alienum quis sciens possideat nulla ex parte fructus suos faciet, quoquo modo sati fuerint, ita qui communem fundum possidet, non faciet fructus suos quo eâ parte quâ fundus ad socium ejus pertinerit.' Again the same rule is used by Celsus: ' Si chorus aut familia legatur perinde est quasi singuli homines legati sint'—and by Paulus: ' Cum hæreditatem peto et corpora et actiones omnes quæ in hæreditate sunt videntur in hæreditatem deducta.' Three arbiters are chosen; one condemns the defendant to pay fifteen ' aurei, another ten, another five. The question is, what is he to pay? or is he to pay anything? ' Et Julianus scribit quinque debere præstari quia in hanc summam omnes consenserunt.' There are several exceptions to this rule; one is, that a bequest to a corporate body is not a bequest to the individuals of whom it consists: ' Si quid universitati debetur —singulis non debetur—nec quod debet universitas singuli debent.'g Nor was the representative of the body the representative of its members: ' Si municipes vel aliqua universitas ad agendum det actorem—non erit hic dicendum quasi a pluribus datum sic haberi. Hic enim pro republicâ vel universitate intercedit non pro singulis.'h   Again—' Universitatis sunt non singulorum veluti quæ in civitatibus sunt, ut theatra et stadia et his similia.'i   So if the father ordered the son to accept an inheritance as the sole heir, ' quasi ex asse,' and he accepted it as heir of a part, the acceptance was invalid: ' Si pater filio mandavit quasi ex asse instituto et inveniatur ex parte—non puto ex jussu adiisse.'k

---

g *Dig.* ii. 3. 4. 7, § 1.   h *Dig.* ii. *id.* tit. 2.
i *Dig.* i. 8. 6, § 1.

k *Dig.* xxix. 2. 25. And see the law, *Dig.* xxx. 5, § *fin* : ' Cum fundus *communis*, legatus sit non adjectâ portione, sed *meum* nominaverit portionem deberi constat.' This is the meaning of the passage, which at first sight is not obvious. Titius leaves all an estate, of which being only joint proprietor he could only give a part ; he describes it all as ' meum.' This false description invalidates the bequest ' pro tanto ' as to the part not belonging to him, and the heir is not bound to give its value to the devisee. Here the rule, ' Falsa demonstratio non nocet.' does not operate ; but if no part of the farm had belonged to the

VIII.

ARGUMENT FROM THE PART TO THE WHOLE.

If an estate is bequeathed to me, by taking possession of a part, I take possession of all: 'Si solus hæres ex pluribus partibus fuero institutus, unam portionem adeundo omnes acquiro.'[1] ' Si cui res legata fuerit et omnino aliquâ ex parte voluerit suam esse totam adquirit.'[m] ' Si patre filio mandavit ex parte adire, potest ex asse adire.'[n]

Where one of the parts is wanting, the whole is incomplete: ' In omnibus rebus animadverto id perfectum esse quod ex omnibus suis partibus constat.'[o]   Paulus says: ' Meum esse cujus non potest ulla pars dici alterius esse.'[p]

A body of which the parts alter, is legally the same.   The law illustrates this (*Dig. de judiciis,* 76).   In answer to a question as to how far a substitution of some for other judges changed the identity of the tribunal, Alfenus says: ' Non si modo usus aut alter sed etsi omnes judices mutati essent, tamen et rem eandem et judicium idem quod antea fuisset, permanere— neque in hoc solum evenire ut partibus commutatis eadem res esse existimatur, sed et in multis cæteris rebus—nam et legionem eandem haberi ex quâ multi decessissent, quorum in locum alii subjecti essent—et populum eundem hoc tempore putari quam abhinc centum annis fuisset cum ex illis nemo nunc viveret—itemque si navis adeo sæpe refecta esset, ut nulla tabula eadem permaneret, quæ non nova fuisset—nihilominus eandem navem esse existimari.'[q]—κ. τ. λ.

To the same effect is the law—' Si grege legato aliqua pecora vivo testatore mortua essent, in eorumque locum alia essent subtituta eandem gregem videri.'[r]   So ' Si navem le-

---

testator, it would have operated, and the heir would have been obliged to purchase the estate, or give its value to the devisee—' Demonstratio in totum falsa non vitat legatum, pro parte falsa, vitat pro parte.'— *Vigelius de Dreisâ,* p. 185.

[1] *Dig.* xxix. 2. 10.   [m] *Dig.* xxix. 2. 79.
[n] *Dig.* xxxi. 60.   [o] *Dig.* i. 2. 1.
[p] *Dig.* l. 16. 25.   [q] *Dig.* v. l. 76.
[r] *Dig.* xxx. 22, § 1.

gavero et specialiter eam ascripsero, eamque per partes totam refecero, *carinâ eâdem manente,* nihilominus recte a legatario vindicabitur.'[s]   So ' Si domus fuerit legata, licet particulatim ita refecta sit, ut nihil ex pristinâ materiâ supersit, tamen dicemus utile manere legatum—at si eâ domo destructâ aliam eodem loco testator ædificaverit dicemus interire legatum—nisi aliud testatorem sensisse fuerit approbatum.'[t]

IX.

ARGUMENT FROM THE CAUSE.

1. Such as the cause, such is the effect, e.g., the children of a slave are slaves—the children not born in matrimony are illegimate—from the ' prætorian' stipulation, a ' prætorian ' action.   Hence ' posito uno absurdo, [e. g., that the crier of the court could vouch for an estate he never heard of] multa sequi absurda.'—*Novell.* 18.   ' Concesso uno inconvenienti sequi aliud.' 7 *Cod. de rescind. Vind.*   So the Canon Law says: ' Quæ malo inchoata sunt principio vix est ut bono peragentur exitu.'

2. The cause of a cause is the cause of the effect of that cause. There is an illustration of this argument in the *Lex Julia de adulteriis* :[u] ' Si in domum aliquam soliti fuerint convenire ad tractandum de adulterio etsi eo loci nihil fuerit admissum— verum tamen videtur is domum suam ut stuprum adulteriumve committeretur præbuisse, quia sine colloquio illo adulterium non committeretur.'   And on the *Leg. Aquiliam*—' In hâc actione dolus est culpa punitur—ideoque si quis in stipulam suam vel spinam, comburendæ ejus causâ ignem immiserit, et ulterius evagatus et progressus ignis alienam segetem vel vineam cæserit — requiramus nunc negligentiâ ejus vel culpa id accidit nam si die ventore id fecit culpæ reus est—nam et qui

---

[s] *Dig. id.* tit. 24, § *fin.*

[t] *Dig. id.* tit. 64, § *fin.* And the law as to the team—' Quadrigæ legatum equo posteâ mortuo, perire quidem ita credunt, si equus ille decessit, qui demonstrabat quadrigam sed si medio tempore deminuta suppleantur ad legatarium pertinebit.' *Dig.* xxxi. 67, § *quadrigæ.*

[u] *Dig.* xlviii. 5. 9.

occasionem præstat damnum fecisse videtur in eodem cri-
mine est et qui non observavit ne ignis longius procederet,
at si omnia quæ oportuit observavit, vel subita vis venti longius ignem produxit, caret culpâ.'[x]

'It were infinite,' say Lord Bacon, 'for the law to consider
the causes of causes and their impulsions one of another,
therefore it contenteth itself with the immediate cause, and
judgeth of acts by that without looking to any further degree.'
In 'jure non remota causa sed proxima spectatur.'

This topic is in our law well illustrated by the risks of
carriers and insurers. In Powell v. Salisbury,[y] it was held that
where, in consequence of the bad condition of fences, which
the defendant was bound to repair, the plaintiff's horses es-
caped into defendant's close, where they were killed by the
falling of a hay-stack, that the defendant was liable; and the
person who sets in motion the cause of evil will be held
responsible for its effects.[z] 'I look,' says C. J. De Grey, 'upon

---

[x] *Dig.* ix. 2. 30, § 3.

[y] 2 Yo. and J., 391 ; SMITH's *Leading Cases*, KEATING and WILLES, p.
210.

[z] Scott v. Shephard, 2 W. BL. Blackstone's argument turns upon
the important question, whether the letters t r e s p a s s or c a s e
also should be used.

'We must keep up the boundaries of action,' said Lord Raymond,
'otherwise we shall introduce the utmost confusion !' *i. e.*, he must ruin
suitors for the unmeaning jargon of a barbarous age, contrived by
practitioners for the benefit of sheriffs' officers, interpreted by men
for the most part narrow-minded and illiterate (as the results shew), to
an almost incredible degree. Let any one read MEESON and WELSBY,
and say whether worse confusion can be imagined—'Confusum est
quicquid in pulverem sectum est.'

'It was long,' says Bayley, J., 'a vexata quæstio [what was this important question which the judges of England left unsettled as a refuge
for pettifoggers?] whether *case* could be brought [*i.e.*, whether the four
letters which make up the word 'case' must or must not be inserted,
in order to enable a man whose eye had been poked out, or limb
mutilated, or property destroyed by the negligence of another, to obtain redress] when the defendant was present. Early in my experience,
'case' *was* the form. In Lord Kenyon's time, a doubt was raised, and *he*
thought 'trespass' was the only action ! Leame v. Bray, was an action of

all that was done subsequent to the original throwing as a continuation of the first force and first act.[a] The cases on insurance are explained with much ability in BROOM's *Legal Maxims*, p. 165.

X.

PARITY OF REASON.

Julianus, proving that the 'usufruct' of a runaway slave was not lost, says: ' Quâ ratione retinetur a proprietario possessio etiam si in fugâ servus sit, pari ratione etiam ususfructus retinetur.'—*Dig.* vii. 1. 12, § *de illo*.

Again, Ulpian: ' Sicut in negotiis gestis vivorum sufficit negotium utiliter cæptum ita et in bonis mortuorum licet diversus exitus sit secutus.'—*Dig.* iii. 5. 11.

Paulus: ' Cum in hæreditatis petitione quæ et ipsa in rem est, dolus præteritus refertur, non est absurdum per consequentiam, et in speciali in rem actione dolum præteritum deduci.'— *Dig.* vi. 1. 28.

Other instances are—

' Ratihabitio mandato æquiparatur.'—*Dig. de Reg. Juris*, 194.

' Servitutem mortalitati fere comparamus.'—*Ib. antepen.*

' Parem esse conditionem oportet ejus qui quid possideat vel habeat, atque ejus cujus dolo malo factum est, quominus possideret vel haberet.'—*Ib.* 192.

' Quæ de tota re vindicanda dicta sunt eadem et de parte intelligenda sunt.'—*Dig.* vi. 1. 75.

---

trespass. Lord Ellenborough thought it should have been 'case''! etc.— (C. Baron Parke ('here are his very c's, and m's, and t's,'), 5 M. and W., 587.) And so steeped in technicalities are the faculties of those who gravely give this history of mischievous folly, that it never occurs to them to think that they are pronouncing as bitter a censure on the law and its expounders, as (short of corruption) it is in the power of words to convey. They no more perceive the evil, than a tallowchandler does the odour of his candles, or a Hottentot the deformity of the rings he carries in his nose and upper lip.

Piggott *v.* Eastern Counties Railway Company, 3 C. B., 229. Damage caused by spark from engine.

[a] Devaux *v.* Salvador, 4 AD. and ELLIS ; controverted, 14 PETERS, 111 ; Redman *v.* Wilson, 14 M. and W., 476 ; Laurie *v.* Douglas, 15 *ib.,* 746.

3. 'A pari causâ par procedit effectus.' On this maxim rests the law: 'Inveterata consuetudo pro lege non immerito custoditur et hoc est jus quod dicitur moribus constitutum— nam cum ipsæ leges nullâ aliâ ex causâ nos teneant quam quod judicio populi receptæ sunt, merito et ea quæ sine scripto populus probavit, tenebunt omnes—nam quid interest suffragio populus suam voluntatem declaret, an rebus ipsis et factis.'[a]

4. If many causes produce the same effect, it matters not which is set in motion. So 'Contrahitur hypotheca per pactum conventum—nec ad rem pertinet quibus fit verbis ... et ideo et sine scripturâ si convenit ut hypotheca sit et probari poterit res obligata erit.'[b] So in the *Instit. de Legatis* : 'Nomina significandorum hominum gratiâ reperta sunt, quod si alio quolibet modo intelliguntur nihil interest.'

5. From cause to effect: 'Qui actionem habet ad rem recuperandam ipsam rem habere videtur.'[c] If several causes are requisite to produce an effect, the absence of any one is fatal: 'Ubi lex inhibet usucapionem bona fides possidenti nihil prodest.'[d]

6. From a cessation of the cause to a cessation of the effect. So Papinian says, that with the power of the adopted father all the rights arising from the relation so created are at an end: 'In omni fere jure finitâ patris adoptivi potestate nullum ex pristino jure retinetur vestigium denique et patria dignitas

---

[a] *Dig*. i. 4. 32, § 1.

[b] *Dig*. xx. 1. 4. 'Mortgages may not only be created by the express deeds and contracts of the parties, but they may also be implied in equity from the nature of the transaction between the parties, and then they are equitable mortgages. Thus it is settled, that if the debtor deposit his title-deeds with a creditor as a security, it is a valid agreement for a mortgage, and not within the Statute of Frauds.' 1020, STORY, *Equity Juris*. Ex parte Coming, 9 VESEY, 116. Russell *v*. Russell, 1 B. *Chan. Reports*, 269.

[c] This sounds an extravagant proposition to the countrymen of Vesey, junior, and of Meeson and Welsby, and of the late Lord Abinger, who said he never knew a case considered from beginning to end simply with reference to its merits.

[d] *Dig*. xli. 3. 24.

quæsita per adoptionem, finitâ eâ deponitur.'[e] Ulpian says: ' Qui in servitute est usucapere non potest, nam cum possideatur possidere non videtur.'[f] So ' Tamdiu clarissima fœmina erit, quamdiu senatori nupta est vel clarissimo.'[g] In the *Institutes de success. cognat.*: ' Vulgo quæsitos nullos habere adquatos cum adquatio a patre sit. Hi autem nullum patrem habere intelliguntur'; and the reasoning of Proculus: ' Si is qui animo possessionem saltus retineret, furere cœpisset non potest dum fureret ejus saltus possessionem amittere, quia furiosus non potest desinere, animo possidere.'[h] So as to the rights of third parties which fail with the right from which they are derived, Papinian says: ' Si medio tempore pignus creditor pignori dederit—domino solvente pecuniam quam debuit, secundi pignoris, neque persecutio dabitur neque retentio relinquetur';[i] and if land was let on condition, that if the rent was in arrear it should return to the owner, and the rent so let was mortgaged, on failure of payment, the right of the mortgagee expired: ' Si vectigali non soluto jure suo dominus usus esset, etiam pignoris jus evanuisse' (*Dig.* xx. 1. 31). So money paid for the ' dos' was of necessity to be returned, if the marriage did not take place.[k]

7. From the final cause, when the end is accomplished, the power or action, granted for the purpose of attaining it, ceases also. So the ' curator,' appointed to conduct a suit between the ' tutor' and ' pupillus,' ceased to be curator when the suit was ended: ' Eo peracto curator esse desinit.' A partnership ceased if the business, for which it was entered into, was terminated: ' Si alicujus rei societas contracta sit et fini negotio impositus, finitur societas.' So ' Quod meum est usucapere me intelligi non potest.' This principle (after the disregard of it had caused an Iliad of calamities to all Englishmen not lawyers)

---

[e] *Dig.* xlvi. 4. 13.
[f] *De Reg. Juris.*, 160.   [g] *Dig.* i. 9. 8, et 6 *id.* tit.
[h] *Dig.* xli. 2. 27.   [i] *Dig.* xx. 1. 40.
[k] *Cod. de condict. ob causam*, l. 1. 'Pecuniam quam te ob dotem accepisse pacto interposito proponis impediente quocunque modo juris authoritate matrimonium jure condictionis restituere debes.'

has at last been adopted with regard to outstanding terms assigned in trust to attend the inheritance (8 and 9 Vic. c.112).[1] By a recent change in the law, the practice of assigning satisfied terms is now at an end. ' For the protection afforded (why should it have been wanted?), by that practice being for several reasons precarious!!! and even, when effectual, being obtained at the expense of an innocent party!!! (what a picture of the results of *practical* sense!) it has been with great wisdom provided (A.D. 1845), with respect to satisfied terms of years, that such as should, by express declaration or construction of law, on the 31st Dec., 1845, be attendant upon the inheritance or reversion of any lands, should on that day absolutely cease,' etc.[m]

8. That which is contrary to the end for which anything is instituted is invalid. There is on this topic a remarkable law in the Pandects. ' Solent,' says Ulpian, ' præsides in carcerem continendos damnare ut in vinculis contineantur—SED ID EOS FACERE NON OPORTET—nam hujus modi pœnæ interdictæ sunt[n]—carcer enim ad continendos homines—non ad puni-

---

[1] Doe *v.* Price, 6 M. and W., 603 ; Hall *v.* Monsdale, *ib.,* 689 ; Doe *v.* Phillips, 10 *Q. B. Reports,* 130 ; Gaward *v.* Tuck, 8 C. B., 231. Well may Chancellor Kent exclaim at the immeasurable folly of allowing disputes on such a subject for 150 years (4 KENT *Comm.,* sect. 58) : ' A very vexatious question has been agitated . . . . it is worth a moment's attention, as a legal curiosity, and a sample of the perplexity and uncertainty,' etc.

[m] STEPHENS' *Blackstone,* i. 365. STORY, *Equity Juris.,* 1001.

[n] This passage will surprise many who look on the Roman law (contained in all the *Codes,* the *Digest,* and the *Institutes*), as a mere repertory of despotic maxims, as Junius, relying with well-grounded confidence on the profound ignorance of his countrymen, described it in his absurd and much-admired letter to Lord Mansfield. Perhaps the magistrates, who punished the keeper of a prison for allowing a person, innocent in the eye of the law and of reason, as he had not been tried, to see his wife, who happened to be a lady, as well as a generous, constant, and high-minded woman, might have been a little wiser if they had considered it ; certainly, if it had been acted upon in the time of the Stuarts (I fear a good deal later, see the cases of Arne and Huggins in the *State Trials*), it would have prevented many murders. Imprisonment might, at the will of the Crown, be death. See Mrs.

endos haberi debet';° and again, 'Factum a judice quod ad *officium* ejus non pertinet ratum non est.'ᴾ

XI.

EFFECT OF EXCEPTIONS.

(To this rule I have already had occasion to advert.)

EXCEPTIO firmat regulam in casibus non exceptis.

So Paulus applies it (*Dig. de Judiciis*, 12): 'Cum Prætor unum ex pluribus judicare vetat—cæteris id committere videtur.' So as the *Lex Julia* forbade an adulteress to give evidence, it was inferred that the evidence of other women might be received: 'Ex eo quod prohibet lex Julia de adulteriis testimonium dicere condemnatam mulierem, colligitur etiam mulieres in judicio testimonii dicendi jus habere' (*Dig. de testibus*, 18). So Ulpian says: 'Cum lex in præteritum quid indulget in futurum vetat.'

There are some exceptions to this rule in the Pandects. A testator left his wife the 'usufruct' of his house, and everything it contained, 'argento excepto.' Scævola held that the exception did not extend the legacy to things which it would not otherwise include: 'Uxori usumfructum domus et omnium rerum quæ in his domibus erant, excepto argento, legaverat— quæsitum est, an lanæ cujusque coloris *mercis causâ* paratæ item purpuræ quæ in domibus erant, ususfructus ei deberetur— respondi, excepto argento, et his quæ mercis causâ comparata sunt—cæterorum omnium usumfructum legatariam habere' (*Dig.* xxxiii. 2. 32, § 2); to which may be added the law (*Dig.* xxxvi. 1. 78, § 'pluribus'). Another instance, where it is superseded, is where there is an accessory to the thing ex-

---

Hutchinson's account of the prison by which her noble husband was destroyed. 'Mr. William Jenkins, 1684, on refusing the Oxford oath, was committed to Newgate, where he died. When he had been prisoner four months and one week, a little before his death, he said, a man might be as effectually murdered in Newgate as at Tyburn.'—NEAL, *History of the Puritans*, vol. iv. p. 529.

    ° *Dig.* xlviii. 19. 8.   ᴾ 129, *De Reg. Juris.*

cepted. In that case the accessory, though not specified, follows
the principal, *e. g.* (*Dig.* xxxiii. 8. 25, § 2): ' Quum instrumentum omne legatum esset excepto pecore, pastores oviliones,
ovilia quoque legato contineri—Ofilius *non* recte putat.'

Another rule, with regard to exceptions, is where it limits a
preceding clause, for instance (*Dig.* xxxiii. 9, § 4, *de penu legatâ*):
' Si ita sit scriptum, omnem penum præter vinum quod Romæ
erit, do, lego, sola penus quæ Romæ est legata videtur.'

XII.

INSTANCES OF INDUCTIVE REASONING.

Ulpian infers the general rule from the enumeration of par-
ticulars in this remarkable law :—

(*Dig.* ii. 14. 7) ' Si paciscar ne judicati vel incensarum ædium
agatur hoc pactum valet. Si paciscar ne operis novi nuncia-
tionem exequar—si quidem ex re familiari operis novi nuntiatio facta sit, liceat pacisci; et de furto pacisci lex permittit.
Si quis paciscatur ne depositi agat, secundum Pomponium
valet pactum—item si quis pactus sit ut ex causâ depositi
omne periculum præstet, Pomponius ait pactionem valere,
nec quasi contra juris formam factam non esse servandam, et in
cæteris *igitur* omnibus ad edictum prætoris pertinentibus, quæ
non ad publicam læsionem sed ad rem familiarem respiciunt
pacisci licet.'

MODESTINUS (*Dig.* xli. 1. 54, § 1). ' Item promittendo nobis
liber homo qui bonâ fide nobis servit, vel emendo, vel vendendo, vel locando, vel conducendo, obligari ipso jure poterit.'
The argument from custom and precedent rests upon this basis:
' rerum perpetuo similiter judicatarum authoritatem vim legis
obtinere debere.' (*Dig.* i. 3. 37; see too *Instit. de fideicom.*
Hæred., § *postea divus.*)

The negative argument is exemplified (*de Reg. Juris. Dig.*
xlv.) : ' Neque pignus, neque depositum, neque precarium, neque
emptio, neque locatio rei suæ consistere potest.' Therefore,
' nullus contractus rei suæ consistere potest.' ' Hæres qui legatum debet, neque ex contractu, neque ex maleficio obligatus
esse intelligitur—igitur ex quasi contractu erit obligatus.' (*Dig.*

xliv. 7. 4.)   So, from the receipts of the three last years, it was inferred that all former dues had been paid to the imperial treasury. (*Cod. de Apoch. Public.* c. 3.)

XIII.

INSTANCES OF THE SYLLOGISM.

Affirmative Form:—Morbus sonticus diem judicii differt
        Febris est morbus sonticus
        Febris diem judicii differt (*Dig.* xlii. 7. 60).

Negative:—'Cujus dolo malo sepulchrum violatum esse dicitur in eum sepulchri violati actio datur.'

' Impuberes et omnes qui non violandi animo sepulchrum violant dolo malo cavent.'

' In impuberes et omnes qui non violandi animo sepulchrum violant, sepulchri violati actio non datur.' (*Dig.* xlvii. 12. 3.)

The argument is stated as an enthymem; *e.g., Dig. de Publiciana in rem actione,* 8.

' Marcellus ait, eum qui a furioso ignorans eum furere, emit posse usucapere.'   ' Ergo et Publicianam habere.'   The major premise ' Quicunque potest usucapere Publicianam habet,' is omitted.

The minor premise is omitted in this instance (*Dig.* xlvii. 1. 137), ' Stipulatione quæ utriusque consensu non fit, nihil agitur. ' Ergo si hominem stipulatus suis et ego de alio sensero, tu de alio nihil agitur.'   The wanting premise being 'hominis stipulatio in quâ ego de alio sensero tu de alio, utriusque consensu non fit.'   Sometimes the conclusion is omitted (*de ritu nuptiarum, Dig.* xxiii. 2. 14. §1): ' In contrahendis matrimoniis, naturale jus et pudor inspiciendus est.   Contra pudorem autem filiam suam uxorem ducere.'   So again (*Dig.* xii. 6. 23): ' Si quis repeti non solet, quod ob causam datum est causâ secutâ.   Sed hic non videtur causa secuta cum transactioni non stetur.'   The law (*Dig.* xxxiii. 7. 29), contains an inverted syllogism, of which the conclusion is: ' Scapha navis non est instrumentum navis,' because 'mediocritate non genere ab eâ differt.' 'Instrumentum autem cujusque rei necessæ est alterius generis esse atque ea quæque sit.' So Ulpian (*Dig.* i. 8, 9), 'Leges sanctæ sunt sanctione enim quâdam subnixæ sunt—quod autem sanctione quâdam subnixum est—id sanctum est etsi deo non sit consecratum.' The argument of Papinian (xxxv. 1. 98) is this: 'Non potest eadem ut vidua et ut nupta legatum petere.' 'At si Titiae ducenta legata sint si nupserit—centum si non nupserit eaque nupserit, ducenta ut nupta petere potest,'

ergo—'Centum ut vidua petere non potest.'

So (*Dig.* l. 16, 148),in order to shew that a man with one child did not fall under the category of those who were 'sine liberis.' Gaius argues in this way: 'Aut liberos quis habet aut est sine liberis.'

'Qui unum filium habet sine liberis esse dici non potest,'

ergo:—' Qui unum filium habet liberos habere dicendus est.'

As an instance of an hypothetical argument:—

'Si posteriore pacto satisfactum non fuerit ex primâ cautione petitio erit totius debiti.

At posteriore pacto satisfactum non est—

Ex primâ igitur cautione petitio erit totius debiti.' (*Dig.* ii. 14, 47.)

Again: 'Si tantum ratio accepti atque expensi est computata in epistolâ debitori datâ cæteræ obligationes manent in suâ causâ.'

     'At illud'

     Ergo:—' hoc'

which is another argument of the same law (*Emptor. Dig.* ii. 14.47).

Again: if the consequence is false, the antecedent is false, but the consequence is false, therefore, etc.

'Si earum rerum quæ pondere, numero, mensurâ constant datione; in creditum ire possumus '—then 'invito creditore aliud pro alio solvi potest'—

     'At non hoc'—

     Ergo:—' non illud:'

and which is the argument of the law (§ *Mutui, l. si certum petatur*).

To illustrate this subject more thoroughly, I will give an analysis of Ulpian's reasoning, in the law ' ex facto ' (*Dig.* xxviii. 5. 35).

There are three parts into which it may be distributed.

The Fact.

The Question.

The Solution.

The Fact was this: A man had appointed two heirs; one for his Italian property, the other for his property in the provinces. He was in the habit of sending money from Italy to buy merchandise, which was to be brought to Italy. He had done this before his death; the merchandise had been purchased, but not yet brought into Italy.

The Question was: To which of the two heirs did this merchandise belong ?

A Preliminary Question being, Was the appointment of the heirs ' certarum rerum ' (instead ' ex semisse,' etc.) valid? This is answered in the affirmative, from which Ulpian draws several conclusions.

1. That they have ' actionem familiæ erciscundæ.'

2. That they are heirs as ' pro semisse,' and liable, in that proportion, to the debts of the testator.

3. That each takes the land as it was bequeathed to him.

4. That the bequest, if it violates the Falcidian law, is to be rescinded for so much, and security is to be given for complying with that law.

The syllogisms by which the main question is answered, are:—

The will of the testator is the only thing to be considered: ' Totum facit voluntas defuncti, nam quid senserit spectandum est,' and here there is an argument as to the purport of the will. Suppose the testator had sent a slave from Italy to Gaul to buy goods and then return, the slave would have been part of the Italian estate.

This is laid down by Mucius: ' Agasonem enim missum in villam a patrefamilias non pertinere ad fundi legatum,' because he was not sent to reside there, ' quia non idcirco illo erat missus ut ibi esset.' Therefore the question is, as to the purpose of the testator: ' ut Italicarum rerum esse credantur hæres quas in Italiâ esse testator voluit.'

In this case it was the will of the testator that the goods should be brought to Italy.

Therefore they belong to the Italian property:—' Igitur effici dixi ut merces quoque istæ quæ comparatæ sunt ut Romam veherentur, sive provectæ, sunt eo vivo sive nondum et sive sit, sive ignoravit ad eum hæredem pertineant cui Italicæ res sint ascriptæ.'

As another specimen of this logic, I will give an analysis of the famous law as Savigny somewhere calls it—' Frater a Fratre.' Premising that the ' peculium ' of an unemancipated son belonged generally speaking to the father, and was on the death of the father divisible among his heirs.

The facts in this case were these—one brother being unemancipated, had borrowed, during his father's life, from his brother, also unemancipated, a sum of money. This debt the borrower repaid after the father's death. The brothers were joint heirs to their father.

The question of law was, whether the borrower could recover the money so repaid as not due ' condictione indebiti.'

The decision was, first, that the borrower as heir to his father, might recover so much of the money repaid, as was in proportion to his share of the paternal inheritance—conditionally, that the share of the ' peculium ' which fell to the lending brother was not thereby diminished.

Suppose Primus has a ' peculium ' of four shares, and Secundus one of four shares. Primus borrows two shares of Secundus. On the father's death, the ' peculium ' of Primus is divided between him and Secundus. Secundus now has four shares, and Primus two, of the ' peculium ' of Primus. Afterwards Primus pays to Secundus the two shares he had borrowed of him, so that to Secundus has now six shares. Thus Primus has

made a double error—in the first place, he has not taken his
share of the 'peculium' of Secundus; and in the next place,
he has not deducted what he was entitled to from the debt
(consisting of 'peculium' to part of which he was therefore
entitled), which he paid Secundus.   Primus can recover only
one share of what he has paid from Secundus, for to one share
of the two Secundus was entitled.   And the share of the
'peculium' of Secundus he will recover 'judicio familiæ erciscundæ.'   The blending of the 'peculium' into one body, to
be divided between the heirs, extinguishes the obligation of
the debtor to the creditor, 'naturalem enim obligationem quæ
fuisset hoc ipso sublatam videri, quod peculii partem frater sit
consecutus,' for said Africanus, if Primus had owed and paid
the money not to his brother, but a stranger, he would have
been entitled to compensation from the estate, according to
Julianus—' Porro eum quem adversus extraneum defendi
oporteret longe magis in eo quod fratri debuisset.'

The second and third parts of the law are answers to the
questions:—

1. Whether, if a father lend money to his son, and the son,
being afterwards emancipated, repay the father, the son can recover the money?   The answer is, No.

2. Whether, if the father pay the emancipated son a debt;
the father can recover the money?   The answer is, No; and in
both cases for the same reason.   That where there is a 'naturalis obligatio,' money paid in conformity with it cannot be
recovered.

Another specimen may be given from the 'nobilissima lex'
(*Dig.* xxviii. 2. 29, Gallus).

Before I enter upon the analysis, I wish to place the definition of ' suus hæres ' under the reader's eyes.

' Suus hæres est qui in morientis familiâ proximum ab eo
gradum obtinet,' two things were requisite; first, that he
answered this definition; next, that he was 'in potestate of the
deceased.'

A person born after the testator's death might be ' suus ' or

' alienus.' ' Suus' if, supposing his birth had taken place during the life of the testator, he would have fulfilled these conditions; 'alienus,' if he would not: only the former could be heir, ' Posthumi non sui institutio inutilis est.'

A testator, who had a son, and a daughter-in-law pregnant by the son, made this bequest.

' Filius hærès esto.' ' Si non erit Titius hæres esto.' After the will was made, the son died, then the testator died, and Titius took the inheritance. After this, the daughter-in-law brought forth a grandson to the testator, who maintained that his birth cancelled the will. For it was a rule of the Roman law, ' Agnatione sui (hæredis) præteriti rumpi testamentum.

' I,' said the grandson, ' am suus hæres; first, because I represent the testator; next because concepti pro natis habentur.'

' Certainly,' said Titius, 'testamentum rumpiter agnatione sui; but you are not in the category of a ' suus hæres.' For, ' suus' is, he who, if he had been alive when the will was made, would have represented the testator, *i. e.* principem in familiâ gradum occupâsset. That is not your case, therefore you are not suus hæres.

To which the grandson answered. ' Is qui natus primum gradum inanem vacuumque offendit suus est;' whether he is born before or after the will. ' Ego locum vacuum offendi;' therefore I am suus hæres.'

Cervidius Scævola proposed a formula to meet this difficulty—it is this.

' Filius hæres esto—si filius meus vivo me morietur tum quicunque natus erit si suus nascitur, hæres esto.'—*Dig.* xxviii. 2; xxix. 6.

' Melius ergo est ut in ejusmodi utilitate præsertim post legem Velleiam—interpretatio admittatur ut instituens nepotem qui sibi post mortem suus nasceretur recte instituisse videatur, quibuscunque casibus nepos post mortem, natus suus esset, rumperetque præteritus.'

In this law, the formula of Aquileius and of the Velleian law are examined with great minuteness, but to recapitulate the arguments would require a larger space than my limits allow, or indeed, than is consistent with my object; which was to exemplify the ' manner' of the Roman jurists.[a]

In the law Callimachus (*Dig.* xlv. 1. 122, § 1), it is decided, that an agent sent to receive money from a debtor, has no authority to prolong the time of payment.

Another remarkable law is the ' Tres fratres' (*Dig.* ii. 14. 35). Mævius and Seia, the brother and sister of Titius, complained that he had withheld money, in the division of a joint inheritance, of which there was no mention ' instrumento divisionis.'

Titius answered, that there was a general compact as to all matters concerning the inheritance by which his brother and sister were bound.

It was answered, that if the compact had been made in

---

[a] See 10 and 11 Wm. III. c. 16, As to the Right of Posthumous Children. The Court of Common Pleas, in Blakiston *v.* Haslewood, 10 C. B., 544, overruled the law laid down in 5 BURROW, 2703, White *v.* Barber. In that last decision it was held, in obvious conformity with reason and justice, that a devise by a testator ' in case his wife should be *enceinte* with one or more children, to such child or children, implied a gift to any child born after the date of the will, but before the death of the testator. This was overruled, for reasons ludicrously insufficient, by the Common Pleas. Fortunately, this contracted and hard doctrine has been contradicted by the Lord Chancellor of Ireland (Blackburne), Re Lindsay, *Irish Jurist* ; Alleyne *v.* Alleyne, 2 Jo. and LAT., 558 ; see JARMAN *On Wills*, vol. i., p. 453.

The beneficial rule laid down in the Will Act, sec. 32, had been suggested by MURATORI, *Difetti della Giurisprudenza*, p. 162, c. 19, he proposes this rule, which, if it had fallen under the notice of the Judges of the Common Pleas, might have prevented the decision in Blakiston *v.* Haslewood. ' Venendo uno istituito erede, e in caso ch'egli muoja senza figlio o descendenti, venendo sustituite altre persone, ancorchè esso erede manchi di vita prima del testatore ciò non ostante i di lui figli o nipoti escluderanno nell' eredità i sustituiti, è chiunque viene *ab intestato*.

' Esige il ben pubblico che si tronchi si gran lite è che sabbia a decidere nella forma suddetta lo persuade la ragione *essendo evidente che il testatore più de sustituiti e di quei che vengono ab intestato predilige i figliuoli dell erede istituito*.'

ignorance of the fraud, it might be withdrawn by the ' exceptio doli mali.'

The law (*Dig.* iv. 2. 12) may be thus analysed: ' Creditor qui vim adhibuit debitori suo ut solveret in legem Juliam de vi incidit, et jus crediti amittit.

      ' Meus creditor vim talem mihi ferit,
      ' Ergo:—jus crediti amisit.'

Answer of the Creditor.

    ' Vim facit qui vulneret hominem
     ' Ego debitorem non vulneravi
   ' Non ergo vim illi feci.'

Replication of the Debtor.

' In vim esse putas solum cum homines vulnerentur? Vis est tum quoties quis id quod sibi deberi putat non per judicem reposcit.'

    ' In pecuniam a me debitam sine judice accepisti—tibi que jus dixisti.'

    ' Vim ergo fecisti.'

Some instances are found where difficulties are balanced, *e.g.* (*Dig.* xxxix. 3. 1, § ' denique'). Ulpian answers one argument of hardship by another. If it is hard, ' Agrum inferiorem superiori sine speciali pacto servire,' it is hard, too, that the fatness of the upper should be carried down to the lower: ' Atque hoc incommodum naturaliter pati inferiorem agrum a superiore compensareque debere eum alio commodo'; and in *Dig.* ix. 3. 51, § 2, where Julianus assigns the degree of compensation due from several persons who have killed a slave, and it does not appear which blow was fatal. If any one, he adds, thinks this absurd, let him recollect that it would be much more absurd if all or any of the malefactors were to escape: ' Quum neque impunita esse maleficia oporteat nec facile constitui possit uter potius lege teneatur.' Another example will be found (*Dig.* xlvii. 2. 63, § 5), where Africanus reasons in this manner, as to the liability of a person who has ordered a particular slave to be purchased: ' Licet alioquin æquum videatur non oportere cuiquam plus damni per servum evenire quam quanti ipse servus sit, multo tamen æquus est, nemini officium si suum quod ejus cum quo contraxit non etiam sui commodi causâ susceperit, damnorum esse.' I conclude with a curious example of a subtilty well known in the schools. The reader will remember that by the Falcidian law the testator was bound to give a fourth part of his estate to his heirs: ' Ita ne minus quam quartam hæreditatis ex eo testamento hæredes caperent' (*Dig.* xxxv. 2. 1). The difficulty proposed was this: a man with an estate worth 400 aurei, after disposing of 300, left the other 100 to Titius, on condition that the Falcidian law was not applied to his will. What was to be done? If the legacy was valid, the Falcidian law did apply, and, therefore, it was not due; if the legacy was not valid, the Falcidian law could not apply, and, therefore, the legacy became due. , Dixi τῶν ἄκρων hanc quæstionem esse qui tractatus apud dialecticos τοῦ ψευδομένου .. dicatur. Etenim quicquid constituerimus verum esse falsum reperietur—namque si legatum tibi datum valere dicamus, legi Falcidiæ locus erit—ideoque deficiente conditione non debebitur—rursus si quia conditio deficiat legatum valiturum non sit legis Falcidiæ locus non erit. Porro si legi locus non sit existente conditione legatum tibi debebitur —cum autem voluntatem testatoris eam fuisse appareat, ut propter tuum legatum cæterorum legata minui nollet—magis est ut statuere debeamus tui legati conditionem deficere '[q] (*Dig.* xxxv. 2. 88).

I have thus endeavoured to show the manner in which the Roman jurists flung what Lord Bacon calls the ' lumen siccum' on public business; in other words, in which they applied the eternal principles of reason to the ever-changing objects of daily life. Human affairs were the elements and letters, which were ranked and ordered by their art and wisdom. No word contains every single letter—no particular case furnishes an

---

[q] AULUS GELLIUS, *Noct. Att.*, v. 10 ; VAL. MAXIMUS, vii. 3.

opportunity for the application of all these rules; but as there can be no word without some letters, there can be no case which does not require the application of some of those general notions without which reasoning and science are impossible. It has been well said by a modern commentator on Aristotle: 'La polémique des sciences révèle plus nette-ment le procédé qu'elles suivent.'[a] I know not if better instances than those I have quoted can anywhere be found of the logic which, in spite of the ignorant demagogues of literature,[b] is the essence of all attempts to reason, and without the aid of which all science must fall into the most inextricable confusion.[c] 'La logique des géomètres,' says Leib-nitz, 'est une promotion particulière de la logique générale.'

The schoolmen, indeed, dealt with Aristotle as the priests of the dark ages did with the Bible. They preferred the commentary of the follower to the text of the master, wrested to their own purposes its plainest maxims, and heaped gloss upon gloss, until, under the strange garb by which it was disguised, an eagle eye was requisite to discover the gracious and noble features of the original. Ramus led the attack on their authority, and he met with the fate of most reformers in that day. In the nineteenth century, in England, he would have been insulted by blockheads, postponed to dunces, and left to starve. In the sixteenth, in France, he was only denounced by priests, and torn to pieces by a mob. This, how-ever, is not the place to dwell on the evil effects which the exces-sive reaction against the schoolmen produced on education, to show how Bacon's real object was to put a stop to metaphysical abstractions and speculative inferences—about complex and con-

---

[a] BARTHÉLEMY DE SAINT HILAIRE, Préface 38, *Logique D'Aristote*; and see the *Prolegomena Logica* of MANSEL, a work of which Oxford may be proud.

[b] οὐκ ἄρα διὰ τὴν ὑπὲρ τῶν ξυλίνων σκευῶν ἐπιστήμην βουλευομένη ὡς ἂν ἔχοι βέλτιστα σοφὴ κλητεά πόλις.'—PLAT. *Pol.* iv.

[c] MELANCTHON, *Erotemata Dialectices*, vol. xiii. p. 514: 'Dialectica est ars et via recte ordine et perspicue docendo, quod fit recte defini-endo, dividendo, argumenta vera connectendo, et male cohærentia seu falsa vetescendo et refutando.'

crete subjects—about matters that can be touched and weighed, and measured and counted, and how utterly he has been misunderstood and misrepresented by half-taught empirics.   But my task would have been incomplete if I had not placed the refined, close, and vigorous reasonings of the Roman jurists in immediate contact with the wretched conceits, captious distinctions, transparent fallacies, clumsy subtleties, and provoking pedantry incorporated with the English law.[d] These are the causes which make the details of that law laborious to search, ignoble to meditate, harsh to deliver, and too often illiberal to practise.[e] These are the causes which, as our books too plainly show, have led to that which is the greatest reproach to all laws and all tribunals — reiterated violations of substantial justice.[f] May they speedily cease from out of the land.

---

[d] 'Ineptæ affectant laudem subtilitatis.'—MELANCTHON, vol. xiii. p. 462, ed. Schneider.

[e] On the other hand, if the law were what it might be made, we might, in the eloquent language of SIR JOHN DAVIS, in the preface to his *Reports*, 'affirm confidently that the profession of the law is to be preferred before all other human professions and sciences, as being most noble for the matter and subject thereof, most necessary for the common and continual use thereof, and most meritorious for the good effects it does produce in the commonwealth.

[f] Οὗ δὴ ἕνεκα πάντα ζητοῦμεν δικαιοσύνη.—PLAT. *Pol.* iv. 430.

To how many who have held high place among us is this description applicable : δοκεῖ σοι τούτου αἴσχιον εἶναι τοῦτο ὅταν τις μὴ μόνον τὸ πολὺ τοῦ βίου ἐν δικαστηρίοις φεύγων τε καὶ διώκων κατατρίβηται ἀλλὰ καὶ ὑπὸ, ἀπειροκαλίας ἐπ᾽ αὐτῷ δὴ τούτῳ πεισθῇ καλλπωΐζεσθαι ὡς δεινὸς ὤν περὶ τὸ ἀδικεῖν καὶ ἱκανὸς πάσας μὲν στροφὰς στέφεσθαι.—PLAT. *Pol.* 89.

APPENDIX.

See, as to Jealousy of Foreign Law, King John's Letter to Innocent III. MATTHEW PARIS, 215.

' ET cum archiepiscopi, episcopi, et alii ecclesiarum prelati . . . in omnium scientiarum plenitudine sufficientur abundent—si necessitas coegerit extra terras suas, justitiam vel judicium ab *alienigenis* non emendicabit;' and in 11 Richard II., answer was made by all the estates, that the realm of England never had been, nor hereafter should be, governed by the civil law. The Roman, on the contrary, made all that was good and great in every land his own.

INDEX.

FRAUDULENT CLAIM, 233.
         PURPOSE, 173.

GAIN. *See* BENEFIT.

GAIUS, cited, 17, 164, 188, 255.

GIFT, 59—62,
     in error, 200.

GOOD FAITH.
     gives possessor same rights as valid title, where the law has
         not otherwise provided, 146.
     gives the possessor the same rights as the fact, unless the law
         prevent it, 177.

GOTHOFREDUS DE REGULIS JURIS, cited, *passim.*

' GREATER AND LESS.'
     ' He who can do the greater can do the less,' 78.

GREECE. Love for the great and beautiful, 8.

GROTIUS, cited, 11, 99, 115, 133, 273.

GUARDIAN AND WARD, 298.

IGNORANCE. *See* YOUTH.
     of fact and of law, 96.

INEXPERIENCE. *See* YOUTH.

INFAMY, 223.

INFANT. *See* WARD.

INHERITANCE, Law of, 252.

INJURY.
     purpose not to be changed to the detriment of a legal right, 31.
     ' No man is injured by what he suffers through his own fault,'
         247.

INSTITUTES, cited, 124, 342.

INSURANCE, 378.

INTENTION, 331, 334.
         See AMBIGUITY. FRAUD. OBSCURITY. SALE.

ITALY.
     the instructor of mankind, 13.

JOVELLANOS, cited, 117.

JUDGMENT.
     the judgment of a competent tribunal is taken for truth, 287.
     ' Chose jugée' of the French Code, 291.
     when admitted in evidence, 293.
     In rem. 294.
     no estoppel unless it be pleaded, 296, *n.*

D D

THE END.

CPSIA information can be obtained
at www.ICGtesting.com
Printed in the USA
LVHW110928260223
740447LV00012B/124